The Rites of Labor

"La Réconciliation des Compagnons" after the play by Agricol Perdiguier, *Les Gavots et les Devoirants; ou, La Réconciliation des compagnons* (Paris, 1862). Lithograph by Dorléans. Source: Musée du Compagnonnage, Tours. This lithograph is often believed to be an evocation of the compagnons' reconciliation of 20 March 1848. Perdiguier's play, however, is not set in Paris or in 1848, and no mères or other women accompanied the compagnons during the 1848 demonstration. This recasting of the reconciliation is discussed in the conclusion.

The Rites of Labor

Brotherhoods of Compagnonnage
in Old and New Regime France

CYNTHIA MARIA TRUANT

Cornell University Press · *Ithaca and London*

Copyright © 1994 by Cornell University

First published 1994 by Cornell University Press.

Printed in the United States of America

Library of Congress Cataloging-in-Publication Data

Truant, Cynthia Maria, 1950–
    The rites of labor : brotherhoods of compagnonnage in old and new
regime France / Cynthia Maria Truant.
        p. cm.
    Includes bibliographical references and index.
    ISBN 0-8014-2769-X (cloth)   ISBN 0-8014-8240-2 (paper)
    1. Compagnonnages. 2. Workingmen's clubs—France—History.
I. Title.
HD6464.T74 1994
331'.88'32'0944—dc20   94-3578

⊗ The paper in this book meets the minimum requirements
of the American National Standard for Information Sciences—
Permanence of Paper for Printed Library Materials, ANSI Z39.48–1984.

Contents

Figures and Maps

Acknowledgments

My long journey with compagnonnage comes to an end with deep thanks to the many people who supported the effort along the way. The Georges Lurcy Foundation funded my original research in France, which was continued with summer grants from the American Council of Learned Societies, the National Endowment for the Humanities, and the Academic Senate of the University of California, San Diego. During those early stages of research, Roger Lecotté (1899–1991), the first curator of the Musée du Compagnonnage in Tours, was most helpful both personally and through his bibliographical work on compagnonnage, which remains an essential resource for scholars. The former and present curators, Gabriel Priou and Louis Bastard, have continued this tradition of assistance and have graciously granted me permission to reproduce several of the illustrations that appear in this book. The museum staff in Tours, the personnel at the Bibliothèque nationale and the Archives nationales in Paris, and archivists elsewhere in Dijon, Mâcon, Lyon, Marseille, Toulouse, Bordeaux, and Nantes have similarly been extremely helpful. During my various research trips in France, Maurice Agulhon kindly showed much interest in the project; my participation in his seminar at the École Normale Supérieure in 1974–1975 deepened my general knowledge of French social history and culture. I also cordially thank Jacques Marillier of the Institut français d'histoire sociale for providing access to the letters and papers of Pierre Moreau.

My interest in compagnonnage was initially encouraged by William Sewell, who remained a most committed and helpful reader. Steven Kaplan deserves great thanks for his generous and unfailing support and for his critical reading of the manuscript. He and the other, anonymous, reader of the manuscript for Cornell University Press have much improved it. John Ackerman, director at Cornell University Press, has been a wise and supportive editor, and I am most grateful for his advice and assistance. Portions of Chapter 5 were revised from an article, "Independent and Insolent: Journeymen and Their 'Rites' in the Old Regime Work Place," which appeared in *Work in France: Representations, Meaning, Organization, and Practice,* ed. Steven Kaplan and Cynthia Koepp (Ithaca, 1986), pp. 131–75. I thank Cornell University Press for permission to use this material.

A pivotal point in the life of this project came when I received a Monticello College Foundation Fellowship for Women from the Newberry Library in Chicago in 1985–1986. There I greatly benefited from the enthusiasm and encouragement of Richard Brown, Paul Gehl, and Mary Beth Rose. I continued the work in the women's studies and history departments at San Diego State University, where I was fortunate to be part of an active community of scholars and companions. Special thanks go to Marilyn Boxer, then dean of the College of Arts and Sciences, who continues to be an inspiration. I also owe a large debt to my present university, the University of California at San Diego, and particularly the members of the history department, whose strong support provided the time and funding I needed to complete the book.

The assistance of many people away from home has been vital. Michael Sonenscher deserves thanks for amiably agreeing to read a late draft at very short notice. His comments and advice, as well as his own work, have illuminated many issues for me, even when our directions have taken a different turn. Jacqueline Lalouette, whom I first met in Maurice Agulhon's seminar, has given me generous hospitality and friendship. She has answered so many questions about so many things over so many years that I can never repay her, but thank her for all her kindness. Nancy Green and Pierre Bouvier have kept me convinced that this work was worth doing as I benefited from their own fine scholarship, hospitality, and friendship. I thank Jean-Yves Jeanneau and Anna Jalar Jeanneau, who gave me invaluable aid in obtaining copies of several of the illustrations. They and their daughters, Katarina and Anne-Marie, gave me a wonderful welcome to the charms of life and language in France. Jacques Selamé and Suzy Selamé sharpened my French and my wits and let their warm and lively home be mine as well.

Others near and far have shared information and advice, suggested rhetorical strategies, invited me to give talks, taught me about archives, and generally furthered this work in countless ways. For these many kindnesses I warmly thank Elinor Accampo, Keith Baker, Kathleen Beatty, Susan Cayleff, Martha Cowan, Natalie Zemon Davis, Barbara Day, Chris Ferguson, Frances Foster, Luce Giard, Carlo Ginzburg, Jan Goldstein, Steve Hahn, Howard Kushner, Kathleen and Peter Koch-Weser, Cynthia Koepp, John Martin, John Merriman, Allan Mitchell, Alden Mosshammer, Joséf Nagy, Jann Pasler, Michelle Perrot, Jeremy Popkin, Joan Kling-el Ray, David Ringrose, Roy Ritchie, Susan Rogers, Theda Shapiro, Michael David Sibalis, Robin and David Van Meter, and Bonnie Zimmerman. Special thanks go to Ann Elwood for her painstaking work on the maps, her research assistance, and her stimulating comments in our many discussions.

Most of all, I thank John Marino for being my companion on some of the roughest parts of this journey. His own scholarship has been brought to bear in innumerable close and critical readings of many drafts of the manuscript. Always an enthusiastic fan of the compagnons, he encouraged me and kept our household going so I could tell this story. Our children, Sara and Marc, have connected me more to life and history with their own lives and love. Sandra Truant, Marc Truant and Alida Truant, Mary and Raymond Timmerman, and Ermes Truant have gone beyond family ties with their interest in and understanding of this project. I am especially appreciative of the generous support and intelligent advice my mother, Lelia Serena Truant, and my late father, Aldo Truant, have given me. I end with their names and those of my grandparents: Liberale and Adele Truant, and Pietro and Philomena Serena, who made their own challenging journeys and inspired my own.

C. M. T.

Abbreviations and Note on Translations

ADG   Archives départementales, Gironde
ADSL   Archives départementales, Saône et Loire
AMD   Archives municipales, Dijon
AML   Archives municipales, Lyon
AMM   Archives municipales, Mâcon
AMN   Archives municipales, Nantes
AN   Archives nationales, Paris
BN   Bibliothèque nationale, Paris

For municipal and departmental archives that are less frequently cited, the abbreviations AD (archives départementales) and AM (archives municipales), followed by the place name, will be used (e.g., AD Côte d'Or).

I have retained the original spelling but modernized the punctuation in French quotations. Unless otherwise stated, all translations are my own.

The Rites of Labor

Introduction

In his *Mémoires d'un compagnon* (1854–1855) Agricol Perdiguier made a compelling plea for a more impartial study of *compagnonnage*, semi-clandestine brotherhoods of young, unmarried journeymen artisans which originated at least as early as the seventeenth century.[1] At nineteen Perdiguier, a joiner by trade who later became a noted worker-poet and man of 1848, was initiated into one of compagnonnage's three major sects, the children of Solomon. Known by the name *Avignonnais la vertu* (The Virtue of Avignon), Perdiguier began his *tour de France,* an experience of work and travel throughout France (see Map 1) around which he built his whole life. He spent the years from 1824 to 1828 being a compagnon and much of the rest of his life writing about what it meant to have been one.[2]

1. Because compagnonnage was never administratively centralized and was divided into three major sects, many historians prefer to use the term *compagnonnages*. Compagnons who were members of these sects, however, generally used the term in the singular. Some, like Perdiguier, believed all the sects had once been united and could be reunited. Others simply claimed their sect was the only true compagnonnage. From the seventeenth through most of the nineteenth century, noncompagnons, especially the police, also most commonly used the singular.

Such apparently trivial issues cannot be dismissed in a book that focuses on the use of language. I often use *compagnonnages* as a shorthand for "sects or brotherhoods of compagnonnage," but when I am interpreting compagnons' accounts or describing the cultural and structural correlations among the sects, I use the term in the singular.

2. Jacques Rancière makes the provocative argument that, like many other worker-poets, Perdiguier hated his work, had minimal skill and an undistinguished artisanal career. "The Myth

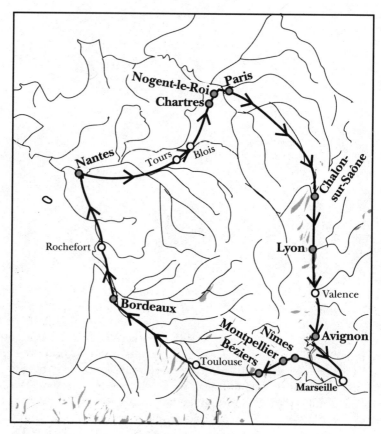

☆ Start of tour
⟶ Direction of travel

⬤ Places in or near which Perdiguier worked.
◯ Places Perdiguier visited or passed through.

Source: Agricol Perdiguier, *Mémoires d'un compagnon*, ed. Alain Faure (Paris, 1977).

MAP 1. Tour de France of Agricol Perdiguier (1824–1828)

Perdiguier had reason to be dissatisfied with the public accounts of compagnonnage which contrasted so sharply with his own knowledge of the association. Perhaps a foreigner or a stranger to modern society could provide a more sensitive analysis. Whimsically he asked if "perhaps in some Chinese, Tartar or Mongol documents there are some very complete, interesting details concerning its values, holidays, customs, past eccentricities, . . . particulars very true and seen in a positive light [which] our own knowledgeable antiquarians, all our learned and sagacious observers judge to be stupid fables or horrible lies."[3] Perdiguier recognized that human perception was limited and shaped—in our terms, constructed—by culture. He could be at once the articulate "native informant" and the "outsider," the ethnographer and interpreter, whereas the scholars of his time regarded the enigmatic and esoteric with suspicion.

Beginning in the nineteenth century, criticisms of compagnonnage often focused on the theme of primitivism. One critic attacked compagnonnage's "superstitious practices" and "crude initiations," customs thought to "denature the association and deprive it of any value whatsoever." Another observer, condemning the frequent, bloody brawls (*rixes*) between sects of rival compagnons, declared that they were "not of the modern age" and originated from the "most ridiculous of reasons." The noted late nineteenth-century sociologist Pierre du Maroussem thought the compagnons' funeral rites had "an archaic cachet that closely parallels ceremonies fit for the primitive races."[4] Such condemnations of compagnonnage could not help but intrigue the general public. The perception of compagnonnage as primitive and archaic endured into the twentieth century. A 1901 work concluded that compagnonnage had "played an important role in the history of the working class [but] now appears only as a curious vestige of the past. The connoisseurs of the picturesque study it with the satisfaction of the antique collector who contemplates an old work of art in a museum."[5]

---

of the Artisan: Critical Reflections on a Category of Social History," in *Work in France: Representations, Meaning, Organization, and Practice*, ed. Steven Laurence Kaplan and Cynthia J. Koepp (Ithaca, 1986), pp. 323–24. Rancière's conclusions are meant to shock his readers; yet he forces us to recognize the worker-poets' ambivalence toward work itself and not just its conditions. Whatever the stimulus for Perdiguier's writing, he indeed created "other" work and a distinguished career out of his "real" work. Ben Hamper, whose fictional *Rivethead* (New York, 1991) is based on his experiences as an auto worker, is a rare contemporary example of a worker who gets out of the shop by writing about it.

3. Agricol Perdiguier, *Mémoires d'un compagnon*, ed. Alain Faure (Paris, 1977), p. 193.

4. Adrien-César Egron, *Le Livre d'ouvrier: Ses devoirs envers la société, la famille, et lui-même* (Paris, 1844), p. 141; review of Auguste-Ambroise Giraud, *Réflexions philosophiques sur le compagnonnage et le tour de France* (Paris, 1846), in *Le Censeur de Lyon*, 14 October 1846; and Pierre du Maroussem, *Charpentiers de Paris: Compagnons et indépendents*, vol. 1 of *La Question ouvrière*, 4 vols. (Paris, 1891–94), p. 140.

5. Alfred Kirch, *Le Compagnonnage en France* (Paris, 1901), p. 154.

The first wave of modern social history also tended to categorize the rituals, iconography, and myths of compagnonnage as primitive hold-overs from the past, curiosities that attracted renewed scholarly atten-tion. Early social historians, however, focused primarily not on the meaning of symbolic practices but on their function, function usually being rather narrowly defined as reduced or related to some aspect of material interest. Scholars asked, for example, if a particular practice—such as brawls—enhanced the competitive edge of the compagnons in the labor market. If no such useful purpose was manifest, the particular practice was judged vestigial. Scholars saw rigid adherence to symbolic forms they considered outmoded as evidence that nineteenth-century compagnonnage was too primitive to be of more than marginal impor-tance in French society.

In *Primitive Rebels* (1959) E. J. Hobsbawm found nineteenth-century compagnonnage overgrown with complicated symbolism, and its "ritual requirements were so numerous and strict that they probably represent a stage in the societies' evolution when they had nothing better to do." Both bemused and impatient at this waste of time, Hobsbawm "spared [the reader] the symbolic significance of all this" and moved on to dis-cuss the relationship of compagnonnage to secret societies he consid-ered more important, such as the Carbonari.[6] Charles Tilly finds evidence of compagnonnage's marginality in its violent brawls without examining their symbolic content. He considers these brawls sociological manifestations of violent collective action, which he originally labeled primitive. Limited in scope and size; generated by participants with prior group ties; and market by inexplicit, obscure, or nonpolitical motiva-tions, the compagnons' violence, he believes, was a legacy of the past which marginalized their brotherhoods and alienated more progressive workers.[7]

By the nineteenth century, the period usually studied, these brother-hoods may indeed have seemed archaic. Compagnonnage had the dis-tinction (or onus) of being one of the few *corps* to survive the French Revolution—its members apparently having learned nothing about modern political culture and having forgotten nothing about the old regime. Certainly, no one would claim that compagnonnage played a key role in the modern organization of labor or that all its practices were progressive. Nevertheless, it is not enough simply to assign the brother-hoods to the category "primitive," with its teleological implications and

6. Eric J. Hobsbawm, *Primitive Rebels: Studies in Archaic Forms of Social Movement in the 19th and 20th Centuries* (New York, 1959), pp. 154, 155, 157, 159.

7. Charles Tilly, "Collective Violence in European Perspective," in *Violence in America: Historical and Comparative Perspectives,* ed. Hugh Davis Graham and Ted Robert Gurr, 2 vols. (Wash-ington, D.C., 1969), 1:5–34; and Charles Tilly et al., *The Rebellious Century, 1830–1930* (Cam-bridge, Mass., 1975), pp. 49–50.

its tendency to foreclose discussion and dismiss such "weapons of the weak." In fact, both Tilly and Hobsbawm have revised their earlier views on the symbolic and the primitive to some extent, although not particularly with regard to compagnonnage.[8]

Moreover, scholars who study compagnonnage in its prerevolutionary incarnation usually depict a far more dynamic and effective organization. Archival evidence demonstrates that compagnonnage was widespread from about 1650, and that in many old regime cities outside Paris compagnons took the lead in labor conflicts and organization. Some of the best-documented work rivets our attention on the social and economic life of these brotherhoods and sees them as possible precursors of the modern labor movement. Simultaneously, they ignore or downplay the significance of symbolic practices.[9] Both Henri Hauser and Jean Cavignac, for example, follow an essentially evolutionary model: they attempt to increase respect for compagnonnage by insisting on its surprisingly modern concern with labor and economic issues. From the very first page of his important (1907) work on the compagnonnages in Dijon, Hauser firmly dismisses the picturesque, mysterious, and secret aspects that had so long "seduced" historians and scholars. Instead, he intends to prove "by means of the evidence" that even in the seventeenth and eighteenth centuries "compagnonnage was, above all . . . an institution of the economic order, an instrument of workers' solidarity."[10]

The lexicologists of the *Larousse du XXe siècle* followed Hauser's lead. They stress the role of the early compagnonnages in labor activities and minimize the importance of the regrettably "bizarre ceremonies" with which "the compagnons' initiation was surrounded."[11] In 1968 Cavignac's major article on compagnonnage in eighteenth-century Bordeaux described an "institution created by and for workers to defend their material situation, their salaries, and standard of living." These aspects made compagnonnage significant and worthy of study, not the "secrecy and strange ritualism which has excited the curiosity of the proponents of the picturesque and mysterious."[12]

8. Eric J. Hobsbawm and Terence Ranger, eds., *The Invention of Tradition* (Cambridge, 1983), Introduction; and Tilly et al., *Rebellious Century*, pp. 49–50. Hobsbawm more than Tilly acknowledges the great importance of symbolism in even the most secular, republican, and socialist of working-class movements to at least the end of the nineteenth century. Many articles in this collection document the pervasive and tenacious grip of symbolic practices. See Cynthia M. Truant, "Fracas et fraternité: Des compagnons du tour de France et des compagnies de pompiers volontaires de Philadelphie au première moitié du dix-neuvième siècle," in *Travail et production en France et aux USA*, ed. Pierre Bouvier et al. (Paris, 1988), pp. 12–28.

9. Henri Hauser, *Les Compagnonnages d'arts et métiers à Dijon aux XVIIe et XVIIIe siècles* (Paris, 1907); Jean Cavignac, "Le Compagnonnage dans les luttes ouvrières au XVIIIe siècle: L'Exemple de Bordeaux," *Bibliothèque de l'École des chartes* 126, no. 2, 1969 (1968): 377–411.

10. Hauser, *Compagnonnages*, p. 1.

11. "Compagnonnage," *Larousse du XXe siècle*, ed. Paul Augé, 6 vols. (Paris, 1928–33), 2:376.

12. Cavignac, "Compagnonnage," p. 377.

Thus, scholars who wished to "rehabilitate" compagnonnage pursued the largely successful strategy of avoiding or deemphasizing the rites of labor. Yet, this strategy is no less problematic than the devaluation of compagnonnage because of its "primitive" practices. Hauser and Cavignac minimize the centrality of its ritual to assert the importance of compagnonnage; Hobsbawm and Tilly minimize the importance of compagnonnage because of its ritual practices. Both viewpoints create a rupture between the symbolic and the socioeconomic life of compagnons. I construct a more nuanced understanding of compagnonnage and its relationship to other contemporary social groups—elite and popular, male and female, corporate, republican, or socialist—in France from the seventeenth to the nineteenth century.

The symbolic practices of compagnonnage, in the context of an essentially corporate, Catholic old regime, fell within an acceptable range of contemporary cultural practices. Both elite and popular cultures in the old regime were rife with symbol and ritual, from the *lits de justice* and aristocratic *courtoisie* to cat massacres and charivaris. Yet, compagnonnage did not necessarily "fit" the old regime better than the new.

These brotherhoods were always illegal, even if they were tolerated to a greater or lesser extent by a police that often lacked the force to contain them. Almost all secular and clerical authorities and most masters regarded compagnonnage as a perversion of legitimate corporate institutions. In the particularistic world of the old regime, organized compagnons often came into sharp conflict with other corporate bodies such as *corps des métiers* (guilds), confraternities, and rival journeymen's brotherhoods. And, like the other corps, the compagnonnages practiced inclusion and exclusion. Steven Kaplan has persuasively demonstrated the necessary interrelationship of social organization and classification as well as the important links between self-perception and the exercise of power in the old regime. Similarly, Susan Davis, in a nineteenth-century American context, has analyzed the critical dynamic that selection exercises in cultural construction. Choices to include and exclude, silences and omissions are all essential to the creation of culture.[13] Using symbolism, signs, secrecy, and rituals, compagnons fashioned a solidarity that enabled them to control aspects of their work experience as well as to create distinctive social and personal identities. Nor were such usages really so odd in the early decades after the Revolution: compagnonnages

---

13. Steven Laurence Kaplan, "Social Classification and Representation in the Corporate World of Eighteenth-Century France: Turgot's 'Carnival,' " in Kaplan and Koepp, *Work in France,* pp. 176–228; and his important and detailed study of social control in the world of work, "Réflexions sur la police du monde du travail, 1700–1815," *Revue historique* 261 (December 1979): 17–77; Susan G. Davis, *Parades and Power: Street Theatre in Nineteenth-Century Philadelphia* (Philadelphia, 1986), p. 15.

remained vital and empowering associations until at least the 1830s.[14] At the very least the study of compagnonnage is vitiated by ignoring its symbolic side or dividing it sharply between old and new regimes.

Eventually, the "tools" compagnons used to construct their associations isolated them. Their rituals tended to alienate nineteenth-century proponents of rationality, progress, and efficiency, and "overall," as Stephan Zdatny notes, "secret handshakes, mysterious titles, and fancy funerals proved a poor match for the syndicates' promise of shorter hours and higher pay."[15] Nonetheless, it took artisans a long time to come around to that view, if indeed shorter hours and higher pay were the primary lure of the new syndicates. Marcel Bris, perhaps drawing too uncritically on Agricol Perdguier, estimates that at the height of compagnonnage in the nineteenth century, the various sects had about 250,000 adherents, and these numbers declined significantly only in the 1890s. Membership dropped rapidly thereafter, and by the early twentieth century only about 20,000 to 25,000 followers remained.[16] Even a reformed compagnonnage could never be as "modern" as the workers' syndicates legalized in 1884, and more traditional societies of compagnonnage often accentuated their differences from other workers' groups. In 1907 a compagnon hatter insisted that a compagnon

> should not consider himself a simple trade unionist. He bears a symbolic name and should practice the virtues that it implies. It is not enough for him to go to the *Mère* [the compagnons' inn], attend meetings, and pay his dues regularly. He must, above all, instruct himself in the mystical things of the society. . . . all its attributes and insignias have a meaning [and] great moral significance. [They are] exterior signs that remind the initiates of their mutual duties toward and distinguish them from the profane.[17]

Late nineteenth- and early twentieth-century compagnons were thus increasingly marginalized by modern trade unionists, who rejected their symbolism as inappropriate to their goals.

14. Michael Sonenscher, for example, has called the period from the mid-eighteenth century to the July monarchy "the golden age of the *compagnonnages*." See "Mythical Work: Workshop Production and the *compagnonnages* of Eighteenth-Century France," in *The Historical Meanings of Work*, ed. Patrick Joyce (Cambridge, 1987), p. 32.

15. Steven M. Zdatny, *The Politics of Survival: Artisans in Twentieth-Century France* (Oxford, 1990), p. 18.

16. Marcel Bris, *Le Compagnonnage: A la recherche de sa vocation, 1900–1946* (Paris, 1984), p. 29. Zdatny accepts the Bris estimate as plausible (*Politics of Survival*, pp. 18–19), and he does not mention that Bris based his figure on Perdiguier, who would not always have been able to confirm his estimates with great precision. More concrete research on the local level would be necessary before accepting these numbers with complete confidence. For the twentieth-century estimate, see Emile Coornaert, *Les Compagnonnages en France du Moyen Age à nos jours* (Paris, 1966), p. 123.

17. Milicent, compagnon hatter, in *Union compagnonnique*, 2 June 1907.

Symbolic practices did not disappear in nineteenth- and early twentieth-century French society, of course.[18] Nor did the republican and socialist workers ever reject the use of symbolism, particularly in their staging of funerals for deceased members. More "modern" workers tended, however, to divest their symbolism of mystery and make it a less obvious part of their lives, but compagnonnage nonetheless remained viable in some trades until the first decade of the twentieth century, even in its more traditional versions. Disturbed and somewhat confounded by this tenacity, syndicalist organizers thought compagnonnage worthy of serious attack. The syndicalist Union des charpentiers de la Seine, for example, worked to undermine the credibility and minimize the attractions of the particularly rigid brotherhood of carpenters, the enfants de Père Soubise. Despite the harsh initiations of this sect of compagnonnage, moreover, it survived while the more liberal compagnon carpenters *du devoir de liberté* virtually faded away.[19]

In sum, inasmuch as the compagnonnage did persist in significant numbers and trades well into the nineteenth century, it is essential not to explain away its ritual practices or to label them primitive or residual but, rather, to interpret them. The development of what is loosely termed "cultural history" has had important implications for the study of compagnonnage. Scholars are less likely to dismiss or deemphasize the meaning—political, symbolic, gendered—of various forms of language and practice.[20]

Michael Sonenscher's extensive body of work, for example, provides

18. See, for example, Edward Berenson, *Populist Religion and Left-Wing Politics in France, 1830–1852* (Princeton, 1984); William Reddy, *The Rise of Market Culture: The Textile Trade and French Society, 1750–1900* (Cambridge, 1984), especially chaps. 9 and 10; William H. Sewell, Jr., *Work and Revolution in France: The Language of Labor from the Old Regime to 1848* (Cambridge, 1980); and Eugen Weber, *Peasants into Frenchmen: The Modernization of Rural France, 1870–1914* (Stanford, 1976).

19. Bris, *Le Compagnonnage*, pp. 31–37, finds that compagnonnage survived fairly well in the building trades and in rural areas into the early twentieth century. See also Zdatny who provides a brief summary of its status from the late nineteenth to the mid-twentieth century. *Politics of Survival*, pp. 18–20.

20. See, for example, Keith Michael Baker et al., eds., *The French Revolution and the Creation of Modern Political Culture*, 3 vols. (Oxford, 1987–89); Berenson, *Populist Religion;* Roger Chartier, *Cultural History: Between Practices and Representations*, trans. Lydia G. Cochrane (Ithaca, 1988); Mary Ann Clawson, *Constructing Brotherhood: Class, Gender, and Fraternalism* (Princeton, 1989); Robert Darnton, *The Great Cat Massacre and Other Episodes in French Cultural History* (New York, 1984); Natalie Zemon Davis, *Society and Culture in Early Modern France* (Stanford, 1975); Lynn Hunt, *Politics, Culture, and Class in the French Revolution* (Berkeley, 1984); Lynn Hunt, ed., *The New Cultural History* (Berkeley, 1989); Carlo Ginzburg, *The Cheese and the Worms: The Cosmos of a Sixteenth-Century Miller* (New York, 1982); Joyce, *Historical Meanings of Work;* Kaplan and Koepp, *Work in France;* Mona Ozouf, *Festivals and the French Revolution*, trans. Alan Sheridan (Cambridge, Mass., 1988); Sewell, *Work and Revolution;* and Michael Sonenscher, *Work and Wages: Natural Law, Politics, and the Eighteenth-Century French Trades* (Cambridge, 1989). See also the revival of Norbert Elias's work, e.g., *The Court Society* (New York, 1983 [1969]), and *The Civilizing Process*, vol. 1: *The History of Manners;* vol. 2: *Power and Civility* (New York, 1978 and 1982 [1939]).

a rigorous and nuanced interpretation of the complex interrelationships between material and cultural worlds in eighteenth-century France. He traces the rise of compagnonnage to an erosion of the legal provisions that had granted journeymen certain rights with regard to their work in urban centers.[21] But not all journeymen were equal: Sonenscher contends that younger, itinerant, unmarried journeymen had far fewer legal rights than older, sedentary, married ones. According to Sonenscher, rituals in the compagnonnages functioned as a sort of "informal counterpart" to legal rights held by older journeymen. This analysis makes a critical contribution by revealing the active relationship that "ordinary" people had with the law and the courts. It is problematic, however, to locate the origins of compagnonnage in the erosion of rights that most itinerant journeymen never had. Furthermore, Sonenscher notes that legal protections for apprentices and journeymen were much more common in Paris than in the provinces, where compagnonnage had its greatest strength.[22] In his analysis of the differentiation of compagnonnage into rival sects (each with increasingly elaborate symbolism), he maintains that this process elevated some workers and lowered others in an increasingly competitive job market where many journeymen competed for the same relatively unskilled work. This functional analysis of the compagnons' system of social classification provides another dimension to our knowledge, but it neglects the role of these rituals in creating fraternity and solidarity.[23] Further, in stressing the conflict between rival groups of compagnons rather than the cohesion within such groups, Sonenscher ignores the persistent and often successful struggles of compagnons against masters. Finally, his conclusion that compagnons increasingly differentiated themselves by symbolic markers and not skill, that the "rituals of the *compagnonnages* . . . were an inverted acknowledgment of the wide dissemination of ordinary abilities," is troubling.[24] He argues from the alleged results of rituals rather than from a reading of the narrative and structure of rituals that provided a context within which itinerant compagnons could assert their demands.

21. Michael Sonenscher, *The Hatters of Eighteenth-Century France* (Berkeley, 1987); Sonenscher, *Work and Wages*, especially chap. 9, which is a revised version of his "Mythical Work"; Sonenscher and David Garrioch, "*Compagnonnages*, Confraternities, and Associations of Journeymen in Eighteenth-Century Paris," *European History Quarterly* 16 (1986): 25–45.

22. Sonenscher, *Work and Wages*, chap. 3. In the event, he concludes that the status of sixteenth- and seventeenth-century journeymen requires further study (p. 79). Sonenscher also describes changes in labor-related law in the decade before the French Revolution, but these also affected the compagnonnages less than other journeymen's brotherhoods. "Journeymen, the Courts, and the French Trades, 1781–91," *Past and Present* no. 114 (1987): 100–106.

23. See Cynthia M. Truant, "Solidarity and Symbolism among Journeymen Artisans: The Case of *Compagnonnage*," *Comparative Studies in Society and History* 21 (1979): 214–26.

24. Sonenscher, *Work and Wages*, p. 323.

We must, for example, ask if the rituals encode patterns of exclusion or rank. Does the symbolism used in the ritual relate to concepts of skill or the dignity of labor? How are rituals related to their particular and general economic, political, and cultural contexts? I do not mean to deny the importance of the "function" of ritual and other symbolic practices, but to define these practices in ways less obviously or directly tied to material interest. The symbolic practices of compagnonnage also operated as texts that created meaning. What I am piecing together from my reading of these symbolic practices, then, is an understanding of the culture of compagnonnage, a culture that adapted to both pre- and post-revolutionary society.

Some studies of compagnonnage have recognized that economic and social life could not be separated from symbolic practice. Etienne Martin Saint-Léon, in his scholarly and extremely well-documented study of compagnonnage, gives sympathetic attention to its rituals, myths, and symbols. These, he says, helped create social solidarity during the height of compagnonnage, but by the nineteenth century, they had undesirable consequences. Emile Coornaert owes much to Martin Saint-Léon's evidence, but he reorganizes these data in an analytically provocative way. Coornaert divides his study into three parts: the historical evolution of compagnonnage, the "constants" (organization, "life," secrecy), and the compagnons' associational behavior and interaction with the environment. This division implies a dynamic among the three parts and certainly gives great weight to the role of symbolic practice, but Coornaert never truly develops his analysis of this interaction.[25]

Jean Lecuir contends that the compagnons' symbolism and ritual must be seen in the context of the popular culture of early modern France. He links compagnonnage to associations such as confraternities and youth groups with which it shared many beliefs and practices rooted in institutional Christianity. The rituals of compagnonnage, in his view, created vital networks of solidarity for itinerant journeymen.[26]

William Sewell's *Work and Revolution: The Language of Labor from the Old Regime to 1848* provides a wider context for my exploration of the culture of compagnonnage. His analysis of workers' associations in France before

25. Etienne Martin Saint-Léon, *Le Compagnonnage: Son histoire, ses coutumes, ses règlements, ses rites* (Paris, 1901); and Coornaert, *Les Compagnonnages.* Unfortunately, Coornaert provides very few footnotes and almost no direct archival references.

26. Jean Lecuir, "Associations ouvrières de l'époque moderne: Clandestinité et culture populaire," *Revue du vivarais,* special issue of *Histoire et clandestinité du Moyen-Age à la Première Guerre Mondiale,* ed. Michèle Tilloy et al., pp. 273–90 (Paris, 1979). In addition to the solidarity within each sect, I have noted elsewhere that symbolic practice also established boundaries and acted as "a charter for legitimizing both opposition and alliance between *rites*" (Truant, "Solidarity and Symbolism," p. 224).

and after the Revolution focuses on their culture and language in a
crucial transitional era of French history. Sewell was among the first to
insist on careful attention to workers' discourse—speeches, writings, and
practice—"texts" in which they articulate their understanding of their
roles as producers and consumers. Sewell is interested in the origins of
compagnonnage and its role in postrevolutionary society. He focuses on
ways the compagnons created their own particular organizations by drawing on the vocabulary they shared with other corporate groups.[27] Sewell
cogently argues that compagnonnage, as one of the few corporate associations to survive the Revolution, was an important repository of
corporate language, ideals, and practice. Although the sects of compagnonnage were never able to reform themselves fundamentally or to become major participants in the organization of labor, their ability to
transmit the "corporate idiom" into the new regime aided in the process
of rethinking the meaning and form of association.

Sewell's central point about "the creative adaptation of workers' corporate mentality and institutions to the new legal regime of property
emerging out of the French Revolution" has generated some stimulating
responses. Lynn Hunt and George Sheridan, for example, in their re-
examination of Sewell's interpretation of the practice of association and
its ideological content, question his conclusion that compagnonnage or
related associations provided "the bridge between corporatism and the
liberal revolutionary heritage." Finding his conclusion "a highly selective understanding of the workers' movement of the 1830s and 1840s,"
Hunt and Sheridan maintain that no single coherent ideology of association emerged in this period. Although they agree that worker thought
and autonomy must be introduced into the debate on class formation
and consciousness, they also insist that "rather than making history entirely in their own image, workers discovered how much of their identity
was shaped by other histories once they resolved to become actors on
that stage."[28]

Here, I examine specifically how compagnons' identities were shaped
by other histories and, even more, by the subtle interplay between representation and practice. This sort of study entails the interpretation of

27. Sewell, *Work and Revolution*, especially chaps. 2, 3, and 8. Sewell mentions Freemasonry
as one of the old regime corps with which compagnonnage shared a common vocabulary (p.
60), but Masonic influence on the compagnonnages was much more a nineteenth- than an
eighteenth-century phenomenon.
28. Lynn Hunt and George Sheridan, "Corporatism, Association, and the Language of Labor
in France, 1750–1850," *Journal of Modern History* 58 (December 1986): 837, 839, 843–44. See
also Sonenscher, "Mythical Work," p. 32, and "Journeymen, Courts, and French Trades," pp.
100–107. Sonenscher's discussion of legal redress adds a critical dimension to Sewell's analysis
of worker protest. None of these studies, however, examines the gendered aspects of workers'
associations.

texts whose contents and contexts are not easily deciphered. Roger Chartier outlines three valuable strategies for the reading of such texts:

> First, to take the text as a text and to try to determine its intentions,
> its strategies and the effects produced by its discourse; next, to
> avoid supposing a stable, full value in its lexical choices, but to
> take into account the semantic investment or disinvestment of its
> terms; finally, to define the instances of behaviour and the rituals
> present in the text on the basis of the specific way in which they
> are assembled or produced by original invention, rather than to
> categorize them on the basis of remote resemblances to codified
> forms among the repertory of Western folk-culture.[29]

To understand the complexities and dynamic of the culture of compagnonnage I propose a history from the inside out, using the terms the
actors employed to structure and give meaning to patterns of belief and
behavior. My history is largely based on a close reading of as many of
the compagnons' own texts as possible. As Chartier warns, we must recognize the dangers in "reading" this material. No text is a transparent
or objective rendering of reality. Even rich and complex accounts, like
those of Perdiguier, have biases, ambiguities, and silences, which can be
revealed and revealing. Interpreting texts that recount ceremonies are
doubly difficult.[30] Such evidence, nonetheless, sharpens our insight into
the ways compagnons perceived or experienced particular configura-
tions of language, ritual, and work. Yet, even as I attempt to provide the
compagnons' version, my own voice intrudes and interprets. My explanations do not disregard the compagnons' views, but rather compare my
informants' accounts and open them up to another level of analysis.

The rationale of voluntary associations such as compagnonnage was
to create a culture of solidarity and brotherhood. The compagnons drew
elements from a variety of corporate and fraternal institutions to construct brotherhoods that were impelled by particular economic and social conditions. Their culture mimicked and paralleled but also

29. Chartier, *Cultural History*, p. 109. My interpretive strategies have also been greatly informed by works like those by Davis, *Society and Culture*; Darnton, *Great Cat Massacre*; Ginzburg,
Cheese and Worms; and Hunt, *Politics, Culture, and Class*.

30. Chartier is particularly wary of interpreting action recounted in texts. See the Chartier-
Darnton debate: Chartier, "Text, Symbols, and Frenchness," in *Cultural History*, pp. 94–111; and
Robert Darnton, "The Symbolic Element in History," *Journal of Modern History* 58 (1986): 86–
93. I agree with Chartier that definitions and uses of "texts" (particularly texts of rituals) must
be more precise but also think he too radically circumscribes our speculations on the social
action represented in these texts. Moreover, unlike the case of the "cat massacre," I generally
know whether or not certain rituals were performed and have other forms of corroborating
evidence to assist my textual interpretation.

transformed the solidarity of the family and of traditional corporate organizations: corps des métiers, religious brotherhoods, confraternities,
and youth groups such as the lords of misrule. Sometime in the late
eighteenth century, elements of Masonic language and practice crept in,
becoming more pervasive in the nineteenth century.[31]

Nor is it insignificant that the compagnons expressed their solidarity
in the form of *brother*hoods. Although the term *brotherhood* is not used by
the compagnons to name their associations, I believe it is, in this case,
a particularly suitable analytical category. The initiation rituals of compagnonnage made unrelated men into fictive kin, specifically, brothers,
who symbolically rejected their families of origin and took on new names
and nicknames. Nicknames tended to be strongly gendered, whether
celebrating virtuous fidelity to the sect or male bravado and virility. Compagnons who worked, ate, lived, and performed rituals together reinforced these bonds of brotherhood. Originally, compagnonnage was
meant to be a liminal and temporary stage for young unmarried men
usually between the ages of eighteen and thirty—a passage between
childhood, apprenticeship, and dependence on the one hand, and adulthood, mastership, and independence on the other.

In the early modern era brotherhoods, including compagnonnages,
were at first closely linked to the patriarchal household, but that link
weakened with the growth of markets and the intensification of economic competition in the seventeenth and eighteenth century. Access
to mastership and, thus, to formal adulthood and male privileges was
curtailed and the semidependence of the journeyman prolonged, sometimes indefinitely. Mary Ann Clawson's work on fraternalism and patriarchy convincingly argues that, in these conditions, fraternal associations
in general "provided their participants with institutionalized ways to intervene in the patriarchal system in defense of their own interests."[32] For
compagnons this defense took the form of frequent labor conflict with
master artisans. In addition, almost from the beginning there was intense
rivalry among the compagnons. By the nineteenth century compagnonnage was split into three major sects and many subdivisions, limiting any
broad concept of fraternity. Yet, division and differentiation, rather than

31. Perdiguier himself became a Freemason in 1845 but remained essentially opposed to
Masonic influence within compagnonnage itself. For an incisive work on social fraternal orders
such as the Masons and their connections to craft brotherhoods, see Clawson, *Constructing Brotherhood.* Although the brotherhoods she studies "valoriz[ed] craft labor and material productivity"
(p. 14) and shared some features with compagnonnages, their primary meaning and function
was social.
32. Clawson, "Early Modern Fraternalism and the Patriarchal Family," *Feminist Studies* 6
(1980): 368–91, p. 374. See her *Constructing Brotherhood,* pp. 25–33, for a useful discussion of
kinship within the patriarchal household.

extended group solidarity, was a common fact of old regime life which was never completely eliminated in more modern associations.

Even as the compagnons attempted to assert their male identity, male-female relations inside and outside the workshop limited the ability of young journeymen to differentiate themselves from women and assert their superiority. Recent scholarship reveals the important interdependence of male and female workers in production. Whereas most women might be considered less skilled than the compagnons, there was at least one woman who could not be treated as a subordinate: the master's wife. She often played a major role in hiring, training, and disciplining journeymen, and she took her husband's place in the workshop during his absence.[33]

Outside the workshop, compagnons tended to view women in traditional ways, as whores, virgins, or mothers. In song compagnons portrayed themselves as dashing swains always ready and willing for diversion. In his memoirs Jacques-Louis Ménétra, an extraordinary eighteenth-century compagnon glazier, boasts of enjoying more than fifty-two affairs before marriage. Some of his conquests were "charming widows."[34] However much reality or fiction informs Ménétra's account, women always played crucial roles in compagnonnage. Members reinforced their brotherhood by living together at inns, usually run by women called *mères* (mothers), who were ideally expected to behave as surrogate mothers. Even when male innkeepers, called *pères* (fathers), ran these lodgings, the inn itself was always called the *Mère,* one of the earliest terms linked to compagnonnage. The powerful imagery of this brotherhood often works to construct relationships—real or metaphorical—to maternal and paternal authority.

My investigation begins with the decades leading up to 1848, when changes in production methods generated a major debate over the organization of labor. The role of compagnonnage in this debate illustrates clearly that this apparently esoteric association was in fact aware of and involved in contemporary economic, social, and cultural transformations. Indeed, the debate on the "social question" included a consid-

33. See, e.g., Natalie Zemon Davis, "Women in the Crafts in Sixteenth-Century Lyon," *Feminist Studies* 8 (Spring 1982): 46–80; Barbara Hanawalt, ed., *Women and Work in Pre-industrial Europe* (Bloomington, Ind., 1986); Martha C. Howell, *Women, Production, and Patriarchy in Late Medieval Cities* (Chicago, 1986); and Merry Wiesner, "Women's Work in the Changing City Economy, 1500–1650," in *Connecting Spheres: Women in the Western World, 1500 to the Present,* ed. Marilyn Boxer and Jean Quataert (Oxford, 1987), pp. 64–74; and Wiesner, *Working Women in Renaissance Germany* (New Brunswick, N.J., 1986). Sonenscher, *Hatters,* pp. 20–25, explains that women made up two of the five major groups of workers involved in hat production in the eighteenth century and did much of the labor-intensive work of preparing and finishing hats.

34. Jacques-Louis Ménétra, *Journal of My Life,* ed. Daniel Roche, trans. Arthur Goldhammer (New York, 1986), p. xi and passim.

eration of the role of compagnonnage in French society. Some saw only a primitive, outmoded organization, but others believed its sects could overcome their divisions to expand their fraternity in a national context and create a foundation for a united working class. Thus, 1848 was perhaps the "political" apogee of compagnonnage, generating the point of most intense connection between it and the wider culture, and the most explicit articulation of this relationship.

The failure of the hopes raised in 1848 made that revolution a critical point in the life of compagnonnage just as it more obviously was for French society in general. In the aftermath of 1848, the importance of compagnonnage for laboring men was vastly reduced; 1848 also put an end to any notions that compagnonnage could become a vehicle for a more broadly based labor movement. The Revolution of 1848 did not, of course, put an end to compagnonnage itself and the logic of my interpretation of ritual and myth takes me beyond 1848 to the end of the nineteenth century.

The brotherhoods of compagnonnage, despite the limitations of internecine warfare and a membership technically limited to unmarried men, were extraordinarily resilient and effective for at least two hundred years. Compagnonnage provided one of the few comprehensive associations for the organization of skilled workers in many trades until at least 1830. The two major sects of compagnonnage certainly had the most solidly established and widely extended interregional network of any workers' association up to that time, providing a valuable system of mutual aid, placement, and social integration at each stop on the migratory compagnon's route through France. These brotherhoods also gave their members some degree of leverage in the labor market. In certain trades compagnonnage remained a viable labor organization to the end of the nineteenth century. To relegate compagnonnage to the realm of the vestigial obscures the importance of an early, persistent, and complex form of voluntary association and limits our understanding of the changing character of and attitudes toward ritual, myth, and secrecy in both early modern and modern culture.

In this book I am less interested in the success or failure of the societies of compagnonnage as labor organizations, or in the modes of production, structure, and technology of the crafts, than in how compagnons in a wide variety of trades created and maintained their brotherhoods throughout France. I want to understand the ways that the practice and practices of compagnonnage were constructed both by members and outsiders. Thus, I begin with 1848 to demonstrate that any interpretation of compagnonnage must travel backward and forward in time. This unusual chronology also enables me to bypass a rigid teleological framework and to avoid isolating compagnonnage from the wider society. In subsequent chapters, I address the questions about the nature of compagnonnage provoked by the ferment of the 1830s and 1840s by returning to the origins of these brotherhoods in the seventeenth century (Chapters 2 and 3) and to their growth and consolidation in the eighteenth century (Chapters 4 and 5). In the final chapters the analysis returns to the nineteenth century to reconstruct the compagnons' responses to the postrevolutionary world.

My strategy represents the subject from multiple vantage points because the various components of compagnonnage had diverse—and sometimes conflicting—meanings and functions. These brotherhoods changed over time and not always in uniformly progressive or retrogressive ways. My particular itinerary through the centuries of compagnonnage allows me to be attentive to these complexities in the compagnons' "practice of everyday life," to recreate the multifaceted existence of their brotherhoods, and to understand what they produced—not so much in wood, stone, or metal as in words, images, and practices.[35]

35. Michel de Certeau uses the concept "the practice of everyday life" in his investigation of the "ways in which users—commonly assumed to be passive and guided by established rules—operate" (*The Practice of Everyday Life* [Berkeley, 1984], p. xi). His approach is not a return to a simple notion of the individual will but a study of action within the context, limits, and possibilities of society and culture. Although Certeau here was more concerned with consumers than producers and my emphasis is the reverse, his ideas on the *arts de faire* and "ordinary" language and culture have been very influential.

CHAPTER 1

Scenes and Seeing from the Outside: Toward 1848

If this Republic we have proclaimed, blackened with the
gunpowder of the barricades, ever needs our support to repulse any aggression . . . all our little Republics [of compag-
nonnage] will form but one to serve as a shield for our
common Mother, and Tyranny will never touch her until it
has crushed our bloodied bodies.

—Les Compagnons réunis, 1848

On 20 March 1848 some eight to ten thousand compagnons gathered at the place de la République for a historic reconciliation of the
three major sects of compagnonnage. Their frock coats and top hats
were adorned with elaborate and colorful ribbons and sashes, the symbols of their many trades and societies. Ignoring these distinctions, the
compagnons formed a long column, linked arms, and advanced to the
Hôtel de Ville. The press was enthusiastic. The *Gazette des tribunaux*, a
major journal of legal and crime news (formerly a harsh critic of these
brotherhoods), declared the reconciliation "one of the greatest acts in
the history of Compagnonnage . . . not for a moment did this beautiful
legion of workers cease to observe the most perfect order." United by a
"holy and solemn oath . . . the brothers wished all Paris to bear witness
to this great act."[1]

Who were these men, organized as brothers into what they called "little republics" pledged to the defense of the new national republic, which
they hailed as their common mother?[2] Less than a decade earlier, the

1. "Chronique de Paris," *Gazette des tribunaux*, 22 March 1848, p. 513.
2. AN, BB[30] 300, piece 1948, 20 March 1848, address to the Provisional Government by the
"compagnons réunis." Family metaphors were common in 1848, but their use and meaning
could and did differ. For a compelling discussion of the framing of this discourse among male
and female garment workers in 1848, see Joan Wallach Scott, *Gender and the Politics of History*
(New York, 1988), pp. 93–112.

public had still viewed compagnons as inhabiting a rather separate space, both exotic and dangerous, within French society. Now they seemed to speak a common language and be pledged to a common national purpose. In 1839 Agricol Perdiguier, as a former compagnon, had written that "compagnonnage has very particular customs and habits; it forms a striking contrast to everything else around it. However, no one seems to have really seen it or talked about it at all."[3] Perdiguier meant that no one had seen it or talked about it with the knowledge and from the perspective of the compagnons, despite the fact that the police and the public had always known something about compagnonnage.

Members of the semiclandestine brotherhoods of compagnonnage were journeymen in the skilled trades, especially joiners, locksmiths, metal workers, stonecutters, and carpenters. These young, unmarried workers, hailing from almost all regions of France, had completed their apprenticeships and were now on the tramp—the tour de France. Almost all journeymen, whether compagnons or not, traveled and worked throughout France for about three years before attempting to become masters. The tour was a means to gain and perfect the skills of their trades as well as to distribute the labor market. For the youthful compagnons these travels also constituted a poor man's grand tour. Diverting, empowering, at times dangerous, the tour was always an education.

Compagnons were thus not an uncommon sight. They tramped the roads of France, flourishing long canes or walking sticks; they labored in French workshops; they drank, sang, and brawled in cabarets and on the streets. People heard about their mysteries and about their walkouts and plots against the masters. Some witnessed acts of mutual aid and friendship in the compagnons' public ceremonies. Others considered these rituals of solidarity the prelude to the bloody brawls of rival sects. The public, then, had some knowledge of compagnonnage but, as Perdiguier would say, had not *really* seen it. The French public began to know more about it beginning in the 1820s, from the police reports and dispatches picked up in the press, especially in the new *Gazette des tribunaux,* founded in 1825.

In the 1840s, after the publication and serialization of Perdiguier's *Livre du compagnonnage,* information multiplied rapidly. Newspapers of all political persuasions devoted feature articles to compagnonnage, and novelists, playwrights, and social critics contributed serious and popular

3. Agricol Perdiguier, *Le Livre du compagnonnage, contenant des chansons de compagnons, un dialogue sur l'architecture, un raisonnement sur le trait, une notice sur le compagnonnage, la rencontre de deux frères, et un grand nombre de notes,* 2d ed., 2 vols. (Paris, 1841), 1:7. Pierre Zaccone was similarly struck by this passage and echoed Perdiguier's view that foreigners might appreciate compagnonnage more than French scholars. *Histoire des sociétés secrètes,* 2 vols. (Paris, 1866 [1847]), 2: 622.

works. Publicity had complex effects beyond merely satisfying the curiosity (or even voyeurism) of a widening audience. The discourse on compagnons, and workers in general, also served a policing function, voicing warnings and criticisms about the allegedly antisocial conduct of this class and augmenting the state's police powers by keeping workers under a potentially vast public surveillance. Increasingly, too, publicity became a means to garner public support for the reform of political and social evils, not merely a tool for criticizing the unruly and seditious individuals or groups within the working classes.[4]

In this chapter I explore changes in outsiders' perception of compagnonnage and the nature of their contacts with compagnons in the decades before the Revolution of 1848. Three major "texts" in the life of compagnonnage frame my discussion of its public face in these decades: its *rixes* and *conduites* (brawls and public ceremonies); the publication and reception of Perdiguier's *Livre du compagnonnage;* and the Parisian carpenters' strike of 1845. I use and deconstruct these texts both to link compagnonnage to the wider French society and culture and to represent the context within which compagnons constructed their associations.

These three points of entry into the life of compagnonnage all contribute to an understanding of the dramatic public appearance of a united compagnonnage in 1848. Each episode illustrates the tensions imbedded within the culture of compagnonnage: between group solidarity and individual liberty; between hierarchy and equality; and between fratricide and fraternity. This chapter introduces that culture; subsequent chapters explore its creation and persistent tensions.

SAVAGE LEGACIES AND PHILANTHROPIC SENTIMENTS

On 1 September 1825 a serious brawl broke out between rival groups of stonecutters working on the outskirts of the small town of Tournus, an important center for granite quarrying north of Mâcon. The prefect of the Saône et Loire immediately reported to the minister of the inte-

4. See Dan Schiller, "From Rogues to the Rights of Men: Crime News and the *Police Gazette* (1845–1847)," *Media, Culture, and Society* 2 (1980): 377–88, esp. 386–87, for an innovative analysis of the social-political role created by a national, relatively inexpensive crime news journal in the United States. The *Police Gazette*, while focusing much attention on lower-class "rogues," simultaneously voiced a more democratic discourse—one critical of all corruption that lay at the root of class divisions. On the *Gazette des tribunaux*, see Claude Bellanger et al., eds., *Histoire générale de la presse française*, 5 vols. (Paris, 1969), 2:87, 89, 115, 146. The *Gazette des tribunaux* was relatively expensive in this era and directed toward a more middle-class readership than the U.S. *Police Gazette.*

rior, describing a fight involving about two hundred compagnon stone-cutters "du devoir de Salomon," who urged their comrades on with cries of "charge, charge" and "brother" ("zou, zou," "cotterie"), against roughly sixty stonecutters "du devoir de Saint Jacques." To restore order, the prefect called in the nearby gendarmerie to aid Tournus's small "police" force of forty firemen. The enraged compagnons du devoir de Salomon turned their attack against these new opponents, shouting, "Close down the workshops. . . . Long live *les enfants de Salomon!* Death to the authorities! F... the authorities, fight to the bitter end. Down with the authorities!"[5] To the consternation of the inhabitants of Tournus, the compagnons' "sedition" soon spilled onto public streets. By day's end new fears arose as the compagnons of Solomon, now four hundred strong, threatened to torch the city. Late that night, although ten men had been arrested, the insurrection's leaders (*moteurs*) were still at large and new troubles were expected. When two days passed with no new fighting, the prefect felt assured that "complete tranquility had been reestablished in Tournus."[6]

Unknown to the prefect, however, the leaders of the compagnons of Solomon had hidden themselves in the quarries outside the city. They wrote to their comrades on the tour de France and asked them to "lend us a hand as we would do for you if you were in our position." The request for help—"send at least thirty stonecutters and more if there are any"—was swiftly answered, and trouble soon broke out anew.[7] On 16 September a troop of seventy to eighty compagnons du devoir de Salomon arrived from Paris, Versailles, and other towns near the capital. Some took public carriages to speed their arrival, not bothering to hide their distinctive insignia—earrings shaped like hammers, ribbons, boutonnieres. Others were openly armed with long canes and iron compasses, the tools of their tramp and their trade transformed into threatening weapons. Arriving on the outskirts of Tournus, the stonecutters "passed muster," were "divided into platoons," and marched like soldiers into the town, singing battle songs that "provoked dread among all."

> Forward march, on the double
> assassinate all these brigands
> with blows of our canes,

5. AN, F⁷ 9787, dos. Saône et Loire, 1 September 1825, "Compagnons tailleurs de pierre, enfants de Salomon," report of prefect to minister of the interior.

6. AN, F⁷ 9897, dos. Saône et Loire, 3 September 1825

7. AN, F⁷ 9898, dos. Saône et Loire, Lyon, 22 September 1825, procès-verbal, commissioner of police, containing a letter by the compagnons du devoir de Salomon dated 3 September 1825.

with blows of our compasses. . . .
destroy these scoundrels
and their supporters.

This time, however, the police were prepared and launched a preemptive strike, arresting a number of the principal leaders and charging them with "attacks and opposition against police agents, the judiciary, and agents of public order."[8]

The stonecutters insisted they were defending their rights. The prosecution's brief alleged that the cause of the violence lay "in the pretension, long claimed by a certain corporation of Compagnonnage, called 'du devoir de Salomon,' exclusively to exploit the workshops of this city, to drive out workers of any other devoir, and to fix irrevocably the price of work based on the caprice and the interest of the association and the pressure of circumstances."[9] The trouble had begun when a master named Brocard had attempted to break this monopoly. He sent for stonecutters of another brotherhood, the enfants de Maître Jacques, who agreed to lower pay than their rivals. The ensuing brawl was a ritualized defense of the prerogative claimed by the devoir of Solomon to set the price of labor and in effect impose a closed shop in the quarries of Tournus. The fight began with economic and social roots, and ended in opposition to the police, making compagnonnage appear very dangerous. Although the compagnons' economic demands were clear and their tactics not unlike those used by more modern labor associations—boycotts and closed shops—their defense was based on rights that derived from their traditions and *devoir* (or code of duty). The compagnons on trial reiterated their right to settle economic issues and uphold their honor without intervention from those outside their association. The authorities, of course, denied that any workers had such rights. Trouble among the devoirs of compagnonnage continued to erupt in Tournus after September, although the compagnons of Solomon generally dominated the work force and controlled prices in stonecutting.

Later that year rival devoirs of stonecutters in this region sought to resolve their differences peacefully in a *concours*, a competition of skill. The most proficient member of each devoir was to create a chef d'oeuvre to be judged by an impartial jury of experts. The victors would "win" Tournus and its lucrative quarries; the losers would be banned from

8. AN, F⁷ 9897, dos. Saône et Loire, Tournus, 16 September 1825, mayor to prefect, and 9 November 1825, minister of the interior to minister of justice.

9. AN, F⁷ 9787, dos. Saône et Loire, 20 November 1825, "act of accusation against the workers of Tournus."

working there for a number of years—traditionally as long as a century.[10]
The prefect was favorably inclined toward the proposal but remained
cynical: "If this struggle, which has been threatening to become bloody,
. . . is ending in such an honorable way, one must praise this. Yet, at the
same time, one is astounded that such honorable feelings can arise from
such coarse souls, who would have but lately massacred their enemies
without mercy."[11] Could apparently base and violent men respect skill
and professionalism? If there were such qualities hidden in these "coarse
souls," the prefect never discovered them. His suspicions were confirmed when the competition was unmasked as a ruse by the compagnons of Solomon to ambush their rivals.

The press, especially before the 1840s, would generally have agreed
with the prefect's representation of the events of Tournus as a savage
brawl. Journals would also have viewed the rituals of the brotherhoods
as bizarre. One such rite, the *conduite* (literally "conduct"), or leave-
taking ceremony, one of compagnonnage's most fraternal rites, was often the prelude to rixes.[12] All the compagnons of a sect would gather,
usually near the edge of town, to give a departing compagnon a rousing
send-off (see Figures 1 and 2). The ceremony was preceded by a great
deal of eating and especially drinking, which continued during the ceremony as compagnons drank toast after toast and sang warlike songs
vaunting their prowess and denigrating that of their opponents. Innocent bystanders, unaffiliated workers, and rival compagnons were often
drawn into the melees that followed these spirited celebrations of group
solidarity. Sometimes rival compagnons or other workers actually initiated brawls by staging a "false conduite": they marched alongside the
first group of compagnons, mimicking and ridiculing their rivals' performance.

One such event occurred in Bordeaux in 1824 as several ironworkers
and locksmiths were accompanying a fellow compagnon to the city limits.
En route they were assailed by roughly sixty compagnons of an opposing
sect, who wounded one of the first group and set the rest to flight.[13] The

10. Such competitions can be documented: e.g., in Marseille in 1809 the compagnon locksmiths du devoir won a concours with the masterpiece created by one Angle-le-Dauphiné. His
lock, known as the "légion d'honneur," was exhibited at the Exposition universelle in 1900.
Roger Lecotté, *Les Archives historiques du compagnonnage* (Paris, 1956), p. 117. Even if a victor
could be agreed upon, however, the losers rarely observed the full term of the ban.
11. AN, F⁷ 9797, dos. Saône et Loire, 28 November 1825, prefect to minister of the interior.
12. Cf. Cynthia M. Truant, "Fracas et fraternité: Des compagnons du tour de France et des
compagnies de pompiers volontaires de Philadelphie au première moitié du dix-neuvième siècle," in *Travail et production en France et aux USA*, ed. Pierre Bouvier et al. (Paris, 1988), pp. 12–
28. In the 1820s and 1830s compagnons commissioned elaborate paintings of these rites; their
iconography is discussed in Chapter 6.
13. AN, F⁷ 9786, dos. Gironde, 10 December 1824, report of gendarmerie.

Figure 1. Conduite of DeBlois l'aimable, "le soutien de Père Soubise," Compagnon roofer, bon drille, in Bordeaux, ca. 1825. Watercolor by Etienne Leclair. Source: Musée du Compagnonnage, Tours.

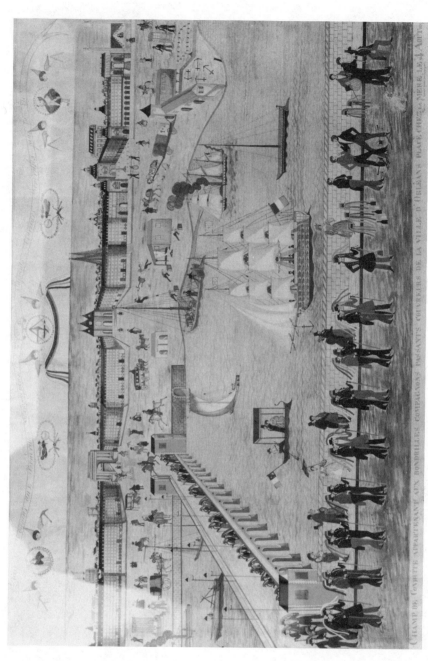

Figure 2. Conduite of the compagnon roofers du devoir, bon drilles, in Orléans, 4 August 1839. Watercolor by Auguste LeMoine. Source: Musée du Compagnonnage, Tours.

unequal numbers, the dishonorable nature of the attack, and the intensity of such battles gave the compagnons the reputation of being violent, unprincipled men. The major liberal newspaper *Le Constitutionnel* called compagnonnage "a savage legacy of the barbarian eras, an association in the state of resistance, fierce, turbulent, hateful, exclusive."[14]

Many papers of the 1820s and 1830s devoted extensive coverage to the unsavory features of compagnonnage, capturing the bourgeois imagination and inflaming its fears. Jean Briquet in his work on Perdiguier reports the impression from those decades as one where "everyone complains about [compagnonnage's] excesses, which fill the pages of the judicial chronicals," such as the widely read *Gazette des tribunaux*.[15] Louis Claays found widespread hostility to compagnons' brawls in Toulouse (1800–1848), as reflected in newspaper articles and letters to the editor. The Toulouse press condemned compagnonnage for its exclusivity, echoing the growing complaints of workers themselves. Compagnons, said the *Journal de Toulouse*, were "spirits hardened to any type of progress . . . assassins of the open road [who] carry out veritable ambushes . . . [and have] a fanatical ardor for forms whose sense they do not even understand."[16]

The police and judicial authorities were interested in the motivations behind what they, too, tended to view as savagery. These officials had been the principal outside "experts" on compagnonnage before the advent of crime-reporting newspapers. Their reports expressed more ambivalence and presented more balanced interpretations of compagnonnage than the press of the 1820s and 1830s.

Toward the middle of the first decade of the nineteenth century, as compagnonnage began a dynamic revival after the disruption of the Revolution, extensive official reports and notes reveal efforts to understand compagnonnage and a debate on whether to eliminate it entirely or to try to tame it. From the time of Louis XIV and Colbert the French police and judiciary had been interested in regulating and supervising the working classes, the poor, and all those considered potentially dangerous to good order. In the nineteenth century, nostalgia for the old regime and the sense that compagnonnage might actually help to restrain labor disorders produced somewhat more tolerant views of the officially illegal association. In any event compagnonnage's real and growing presence in the world of work stimulated detailed police accounts and analysis,

14. *Le Constitutionnel*, 2 February 1841, cited in Perdiguier, *Livre du compagnonnage*, 2d ed., 1: 96.

15. Jean Briquet, *Agricol Perdiguier: Compagnon du tour de France et représentant du peuple (1805–1875)* (Paris, 1955), p. 181.

16. Louis Claays, "Le Compagnonnage à Toulouse de 1800 à 1848" (Maîtrise, Université de Toulouse, 1969), pp. 65–66, citing *Journal de Toulouse*, 27 July 1829.

particularly in the context of the reorganized and highly structured Napoleonic system.

Detailed descriptions of the practices of compagnonnage, beyond or unrelated to any labor disturbances, proliferated in this era. In 1809 the attorney general of the Gironde told the minister of police in Paris that "everyone knows [members of compagnonnage] by the ribbons on their hats and their canes. No one, however, except the members of this brotherhood knows the meaning of their mysterious signs." The commissioner general of Lyon reported that on patron saints' days and before the "ceremony of the conduite" compagnons had masses said for them; they held meetings and "ran around the streets with their multicolored ribbons, according to their class and rank." In their public processions compagnons wore distinctive ribbons, sashes, and earrings and carried canes and bouquets. These parades, accompanied by bands playing lively music, included the proud display of large-scale masterpieces of their trades, borne aloft on platforms. The subprefect of the Rhône described a patron saint's day in 1809, "a solemn occasion" when the compagnons marched "in a row, like troops, preceded by military firemen [*sappeurs*] and a drum major *in costume* and drummers who beat the rhythm."[17] In 1824 the prefect of the Loire Inférieure discussed workers in Nantes who were "given over to the dangerous customs of compagnonnage": rope makers adorned themselves with ribbons, "signs of recognition among members of compagnonnage"; nail makers carried long canes of four to five feet in length "and had masters in the art of wielding these weapons to train them."[18] Elements of an older popular culture mingled with aspects of a newer national culture drawn perhaps from military drill and service in the wars of the Revolution and Empire. Such cultural fusion was even more evident in the Tournus rixe.

Even when official reports told their tales without extensive comment, they still made judgments: acts that compagnons viewed as joyous fraternal demonstrations, the police labeled "debauchery and sedition." When commentary exists, more overt biases emerge. Reports frequently linked the customs of compagnonnage to demonstrations that endangered public order, again, as had been the case in Tournus.[19] Nonethe-

17. AN, F⁷ 4236, dos. Gironde: 1809–11, Bordeaux, 8 November 1809; dos. Rhône, Lyon, 3 January 1812, commissioner general to councillor of state, 14 May 1809, subprefect to councillor of state.

18. AN, F⁷ 9787, dos. Loire Inférieure, Nantes, 15 November 1824, prefect to minister of interior.

19. According to Yves-Marie Bercé, early modern authorities were convinced that all popular festivals were serious threats to social order and political hierarchy. *Fête et révolte: Des mentalités populaires du XVIe au XVIIIe siècle* (Paris, 1976), pp. 13–18, 74–82. Although unruly festivals rarely evolved into major revolts, the pervasive belief that they could easily do so shaped responses to them. Sometimes festivals embraced acts of defiance or were read as persistent expressions of

less, official interpretations of compagnonnage could be nuanced, at least by contrast with press reports before the late 1830s. Not all authorities who came in contact with it, particularly in the Restoration era, considered its activities dangerous or its members debauched. On the local level compagnonnage was sometimes condoned or tolerated because of economic conditions, pragmatic views about its utility as a vehicle of social control, or ambiguities in the legislation on association. Some officials even evinced a more sympathetic, albeit paternalistic, vision of workers' needs—although not of workers' rights.

The prefect of the Charente, for example, expressed his favorable views of the statutes of a group of compagnon shoemakers in Angoulême in 1813. Their regulations revealed nothing he considered in any way reprehensible. Indeed, he reported, they seemed "to have their basis in those sentiments of philanthropy which tie men more closely together than for [just] their mutual aid."[20] Similarly, a long report of the special commissioner of police in Toulouse in 1811 had evoked the deplorable condition of workers and recognized the ability of compagnonnage to alleviate poverty: "One of the bases of this institution is its charitable role, one precious to preserve because a destitute worker, arriving in a town, finds food, shelter, and very soon afterward, work. One cannot deny, that in this respect it is a very great source of assistance for this very numerous class." Yet, the special commissioner's sympathy was strongly tempered by other considerations: he added that compagnonnage "contributes in an important way to diminishing the number of vagabonds and brigands."[21] Official tolerance tended to be linked to the potential use of the brotherhoods for social and economic control of an "unruly" class of men now that the trade corporations (the corps des métiers) no longer existed. With the abolition of the guilds in 1790, workers had lost their clearly defined status in French society. Some officials reasoned that campagnonnage, one of the few remaining links to the trade corporations, could serve to discipline workers and subordinate them to the needs of society.

Similar ambivalence and self-interest persisted and grew in the restoration era. In 1820 the prefect of the Gironde, although he claimed to deplore its violence, stated he was reluctant to prohibit the association,

---

resistance. See, e.g., Philip Hoffman on Counter-Reformation curbs on popular culture, *Church and Community in the Diocese of Lyon, 1500–1789* (New Haven, 1984), pp. 90–95. We cannot thus dismiss such practices as mere entertainment or traditional mechanisms to control popular rebelliousness without further investigation.

20. AN, F⁷ 4236, dos. 9897/P², Charente, Angoulême, 3 March 1813, prefect to councillor of state, 2d arrondissement.

21. Ibid., Haute-Garonne, 9 November 1811, "Désordres commis à Toulouse," special commissioner of police to councillor of state, 2d arrondissement.

at least in Bordeaux. Technically, all workers' organizations were already outlawed by the provisions of the Napoleonic Code, which superseded the Le Chapelier Law of 1791. Ambiguities, however, remained. A decade earlier the attorney general of the Gironde wrote that compagnonnage had not been punished or repressed for ten years; rather, it had been openly tolerated as a result of legal loopholes. Unlike the Le Chapelier Law, the present laws failed to use the word *corporation,* the form the attorney general thought best defined compagnonnage. The chief justice of the Empire, responding to queries on the subject, recommended that compagnonnage be prosecuted only in "cases of excesses or other crimes . . . without discussing the group in itself, or its assemblies or other factors mentioned in the law of 1791."[22]

By 1820 the prefect of the Gironde developed these opinions into the conviction that the principles of compagnonnage were not inimical to those of the restored monarchy. Indeed, he insisted that it was "an association that resisted the Revolution." The perfect (and other officials) conveniently ignored that sects of compagnonnage had always been illegal, had always been organized by workers to defend their own interests and oppose those of old regime authorities. The prefect was interested only in the corporate form, which he saw as a means of reinforcing the restoration. He thus urged a serious examination of measures to "regulate and contain" but not destroy compagnonnage.[23]

While some Restoration officials used legal confusion about the status of compagnonnage to grant it de facto legitimacy, others persisted in condemning the association. In 1825 the minister of the interior conceded that "several tribunals have determined that the associations of compagnonnage do not fall under the jurisdictions of associations prohibited by article 291 of the Penal Code."[24] Despite these rulings, the minister believed that the law was in fact applicable. Nonetheless, attempts to enforce his interpretation were not entirely successful. Whatever the legal status of compagnonnage, police used the existing structure of its branch associations to monitor labor and economic conditions, for as the prefect of the Bouches-du-Rhône noted, compagnonnage "offers an easy means of surveillance for this mass of journeymen who are constantly on the move from one place to another. The police could perhaps tolerate the institution of *Mères* [compagnons' inns] because of their resultant utility."[25]

22. Ibid., dos. 9786/P², Gironde, Bordeaux, 8 February 1810, letter to mayor of Bordeaux, copy to prefect.
23. Georges Bourgin and Hubert Bourgin, *Les Patrons, les ouvriers, et l'état: Le Régime de l'industrie en France de 1814 à 1830,* 3 vols. (Paris, 1912–41), 1:286, quoting report of prefect to minister of the interior, 24 January 1820, AN, F⁷ 9786, dos. Gironde.
24. AN, F⁷ 9787, dos. 4431, Rhône, 1 October 1825.
25. AM Marseille, I², dos. 137, 17 April 1818. Another "great advantage," he noted, was that

Competing views made headway in the 1820s and 1830s, although the public generally continued to perceive the association in negative terms. Yet, in 1829 one condemnation met with strong opposition in the National Assembly. Presented by one Martin, a worker from Lyon, on 21 February 1829, the petition declared compagnonnage engendered violence, fostered rivalries, and tyrannized its young novices. Charles Dupin, a deputy who had made his own "tour de France" to gather information on the state of technical instruction, disagreed. He had met many compagnons during his travels, and he rose to defend them. "Compagnonnage in itself is a very moral institution," Dupin declared, "very beneficial for the working class; we must be careful not to break this social tie."[26] Admitting the need for reform, he asserted that many of its societies were already undertaking such changes. Martin's petition was defeated and removed from the agenda.

COMPAGNONNAGE REVEALED

Martin was not the first worker to appeal to the authorities to destroy compagnonnage; workers in both the old and new regimes, had objected to its tactics of domination and force. But these complaints should have had particular weight in the postrevolutionary era, after the abolition of corporations. The police received several petitions and grievances from workers in the Napoleonic era who protested that they were forced to join compagnonnage, adhere to its regulations, and pay dues.[27] In Tarascon five men ("fathers of families") wrote to the minister of the interior in 1824 to describe the long history of a "compagnonnage which is often the ruin of the young men who wish to go on the Tour de France." One man's son had been sentenced to five years' hard labor for his involvement in a violent incident of compagnonnage. The petitioners pleaded for the end of this "damnable compagnonnage" and "its assassins" or at least the reform of its most flagrant abuses. While condemning compagnonnage, the men supported the practice of the tour de France, which enabled young artisans to learn their trade well. They emphasized, moreover, that they were not opposed to the principle of association as such, only its "excesses." In 1825 several workers in

---

compagnonnage kept "workers from turning into beggars and vagabonds and [obliged] them to continue on their route . . . when they cannot find work." With far less empathy, he echoes the sentiments of the special commissioner of Toulouse.

26. *Le Moniteur universel*, 23 February 1829. Many workers rejected Dupin's paternalism: in October 1840 the workers' newspaper *L'Atelier* published an ironic thanks to Dupin, sharply critical of his continuing advice to the working class.

27. See, e.g., Dijon, 30 July 1805, AD Côte d'or, U II A b/13, and Toulouse, 11 July 1803 and 11 March 1811, AM Toulouse, liasse 77 and liasse 81.

Arles likewise called for the "destruction of perhaps the reform of the regulations of compagnonnage."[28] Much like the five men in Tarascon, they opposed its exclusivity, not the organization of labor itself.

The beginnings of reform and reevaluation in compagnonnage were affected only marginally by such criticism, however, before the 1830s. Greater impetus came from changes in postrevolutionary France itself, both the general political changes and the economic and social dislocations evident in workshop production in the first half of the nineteenth century. Compagnons who prided themselves on their skills and insisted on rigorous requirements for entry into their association seemed somewhat incongruous in a world where work was requiring less and less skill and training. Newer forms of industrial and capitalist production did not eliminate artisanal production and the need for skilled or semi-skilled labor, but they created a more competitive framework and established new relations among levels or types of workers. For example, as Ronald Aminzade notes, the increasing use of subcontractors by merchant capitalists in many trades to "organize different stages of the production process" undermined the independence not only of the small masters but of compagnons, who had to rethink their relationship to one another and to the new bargaining unit.[29]

Compagnons began to work out responses to these conditions in a context that increasingly viewed their brotherhoods as outmoded or even ridiculous. Some compagnons shared this perception. A reforming *blancher-chamoiseur* (chamois dresser), Jean-François Piron (called Vendôme la clef des coeurs), claimed his society had proposed a new devoir (code of duties) and new regulations as early as 1816. He explained that changes would have to be made "at least in terms of the language used, for its style, old and outmoded, is no longer that of our time."[30] Vendôme's argument has an Enlightenment resonance: words and things no longer corresponded and to change things it was necessary to change words. Jacques Gosset, known as the Père des forgerons (ironsmiths),

28. AN, F⁷ 9786, dos. Bouches-du-Rhône, Tarascon, 7 November 1824, "cinq pères de famille" to minister of interior, and Arles, petition, 20 January 1825.

29. Ronald Aminzade, "Reinterpreting Capitalist Industrialization: A Study of Nineteenth-Century France," in *Work in France: Representations, Meaning, Organization, and Practice,* ed. Steven Laurence Kaplan and Cynthia J. Koepp (Ithaca, 1986), pp. 413, 415–16.

30. AD Seine, 4 AZ 1068, five ms. registers [1840], "Devoir des compagnons blanchers et chamoiseurs réunis," register 2, p. 1. Police seized these registers some time in the 1840s. They are now in print: J[ean]-F[rançois] Piron, *Devoir des compagnons blanchers et chamoiseurs réunis* (Paris, 1990). *Blanchers-chamoiseurs* were dressers (and "whiteners") of delicate animal skins such as chamois. Two other trades of leather workers participated in compagnonnage: *mégisseurs,* dressers of heavier, more durable leathers, and *tanneurs-corroyeurs,* tanners and curriers of animal hides. The chamois dressers and tanners have left the more complete record of their involvement in compagnonnage. All of these trades shared some production techniques, but in the (especially French) world of artisanal production maintained distinctions and barriers between their crafts.

who wrote on the reform of compagnonnage in the early 1840s, thought it might be best to suppress the public rites such as the conduite rather than display them "in front of a mocking public."[31] Sounding a similar theme in his *Mémoires*, Agricol Perdiguier traced the origins of such ridicule and its dangers to the 1820s: "At first the public looked at us with wide-eyed astonishment and amazement, they marveled at us; soon, however, they ended up by laughing at us and compagnonnage lost its prestige."[32]

Pierre Moreau, who had been a novice compaganon but had quit and helped found and lead the rival Société de l'Union, thought it absurd that a worker should be stopped from working wherever he pleased by a man who "idiotically attaches a scrap of ribbon to his buttonhole."[33] His words acknowledge the power of compagnonnage while affirming his scorn of the forms this power took, for without that little "scrap of ribbon," many workers could not gain entry to the workshop. Thus, while ridicule of such customs turned some workers away from compagnonnage, fear and envy of its power remained potent attractions.

The internal critique of compagnonnage became more intense after 1830. As the works of Bernard Moss, John Merriman, William Sewell, and Maurice Agulhon have demonstrated, the Revolution of 1830 and its aftermath had decisive effects on the political and social organization of the working class.[34] Many individual compagnons as well as many societies of compagnonnage eagerly joined the debate on the organization of labor. Then, after nearly a decade of immersion in the new political and social ideas and encouraged by the favorable reception of two smaller projects on compagnonnage, Agricol Perdiguier published the *Livre du compagnonnage* in 1839. The book had a tremendous impact, as Etienne Martin Saint-Léon notes: "An immense mass of workers, hardly thought of by the upper classes, appeared all at once in full view. It seemed as if a State within a State, a sort of kingdom of labor with its institutions and laws, had been discovered by a poor man's Christopher Columbus."[35]

31. Jacques [a.k.a. Jean] Gosset, *Projet tendant à régénérer le compagnonnage sur le tour de France: Souvenir à tous les ouvriers* (Paris, 1842), p. 5.

32. Agricol Perdiguier, *Mémoires d'un compagnon*, ed. Alain Faure (Paris, 1977), p. 232.

33. Pierre Moreau, *Un Mot aux ouvriers de toutes les professions, à tous les amis du peuple et du progrès, sur le compagnonnage; ou, Le Guide de l'ouvrier sur le tour de France* (Auxerre, 1841), p. 28. Moreau wrote several works critical of compagnonnage.

34. See, e.g., Bernard Moss, *The Origins of the French Labor Movement, 1830–1914: The Socialism of Skilled Workers* (Berkeley, 1976); John Merriman, ed., *1830 in France* (New York, 1975); William H. Sewell, Jr., *Work and Revolution in France: The Language of Labor from the Old Regime to 1848* (Cambridge, 1980), esp. chap. 9; and Maurice Agulhon, *Une ville ouvrière au temps du socialisme utopique: Toulon de 1815 à 1851* (Paris, 1970), esp. pp. 125–53, 197–265.

35. Etienne Martin Saint-Léon, *Le Compagnonnage: Son histoire, ses coutumes, ses règlements, ses*

Parts of the book were serialized in 1840 in the major republican newspaper *Le National* and in the first and subsequent issues of the important monthly workers' newspaper *L'Atelier: Organe des intérêts moraux et matériels des ouvriers* ("The workshop: Organ of the moral and material interests of the workers"), expanding its readership among both elite and popular classes.[36] The *Livre du compagnonnage* described in detail the legends and customs—but not the initiations—of the brotherhoods, their labor activities and technical training. Above all, it was an impassioned plea for the unity of all compagnons and a testimony to the possibility of progress and enlightenment among workers. Perdiguier eloquently endorsed the basic principles of compagnonnage—solidarity, fulfillment of duty, artistry in work, and the dignity of labor. He was confident that its schisms could be healed and convinced that it was the attitudes of compagnons—and not their associations—that most needed change. And inspired by the growing power of republican sentiment and post-1830 fraternity, Perdiguier had great faith in the compagnons' ability to change.[37] Perdiguier's partisan, yet candid assessment of an association of which he himself was a member, his message of fraternity, and his authentic literary style fascinated and charmed his readers.

The literary "greats" of the time—Lamennais, Chateaubriand, Lamartine, Beranger—were lavish in their praise. All wrote extremely flattering letters to Perdiguier. Lamennais called the *Livre du compagnonnage* "one of the most useful books one could read these days"; Lamartine eagerly congratulated the author on attempting this "noble task" of "extinguishing the hatred between the various trades."[38] Although some opposition papers (the *Courrier,* the *Siècle*) remained silent, the conservative press generally lauded Perdiguier's work. The view of the influential *Journal des débats* was typical: "As a collection of historical and statistical information on compagnonnage, M. Perdiguier's publication is remarkable, because it is a little-known, little-studied subject. . . .As an expression of sentiments of order, it deserves to be welcomed with great

rites (Paris, 1901), p. 240; quoted in Jean Briquet, "Signification sociale du compagnonnage," *Revue d'histoire economique et sociale* 23 (1955): 329.

36. Briquet, *Agricol Perdiguier,* p. 240. Serialization in these two papers may not have been accidental: the democratic *Atelier* had some links with the republican *National.* Bellanger et al., *Histoire générale de la presse française* 2:210.

37. Only a few years later Perdiguier confessed his inability to counter growing factionalism (often based on seniority). "It is very certain," he declared, "that in former times compagnonnage was not fragmented as one sees it in our day" (Agricol Perdiguier, *Histoire d'une scission dans le compagnonnage* [Paris, 1846], p. 7).

38. Lamennais to Perdiguier, 22 December 1840, and Lamartine to Perdiguier, 23 November 1840, in Perdiguier, *Livre du compagnonnage,* 2d ed., 1:19, 18.

favor."[39] The timeliness of Perdiguier's topic made the work all the more welcome.

On the Left the *National* warmly praised Perdiguier's book for raising "a question of humanity. . . .one might ask if it is the hand of a worker who traced these lines, and one does not know what to admire most— the depth and freshness of thought or the originality and even eloquence of style."[40] Evidently perplexed by a worker's eloquence, the *National* never acknowledged Perdiguier's authorship when it serialized excerpts.

Perdiguier was far from the only worker-poet to attract the admiration of elite audiences.[41] The weaver Magu, the wigmaker Jasmin, the seamstress Marie Carre, and the joiners Durand and Roly were enjoying a great wave of popularity at this time, reinforced by the vigorous presence of working-class newspapers. The most important were *L'Atelier* and *La Ruche populaire,* and Perdiguier wrote many articles for both. He served as a bridge between classes, particularly on the issue of the organization of labor, a question of growing concern to all socioeconomic classes. Although a wide range of authors, working and upper class, were fascinated by compagnonnage, however, it was primarily elites—literary figures, philanthropists, and some socialists—who kept public attention on these associations. By 1845 press and public had generally come to view compagnonnage not as an invidious social force but as a potentially ameliorating one.

One of the most ardent supporters of compagnonnage was George Sand. Soon after reading Perdiguier's book, she produced *Le Compagnon du tour de France,* a novel that portrays compagnonnage as the ideal organization of the community of workers. So intelligent and civilized was her protagonist, Pierre Huguenin, that critics attacked the portrayal for its lack of verisimilitude. In the preface to the 1841 edition Sand defended her characterization, assuring readers that although Huguenin might appear embellished to those who had never had contact with workers, he had an excellent and virtuous model in the real world— Agricol Perdiguier. Sand had taken the trouble to make Perdiguier's acquaintance and was duly impressed by the man and his ideas. In the preface and the text of the novel Sand emphasized what she considered the single most important doctrine of compagnonnage, "the principle of association itself."[42] Not content simply to write about the brother-

---

39. Quoted in Anfos Martin, *Agricol Perdiguier, dit Avignonnais-la-vertu: Sa vie, son oeuvre, et ses écrits* (Cavaillon, 1904), p. 115, date of review not given.

40. Ibid.

41. Briquet, *Agricol Perdiguier,* 171.

42. George Sand, *Le Compagnon du tour de France* (Paris, 1841), pp. 2, 9.

hoods, she funded a second "tour de France" for Perdiguier, enabling him to spread his message of reconciliation to all compagnons.

Although Sand was perhaps the most vocal and renowned publicist of compagnonnage, both Honoré de Balzac and Eugène Sue were intrigued with its literary potential, and each devoted a major subplot of a novel to the subject. Both authors, however, primarily depicted their fictionalized compagnons as the embodiment of the "dangerous classes." Balzac's chief compagnon was Ferragus, leader of the warlike and highly secretive sect of the compagnons du devoir, who appeared in the *Histoire des treize* (1842–1848), part of Balzac's *Comédie humaine*. Sue elaborated on these aspects of compagnonnage in *Le Juif errant,* the tremendously popular novel first serialized in *Le Constitutionnel* (1844).[43] In a subplot Sue vividly recreated the violence of compagnonnage. As in Balzac's novel, the "blood thirsty" villains were meant to be compagnon stonecutters du devoir, whom Sue called the *loups* (wolves), although the actual nickname of compagnon stonecutters du devoir was *loups-garoux* (werewolves).[44] But whether they were to be called wolves or werewolves, one of Sue's illustrators, in an 1845 edition, provides a powerful interpretation of the underlying message: his compagnon du devoir is a human wolf, barbaric and cannibalistic (see Figure 3). To the savagery of this depraved sect Sue opposed its noble twin, whose hero was a young, intelligent, and progressive worker, Agricol Baudouin (another thinly disguised Perdiguier), who epitomized the worth and potential of these associations. Baudouin notwithstanding, however, Sue's lurid depiction of the brutal and despotic wolves left readers with the dominant impression of a retrograde association. In a footnote Sue acknowledged that the frequency of brawls was declining as compagnons "became more enlightened and . . . gained a greater consciousness of their own dignity," thanks in great part to Perdiguier's "excellent book."[45] Undoubtedly, the brutishness of Sue's compagnons reflected certain realities; also undoubtedly, it made for popular reading and contributed to the novel's commercial triumph.

A number of light romantic comedies based on compagnonnage likewise enjoyed a lively success in the 1840s by playing on some similar themes.[46] *Les Dévorants* (1843) *Deux compagnons du tour de France* (1845),

---

43. Briquet, *Agricol Perdiguier*, p. 386. René de Livois notes that the serialization of Sue's *Mystères de Paris* and *Le Juif errant* secured a popular audience and the highest circulation figures of the time. *Histoire de la presse française*, 2 vols. (Lausanne, 1965), 1:233.

44. Eugène Sue, *Le Juif errant*, 2 vols. (Paris, 1845), 2:112–13; Perdiguier, *Livre du compagnonnage*, 2d ed. 1:31, 37. Perdiguier belonged to the opposing sect, the compagnons non du devoir, whose *loups* were joiners and locksmiths.

45. Sue, *Juif errant* 2:114.

46. The theme of work and workers had already become something of a preoccupation

Figure 3. The *Loup*, compagnon du devoir. Illustration by A. Ferdinandus, from Eugène Sue, *Le Juif errant*, 2 vols. (Paris, n.d. [1845]), 2:113.

Les Compagnons; ou, La Mansarde de la cité (1846), and *Les Charpentiers* (1847) all helped keep compagnonnage and the question of association before the public.[47] And the message of such plays reached beyond theater audiences in the weekly theater column of the popular journal *L'Illustration,* which reviewed and often summarized the plots of current plays. The intent of these plays, with the exception of a few scenes and songs, was generally not to describe the societies or their practices with any accuracy. All gave some emphasis to the violent or "archaic" aspects of the compagnonnages and drew on comic or negative stereotypes of workers, depicting their carousing, their drinking, the dangers of their antisocial behaviors, and particularly their penchant for indolence, brawls, and strikes.

The plays also tended to conform to the stock plots of contemporary melodrama, presenting star-crossed lovers, male rivalries, and the evil machinations of unsavory characters—albeit in a working-class setting. With the possible exception of *Deux Compagnons du tour de France,* none of the plays could be said to have been deeply informed or influenced by Perdiguier's work. Théodore Barrière may have read the *Livre du compagnonnage,* but his dramatization of the carpenter's strike of 1845, *Les Charpentiers,* is in fact, a strong anticoalition statement. Each play, nonetheless, provides some sympathetic portrayals of the world of work as seen from the perspective of organized workers. All to some degree explore the meaning of brotherhood among workers, the resolution of conflicts between the individual and the group, and the importance of bonds of sentiment—between individual compagnons, among groups of compagnons, and between compagnons and their sweethearts. A particularly powerful theme in all the plays is the "civilizing" and redemptive power of love and marriage or domesticity in general, as at the lodging house of the *mère.*

Joseph-Philippe Lockroy and Jules de Wailly make more effort than the other playwrights to describe some of the practices and beliefs of

---

among popular playwrights of the Restoration. Louis Allard, *La Comédie de moeurs en France au dix-neuvième siècle: La Vie, les théâtres, les auteurs* (Paris, 1933), 2:471. One of the earliest nineteenth-century plays to focus on compagnonnage was *Les Compagnons du devoir* by W. Lafontaine, E. Vanderburck, and Etienne (Paris, 1827).

47. C.-H.-Edmond Desnoyers [a.k.a. E. D. de Biéville], *Les Dévorants* (Paris, 1843), "Comédie-vaudeville en deux actes," presented at the Folies dramatiques, August 1843; Joseph-Philippe Lockroy and Jules de Wailly, *Deux compagnons du tour de France* (Paris, 1845), "comédie-vaudeville en deux actes," presented at the Variétés, November 1845; Adolphe Philippe Dennery [a.k.a. D'Emery or D'Ennery] and Pierre-Etienne Piestre [called Eugène] Cormon, *Les Compagnons; ou, La Mansarde de la cité* (Paris, 1846), "drame mêlé de chants, en cinq actes et sept tableaux," presented at the Gaîté, February 1846; and Théodore Barrière, *Les Charpentiers* (Paris, 1847), "drame en quatre actes et cinq tableaux," presented at the Théâtre Beaumarchais, September 1847.

compagnonnage as well as the origins of the two major sects. *Deux compagnons du tour de France* focuses on the bitter rivalry between compagnons du devoir ("the *dévorants*"), and compagnons non du devoir ("the *gavots*"). The dévorants (followers of the duty or "devourers" to their enemies) and the gavots (mountain people or "heretics" to their antagonists) decide to end their long-standing opposition by means of a peaceful competition of skill, "worthy of civilized compagnons." One of the competitors, Le Corinthien, is betrayed by his own brother, Le Pensif (both gavots), because he believes his brother has stolen the affections of his sweetheart. Le Corinthien is unjustly expelled from the gavots; Le Pensif is racked by guilt. Although the quarrel between the dévorants and the gavots remains unresolved (the dévorants essentially remain the villains), Le Pensif confesses and Le Corinthien is fully reinstated by the gavots as a friend and a brother. Le Pensif discovers his sweetheart loved him all along, and as the play ends, he expresses his greatest joy in having what he had always lacked: a family. The play thus ends by underscoring the ultimately limited nature of the family of compagnonnage: even though Le Pensif had always had his brother, had been part of the family of the gavots, a son of Solomon, he still felt he had no family. For Le Pensif a real family could exist only once he had the love of a woman— perhaps, once he had grown up.

Outside the more purely literary realm, a number of bourgeois social critics and philanthropists of the 1830s and 1840s wrote fervently about the capacity of compagnonnage to ameliorate workers' material and spiritual condition. In speeches and books that enjoyed a certain prominence in their day, men such as François-Félix de la Farelle, a member of the old nobility and former deputy, and Ange Guépin, a medical specialist involved in liberal politics, praised the high standards of compagnonnage and its organization. De la Farelle, however, thought compagnonnage might be further improved if it were directed by the upper classes of society. Some bourgeois philanthropists believed it might be used to resolve the class tensions in French society. August-Ambroise Giraud's *Réflexions philosophiques sur le compagnonnage* stressed that its Christian and ethical nature might "moralize" the working class and "harmonize" it with the rest of society.[48] To Giraud, and many others in the 1840s, a reformed compagnonnage seemed a ready-made solution to the *question sociale*.

48. Giraud, *Réflexions philosophiques sur le compagnonnage et le tour de France* (Paris, 1846). The Christian symbolism in compagnonnage may have been among its chief attractions to philanthropists such as Giraud and Lamennais, who also had strong ties to the liberal Christian movement. Christian symbolism also remained significant to wider segments of the populace. See Edward Berenson, *Populist Religion and Left-Wing Politics in France, 1830–1852* (Princeton, 1984).

Socialists, by contrast, with both a more complete view of compagnonnage and more contact with workers, were skeptical about the potential
of even a transformed compagnonnage to participate in a social and
democratic republic. Most socialists did not discuss the brotherhoods
directly, but there were notable exceptions. Flora Tristan felt she had
been enlightened by reading Perdiguier's *Livre du compagnonnage,* and
corresponded with him in the early 1840s. In January 1843 she told
Perdiguier in a letter that her idea of the *union universelle* of all workers—
men and women—had come to her while reading his book. The two
disagreed, however, on the ability of compagnonnage to lead to working-
class unification. Later in 1843 Tristan wrote to the ex-compagnon
Pierre Moreau that she remained convinced of the "insufficiency of the
societies of compagnonnage" to "constitute" the working class because
they operated within the framework of "the personal order."[49] She nonetheless applauded Perdiguier's attempts to unite compagnonnage and,
like many others, valued what he revealed about that vast network.

Louis Blanc, too, declared himself convinced of the significance of the
Livre du compagnonnage and the soundness of Perdiguier's ideas. In the
Revue du progrés Blanc wrote that the compagnons could be looked to
for "examples of devotion."[50] He also included Perdiguier's "Projet de
règlement." a plan for regulating work and the means of production
through the formation of producers' cooperatives, in his own book
L'Organisation du travail (1848). No other author received this distinction
in Blanc's work. With such ideas, Blanc, believed, "all good citizens
should be concerned."[51] Later editions of *L'Organisation du travail* drew
on Perdiguier's research to demonstrate the nineteenth-century decline
in real wages in various trades.[52] Blanc apparently learned much about
organic modes of social organization from studying compagnonnage.
Despite its disunity, he thought that compagnons had profited from
many of the benefits of association. In some ways they were more advanced than other workers: they already practiced what Blanc called the
"voluntary association of needs and pleasures."[53] What remained was for
compagnonnage to resolve its internal quarrels and extend its benefits
to all workers. Perhaps Blanc drew on his observations of the compagnon

49. Briquet, *Agricol Perdiguier,* p. 222, quoting Flora Tristan to Perdiguier, 25 January 1843.
Tristan to Pierre Moreau, 7 April, and 24 June 1843, in Archives Pierre Moreau, Institut français
d'histoire sociale.
50. Louis Blanc, *Revue du progrès,* 15 December 1839, p. 486.
51. Louis Blanc, *L'Organisation du travail* (Paris, 1848), p. 278.
52. Ibid., 2d ed. (Paris, 1882), pp. 35–37. Perdiguier published his research separately as
Statistique du salaire des ouvriers, en réponse à M. Thiers et autres économistes de la même école (Paris,
1848).
53. Blanc, *Organisation du travail,* p. 90.

carpenters who in 1845 had united their warring sects and led an orderly strike, directed in part against the erosion of artisanal values. Their accomplishments in that mass strike seemed to confirm the possibility of a new sort of compagnonnage.

RIVALS UNITE: CARPENTERS ON STRIKE

On 11 June 1845, *La Démocratie pacifique* reported, "all the carpenters in Paris ceased working."[54] The sense that nearly all the carpenters in Paris were on strike was well founded, for of roughly four to six thousand carpenters normally working in the city, between four and five thousand—compagnons du devoir, compagnons du devoir de liberté, and unaffiliated workers in the trade—joined the generally nonviolent strike before it ended three months later.[55] Almost from the start, the carpenters found support for their cause in the opposition press—from the *National* and *Démocratie pacifique* on the Left to the *Quotidienne* on the Right.[56] The *Atelier* and some of the more radical press went farther, dramatically calling the strike the beginning of the struggle between labor and capital—a view the police were all too ready to accept.[57] Although the strikers themselves would not have taken such a broad view, they considered their demands important. On the first day the strike leaders—members of the "society of the compagnons du devoir"—called for a minimum wage of five francs per day and the establishment of a bargaining commission to negotiate between the two sides. If these demands were not met, all unmarried carpenters would leave Paris. The compagnon Vincent (nicknamed "Condon"), secretary of the compagnons du devoir, was delegated to take charge of all official matters—printing circulars, conducting negotiations, organizing the strike fund.[58]

The compagnons du devoir had consented to lead the strike only after gaining agreement that the masters, patrons, and entrepreneurs first be warned of their intentions. Thus, on 17 May 1845 Vincent presented himself at the *chambre syndicale,* a legally authorized employers' associa-

54. *La Démocratie pacifique,* 11 June 1845.

55. Dudley Channing Barksdale, "Parisian Carpenters and Changes in Forms of Work, Culture, and Protest, 1789–1848" (M.A. thesis, University of North Carolina, Chapel Hill, 1978), pp. 24–25. Also Michael David Sibalis, "The Carpenters of Paris, 1789–1848," revised version of a paper originally given at the annual meeting of the Society for French Historical Studies, Minneapolis, Minnesota, March 1987, esp. pp. 1–5, 9, 12–13.

56. Ernest Labrousse, *Le Mouvement ouvrier et les théories sociales en France de 1815 à 1848* (Paris, 1965), p. 174.

57. "Luttes du travail contre le capital," *L'Atelier* 5, no. 10 (July 1845); Sibalis, "Carpenters of Paris," p. 1.

58. *La Démocratie pacifique,* 11 June 1845.

tion, to give official notice (*préavis*) that the workers would strike unless
an original demand for a ten-centime-per-hour across-the-board increase
was met. The compagnons claimed "they did not want to start any trouble. . . . they had no other intention vis-à-vis the masters than to exercise
their rights."[59] But what rights did workers have? How could a strike
eventually involving thousands of carpenters be organized and led when
all such activity was illegal in 1845? Despite legal prohibitions against
labor associations, they were in fact tolerated in the guise of mutual aid
societies. Strikes, however, particularly in the construction industry, were
a different matter. Nonetheless, carpenters, under the leadership of compagnons, had struck before. Among the rare strikes in the era were major, long-term, and relatively successful strikes in 1822 and 1832–1833,
led by united compagnons. When the carpenters' first demand was flatly
rejected in May 1845, the carpenters quickly reached a decision.

A strike in carpentry was always critical, particularly in Paris, where
construction accounted for roughly 10 percent of all business. As in
many economies, building was closely tied to other sectors—mining,
metallurgy, wood processing, chemical refining—and a long-term strike
among carpenters could cause serious economic dislocations. Nevertheless, the 1845 strike and the subsequent trial of its leaders aroused public
sympathy. As in prior actions, the two major sects of compagnonnage,
du devoir and non du devoir (or de liberté) declared a truce in order
to present a united front. Compagnons outnumbered independent carpenters by roughly five to one.[60]

Pierre-Antoine Berreyer, the noted legitimist lawyer who defended the
compagnons arrested in the strike, outlined and then justified the role
of compagnonnage for the court. He pointed out that no new labor
agreement had been negotiated since 1833, and real wages were drop-
ping. "In 1845," Berreyer later recalled, "the situation worsening, the
workers addressed themselves to the compagnons du devoir and begged
them to serve as intermediaries between the masters and themselves."
Already in 1844 and earlier in 1845, groups of independent carpenters
had approached the compagnons du devoir about a united strike action.
Success, they believed, would require the backing of compagnonnage:
"The society of the compagnons du devoir is the oldest group in Paris,
it has a large membership, and naturally other workers came to it when
it concerned a matter pertaining to the general interest."[61]

59. Pierre-Antoine Berreyer, *Affaire des charpentiers: Plaidoyer en faveur des ouvriers accusés du délit
de coalition (23 août 1845)* (Paris, 1845), p. 14. In the Second Empire the term *chambre syndicale*
was "appropriated by workers' societies to give them parity in negotiations with employers,"
according to Moss, *French Labor Movement*, p. 53.
60. Barksdale, "Parisian Carpenters," pp. 13–14, 25.
61. Berreyer, *Affaire des charpentiers*, p. 14.

The strike gained momentum in the early summer and spread to Versailles, Tours, and Blois. In addition to their key demand of a five-franc-
per-day tariff, agreed to and signed by the entrepreneurs, the carpenters
presented new demands. They wanted the work day shortened to ten
hours and subcontracting suppressed. Subcontracting was an especially
sore point. The compagnons believed they had more power to negotiate
work conditions with individual masters than with subcontractors. The
use of subcontracting, moreover, was gradually removing small producers from the building trades and further eroding their status and the
need for their skill. Gradually, through the months of June and July a
number of patrons agreed to the new wage, but workers held fast to
their demand for a general increase. On 28 June the government re-
cruited soldiers to man the workshops—a move that the press generally
criticized.[62]

Up to this point the nonviolent conduct of the strike had kept public
sympathy high, turned the strike into a *cause célèbre*, and frustrated government attempts to end it. Matters were brought to a head on 17 July,
when the police raided the Mère of the compagnons du devoir. They
seized the strike fund—between twenty-five hundred and thirty-five hundred francs—and confiscated papers. They also arrested Vincent as well
as the mère and père Lénard, who ran the compagnons' inn; the court
set no bail for the accused. The compagnons remained calm, but the
press was incensed. The *Démocratie pacifique* declared the compagnons
heroes and praised their "upright, honorable, and peaceful" conduct.
Compagnonnage was "this cult of the corporative family, ceding to a
respect for order. What a beautiful sight and what a lesson."[63]

The real issue had become the right of association. The *Démocratie
pacifique* concluded that the serious increase in labor unrest in the 1840s
resulted directly from the lack of organized relations between employers
and workers. The law against coalitions, moreover, presented gross injustices. Collusion between masters and entrepreneurs plainly existed but
was rarely if ever prosecuted, whereas workers' attempts to organize met
with constant harassment.[64] Even the conservative *Quotidienne* called association a positive force in the fight against the worst problem of the
age: "Individualism, detestable in politics, is not less so in industry. . . .
[it] is the most profound evil of industry."[65]

Seventeen of the alleged strike leaders went on trial on 20 August,

62. *La Quotidienne*, 28 June 1845.
63. *La Démocratie pacifique*, 18 July 1845.
64. Ibid., 12 June 1845. See, e.g., Theodore Zeldin, *France, 1848–1945*, 2 vols. (Oxford,
1973), 1:203–5.
65. *La Quotidienne*, 28 June 1845.

charged with the misdemeanor of illegal association. Ten of them bore the distinctive nicknames of compagnonnage, usually indicating their region of origin.[66] Berreyer's defense was two pronged: he championed the principle of association and decried the unequal application of anticoalition laws. Maintaining that association was natural and necessary to human relations, he extolled the carpenters' ability to deal harmoniously with their collective problems. This unity puzzled the tribunal. The presiding judge asked why the two societies of compagnon carpenters, "who have been rivals for as long as can be remembered, find themselves in agreement in this case?" Vincent answered that "they themselves realized, without the need for a written agreement or even a verbal pact, that the general will had made itself felt and had to take precedence above anything else."[67] The carpenters' ability to accept the "general will" and Vincent's eloquent exposition of the Rousseauean concept may have found a resonnance in the social climate of the 1840s. Curiously, however, the carpenters' remarkable solidarity also apparently arose without direct links to the contemporary discourse on reform. The carpenters never mentioned Perdiguier or his work during the strike or the trial; their unity seemed a "natural" product of the political and social ferment, particularly evident in Paris. Nonetheless, Perdiguier's discussion of the origin narratives of the major sects of compagnonnage posited that the two devoirs were originally one and could again be united.[68] Whatever the primary motive, in 1845 compagnon carpenters turned away from their bloody brawls and allowed the general will to supersede longtime hatreds in a way that seemed almost mystical.

Berreyer's second line of defense focused on many cases of employers' coalitions, including the one in the current strike: not one of them had ever been tried as a criminal action. "If you recognize the right of liberty for masters, you must likewise recognize it for workers; the law must be for all, rich and poor alike; but to wish to condemn the worker to an isolated and weak state of individual action is the most unjust, the most despicable act which can occur in human society." The workers' demands were just, Berreyer declared, and their conduct exemplary. Returning to his main theme, he put himself among those seeking an answer to the "social question" when he proposed that society develop a plan for the organization of labor. Knowing the resistance this proposal would meet, the lawyer pleaded: "If until then you can do nothing for

66. *La Démocratie pacifique,* 10 August 1845. Only one of the nicknamed appears to have been a Paris native.
67. *La Quotidienne,* August 1845, trial transcript.
68. The question of compagnonnage's origin narratives is addressed in subsequent chapters, and particularly in Chapter 9.

the workers, at least leave them the means of bettering their lot, leave them this exchange of confidences between themselves, an exchange that aims to show them the means of freeing themselves from poverty." The audience in the packed courtroom greeted Berreyer's words with thunderous applause and unrestrained approval.[69]

The tribunal was far less enthusiastic. Eleven of the carpenters were given jail sentences, and three of them were still serving their terms in 1848. The *Démocratie pacifique* called the unpopular verdict "exorbitant" and announced on 14 September 1845 that the carpenters would appeal the decision. Nothing came of the appeal; yet, the carpenters' spirit remained unbroken.[70] Despite the fact that no general rate increase had been signed, the majority of the entrepreneurs in Paris agreed to the five-franc-per-day rate. By the end of the trial even many entrepreneurs sympathized with the workers' cause. The authorities, however, worried about the vast threat posed by a mass of workers who had overcome their internal differences.

Despite the official view, compagnons had convinced much of the public that they could act reasonably in pursuit of a just cause. After the June strike, articles in two major periodicals reinforced some of these positive themes. In October 1845, an extensive and largely favorable two-part article had appeared in *Le Correspondant,* a biweekly conservative newspaper for "the defense of the Catholic religion." The article by the legitimist attorney and author Henri de Riancey sought to allay elite and clerical fears of the dangers of association while forcefully urging government protection of compagnonnage and the granting of suffrage to compagnons. Riancey was still troubled by aspects of compagnonnage, particularly its rituals. Unlike Peridguier, he quoted at some length from some rare eighteenth-century sources that had revealed the early compagnons' initiations. The unfortunate tendencies of compagnonnage could be mitigated, however, through true Christian sentiment and education, particularly among the popular classes—subjects on which Riancey had written in an 1844 book on public education. Nonetheless, Christian faith was not enough. The people and their leaders had an obligation to ameliorate social ills caused by political and economic neglect. Compagnonnage could be part of the remedy—a social organization that encouraged order and civilization, not disorder. Its quarrels,

69. Berreyer, *Affaire des charpentiers*, p. 9.
70. In gratitude to Berreyer the compagnon carpenters du devoir commissioned Pizargue, one of their most skilled workers, to construct an elaborate masterpiece that was presented to the attorney in 1847. The model was over two meters high, replete with marquetry, engraved figures, and an internal circular staircase. Berreyer kept it in his office for the rest of his life. That only the compagnon carpenters du devoir were involved in the creation and presentation of the model further suggests their commanding role in the whole strike.

Riancey emphasized, were less significant than its strengths, which included its "national" and "cosmopolitan spirit."[71]

A month later, the best-selling weekly *L'Illustration* ran a two-part article that commended "the transformation of [the compagnons'] customs" and attributed the change largely to the work of Argicol
Perdiguier. The anonymous author quoted extensively from an 1842
article in *L'Atelier* which had praised the "moral, humanitarian and mutual aid value of compagnonnage," but went on to dicuss its disadvan-
tages, quoting again from *L'Atelier* and an even sharper critic, Pierre
Moreau. Furthermore, the cariacatures accompanying the article, by the
popular Jules Noël, reinforced negative stereotypes: the compagnons appeared vain and foolish as they conducted their meetings and participated in their rituals. And in contrast to the portrayal of mères in most
of the contemporary theater pieces on compagnonnage, Noël's mères
were homely older women whose demeanor seemed to intimidate the
young compagnons who arrived at their lodgings. The article itself noted
that many warm relationships existed between mères and compagnons
and emphasized how proud mères were of their role. But it also accused
them of "realizing enormous profits" from their "tenderness" by extending credit to bad risks and then holding the whole society responsible for these debts. The article remained especially critical of the most
"radical vice of compagnonnage: a principle of hierarchy and inequality."[72] In 1848, as compagnons attempted to reconcile their sects, it
seemed that this vice might at last be eradicated by a new national spirit
based on the principles of egalitarian brotherhood.

1848: THE APOTHEOSIS

Recognized for their bravery on the barricades of February 1848, compagnons aroused the greatest public sympathy by their willingness to
meet together as brothers with other compagnons and workers on 20
March in the massive demonstration at the place de la République described at the outset of this chapter. Even the iconoclastic and acerbic

71. Henri de Riancey, "Du Compagnonnage: Son passé, son présent, son avenir," in *Le Correspondant: Recueil périodique: Religion, philosophie, politique, sciences, littérature, beaux-arts,* 10 October
1845, pp. 45–80, and 25 October 1845, pp. 202–36; quotation from 10 October 1845 issue, p.
74. *L'Atelier* reprinted excerpts in its December 1845 issue. On initiations Riancey cited Pierre
[Père] LeBrun, *Histoire des pratiques superstitieuses qui ont séduit les peuples et embarassé les sçavans,* 2d
ed. augmentée par J. Bellon 4 vols. (Paris, 1732–37); and Pierre [Père Hippolyte] Helyot, *Histoire
des ordres monastiques, réligieux, et militaires et des congrégations séculières,* 8 vols. (Paris, 1714–19).
72. "Les Compagnons du tour de France," *L'Illustration,* 22 November 1845, pp. 183–85,
and see 29 November 1845, pp. 203–6.

editor of *Les Guêpes*, Alphonse Karr, was impressed: "I am convinced that I was not the only one with tears in his eyes when told of their reconciliation. . . . they have abandoned their ancient hatred [and] have reconciled and intermingled all the devoirs. Here is something great, something noble!"[73] To the "acclamations of the whole population," compagnons presented their respects to the Provisional Government and assured it of their passionate support and devotion. Two key officials responded to the declaration, the deputy mayor of Paris and the general secretary of the provisional government.

The deputy mayor, Philippe-Joseph Buchez, a socialist theorist, told the compagnons that they must use their omnipresent association and their travels throughout France to "carry the sentiments that animate your hearts" all over the country. Compagnons were the fortunate ones, those who already knew that workers must associate. Buchez had long acknowledged the intellectual debt he owed to his collaborations with members of working class on the question of association, which could produce a "common social capital." He was more cautious about the compagnons' zealous pledge to defend the new republic with their lives if necessary. He told them that "if the Provisional Government has need of your arms, of your courage, it will call on you." Buchez checked the rousing response, "You can count on us," and advised the compagnons to wait for the government's call. The history of the First Republic and the troubled past of compagnonnage informed Buchez's rhetoric. He emphasized the orderly, bloodless aim of 1848, a "beatiful Revolution because of the conduct of the workers," and he insisted, "This Revolution will remain pure"—untainted by violence and dissent.[74]

Pagnerre, editor of the 1839 edition of Perdiguier's *Livre du compagnonnage* and general secretary of the Provisional Government, was less restrained in his reply. He praised the compagnons for realizing that they "must not remain separate families" for they were "all members of the same family, the family of workers, and above all, the great national family." He thanked them for their pledge of support: "Yes, if it is necessary, you will be ready to run to the border to defend the *patrie*." The compagnons cheered: "Yes! Yes! We swear it!" Pagnerre ended by telling the compagnons, "We count on you as you can count on us."[75]

Pagnerre's reference to the family of compagnons, the family of the

73. *Les Guêpes*, March 1848, p. 359.

74. *Le Moniteur universel*, 21 March 1848, p. 651. For the complete text of the compagnons' address to the Provisional Government, see Cynthia M. Truant, "Compagnonnage: Symbolic Action and the Defense of Workers' Rights in France, 1700–1848" (Ph.D. diss., University of Chicago, 1978), appendix 1, p. 319. On Buchez's social theory, see Sewell, *Work and Revolution*, pp. 203–4, 211, 234.

75. *Le Moniteur universel*, 21 March 1848, p. 651.

nation, was an important metaphor. Joan Scott provides a valuable analysis of the discourse on family within the broader critique of capitalist political economy in 1848 and notes that "within the body of critical social(ist) theory, there were different emphases and programs but there were also common uses of images of the family and of references to gender. The family was projected as an abstract entity, a place of complete human fulfillment, in opposition to the alienation of capitalist society."[76] For compagnons in the public demonstrations of 1848, the family almost always equated with egalitarian brotherhood.

On 21 May compagnons joined their "families" to the larger family of workers, male and female, in the Fête de la Concorde, the celebration of peace and labor. The *Moniteur* estimated more than 1.2 million spectators lined the extensive parade route as roughly 300,000 participants marched in a procession lasting from early morning to late evening. Each group of compagnons carried its own banners and masterpieces, and harmony prevailed among these formerly bitter enemies. Like other workers' corporations, they joined the procession without concern for hierarchy in the order of march. This unity forged from diversity seemed an excellent model for the new nation, and a major newspaper seized on it: "Compagnons of the devoirs, previously divided, today shook each other's hands under the powerful inspiration of Fraternity."[77]

Members of the Luxembourg Commission, the advisory body formed to deal with workers' issues, however, never really saw compagnonnage as a model for the organization of labor. Sewell analyzes the centrality of the concept of equality in the transformation of corporate discourse in workers' parades and demonstrations in 1848: "Far from recognizing any social or political hierarchy or the authority of the church or the king [as in the old regime], the trade corporations were displaying themselves as equal constituents of the sovereign people, the ultimate source of all political authority."[78] In any event compagnons did not make concerted attempts to exert leadership in the Luxembourg commission. Presided over by Louis Blanc and the worker Albert from the Provisional Government and composed of workers' delegates, the commission was to formulate recommendations and propose candidates for the upcoming National Assembly. Although without real power, the commission played a critical role in organizing workers politically and articulating their views, particularly on the question of producers' cooperatives. Generally, the Luxembourg Commission did not support compagnons' candidacies for the assembly, despite any favorable views Louis Blanc had

76. Scott, *Gender and the Politics*, p. 108.
77. *Le Moniteur*, 23 May 1848, p. 1123.
78. Sewell, *Work and Revolution*, pp. 262–63.

toward their associations. "Immediately rejected," Daniel Stern reports, "were the candidates proposed by compagnonnage, whose former elitist pretensions had not been forgotten and who were believed to be influenced by the clerical party."[79] Exceptions were made for Perdiguier and two other compagnons, based on "personal considerations." All three had promoted unity and reform in compagnonnage; during the Revolution their concern extended to all workers and their relationship to the nation. By 1848 Perdiguier found the framework of compagnonnage too narrow for the "new united organization of the working class."[80] As Flora Tristan might say, he had transcended the "personal order."

The reconciliation of compagnonnage and the public celebration of that unity were neither long-lived nor deeply rooted. Perhaps not surprisingly, the loudest acclaim came from members of middle- and upper-class elites whose interest in compagnonnage may have reflected a nostalgia for corporatism or been encouraged by a romantic interest in the medieval and the folkloric.[81] Perdiguier's enthusiasm for reconciliation reflected an idealized vision of a harmonious community at odds with the realities of the situation. The inspiration of fraternity had no more power to effect a lasting synthesis of the branches of compagnonnage than it had to reconcile the nation. Thus 1848 proved to be the "apotheosis of compagnonnage" and not its transformation.[82] Yet, compagnonnage was remarkably resilient. Both responsive and resistant to change, its societies could be neither united nor completely destroyed. To explore why and how this was so, the following chapters trace how the culture of compagnonnage was constructed.

79. Daniel Stern, *Histoire de la Révolution de 1848* (Paris, 1869), p. 338. For a valuable discussion of the ideas of corporatism in 1848 and the role of the Luxembourg Commission, see Sewell, *Work and Revolution*, pp. 232–36, 245–65.

80. Rémi Gossez, "Le Compagnonnage en 1848 d'après des documents inédits," *Compagnonnage* (May 1950): 7.

81. On the nostalgia for corporatism, see Michael Sibalis, "Corporatism after the Corporations: The Debate on Restoring the Guilds under Napoleon I and the Restoration," *French Historical Studies* 15 (Fall 1988): 718–30.

82. Gossez, "Compagnonnage en 1848," p. 7.

CHAPTER 2

Early Constructions
of Compagnonnage

> Far from the noisy chaos of this vulgar world and its shame-
> ful dealings . . . the mysterious order of which we shall
> speak was born unnoticed, in the shadow of secrecy.
>
> —Joseph Voisin

In his 1931 autobiography Joseph Voisin, a former compagnon carpenter, promised to telln all about the birth of his enigmatic association.
His is a fascinating account, based as it is on myths and legend, which
are often more revealing about the nature of compagnonnage than
"plain" facts would be.[1] Compagnons often blurred the boundaries between fact and fiction as they constructed their associations and experienced their relationship to the wider French culture. These boundaries
remain open in this study as well. Nonetheless, early archival documentation of compagnonnage, despite its filters and limitations, adds a vital
dimension to our knowledge of these brotherhoods in early modern
French culture.

Thus, it is intriguing that some histories of compagnonnage have been
almost as speculative as Voisin's. The most concerted attempts to trace
the origins of the brotherhoods began in the nineteenth century, when
both compagnons and outsiders seem to have been captivated by the
"antiquity" and persistence of compagnonnage. In earlier eras there
seems to have been more interest in activities than in origins. Knowledge
of compagnonnage before 1789, moreover, was largely limited to the
police (in its broadest sense) and to the world of artisanal production.

The *Encyclopédie,* despite its intense concern with manufacturing and
the organization of the artisanal trades, defines *compagnonnage* only

1. Joseph Voisin, *Histoire de ma vie et 55 ans de compagnonnage* (Tours, 1931).

briefly and narrowly, as the stage between apprenticeship and mastership, and a *compagnon* as one who accompanies another, as in travel or
work. In articles on specific trades and on artisanal production (as in the
article "Communautés") the encyclopedists were generally critical of the
guilds, faulting them for excessive regulation, indifference to progress in
their trades, and the tendency to promote the particular over the public
interest. In the article "Maîtrises" (masterships), for example, the author, Faignet de Villeneuve, criticized the obstacles that guilds placed in
the way of becoming a master, especially the high costs and the requirement that the compagnon produce a chef d'oeuvre. The author makes
an important connection between economic status and political rights. It
was particularly unfair to impose such burdens, he writes, because the
compagnon was "as much as anyone else a member of the republic, and
he should benefit equally from the protection of the laws."[2]

Among scholarly works, Pierre Larousse's *Grand dictionnaire universel
du XIXe siècle* states that "it is almost certain" that compagnonnage was
born in the twelfth century, together with the corps des métiers (the
trade associations or guilds), but provides no support for its assertions.
Twentieth-century sources are generally better informed and more cautious. The *Larousse du XXe siécle* (1929) dates the beginning of the actual
practice of postapprenticeship travel to the sixteenth century and says it
was fully established in the seventeenth century, when the corps des métiers were becoming exclusive and masterships were increasingly reserved
for the sons of masters. The result was that "journeymen united into
compagnonnages, which became centers of resistance against the pretensions of the masters."[3]

Curiously, more recent works on compagnonnage returned to earlier
and more sweeping approaches. Emile Coornaert warns that "only God
knows for certain" when and how the institution began but then speculates that it emerged as a secret association among stonecutters working
on the thirteenth-century cathedrals. By the fourteenth century, he says,
compagnonnages had permanent alliances and ordinances, and each
was led by a chief who was "dreaded by all his compagnons" and

2. Denis Diderot, "Compagnon" and "Compagnonnage," in *Encyclopédie; ou, Dictionnaire rai-
sonné des sciences, des arts, et des métiers, par une société de gens de lettres,* 17 vols. text and 11 vols.
plates (Paris, 1751–72), 3:744; and Faignet de Villeneuve, "Maîtrises," ibid., 9:913. This article
is classified both under the categories of arts and commerce and under politics. The encyclopedists' apparent lack of interest in the associations of compagnonnage is not surprising. Eighteenth-century compagnonnage was not widely known to the bourgeois public, and it was much
more a provincial than a Parisian phenomenon.

3. "Compagnonnage," *Grand dictionnaire universel du XIXe siècle,* ed. Pierre Larousse, 17 vols.
(Paris, 1866–90), 4:767–70; "Compagnonnage," *Larousse du XXe siècle,* ed. Paul Augé, 6 vols.
(Paris, 1928–33), 2:376.

"charged with defending their interests and statutes."[4] Coornaert's earlier, extensively documented work on the *corporations* in France lends confidence to his assertions, but his work on compagnonnage is marred by an almost complete absence of the scholarly apparatus of references and notes—archival or otherwise. Historians such as Henri Hauser, Paul Labal, and James Farr present more reliable and verifiable conclusions based on extensive archival research. Using such work and other archival evidence, I want to do a sort of archeology of compagnonnage which moves backward and forward in time to deconstruct the accretions of meaning.[5]

THE ROOTS OF COMPAGNONNAGE

Although many nineteenth-century compagnons preferred to trace their origins to elite and esoteric orders such as the Knights Templar and the Masons and acknowledged no relationship to the corps des métiers and confraternities, it is to these latter bodies that compagnonnage owed its original impetus. Although compagnonnage differentiated itself from other corporate groups in the world of work, all these institutions shared a deeply embedded Christian symbolism and drew on models and practices present in Catholicism and particularly the religious orders.

Corps des Métiers

The corps des métiers began as associations of free artisans in twelfth-century France, organized in response to socioeconomic changes stimulated by the growth of trade and the rise of urban centers.[6] The first

4. Emile Coornaert, *Les Compagnonnages en France du Moyen Âge à nos jours* (Paris, 1966), p. 238.
5. Henri Hauser, *Les Compagnonnages d'arts et métiers à Dijon aux XVIIe et XVIIIe siècles* (Paris, 1907); Hauser, *Ouvriers du temps passé (XVe–XVIe siècles)* (Paris, 1899); Paul Labal, "Notes sur les compagnons migrateurs et les sociétés de compagnons à Dijon à la fin du XVe et au début du XVIe siècles," *Annales de Bourgogne* 22 (1950): 187–93; Labal, "Artisans dijonnais d'autrefois: Notes sur la vie des gens de métiers de 1430 à 1560," *Annales de Bourgogne* 23 (1951): 85–106; and James Farr, *Hands of Honor: Artisans and Their World in Dijon, 1550–1650* (Ithaca, 1988), a valuable study of artisanal culture. See especially pp. 59–75 for the compagnonnages. Jean-Pierre Bayard, *Le Compagnonnage en France* (Paris, 1977), begins with definitions of the various sects of compagnonnage and a general historical overview and account of the legends (pp. 20–61). This direct approach seems helpful at first, but ultimately obscures questions of historicity and contextual meaning. Bayard's minimal use of archival sources further diminishes the book's value and leads to uncorroborated claims about the relationship of compagnonnage to Freemasonry and the Templars.
6. Prior to the twelfth century no evidence decisively supports the existence of organized systems of merchants or artisans. François Oliver-Martin, *L'Organisation corporative de la France d'ancien régime* (Paris, 1938), p. 83.

detailed accounts of these organizations are found in the late thirteenth
century in Etienne Boileau's *Livre des métiers,* an attempt to describe "all
the trades in Paris, their ordinances, the manner of fabrication of each
trade, and their fines."[7] Boileau, provost of the Parisian guilds, examined
trade practices, membership qualifications and restrictions, procedures
for celebrating ceremonies and feast days—in short, anything concerning work and its organization. The *Livre des métiers* was no attempt to
standardize trade organization, however. The organization of work continued to vary from place to place with *jurandes* (sworn trades), *métiers
libres* ("free" trades), and *priviligié* (trades directly licensed by the
crown). But however organized, all work was regulated in early modern
France. Organization in the so-called *métiers libres* differed from the *jurandes* primarily in the specific authority that administered and controlled
them. In practice, as Farr notes, "these pure types did not exist. In Dijon,
a *ville jurée,* the municipal authorities ruled in conjunction with appointed officials from the guilds themselves."[8]

The corps des métiers promoted commerce and organized the work
force. By the fifteenth century artisans were divided into a threefold
hierarchy—apprentice, journeyman, and master—whose numbers were
usually limited by statute. Apprentices learned the rudiments of a trade
during a period of up to seven years, usually in the town where they
hoped to become masters. At about the age of fourteen, they became
journeymen and, in many trades, made a tour de France to perfect their
skills and learn regional variations and trade secrets. Journeymen often,
but not always, owned their own tools. After three to seven years, they
returned home, ideally, to become masters themselves. To be admitted
to the *maîtrise,* journeymen usually had to submit apprenticeship papers,
make a masterpiece (usually under observation), and pay a fee. In practice these requirements varied; many were waived for masters' sons. A
primary consideration was the candidate's *vie et moeurs* and religious orthodoxy—essentially his repute and standing in the community. Although apprentices and journeymen were in principle members of their
trade corporations, masters alone swore an oath to uphold its regulations. New masters usually hosted a dinner for the trade's officials (*jurés*)
and town aldermen and sometimes "offered" gifts or emoluments. Each
sworn trade had legal rights and obligations, many of them related to
the acceptable weights, measures, quality, and price of the objects they

---

7. Etienne Boileau, *Le Livre des métiers,* ed. René de Lespinasse and François Bonnardot (Paris,
1879), p. 1.
8. Farr, *Hands of Honor,* p. 17. See also Farr's discussion of the corporate system, particularly
its range of variations (pp. 16–59); and Henri Hauser, "Des divers modes d'organisation du
travail dans l'ancienne France," *Revue d'histoire moderne et contemporaine* 7 (1906): 357–87.

produced. Trade communities elected or appointed officers charged
with assuring these standards and defending the trade's rights, primarily
a monopoly on its goods and services; they brought serious problems or
infractions of their statutes to the attention of town officials.

Theoretical analyses of the organization of labor began to flourish only
in the eighteenth century. Earlier treatises on social and political organization by Jean Bodin, Jean Domat, and Charles Loyseau, among others
are relatively silent on the question of labor, although inferences about
work and workers may be drawn from them. It is legitimate, too, to
compare the corps des métiers to other corporate institutions in France,
such as estates or parlements. All these institutions were *corps*, organized
on the model of the human body, whose most important principles were
thought to be order and hierarchy.[9] Thus, all French corps ideally shared
common forms and beliefs about the nature of society and man's place
in it. The French jurisconsulist Charles Loyseau elaborated on these
principles in his *Traité des ordres et simples dignitez* (1610), beginning with
the assumption that "it is necessary that there be an order in all things,
for their well-being and for their direction." Yet, men were not naturally
orderly like the physical universe; instead, they were "mutable and subject to vicissitude, on account of the franchise and particular liberty that
God has given them for good and for evil. Nonetheless, they cannot exist
without order."[10] The best order was hierarchical: some men were to
command; others to obey. Whereas the artificial body politic could not
be regulated in the same way as the natural body, each part could be
assigned a specific function. From the head, which commanded, down
through the various members, each part had a role varying in importance but essential for the whole body's existence. Modeling social arrangements on the body produced solidarities of cooperation within a
hierarchical framework.

The corporeal model was complemented by familial models of social
organization, which also had both egalitarian and hierarchical features.
Families could display a certain solidarity based on cooperation and affective ties, especially between brothers, and on authority based on the
father's power and dignity. Wives and mothers could be metaphors for

9. John of Salisbury presents an early formulation of political institutions in terms of the
body in *Policraticus* (1159). "The place of the head in the body of the commonwealth is filled
by the prince. . . .The husbandmen correspond to the feet, which always cleave to the soil, and
need the more especially the care and foresight of the head, since while they walk on earth
doing service with their bodies, they meet the more often with stones of stumbling, and therefore
deserve aid and protection all the more justly since it is they who raise, sustain, and move forward
the weight of the entire body" (John of Salisbury, *The Statesman's Book*, trans. John Dickenson
[New York, 1963], p. 65).

10. *Les Oeuvres de Maistre Charles Loyseau*, ed. Claude M. Joly (Paris, 1665), p. 1.

structures meant to mitigate or reject the absolute authority of fathers.[11] The basic model of the early modern family remained hierarchical and patriarchal, but alternative models suggested ways of thinking about and playing with concepts of authority and equality. Even within the hierarchically organized corps des métiers relationships were not strictly authoritarian.

Moreover, relationships were not (ideally) based solely on economic benefits. Workers owed their masters good service and loyalty; masters were responsible for their workers' actions. The master was obliged to train his workers well and treat them justly, lodging and feeding them in his own house. Gradually, however, as trade corporations became almost exclusively preoccupied with protecting masters' privileges, the importance of the organic model diminished, and labor became more of a market commodity. The selling of masterships, made common in the reign of Louis XI (1461–1483), sometimes placed men with little or no skill in the craft at the "head" of their workers. Normative values such as pride in work and artistry could more easily be subordinated to avarice in such situations. As Natalie Zemon Davis has shown, journeymen were often conscious of and articulate about these work relationships. In Lyon, for example, journeymen printers clearly signaled their desire for a more egalitarian relationship with masters. Their familial model substituted the horizontal solidarities of brotherhood for the vertical ties of patriarchy.[12]

Confraternities

The confraternities, like corps des métiers, appear to have originated in the late Middle Ages. Although legally constituted, they sometimes ran afoul of church and state authorities, and therefore they form a useful comparison with the illegal compagnonnages. Initially, confraternities were religious and charitable organizations for the lay community in a particular locality. *Confrères* dedicated their efforts primarily to the performance of religious duties, among the most important of which were the elaborate ceremonies held on the feast days of their confraternity's patron saint. On these days members would parade through town, adorned with ribbons and other finery, carrying banners and the saint's relics.

11. For such metaphors in a theoretical work, see John Locke, *Two Treatises of Government*, ed. Peter Laslett (New York, 1960): *First Treatise*, secs. 60–65, pp. 220–25, and *Second Treatise*, chap. 6, "Of Paternal Power," which Locke argues should properly be termed *parental* power.

12. Natalie Zemon Davis, "A Trade Union in Sixteenth-Century France," *Economic History Review* 19 (1966): 53.

Theoretically, confraternities could include members from diverse socioeconomic groups as long as they were all dedicated to the performance of their religious duties. In practice, however, they tended to be
segregated by trade, although apprentices, journeymen, and masters
might all be members. The religious aspect of the confraternities was
extremely important, but they often became adjuncts to trade organizations as well. To become an official in a trade community, one might
first have to serve as a *syndic* (trustee) in the trade's confraternity. These
two bodies frequently met together to discuss common problems and
interests, especially those of a financial nature. Somewhat less hierarchical than trade communities, confraternities nonetheless had elected
leaders, each with a specific title or rank. Their statutes were generally
drawn up by the association, subject to higher secular or clerical approval.[13]

Confraternities were primarily under ecclesiastical jurisdiction, which
was most concerned with offenses or infractions committed in confraternal ceremonies. Secular powers were more concerned that confraternities might act as a shield for illegal economic and labor activities. Trade
communities were vehicles for tax collection and assessment and the
control of labor, and royal authorities objected to the existence of any
associations that might interfere with these objectives. Neither religious
nor lay authorities liked the confrères' loyalty oaths. In 1565 a lawyer
named Joachim du Chalard explained why confraternities were abolished by the Edict of Villers-Cotterets (1539):

> All confraternities by the ordinances of King François I are abol-
> ished: because they tend more to create a type of external super-
> stition, monopolies, debaucheries, and expenses than to foster
> good and true religion. But the natural state of such artisans and
> those who practice the mechanical arts is so unruly, [and] they are
> so difficult to govern . . . that no one has ever known how to make
> them observe the ordinances any more than one was able to do
> with the children of Israel in the desert; they run around, dance,
> feast, and get drunk the day of their chosen patron saint under
> the guise and shadow of religion and a divine service.[14]

13. Emile Coornaert, *Les Corporations en France avant 1789* (Paris, 1941), pp. 23, 231.
14. Ibid., p. 234, quoting Joachim du Chalard, *Sommaire des ordonnances du roy Charles IX*. For
the 1539 edict, see François-André Isambert et al., eds., *Recueil général des anciennes lois françaises
depuis l'an 420 jusqu'à la révolution de 1789*, 29 vols. (Paris, 1822–33), 12:638. The edict "pros-
crivent évidemment la confrérie des compagnons, quelle qu'en soit la forme, au même titre que
la confrérie du métier ou confrérie mixte," and was renewed in the codes of Orléans (1560),
Moulins (1566), and Blois (1576). Etienne Martin Saint-Léon, *Le Compagnonnage: Son histoire, ses
coutumes, ses règlements, ses rites* (Paris, 1901), pp. 38–39.

Confraternities (like compagnonnages), although legally abolished, were never effectively suppressed. By the end of the sixteenth century, however, trade confraternities were increasingly divided: those composed solely of masters had a charitable and pious role; those made up of journeymen, while carrying out religious functions, became mutual aid associations and sometimes a cover for labor agitation. By the early seventeenth century, the church tolerated confraternities (under strong episcopal control), and from 1660 on, the state recognized them "on condition of the formality of authorization."[15] Such confraternities were thus rather different in character from the earlier ones. They continued to provide the world of work and the worker with an institution incorporating the principles of charity and religious devotion, but medieval ideals of the organic unity of the spiritual and the temporal in the confraternity were fragmented. Eventually the trade confraternity became more religious "appendage" to the corps des métiers than an independent association. By separating levels of workers, such confraternities further eroded the "corps" in the corps des métiers while giving new scope to the journeymen's aims and ideas.

Religious Orders

The most important of the other corporate organizations that helped inform the organization of confraternities and, in turn, compagnonnages were the religious orders, specifically, the rule of these orders. By the early Middle Ages the Rule of Saint Benedict (compiled about 528) had been adopted in monasteries throughout Europe. This monastic code combined religious and charitable principles in a practical framework, a threefold division of each monk's life into liturgical prayer, reading, and manual labor, which together contributed to the common good of the order. The rule was administered by the paternal authority of an abbot, literally a "father." When a monk took his final vows, however, he made a profession of faith and swore lifelong obedience to the rule itself—the supreme law of the monastery.[16]

The rule regulated every aspect of monastic behavior. Offenses met with a graded system of discipline, conducted by the abbot according to the general precept of firmness tempered by charity. Disciplinary correction began with a monk's exclusion from meals in common and moved to total ostracism from his fellow monks, who were forbidden to associate with the offender. In difficult cases, physical punishment was

15. Martin Saint-Léon, *Compagnonnage*, pp. 39, 235.
16. David Knowles, *Cistercians and Cluniacs* (Oxford, 1955), pp. 6, 13.

meted out. If the offender would not reform, he was expelled from the order.[17]

Just as expulsion from the order was the culmination of graded steps, so too was entry into it. Religious orders were not joined at whim. A supplicant might knock on a monastery's entrance gate for days without response; once admitted, he was put to the test of a yearlong novitiate. If finally accepted, the monk found himself (according to Benedict's original conception) within a "family" of moderate size, a form of continuity between the monk's past and present lives. Although ideally this monastic family was a community of equals, it recognized various ranks—such as dean and provost—granted on the basis of merit and learning, not seniority. Seniority, however, played a certain role: monks were divided into "juniors" and "seniors," ranks partly determined by merit but also by date of entry into the order. Seniors had certain privileges but were not supposed to exploit these rights. Juniors were to honor the seniors—give up their seats to them, for example, and beg the seniors' blessing—and seniors were to love the juniors. Finally, the abbot, elected by a majority vote of all the monks was to be like "a father in whom the members of the family acknowledged, with affectionate respect, the obedience due to our lord Himself because . . . he occupies the place of Christ."[18]

These first straightforward principles were gradually elaborated. Expanded liturgical ritual at Cluny, for example, was accompanied by a ritualization of nonliturgical activities, whereby "the normal activities of everyday life—working, dressing, sitting, eating—became ceremonialized." The use of sign language, extravagant clothing, and fine ceremonial objects were corollaries of the elaboration of ritual found in certain orders.[19] Yet, while certain religious orders strayed from the simplicity of Benedict's original precepts, his rule and the life of religious communities continued to serve as powerful models for lay people seeking to unite their forces in pursuit of their own, secular endeavors. Religious orders, like trade communities, confraternities, and families, incorporated a dynamic interplay between solidarity and hierarchy. Compagnonnage borrowed from these "bodies," and as in these models, principles of brotherhood and love remained in tension—and often erupted into conflict—with those of hierarchy and authority.[20]

17. Benedictus, Abbot of Monte Cassino, *The Rule of Saint Benedict*, ed. Francis A. Gasquet (London, 1925), pp. 79, 55–58.
18. Ibid., pp. 108–10, xxv–xvi.
19. Barbara H. Rosenwein and Lester K. Little, "Social Meaning in the Monastic and Mendicant Spiritualities," *Past and Present*, no. 63 (1974): 7.
20. Cf. Farr, *Hands of Honor*, especially chap. 3, "Hierarchy and Solidarity"; and Mark Motley, *Becoming a French Aristocrat: The Education of the Court Nobility, 1580–1715* (Princeton, 1990), pp.

Origins: The Etymological Argument

My search for compagnonnage begins with the name itself. The etymology of the root word *compagnon* provides some clues about concepts of community; its use informs and helps trace the presence or absence of both itinerant workers and compagnonages before the fourteenth or fifteenth centuries. Worth noting from the outset is the difference in connotation between the French *compagnon* and the English *journeyman*. Both terms define the same stage of the artisanal life cycle, but each rivets attention on a different element in the worker's life. *Compagnon* derives from the Latin *cum panis*, "with bread," those who take bread together. The term is inherently suggestive of community, whether religious or secular, whether of masters and workers or of workers alone. By contrast, the English *journeyman* (or "tramping artisan"), a man who travels from place to place, carries less symbolic baggage, although it can evoke images of the rootless wanderer who must move on to earn his daily bread and of the young adventurer seeking fortune and romance.[21] Whatever the name, the young worker experienced hardship, isolation, some adventure and romance, and some degree of community. The shift from breaking bread with a master in a patriarchal family to breaking it with a fraternal community on the road, however, came only gradually.

Before the fourteenth or fifteenth century French workers were usually divided into two categories: *apprentis*, *valets*, or *garçons*, who were younger, less-skilled workers, and *maîtres*, that is, fully qualified workers. Although an intermediate stage existed, scrutiny of Boileau's *Livre des métiers* reveals a marked absence of the word *compagnon*. Boileau commonly refers those who had finished apprenticeship as *ouvriers* (or sometimes valets or garçons).[22] *Ouvriers*, moreover, are defined not as itinerants but as those practicing the trade before attaining mastership. Etymological dictionaries do not give the meaning of *compagnon* as a worker in the stage after apprenticeship before the fifteenth century. Evidently, the introduction of a "new" word to name this stage demarcates some consciousness of change in the world of work. A. J. Greimas, for example, states that the term *compaing* or *compaignon* can be traced to 1080, when its primary meaning was "associate," "comrade," or follower of a lord, derived from the Latin, "he who shared bread with

---

18–19. Motley analyzes the transition from childhood to adulthood in the aristocracy and argues: "The dialogue between childhood 'nature' and adult 'culture' was in fact an essential way in which relationships of both hierarchy and solidarity could be constructed and expressed, and in which household socialization connected with the principal contexts of adult life."

21. There were journeymen, however, who were primarily resident in one city.

22. In some trades, *valet* and *garçon* were the equivalent of apprentice.

another." At least up to the fourteenth century, the term was *not* used
to mean a worker (itinerant or otherwise) between apprenticeship and
mastership in any sources found by Greimas or by Frédéric Godefroy in
his dictionary of old French to the fifteenth century. Walther von Wartburg traces to 1460 the meaning as a "*garçon* who has finished his apprenticeship but does not yet have the mastership."[23]

The archival sources confirm the dictionaries. Even when sources begin to use the term *compagnon* in the late Middle Ages, it might not be
distinguished from *ouvrier*. Emile Coornaert quotes a fifteenth-century
example: "Many compagnons and ouvriers speaking different languages
and from various nations [i.e., regions of France] came and went from
city to city to work and learn, to meet, to see and to come to know one
another."[24] Jean-Robert Zimmermann's important work on journeymen
artisans in Strasbourg from the fourteenth century to the eve of the
Reformation, uses archival evidence to argue that at the beginning of
this era the stage between apprenticeship and mastership was still one
of service. "The compagnon was a valet . . . the servant of his master."[25]
Only later did this stage of the workers' life cycle take on more independence and acquire a status that differentiated the compagnon from
an apprentice or valet. Such evidence suggests that we must explore what
the term *compagnon* meant to workers who bore the name and to other
members of the artisanal community from the time when it became common.

Zimmermann's argument about service is crucial. As compagnons began to differentiate themselves from valets or less-skilled workers, they
focused on their relationship to masters. Natalie Zemon Davis's work on
Lyon supports this view and demonstrates that journeymen printers en-
visioned a less subordinate relationship: "Given the quality of the parties
involved there should be mutual and reciprocal love between us. Indeed,
above all other Arts, the Masters and Compagnons are or ought to be
only one body together, like a family and a fraternity."[26] For their part,
Davis cogently remarks, "the only family relation that most masters were

23. A. J. Greimas, *Dictionnaire de l'ancien français, jusqu'au milieu du XIVe siècle*, 2d ed. (Paris, 1968); Frédéric Godefroy, *Dictionnaire de l'ancienne langue française . . . du IXe au XVe siècle* (Paris, 1891–1902); Walther von Wartburg, *Französisches Etymologisches Worterbuch* (Basel, 1946).

24. Coornaert, *Corporations*, p. 239. Coornaert believes that the custom of the tour de France was not fully developed until the fifteenth century.

25. Jean-Robert Zimmermann, *Les Compagnons de métiers à Strasbourg au début du XIVe siècle à la veille de la réforme* (Strasbourg, 1971), pp. 9–12.

26. *Remonstrance et Mémoires pour les Compagnons Imprimeurs de Paris et Lyons: Opposans contre les Libraires, maistres Imprimeurs desdits lieux: Et adiountz* (n.p. [Lyon?], n.d. [1572]), quoted in Davis, "Trade Union," p. 53. See also Davis, "Strikes and Salvation at Lyon," *Archiv für Reformations-geschichte* 56 (1965): 48–64, reprinted in Davis, *Society and Culture in Early Modern France* (Stanford, 1975).

willing to have with their workers was that of a strong father to docile obedient sons. But most journeymen wanted to be treated like adults and brothers," if not quite like equals, a word they do not use. Journeymen printers contended they had "old and ancient customs" and "rights" that their masters were conspiring to destroy. Greedy masters and publishers were acquiring "great and honorable wealth at the price of our sweat and marvelous toil . . . yea, even at the price of [our] blood."[27]

As early as the sixteenth century the petitions of the journeymen printers bore witness to a disintegration of the ties between themselves and masters, who no longer wanted to lodge or feed them and fulfil the duties demanded in return for their loyalty and obedience.[28] The master printers emphasized production and were unwilling to permit more fraternal relations with the journeymen. Nor were they any more likely to dispense with hierarchy in the confraternities. Faced with this intransigence, the journeymen formed their own association. Thus, the advent and use of the word *compagnon* reflects the changed material and social circumstance of the worker in transition between apprenticeship and mastership.

Use of the term *compagnonnage* to refer to associations of illegally organized journeymen did not occur until the mid-seventeenth century and was used only relatively rarely thereafter until the nineteenth century. Old regime officials and masters generally called members of these brotherhoods by the names the workers gave themselves—compagnons du devoir or compagnons non du devoir—although they sometimes used *compagnonnage* generically to mean the stage of being a journeyman. Seventeenth-century authorities occasionally use the term *société*. In the nineteenth century authorities used the term *compagnonnage(s)* to designate illegally organized journeymen with a distinct set of common ritual practices. Compagnons likewise seldom called *themselves* a compagnonnage until the nineteenth century.[29] Moreover, they had no single name for their branches; in the old regime, terms such as *chambre* (room), *vacation* (trade or vocation), and *cayenne* (barracks or depot) were common. In the nineteenth century compagnons began to use the term *société* to mean both the local branch and the whole sect, but their older terms (with the exception of *vacation*) remain much more common at least until 1848. Thus, much of the terminology used by scholars of com-

27. Davis, "Trade Union," pp. 54–55.
28. Ibid., pp. 53–55.
29. My conclusion is based on extensive archival evidence, including police interrogations and compagnons' own writings. Jacques-Louis Ménétra generally uses the phrase "compagnons du devoir" to identify his association. A rare use of *compagnonnage* appears in his reference to the "honneur du compagnonnage." *Journal de ma vie*, ed. Daniel Roche (Paris, 1982), p. 132.

pagnonnage(s)—"brotherhood" included—is arbitrary and analytically imposed. Categorizing serves important theoretical and comparative purposes, but it is equally vital to step back from our classificatory schemes and explore how our terms create unintended meanings and mask the flexibility, dis-organization, and capacity for reorganization which existed within and between these associations.

Beyond the root *compagnon,* one other term is central: *devoir,* literally "duty," is one of the earliest defining terms connected with the compagnonnages. "Du devoir" and "non du devoir" are the phrases most commonly used by both compagnons and outsiders from the mid-seventeenth century to the nineteenth century to designate what we now call a compagnonnage. *Devoir* was a powerful and polyvalent term. First, it was a central and shared concept in early modern French society: all had a *devoir* to perform corresponding to their birth and status; *devoir* was also closely linked to honor. Masters had a *devoir* toward their workers, fellow masters, and clients. Likewise, all journeymen had obligations toward their masters and other superiors, which were often reiterated in labor contracts.[30] To "stay within one's *devoir*" was a phrase commonly applied to workers in the trade communities.

Organized brotherhoods, however, usurped the word and used it to mean one's duty to one's brothers and equals. Analytically, this devoir was what David Schneider has called a "code for conduct," a set of rules, customs, or traditions establishing a pattern for behavior among legal kin.[31] The compagnonnages tried to make their members into a network of fictive kin based on their code for conduct, the devoir, which ideally held the force of law. Compagnons tried to transfer to themselves the powerful economic, social, and emotional, ties and duties bound up in the family.[32] In one word *devoir* encapsulated all that was expected of every member of these brotherhoods. The mutual aid and support the devoir offered was enumerated both in ritual practice and in the specific set of obligations and privileges, usually written, regulating the compagnons' conduct toward one another and their work. These written pre-

30. Farr, *Hands of Honor,* p. 178, demonstrates that *devoir* included "assumptions of obligation and hierarchy." Until the sixteenth century the concept of *fidelité personnelle,* a moral obedience the worker owed the master in return for his paternal responsibility, tended to dominate the organization of artisans. After that time this notion was "undermined by growing horizontal ties among journeymen defined in opposition to masters" (p. 23).

31. For David Schneider, relationships of "natural substance," i.e., shared biogenetic material, are more fundamental and enduring than relationships created by a code for conduct. Nonetheless, such codes impose important prescriptive behavior on legal kin. *American Kinship: A Cultural Account* (Englewood Cliffs, N.J., 1968), pp. 25–29, 63.

32. The complex dynamic of family is explored in an important collection edited by Hans Medick and David Warren Sabean, *Interest and Emotion: Essays on the Study of Family and Kinship* (Cambridge, 1984). See especially the editors' introduction and their essay, "Interest and Emotion in Family and Kinship Studies: A Critique of Social History and Anthropology," pp. 9–27.

cepts were called *rôles, règlements,* or *statuts,* but they could simply be called the devoir, thus a third meaning for the term. Fourth, *devoir* was sometimes used to name the local branch of the association. Finally, and more generally, *devoir* was an organizational term that linked all the compagnons throughout France, of whatever trade, who had sworn to uphold a particular set of common beliefs and practices until death. The complex texture of this term emerges in the early documentation.

ORIGINS: JOURNEYMEN'S BROTHERHOODS BEFORE THE 1650S

The most convincing evidence for the existence of compagnonnage-like brotherhoods before the seventeenth century comes from Dijon. Paul Labal's extensive research in the judicial archives of fifteenth- and sixteenth-century Dijon reveals "particular confraternities of journeymen," organized by trade, which he convincingly argues were the basis of compagnonnage. By the sixteenth century these groups had established "fairly well-developed communitarian customs."[33] Further research may well reveal other early compagnonnages, but to date, the likeliest pre-seventeenth-century antecedents were located by Henri Hauser in Troyes in 1583.[34] These early compagnonnages, Labal says, had itinerant as opposed to sedentary members, emphasized secrecy, and used specific terminology and practice to distinguish themselves from other confraternities.

Labal found evidence of these early compagnonnages in the cutlery, saddlery, and shoemaking trades—three of the five trades later condemned by the Sorbonne in the mid-seventeenth century for forming illegal compagnonnages. These communities levied payments on new compagnons in Dijon in return for helping them find jobs and lodging. They also claimed the right to hold assemblies, and they had jealously guarded secrets. Members of these "cabals" were reputed to bear false testimony in official interrogations rather than reveal them.[35]

The payments demanded of incoming compagnons were not simple dues but part of the rituals of *bienvenue* (welcome), *lavez-pied* (washing of the feet), and *droit de pied* (right of entrance), which sanctioned the right of the new man to be integrated into the town. For example, the

33. Labal, "Notes sur les compagnons migrateurs," p. 191.
34. Hauser, *Compagnonnages,* p. 73 (AM Troyes, BB 11), compagnons (various trades) who held assemblies with the object of raising their *salaires* and practiced the custom of the conduite.
35. Labal, "Notes sur les compagnons migrateurs," pp. 191 (14 August 1464 interrogation of Jehan Manière, cutler), 192 (municipal investigations into activities of compagnons in 1466, 1469, and 1502).

"washing of the feet" suggests an important ceremonial link with the Catholic church and French popular culture, although we have no details on how it was performed. Christ washed the feet of the apostles on Holy Thursday, symbolically making himself the "servant of the servants of God" in this ceremony of inversion. The ritual was (and still is) performed by the pope on Holy Thursday, when he washes the feet of the poor and distributes bread to them. In medieval and early modern France this ritual was performed by the high clergy and even city officials. If, as seems likely, the new compagnon washed the feet of the others, he too was humbling himself and agreeing to "serve" them, at least during his temporary stay in the new town.

More explicit hierarchical relations were established with the compagnons' use of the term *autorité première*. In 1464 one Richard Perpillou was accused of taking as "dues" the coat of a newly arrived compagnon cutler by the name of Gautherot. Another compagnon, Jehan Manière, explained that Perpillou "took the said coat by his *autorité première* and his official position."[36] The term is of great interest because it is a link to the mature associations of compagnonnage, which used the term *premier* to designate the "first compagnon," the head of a trade or trades in a particular locale. When these compagnons assembled under the premier's leadership, they usually did so at the *Mère*. This is another link with the mature compagnonnage in which the key term *mère* denoted both the compagnons' lodging house and the woman who ran it.

The 1540 Dijon case involved a newly arrived compagnon shoemaker, Jehan de la Mothe, taken by another compagnon, Robert Ferron, to the shop of Robert de Pontoje, Ferron's master, to ask him if he had any work for de la Mothe. Presumably Pontoje hired the new compagnon, for "after having their noon meal they [Ferron and de la Mothe] set to work until supper when they went to eat at the home of a woman called the mère."[37] The use of these terms, again in addition to an itinerant membership, helps build the picture of an association rather different from a confraternity. Although any older woman might be called mother (for example, Daniel Defoe's, Mother Midnight), the passage does not read quite that way: "a woman they called the mère" presents a very different construction from "Mère ——." Labal reasonably concludes, despite the absence of the term *devoir,* that an embryonic "solidarité compagnonnique" existed before the seventeenth century. James Farr's

36. Ibid., p. 191.
37. Quoted in Roger Lecotté, *Le Compagnonnage vivant* (Paris, 1973), p. 23 n. 63 bis; see also, Labal, "Notes sur les compagnons migrateurs," p. 192 (17 December 1540, AD Côte d'Or, B II 360/33, Tour de France de Jehan de la Mothe, cordonnier).

work on artisans in early modern Dijon confirms the development of the types of groups Labal had earlier discovered.[38]

Hauser's research in judicial and trade community archives unearthed a number of pivotal cases in which organized journeymen opposed themselves to their masters' dictates, particularly on the issue of placement. I want to examine a few of these examples more closely by drawing on a number of primary documents reproduced in Hauser's work although I differ with his terminology to some extent. He considers all the cases he presents, from 1608 on, as compagnonnages; yet, until a pivotal case of 1663, none of his evidence, particularly with regard to language, definitively proves that compagnonnages were concerned. Nonetheless, the pre-1650 evidence is valuable for what it tells about how associations like compagnonnages were "put together." Compagnons were *bricoleurs*, using a range of available ideas, practices, and language to assemble their associations and differentiate them from others.

Hauser presents seven cases of particular interest, all generated by the hiring and organizational practices of journeymen in the trades of shoemaking and joining between 1608 and 1649. In the 1608 case, journeymen shoemakers, still called valets, were accused of "stealing" workers from masters, meeting and socializing at particular inns, and attempting to raise the price of their products. The masters' complaints make no connection between the valets' fraternization and the agitation over prices.[39] The *Chambre du conseil,* the City Council of Dijon, responded with an edict that banned the valets' practices, set the *prix de façon,* and forbade masters from advancing their workers more than twenty sous. All the issues raised in 1608 became persistent themes in the history of journeymen's brotherhoods, particularly the compagnonnages.

It recurs in the case of 1621, which grew out of a complaint of the majority of master shoemakers against their "compagnons and valets." Advances could reveal the power of the workers virtually to extort the best possible cash deal from a master before beginning work, but at other times, they locked the worker into a cycle of debt which kept him from seeking better employment elsewhere. In the 1621 case the balance of power seemed to favor the "compagnons and valets." The majority of the masters complained that some masters were breaking the 1608 ordinance, offering workers more than twenty sous in advance and luring

38. James Farr, "Contrary Loyalties: *Fidelité Personnelle* and *Compagnonnage,* in 16th-Century Dijon," unpublished paper given at the Sixteenth-Century Studies Conference, 26 October 1985, Columbus, Ohio, pp. 7–8. Even in 1588, tailors had a "national" organization and knew of the way station in Dijon. See also Farr, *Hands of Honor,* esp. pp. 59–75.

39. Hauser, *Compagnonnages,* pp. 74–76 (B 246, fol. 115v, and the summary in H 185 bis in the AMD), and see pp. 71–217 (docs. I–XXVI). Hauser reproduces most cases verbatim.

them away from masters unable to afford such enticements. The case suggests an economic context of increasing demand and a sometimes limited pool of labor which put pressure on some masters to conform to the workers' demands.[40]

Hauser found the first indications of organization among compagnon joiners in 1621. This case is particularly significant because it suggests that compagnon joiners had been organized in Dijon long before 1621 and had previously acted to place workers. The official statutes of the joiners, issued on 26 January, prohibited the compagnons from interfering in hiring, holding assemblies, and breaking their labor contracts. These statutes also established an *embaucheur* (placement official), who the masters hoped would circumvent the compagnonnages' control of hiring practices. The dry language of the joiners' statutes reveals little of the more complex plans of the compagnons. Only two years later, in 1626, the masters petitioned the Dijon council to prohibit the *monopolle* (monopoly) and abuses of their compagnons. Masters protested that compagnons controlled the placement of all incoming workers and exacted money from the newcomers for this service as well as for the bienvenue and other *festins;* they also convoked illicit assemblies and engaged in walkouts. A new and crucial piece of evidence emerges: these organized compagnons kept records and allegedly "constrained all who were inscribed on their *rooles* to follow them." The result was "troops" of twenty to thirty compagnons, roaming the city, threatening to assault the masters, and grossly insulting them if they dared to remonstrate.[41]

The rolls, which compagnons were to sign or mark, obliged the members, under pain of severe penalty, "to obey him whom they named [i.e., as leader], to punish . . . and penalize by fines those who contravened [their] resolutions and *particularly those who revealed the secret of their resolutions.*"[42] According to the masters, the compagnons' organization was based on strong leadership, discipline, a written document constituting their association, and a code of secrecy, all of which "subjected the masters to the commands ["word"] of the compagnons." Journeymen's confraternities also had membership lists and written documents, and they also engaged in labor agitation, but their fundamental purpose was religious, even if this ostensible purpose could be used to mask a labor association. More critically, confraternities were primarily organizations of sedentary compagnons.

40. Ibid., p. 76 (AMD, G 25, B 259, fol. 68, and B 190 bis, fol. 73).
41. Ibid., pp. 77–79 (AMD, B 264, fol. 190), 79–85 (AMD, G 10).
42. Ibid., p. 80 (AMD G 10, 28 April 1626, "Supplique des maîtres menuisiers à MM. les Vicomte Mayeur et Eschevins de la ville de Dijon"; my emphasis). The rolls themselves were not impounded.

This case allows us to "hear" not only the masters' interpretation of events but also the interrogations of two compagnons closely associated with the joiners' association—an organization without a name at this point. These two, the alleged "authors" of the compagnons' monopoly and abuses, were arrested and interrogated on 28 April 1626. The first, Roch Pestelet, was asked if there had recently been many meetings of compagnons during which "they decreed, in writing [*par escript*], that in the future no compagnon . . . would be received unless he first paid homage [*fait la révérance*] to a chief *whom they had elected* [my emphasis] and by whose command he would be placed and not otherwise, on pain of being expelled from the town by cudgel blows." Pestelet declared he was working in Paris when these statutes were drawn up but admitted that when he arrived in Dijon the compagnons had read him the statutes. Furthermore, Pestelet conceded he had "promised to obey the words," which in substance were those of the procurer's interrogation. For his *entrée* among the compagnon joiners of Dijon, Pestelet and "Le Normand," another compagnon arriving at the same time, had each paid eight livres "for refreshments." The entrée rite thus combined economic and social functions: the new compagnon was placed in a job acceptable to the resident compagnons, and all then had a chance to fraternize. Pestelet expressed no sense of wrongdoing but agreed that if the "messieurs de la justice" disapproved of the compagnons' statutes, they "should be torn up and thrown in the fire."[43]

Heyle Mignon, interrogated next, was a key figure in the monopoly for he was *premier chef* of the compagnons. Mignon explained that about three months earlier, in February 1626, all the compagnon joiners of Dijon had met in the house of Jean Ligier, a pastry maker. After each laying out a sum of eight livres, they "resolved to make a statute among themselves in order to make themselves obeyed, and this they did. . . .the said statute was written in the hand of one named Pierre de Montauban." Henceforth, any compagnon joiner who came to work in Dijon was obliged "to greet [*dit bonjour à*] Mignon . . . the *premier chef,* by whose command [the compagnon] was placed in any shop that [Mignon] wished." Although new compagnons were obliged to pay eight livres for the entrée, Mignon, contradicting Pestelet, said they were treated to a drink at the premier's expense. Those who refused to cooperate would be chased from the city.

Neither Pestelet nor Mignon had to be greatly pressured to reveal these facts, despite the compagnons' alleged zeal for secrecy. Furthermore, they openly admitted to having a number of written documents.

43. Ibid., p. 82 (AMD, G 10, "procès-verbal d'arrestation").

Pestelet, and particularly Mignon, defended the legitimacy of their customs. Compagnons were honorable men who had rights and should not be subject to the masters' personal grievances. Mignon maintained that he and the others "had done no wrong but rather good to all the compagnons." Later, after he and Pestelet had been imprisoned, they submitted a petition to the lieutenant general of the bailliage of Dijon protesting their incarceration as "hugely scandalous" and an "affront to the honor of the petitioners, who had neither been delinquent nor [committed] any reprehensible act." The two blamed François Sanbin, a master joiner who harbored a "mortal hatred" against Pestelet.[44]

This whole discussion reveals how much compagnons were concerned with the issue of honor. Farr maintains that it "would be difficult to overemphasize the importance of honor in the daily life of the early modern Dijonnais" and notes how master artisans, much like their social superiors, aspired to the ideal of the honorable man. Here and elsewhere we find that "even" compagnons could share in this paradigm, although perhaps they claimed the honor of personal virtue more than that of social status. The preoccupation with honor could subvert social order, for artisans "had notions of their own about who possessed what degree of honor, and independent judgment from the bottom up tended to undermine a rigid hierarchy."[45] When compagnons applied their own code of honor and devoir to social and economic situations, the exercise could be particularly subversive.

A municipal investigation in July 1649 revealed that master shoemakers faced similar insubordination from compagnons who had plans to create a large organization. Anthoine Saviot, innkeeper at the "Sign of the Wolf," declared under questioning that on 28 June 1649 fifty to sixty compagnons came to his inn and requested a room large enough to receive them all. They wanted the room furnished with two beds for the use of sick or newly arrived compagnons. They would meet every fifteen days, each paying dues of five sous, presumably on this semimonthly basis.[46] Although Saviot was not called the père in this agreement, or his inn the Mère, the roots of these institutions are clearly visible.

By the 1620s, then, the structure of the compagnons' association consisted of a strict entry policy codified by statutes, regular meetings at a fixed locale, and a hierarchy based on the authority of a premier chef.

44. Ibid., pp. 82–83.
45. Farr, *Hands of Honor*, pp. 177–78 and, more generally, chap. 4, "Order, Conflict, and Honor."
46. Hauser, *Compagnonnages*, pp. 89–91 (AMD, G 10 and B 287, fol. 88v, Dijon, 16 July 1649, "Extraict des registres de la Chambre du conseil").

The objective was to regulate and facilitate the placement, assimilation, and fraternization of journeymen from various regions of France. These activities must have continued into 1627: an arrêt of 7 October barred "foreign compagnon joiners and others from forming any illegal assembly and monopoly or exacting any sum of money from one another on the pretext of 'bienvenue' or for any other reasons." The question of who was to place compagnons continued to trouble Dijon's corporations, leading to conflict not only between masters and compagnons but between "large" and "small" masters. In 1638 a quarrel erupted among master joiners over whether or not to continue to appoint a placement official. The larger masters, who had more orders to fill and needed more workers, objected to the community's requirement of equal distribution of workers. The smaller masters accused them of favoring the compagnons' placement practices, implying that they had the means to attract compagnons with advances and better pay and working conditions. The case was temporarily resolved in 1639 when a parlementary edict overrode the municipal ordinance and decreed absolute liberty of placement without fee. Simultaneously, however, the edict confirmed any and all edicts against compagnons' associations and banned their interference in placement.[47]

This debate between "freedom" of placement, demanded by the compagnons and some masters, and regulation, supported by the official trade communities, continued to the end of the old regime. It was a crucial issue, and it both preceded and was later influenced by the wider eighteenth-century debate on free trade seen in the work of the philosophes and physiocrats. The more immediate struggle over who was to control—or not control—hiring intensified in cities where trade expanded and the gap between larger and smaller producers widened. For their part, in advocating freedom the compagnons hardly wanted the "open shop": they were demanding control of the labor market themselves.

The cases I have outlined demonstrate a tenacious demand for organization and solidarity—both economic and social—among Dijonnais compagnons even in the early seventeenth century. The cornerstone of their organizations was the principle of control over hiring, which could give them some control over the conditions of their labor. To implement their "right" to control hiring the compagnons in these cases met fre-

47. Ibid., pp. 98–99 (AMD, B 302, fol. 72), 86–89 (AMD, B 275, fol. 230v, G 10, and AD Côte d'Or, B 42243, fol. 271 v, 11 March and 6 April 1638, "Règlement pour les menuisiers au faict du clerc du mestier," and 28 March 1639, "Extrait des registres du Parlement"). For the benefit of any who had forgotten, a municipal ordinance of 7 August 1663 reprinted the 1627 arrêt, declared it still in effect, and reiterated the ban on compagnon joiners' associations.

quently in assemblies, established written statutes, tried to enforce a
"closed shop," and not least of all, "elected" or chose a chief with the
power to carry out the statutes. But in demanding that new compagnons
perform the entrée or bonjour, organized compagnons established more
than economic sanctions on their members. These procedures involved
some kinds of ritual fraternization, though we learn little of the specifics.
We do know that these compagnons did not call themselves a confraternity, but who and what did they think they were? Only from the mid-
seventeenth century on are compagnonnages defined by distinctive
practices and language.

THE "DISCOVERY" OF COMPAGNONNAGE

The first evidence that (over) defines compagnonnage comes from
relatively detailed accounts of its ritual practices brought to light in the
mid-seventeenth century in the context of the mature French Counter-
Reformation (see Appendix 1). During this era, Philip Hoffman writes,
the church hierarchy waged a "campaign against popular culture." But
clerics were seconded and often driven by groups of zealous lay religious
reformers—the *dévots*—intent on stamping out "disorders and impieties," particularly those related to the church and its sacraments and
celebrations. The dévots, emphasizing "good works" and social and
moral conformity over spirituality, considered such "public sins" especially grave, for they openly challenged and eroded religious and civic
authority. In Counter-Reformation Lyon, Hoffman demonstrates, the infamous and influential Company of the Holy Sacrament, founded in
Paris in 1627, "was particularly troubled by the festivities of traditional
communal bodies." Its members "repeatedly voted to battle the popular
customs they abhorred."[48] This campaign was crucial in shaping the perception of compagnonnage, for its customs fell into the category marked
for elimination. Its worst offense was the "abominable" transformation
of licit religious ceremonies for profane purposes, "even more dangerous because they were hidden under the veil of an apparent piety."[49]
Ironically, some of the paraliturgical practices and popular religiosity of
compagnonnage may have been encouraged by Counter-Reformation
piety. Journeymen's participation in Counter-Reformation confraternities gave them not only a new intimacy with and understanding of relig-

48. Philip Hoffman, *Church and Community in the Diocese of Lyon, 1500–1789* (New Haven,
1984), p. 88, and on the Company of the Holy Sacrament, see pp. 73–74.
49. Pierre [Père Hippolyte] Helyot, *Histoire des ordres monastiques, réligieux, et militaires et des
congrégations séculières*, 8 vols. (Paris, 1714–19), 8:179.

ious practices but also access to vestments, chalices, candles, and other sacred objects.

Religious rather than secular institutions led the seventeenth-century attack on compagnonnages in Paris, Toulouse, and Bordeaux.[50] The Sorbonne's interest was generated by the Company of the Holy Sacrament, founded in Paris in 1627. Inquiries into compagnon shoemakers' brotherhoods began in Paris in the early 1630s and led to similar discoveries in Toulouse and Bordeaux.[51] The investigations resulted in a series of decisions, between 1635 and 1655, handed down by the faculty of theology of the Sorbonne and other clerical and municipal authorities against compagnon shoemakers (1645, 1651, 1655), tailors (1655), saddlers (1654 and 1655), hatters (1655), and cutlers (1655).

The investigation of the shoemakers reveals the initial links between confraternities and compagnonnages. The Confraternity of Saints Crispin and Crispinian (the shoemakers' patron saints) had had a long and stormy history.[52] It was originally composed of both masters and journeymen (called garçons in this trade) and was dissolved, along with all other trade confraternities, by the Edict of Villers-Cotterets in 1539. Reestablished two years later, the confraternity continued a pattern of tumultuous dissension. By 1551 the chapter head at Notre-Dame made the masters governors of the confraternity, and the journeymen disputed his order. Once again the confraternity was dissolved, in 1553, only to be revived in 1555. Renewed disagreements forced the chapter head to intervene and instruct masters and garçons to celebrate their festivals separately.[53] Whether or not this resolution suited the majority of the

50. For Toulouse, see [Abbé] Célestin Douais, "Le Pseudo-baptême et les pseudo-serments des compagnons du devoir à Toulouse en 1651,"*Mémoires de l'Académie des sciences, inscriptions, et belles-lettres de Toulouse*, ser. 9, vol. 5 (1893): 432–58, an article based on documents in the episcopal archives of Toulouse. For Bordeaux, see BN, Collection Dupuy [hereafter Coll. Dupuy], no. 775, fols. 272–74, "Serment des selliers de la ville de Bordeaux" and "Note relative au serment secret prêté par les selliers de Bordeaux lors de leurs reception comme compagnons." I cannot verify Douais's mention of similar activities in Nevers and Reims (pp. 438–39).

51. See, for example, Raoul Allier, *La Cabale des dévots, 1627–1666* (Paris, 1902), pp. 193–213; [Abbé] Alphonse Auguste, *La Compagnie du Saint-Sacrement à Toulouse: Notes et documents* (Paris, 1913); Coornaert, *Compagnonnages*, pp. 42–45; and Jean Lecuir, "Associations ouvrières de l'époque moderne. Clandestinité et culture populaire," *Revue du vivarais*, special issue: *Histoire et clandestinité du Moyen-Age à la Première Guerre Mondiale*, ed. Michèle Tilloy et al., pp. 273–90 (Paris, 1979). Martin Saint-Léon, *Compagnonnage*, p. 40, accepts a slightly different version, following F. Rabbe, "Une Société secrète catholique au XVIIe siècle," *Revue historique* 71 (November 1899): 243–302, who says the compagnon shoemakers were denounced in 1639 by a society of dévots called the "confrérie du Saint-Sacrement." According to Martin Saint-Léon the ensuing investigation resulted in several admonitions (*monitoires*) and sentences in 1640–41, but he does not discuss the important documents of 1645 and 1648.

52. Coornaert, *Compagnonnages*, p. 415.

53. Ibid. As with many old regime terms, the meaning and use of *garçon* varied from region to region and trade to trade. *Garçons* could refer to apprentices, but here meant journeymen. Once the devoir was discovered, *garçons* designated unaffiliated journeymen; *compagnons* identified the devoir's adherents.

garçons, some of them seized the opportunity to organize a faction within the confraternity. By the seventeenth century, we learn, largely from Michel-Henry Buch's inquiries, they were calling themselves compagnons du devoir and had developed a number of unconventional practices.

Buch was a shoemaker by trade and lay preacher by vocation. As a journeyman and later as a master shoemaker, "le Bon Henry" spread his gospel on the "science of salvation," good works, and the celibate life. Preaching to apprentice and journeymen shoemakers sometime in the early 1630s, Buch learned of the "execrable and sacrilegious maxims" practiced by some compagnons in the shoemakers' confraternity. When his evangelizing and "charitable remonstrances" failed to convert these wrongdoers, a troubled Buch confided in Baron Gaston de Renty, a friend and high-ranking member of the Company of the Holy Sacrament who belonged to Buch's circle of dévots.[54] In 1635, armed with details of the compagnons' alleged impiety, the governors of the Company of the Holy Sacrament submitted a complaint to the provost of the Châtelet, the seat of criminal jurisdiction in Paris. Ruling for the plaintiffs, the provost issued a sentence against the compagnon shoemakers on 22 August. In the following decade other admonitions and sentences followed.[55] The case developed new dimensions in 1645 when master shoemakers divulged the compagnon shoemakers' initiation ceremony in a petition to the Sorbonne's faculty of theology. The key issue hinged on the explanation of how uninitiated journeymen became "compagnons." The theologians determined:

> 1. The oath that engages the compagnons in the aforementioned practices . . . is full of irreverence and is repugnant to Religion, and obligates the person taking the oath in no way.
> 2. The said compagnons are no longer secure in their conscience,

---

54. Helyot, *Histoire des ordres* 8:179; Coornaert, *Compagnonnages*, p. 43. Coornaert calls this the confraternity of the Holy Sacrament; most sources call it the "company." Renty was a *supérieur* in the organization. René de Voyer d'Argenson, *Annales de la Compagnie du St. Sacrement*, ed. and annotated by H. Beauchet-Filleau (Paris, 1900), p. 61. See also, Allier, *Cabale des dévots*, pp. 193–213, who speculates that the Company of the Holy Sacrament provided Buch with funds for his mastership. Among Allier's sources is Jean-Antoine Vachet, *L'Artisan chrétien; ou, La Vie du bon Henry, instituteur des frères cordonniers* (Paris, 1670). Allier notes that Vachet never mentions the Company of the Holy Sacrament but discusses Buch and Renty's close friendship.

55. Coornaert, *Compagnonnages*, p. 43. His evidence (see his app. VII, pp. 415–24) comes from a "little parchment register with the word *Confrérie* on the back, communicated [to Coornaert] by René Edeline and belonging to M. Centner." Edeline was a compagnon baker and collector par excellence of compagnonnage memorabilia. Coornaert notes that the title "Extraits des registres de l'Officialité du Chapitre de l'Eglise de Paris" appears on p. 99 of the register. He lists the events and provides excerpts for the years 1635 and 1642.

as long as they wish to continue these evil practices, which they must renounce.

3. The journeymen who are not in this devoir cannot join it without committing a sin, if they have been duly warned of the said practices in which they engage which make them part of this Compagnonnage du devoir.[56]

The master shoemakers did not, however, confine themselves to complaints about sacrilege; much of their petition denounced the effects of this compagnonnage on the trade. The compagnon shoemakers insisted that the three key elements of their devoir were blameless: honor God, preserve the well-being of the masters, and maintain the compagnons. The masters retorted that the "quality" of compagnon conferred in such ceremonies created an "offensive and defensive league" which made "laws after [its] own fashion"; the magistrates had banned compagnonnage "for the great inconveniences that it occasions."[57]

Chief among these was the threat of "ruin" for masters. If a compagnon claimed a master had mistreated him, his fellow compagnons could empty the shop of workers for as long as their need for vengeance dictated. The devoir, moreover, generated the kind of rowdy, debauched behavior pious Counter-Reformation laity loathed, and even made life miserable for workers, leading to frequent quarrels based on alleged infractions of the devoir or on a worker's refusal to join it. Compagnons levied fines or otherwise punished and attacked offenders. Apprentices were particularly vulnerable to the abuse of these compagnons, and indeed to journeymen in general. Although unaffiliated workers outnumbered them, compagnons were stronger because their league "nourished among them the fire of violence against others." They took as their symbol Gideon, a judge of Israel who conquered the Midianites, because his feats exemplified the victory of the few and the weak against the many.[58] Finally, the compagnon shoemakers' correspondence revealed a network that informed members in the devoir throughout

56. BN, 4° FM 35348, "Compagnons du devoir, cordonniers," Paris, 21 September 1645, 4-page printed pamphlet (n.p., n.d [Paris, 1645]), p. 3 (see also Appendix 1, no. 1). Another, somewhat abridged version of this piece exists (n.p., n.d. [Paris, 21 September 1645]); it begins with the words "Les Compagnons d'un certain Mestier" (BN, E. 3488). Roger Lecotté reproduced this version in "Les Plus anciens imprimés sur le compagnonnage," *Bulletin Folklorique de l'Île de France (Paris)*, 4th ser., no. 4 (1968): 67–68. In the French text the word *compagnon*, printed in lowercase type, referred to uninitiated workers; capitalized, *Compagnon* referred to initiated workers. I use the word *journeyman* as opposed to *compagnon* to distinguish between the uninitiated and initiated.

57. Ibid., p. 1.

58. Ibid., p. 2.

France of delinquents to be tracked down and, if necessary, exiled from the brotherhood.

Despite new censures in 1646 and 1647, compagnons du devoir persisted in their "damnable and diabolical superstition."[59] In 1648 the archiepiscopal and metropolitan courts in Paris heard a brief that set forth the grievances of the masters, governors, and administrators of the Confraternity of Saints Crispin and Crispinian against the "compagnons du devoir," who were accused of committing innumerable disorders, particularly during the election of confraternal officers. Simultaneously, these compagnons submitted their own petition to the court, in effect requesting permission to secede from the confraternity and hold their own services elsewhere, perhaps in the church of Saint Eustache.[60]

The heart of the problem was the compagnons' search for a satisfactory definition of the roles and rights of masters and journeymen. Even in the seventeenth century, the Confraternity of Saints Crispin and Crispinian was still composed of apprentices, journeymen, and masters; journeymen could play some role and attain some offices in the organization, but the compagnons du devoir wanted more independence. A growing economic and social disparity between masters and journeymen and restricted access to the mastership led to continuing friction in the confraternity. But, although the compagnons du devoir wanted a more egalitarian and less hierarchical organization, they did not base their demand on some "golden age" when the confraternity had been a true brotherhood. The compagnons du devoir became a small but vocal faction within the brotherhood, organizing against the masters and against those journeymen who refused to take a more aggressive stand.

The decision of the ecclesiastical courts, rendered on 13 May 1648, illuminates this split among the compagnons. Levan Isambert, a journeyman shoemaker who had held important offices in the confraternity, was attacked, thrown out of the chapel, and roughly insulted by compagnons du devoir while trying to attend mass on the Sunday after Ascension. The division in the confraternity seems to have been between native journeymen, somewhat older and married (like Levan Isambert), and "foreign" compagnons, younger, single, and on the tour de France, who used their "superstitious and illicit oath" to "league together" as a secret faction within the association "to the prejudice of the other apprentices and garçon shoemakers."[61] All the machinations of the compagnons du devoir were condemned. They were told to renounce their

59. Coornaert, *Compagnonnages*, pp. 415–16 (28 June 1646, "Sentence contre le Devoir").
60. BN, E. 3489, *Extraict des registres de l'Officialité de Paris*, 13 May 1648.
61. Ibid. Coornaert, *Compagnonnages*, p. 419, gives Isambert's first name as "Lenan." The printed document renders the name "Leuan," hence Levan.

oaths; stop their ceremonies of arrival and leave-taking; end their assemblies; elect no Masters and Governors of their "so-called Compagnie du devoir"; and finally, keep no registers, collect no dues, maintain no treasury.

Despite this itemized ban, two petitions in late May 1648 revealed that the compagnons du devoir had won the sympathy and support of Maistre Gilles Poupel, chaplain of the priory of Saint Denis de la Chartre. "With an extraordinary scorn" for the edict against them, the compagnons du devoir planned to celebrate mass at this chapel and offer seven or eight loaves of blessed bread. The chaplain was informed of the sentence of 13 May—it was even read to him—but he reportedly would not desist from celebrating the mass and "favoring the [compagnons'] undertakings." Fearing the compagnons' determination, authorities reissued the sentence of 13 May 1648 on 1 July, ordering all compagnon shoemakers to obey its conditions and renounce their oaths or face excommunication. The compagnons du devoir used the legal system to engage an attorney, Maistre Jacques Bercquel, who declared in their name that they "renounced all allegiance to the so-called Devoir, and all of its bad practices." This declaration kept the compagnons du devoir in check (or at least out of the courts), but only for three years. By 1651 they were again convoking assemblies and initiating new members in cabarets. These "receptions," as their initiations were called, included practices contrary to "divine and human laws."[62]

In a bid to skirt the control of the Paris diocese, the compagnons' brotherhood sought sanctuary in the quarter of the Temple, which had its own canonical jurisdiction. But the bailliage of the Temple issued a sentence on 11 September 1652, expelling the compagnons du devoir who had been meeting and celebrating their holidays in a church in that quarter. The sentence reiterated the earlier prohibitions and cited the pronouncements issued in Toulouse in 1651. This evidence and the compagnons' correspondence reveal that compagnonnage, far from being eliminated in the capital, had spread beyond it.

On 23 March 1651 the bailiffs of the Confraternity of the Conception of Notre Dame and Saints Crispin and Crispinian wrote to the archbishop of Toulouse claiming that "the Compagnonnage du devoir and actions which it commits in the receptions of Compagnons of the said trade of the said devoir are vicious things and things by which God is offended and religion held to scorn." The archbishop hastened to denounce these "sacrilegious" activities. But only three years later, reports

---

62. BN, E. 3485, *Extraict des registres de l'Officialité de Paris*, 1 July 1648; Coornaert, *Compagnonnages*, p. 422 (18 August 1651, "Attestation des chefs de la confrérie").

on compagnon saddlers in Bordeaux disclosed comparable "blasphe-mies," made worse because they involved the threat of Protestantism. It was alleged that the saddlers took oaths and performed initiation cere-monies and commited "other heresies, Huguenots with these evil Cath-olics. And the Huguenots do the same . . . [and] are received Compagnons by these Catholics, and the Catholics by the Huguenots." The triple repetition of this blasphemous ecumenism underscored the chronicler's horror. Whether or not the author was associated with the Company of the Holy Sacrament, his views conform to one of its key ob-jectives: the rooting out and destruction of the reformed faith.[63] Finally, on 14 March 1655, the Sorbonne issued a general denunciation of "the impious, sacrilegious, and superstitious practices that are committed in the trades of shoemaking, tailoring, hatting, saddlery to become Com-pagnons of what they call the devoir." Some sources indicate that com-pagnon cutlers were also condemned at this time. The Company of the Holy Sacrament printed and diffused the decision at its own expense.[64]

The compagnonnage du devoir gravely affronted clerics, masters, and officials, who concurred that the compagnons "greatly dishonor God, desecrate all the mysteries of our religion, ruin the masters, emptying their shops of workers when a member of their cabal complains that he has been wronged, and ruin themselves by the faults of the devoir—they give money to each other which is used for drinking." This grievance, like earlier ones, dwelled almost as much on secular abuses as on blas-phemy. Compagnons had illegally constituted a corps in opposition to the legally established corps des métiers and had used their body to defy

63. Douais, "Pseudo-baptême," pp. 433–34; BN, Coll. Dupuy, no. 775, fol. 274v, "Serment des selliers"; cf. Hoffman, *Church and Community*, p. 73; and Orest Ranum, *Paris in the Age of Absolutism* (Bloomington, 1979), pp. 231–32. The company's maneuvers to deny Protestants civic and professional rights (e.g., entry into guilds and corporations) were particularly widespread in the 1650s.

64. BN, D. 1074, *Résolution des docteurs de la faculté de Paris, touchant les pratiques impies . . . pour passer compagnons, qu'ils appellent du devoir, depuis peu reconnues et advouées par plusieurs desdits Mestiers,* 4-page printed pamphlet (n.p., n.d. [Paris, 14 March 1655]), p. 1; Roger Lecotté, *Archives his-toriques du compagnonnage* (Paris, 1956), n.p., note to piece no. 23. Unless otherwise stated, I use the version of the *Résolution* in the Bibliothèque nationale. This version is found, with slight variations, in various sources, e.g., [Père] Pierre Lebrun, *Histoire des pratiques superstitieuses, qui ont séduit les peuples et embarrassé les sçavans,* 2d ed., 4 vols. (Paris, 1732–37), vol. 4: *Recueil des pièces pour servir de supplément à l'histoire des pratiques superstitieuses,* pp. 54–68. Pierre Varin presents a rather different version, which he says was appended to the statutes of the shoemakers and cobblers of Reims. *Archives législatives de la ville de Reims: Collection de pièces inédites pouvant servir à l'histoire des institutions dans l'intérieur de la cité* (Paris, 1840–52), pt. 2, vol. 2: *Status, 1514–1699,* pp. 249–55. His version includes the documents on the shoemakers cited earlier. Varin also provides details on the hatters' initiations and includes a section on the cutlers, which I have not been able to verify in any other seventeenth-century document. Nonetheless, several scholars use Varin: e.g., Martin Saint-Léon, *Compagnonnage,* pp. 39–42. Emile Levasseur reprinted Varin's account without citation in *Histoire des classes ouvrières en France, avant 1789,* 2 vols. (Paris, 1900), 1:703–7; as does Coornaert, *Compagnonnages,* pp. 350–56.

work regulations. They had assimilated the church's religious prerogatives by conducting their own ceremonies; they had usurped some of the trade corporation's economic role, intervening in their members' placement and working conditions. Compagnons thus presented a serious challenge to the established order of things—religious and secular— even if prosecution was ecclesiastical in that century.[65]

Ecclesiastical prosecution makes sense in a Counter-Reformation context, particularly because the compagnons' acts were regarded as blatant sacrilege. But clerics were almost equally concerned with the economic insubordination, regarded as inevitably leading to moral and spiritual disorder. The close links between the sin of debauchery, for example, and all other transgressions was common in religious (and, later, secular) pronouncements against compagnonnage. Independent brotherhoods, such as the compagnons du devoir had frequent "occasions for sin" at their designated meeting places, and they threatened the privileges of masters—control over production and social definition. The Sorbonne insisted that "this quality of Compagnon does not have anything to do with the achievement of the status of master; to the contrary, this practice has been forbidden by the Magistrates, for the great inconveniences which it creates, only serving as an offensive and defensive league."[66] These leagues enabled compagnons to take concerted action against masters and also kept unaffiliated journeymen from finding employment—effectively punishing those who would not join them or dared betray their "secret."

In theory, ecclesiastical bans against compagnonnage might have extended beyond the capital, but in practice, their influence was limited if secular authorities failed to enforce them. And whereas secular authorities generally supported the church's censure of compagnonnage, they had minimal resources to halt its spread. Nevertheless, ecclesiastical condemnation and intervention was successful in one case, that of the

---

65. Douais, "Pseudo-baptême," pp. 437–38. Michel Foucault says the "parlements showed a certain apathy" in prosecuting workers' assemblies and leagues and sees a "silent conflict opposing the severity of the Church to the indulgence of the Parlements" (*Madness and Civilization* [New York, 1965], pp. 47–48). Recall, however that the parlement of Dijon condemned all such associations in 1639. The parlements had not yet fully involved themselves in the question, but by the late seventeenth century, they vigorously pursued compagnonnages, perhaps signaling a shift from religious to secular power. Apparent toleration can be explained just as well by regional economic needs and the real limitations of the police. More critically, although royal officials theoretically supported regulation for its fiscal advantages, they also recognized some of the benefits of economic liberty. In this complex transition to a "free" economy, compagnonnages could inadvertently aid the state, opening up the corporate system by hammering away at regulations on placement and worker distribution which prevented the growth of larger, more productive shops.

66. BN, 4° FM 35348, "Compagnons du devoir, cordonniers," Paris, 21 September 1645, p. 1.

shoemakers. Recognizing some legitimate mutual aid benefits in compagnonnage, clerics and magistrates in Paris and Toulouse decided to
reorganize the compagnon shoemakers du devoir in Paris. Together,
Buch and de Renty had begun the reform even before the final condemnation of 1655. A new lay religious order called the Communauté des
frères cordonniers des Saints Crespin et Crespinian" was established in
February 1645 and survived until the late eighteenth century. The members promised "constancy, chastity, and renunciation of property"; two
archbishops of Paris reviewed and sanctioned their statutes.[67]

In Toulouse, compagnon shoemakers voluntarily agreed to reform
their organization, submitting their new statutes to the archbishop, who
approved them on 3 May 1651. The masters' confraternity became the
Confrairie de la conception Nostre Dame; the journeymen's confraternity became the Association des serviteurs cordonniers. Regrouping the
compagnons under church tutelage appears to have been a tacit admission of the masters' inability to coexist with the journeymen in a single
confraternity, but the church soon proved no more successful than the
masters in controlling the journeymen. Compagnons in the new association, despite their avowed religious aims, also used the confraternity for
secular ends. Their continual pressure for wage increases resulted in the
establishment of a fixed salary for all journeymen shoemakers in 1702.[68]

This transformed compagnonnage allows us to make some comparisons with confraternities. The association's statutes, although probably
drawn up by the cathedral canon Dufour and not the compagnons, reveal a number of the same principles found in the statutes of the mature
compagnonnage, though the overtly religious element is more fully emphasized. The statutes opened with the shoemakers' desire to establish
a "holy union and association, for the greatest glory to God and for the
assurance of our salvation by means of charitable and mutual assistance
. . . such that being all of the same vocation all will have the same spirit,
according to God, which will animate and fortify us all such that none
of us could henceforth find himself friendless and abandoned in his
extreme need." The concern with mutual aid is given even stronger
voice in the twelfth article, which outlines an essential element of compagnonnage: "We will all have a singular and mutual affection and charitable concern for one another in our needs, be they in health, sickness,
or even after death."[69]

Many articles addressed religious obligations: confrères were to pray
to God morning and night, attend church on Sundays and holy days,

67. Allier, *Cabale des dévôts*, pp. 193–213; Douais, "Pseudo-baptême," p. 439.
68. Douais, "Pseudo-baptême," pp. 457–58.
69. Ibid., pp. 442, 447.

refrain from work on Sundays, attend confession and receive communion monthly, and hear a weekly catechism or sermon. The majority of
the articles, however, concerned the regulation of the *boîte,* the shoemakers' treasury. Each member was to contribute an initial payment of
five sols tournois, followed by dues of twelve deniers to be collected at
the bimonthly assemblies. The association elected two men to guard the
boîte; the elder of the two presided over the assemblies. There was a
secretary, "well instructed in writing." All officers could be replaced at
the discretion of the members. The funds were used for sick or unemployed members, those with "some other great necessity," and for funerals and masses for deceased members.

Equally important were the moral rules: visitation of the sick, advice
and comfort to the troubled, and above all, peace and harmony among
all members. The statutes required the policing of the disobedient or
those caught in other "wrongdoing." Finally, article 10 commanded
confrères to be "faithful to the masters, to work carefully and diligently,"
and enjoined them not to "discuss the masters' affairs in our assemblies
[or] the question of raising wages." As we have seen, the last injunction
was not always obeyed: confrères may have felt it their right to raise such
questions if masters failed to adhere to accepted standards. In the same
vein journeymen exhorted masters to "aid us in keeping to our good
plan for the good of their service, the welfare of their shops, and their
position [*état*] in which we trust by their kindness."[70] The reform of the
illegal associations of shoemakers in Paris and Toulouse essentially
ended compagnonnage in this trade. With few late seventeenth-century
exceptions, shoemakers were almost entirely absent from compagnonnage until the late eighteenth and early nineteenth century. When they
tried to reclaim their original rights as compagnons, shoemakers were
persecuted as frauds by most of the compagnonnages.

The Sorbonne's mid-seventeenth-century condemnations and discussions of these early compagnonnages actually helped define and consol-
idate them. Their most salient features up to this point appear to be,
first, control of worker placement; second, the election or appointment
of a leader responsible for defending this objective; and third, the use
of written regulations, which defined costs for job placement and ritualized welcomes, to which members had to conform. "Membership" was
still quite pragmatic: authorities commonly complained "that the garçons of the trade are solicited and persuaded, even by violence, to become compagnons."[71] Coerced compagnons must eventually have been

70. Ibid., pp. 446–47.
71. BN, 4° FM 35348, "Compagnons du devoir, cordonniers," Paris, 21 September 1645,
p. 1.

converted, for the associations survived and grew into an interurban network, sustained by written and oral communication and shared ritual practices. These early associations of compagnons tended to be eclectic and adaptive, less markedly distinct from other brotherhoods than they would later be. Yet, by the mid-seventeenth century the devoir was distinctive enough for authorities to recognize it and fear the dangers behind it.

CHAPTER 3

Becoming and Being a Compagnon in a Corporate World

He who is to become a compagnon, after having chosen
two of the company for Godfather and Godmother . . .
swears on the Gospels . . . that he will never reveal, even in
Confession, that which he will do or see done. . . .[He] is
received with many ceremonies against the Passion . . . and
the Sacrament of Baptism, which [the compagnons] counterfeit.

—Faculty of Theology, Paris, 1655

The construction of the compagnons' devoir in the last half of the seventeenth century can be traced in the interaction between ritual and the organization of daily life. Ritual practice was at the center of these particular associations and an important point of opposition to them. Recall the Sorbonne's 1655 condemnation of "impious, sacrilegious, and superstitious" ceremonies: the apparent levity involved in imitations of holy rituals rendered them blasphemous and intolerable.[1] Yet, the compagnons' primary aim was not to ridicule but to empower. They acknowledged the force of Catholic ritual and redirected it toward their own ends. Yet, even performed piously, such acts were considered sacrilegious, for they raised the events of the compagnons' life cycle to the level of sacraments.

To interpret how the rituals functioned and what they meant for the compagnons and their brotherhoods, it is useful, following Claude Lévi-Strauss and others, to view ritual as social communication and commentary. For the compagnons, as for any individuals or groups, social communication and commentary developed in the material and cultural

---

1. *Résolution des docteurs de la faculté de Paris,* 14 March 1655, reprinted in [Père] Pierre Lebrun, *Histoire des pratiques superstitieuses qui ont séduit les peuples et embarassé les sçavans,* 2d ed., augmentée par J. Bellon, 4 vols. (Paris, 1732–37), 4:54–60, 55.

context of their wider society. Thus, individuals choose and create what
is meaningful for them, but only within certain limits. Robert Darnton,
for example, comments on Nicolas Contat's account of the "great cat
massacre": "He derived his notions of meaning from his culture just as
naturally as he drew in air from the atmosphere around him. . . . The
subjective character of the writing does not vitiate its collective frame of
reference."[2]

Ritual can be defined broadly here as a set pattern of acts with no
intrinsic relationship between means and ends. This definition permits
us to filter out minor variations and identify major cross-cultural structural similarities. Nevertheless, variations that scholars categorize as superficial are often perceived by the actors as deep and significant.
Focusing on the actors' perceptions helps us better understand what and
how they thought. Attention to variations in elements of the rituals—
physical setting, dress and language—and to changes in content and
structure over time, thus, is critical. The compagnons' ritual practices
grew out of preexisting forms but ended up as original creations.

My comparative and analytical focus prompts me to retain the term
ritual, even though compagnons rarely, if ever, used this word. Particularly before the nineteenth century, this word was more specifically connected with religious practice. In the seventeenth and eighteenth
centuries compagnons called the series of steps which made them a
member of compagnonnage *cérémonies, réceptions,* or *baptêmes.* These
terms persisted in the nineteenth century, but by then some compagnons
also spoke of *initiation* and *cérémonie* or *rite d'initiation.* Remaining aware
of changes in language makes me less hasty to assert "structural similarities" or "fit" between the performances and beliefs of compagnonnage
and other anthropological or folkloric cases of rites of passage. Yet, my
comparative perspective enables me to supplement the compagnons'
perspective without negating it.

The most serious difficulty in the historical study of ritual is that even
the best documentation available is not the ritual itself but only the written version of what was once a performance.[3] Indeed, the existing texts
of compagnonnage are not often that close: they are more likely the
script for a performance (or a version of it) and not the record of an
actual performance.[4] Somewhat closer to the original are accounts of

2. Robert Darnton, "Workers Revolt: The Great Cat Massacre of the Rue Saint-Séverin," in
his *Great Cat Massacre and Other Episodes in French Cultural History* (New York, 1984), pp. 99–100.
Moreover, Darnton convincingly demonstrates that analyzing rituals and jokes "can help one to
see how workers made their experience meaningful by playing with themes of their culture."
3. In analyzing specific cases I often use the terms *text* or *account* of the ritual. In general
discussion, however, I chose the term *ritual* for analytical purposes and for brevity.
4. See Roger Chartier, "Text, Symbols, and Frenchness: Historical Uses of Symbolic Anthro-

the compagnons' "myths," or, more analytically, their origin narratives. These may in fact be the actual accounts told in an initiation chamber or over drinks at a tavern, although the tendency to elaborate or forget in such contexts may well modify the original text. But even a direct transcription of a ritual or an origin narrative cannot recapture the moment of the act, the inflections of the actors, or the responses of the listeners. Did they drink in every word or yawn with boredom? With rare exceptions, the texts of rituals fail to tell us if the initiates trembled with fear, laughed at ritual trappings they thought foolish, or were impressed by the spectacle. Were initiations sacred affairs, following all the scripted details, or makeshift ones apt to miss some of the proper objects, words, and gestures? Even if authors tell us these things, we are still far from the lived experience.

Despite this distance from the acts themselves, I am convinced that it is possible to understand much about these rituals by remaining explicit about the distinction between text and performance and between scripts *for* performances and accounts *of* actual performances.[5] To maintain this distinction between representations and practices means working closely with native accounts, examining their contexts and attempting to understand what compagnons thought they were doing when they counterfeited the ceremonies of the church, took new names, and changed from ordinary journeymen into *compagnons passés*. I look for compagnons' explanations of their intentions and strategies at particular historical moments. Identifying and situating the texts historically, as well as analyzing comments on the text by participants or observers, permits the reader to approach an understanding of how the actors viewed their own performances. Thus, it is necessary to accept the explanations, intentions, and strategies presented in the texts without conflating intention and results or ignoring contradictions within or among accounts.

The demand on the historian to recognize historical context and transformation in analyzing ritual and myth is particularly crucial because those who have written about compagnonnage—scholars and compagnons alike—have tended to accept these symbolic activities as essentially unchanging. Many eighteenth- and nineteenth-century com-

---

pology," in his *Cultural History: Between Practices and Representations,* trans. Lydia G. Cochrane (Ithaca, 1988), pp. 98–110, for an important and persuasive discussion of this point. Cf. Darnton who says that Contat's "written account must be thin compared with the action [the cat massacre] it describes" (*Great Cat Massacre,* p. 100).

5. Although these distinctions seem obvious, it is easy to ignore or blur them. See, for example, Chartier's comments on Darnton's interpretation of Contat's written account of the cat massacre 30 years later. *Cultural History,* pp. 98–110. This last sentence alone is a vivid reminder of the difficulties of sorting out one's accounts—Chartier on Darnton on Contat on the cat massacre.

pagnons claimed to be faithfully reenacting the rituals of earlier eras. In 1850 Victor-Bernard Sciandro, "La sagesse de Bordeaux," a compagnon stonecutter du devoir, declared that "compagnonnage has maintained, in all its private and public ceremonies, the same forms and the same usages found from the beginning of its existence."[6] He and his fellow compagnons considered this timelessness a positive and priceless inheritance.

Some modern scholars would agree with Sciandro that these rituals were unchanging but would not share his evaluation of this legacy. E. J. Hobsbawm saw them as proof of elitism and inflexibility. Yet, even if nineteenth-century compagnonnages were elitist, the question remains: were these rituals really unchanged from the seventeenth century? Michael Sonenscher provides a more productive framework for analysis: "Instead of attempting to discover how a corpus of myth and ritual was passed from one generation to the next as an unvarying totality, it may be more helpful to think in terms of modifications, mutations and accretions to a loosely structured series of stories and ceremonies recognized by journeymen in different times and circumstances in ways which were themselves often very different."[7] Moreover, even if the ritual script and performance changed little, compagnons' interpretation and use of ritual undoubtedly changed in relationship to diverse contexts.

In short, although many elements remained consistent, sometimes identical, in the ritual performances of compagnonnage, their meaning was constructed over time. The growing exclusivity of the nineteenth-century compagnonnages cannot be directly attributed to allegedly seventeenth-century rituals. These later rituals were elaborated, intensified, and modified in response to postrevolutionary changes in artisanal culture and production. The period of rupture in compagnonnage occasioned by the French Revolution rendered strict adherence to tradition problematic in any case and pushed compagnons to reorient and reshape their practices. To trace these transformations I examine the various stages in the ritual life of compagnonnage in chronological context, beginning with the relatively detailed seventeenth-century accounts. But these earliest accounts should not lead us to easy extrapolations about later ritual practices. The drawback to a contextualized approach is the loss of a focused, synchronic comparison of accounts that span more than two hundred years, from the 1640s to the 1890s. I hope to diminish

6. Victor-Bernard Sciandro, *Le Compagnonnage: Ce qu'il a été, ce qu'il est, ce qu'il devrait être* (Marseille, 1850), p. 130.

7. Michael Sonenscher, "Mythical Work: Workshop Production and the *Compagnonnages* of Eighteenth-century France," in *The Historical Meanings of Work*, ed. Patrick Joyce (Cambridge, 1987), p. 37.

this disadvantage by complementing diachronic analysis with synchronic and comparative analysis of ritual practice in the relevant chapters.

EXTANT ACCOUNTS OF INITIATION RITUALS

Any analysis of the rituals of initiation, or *réception*, is limited by the extant source material. I have been able to locate and examine approximately twenty distinct, more or less complete accounts of such rituals, only three of which have not been published in part or in whole (see Appendix 1). I have also examined a number of cases in which compagnons' letters or official reports document the occurrence of a réception. Although none of the twenty or so accounts is wholly unknown to scholars, there has been no attempt to give this body of evidence the rigorous comparative analysis that is required if we are to understand the resiliency and force of compagnonnage and how it relates to other sorts of brotherhoods such as youth groups, confraternities, Freemasonry, and secret societies that employed ritual practices.

The accounts from which I work form a limited but representative sample, and they are authenticated by letters and other writings of past and present compagnons. Especially valuable are the autobiographies of nineteenth-century compagnons such as Sciandro and Toussaint Guillaumou. Significantly, Agricol Perdiguier does not give or explicate an account of an initiation ceremony. Internal evidence and comparison of the rituals provides further verification of authenticity. Finally, all the rituals are structurally similar and are cross-culturally related to other initiation rituals. They can be categorized, following the work of Arnold Van Gennep and Victor Turner, as classic rites of passage with three relatively distinct phases: separation, transition, and incorporation.[8] Using these terms as well as cultural history and anthropological approaches, I want to deconstruct and compare these accounts to reveal meanings and evidence of persistence or change.

Beginning in the seventeenth century, compagnons derived the specific structure, symbolism, and content of their rituals from the wider society, particularly Christian rites and symbols. Ceremonies used in the corps des métiers to mark the transition from apprentice to journeyman and journeyman to master also contributed. By the nineteenth century compagnonnage had similarly integrated some of the symbols of Freemasonry (for example, the square and compass) and some of its prac-

8. Arnold Van Gennep, *The Rites of Passage*, trans. Monika B. Vizedom and Gabrielle L. Caffee (Chicago, 1960), esp. pp. 21, 26, 96; and Victor Turner, *The Ritual Process: Structure and Anti-Structure* (Chicago, 1969), pp. 166–68.

tices (increased emphasis on ranks and titles). As time passed, compagnons reordered and transformed what they borrowed. Historically, then, compagnonnage both simulated other associations and institutions in French society and differentiated itself from them. For compagnons, differentiation was an assertion of the solidarity and dignity of their own devoir and trade. This construction of solidarity and dignity responded over time to external and internal changes and challenges to the existence of compagnonnage.

BECOMING COMPAGNONS IN THE MID-SEVENTEENTH CENTURY

I want to examine two of the more complete and reliable texts of initiation: that of the compagnon shoemakers du devoir (1645) and that of the compagnon saddlers du devoir (1654). The shoemakers' account is especially interesting because this trade's compagnonnage was effectively dismantled until the nineteenth century; its earlier and later rituals can thus be compared as discrete entities. The compagnon saddlers' account is valuable because it is the only one relating the initiation of both Catholic and Protestant members and suggesting some involvement of masters. After I have analyzed these two accounts in Van Gennep's terms, I compare the seventeenth-century initiations of all five condemned trades—tailoring, saddlery, hatting, and cutlery, as well as shoemaking. Unfortunately, none of these texts provides a complete account of the whole initiation. Because the initiation oaths were of most concern to religious and secular officials, the accounts focus mainly on these, and secondarily on how the ceremonies "counterfeited" and profaned Catholic rituals. They give very little information about the compagnons' intentions.

The Compagnon Shoemakers, 1645

In 1645, as noted earlier, the officials of the shoemakers' corporation in Toulouse requested the faculty of theology in Paris to review their compagnons' practices. One journeyman shoemaker had begun to doubt the propriety of the oath he had taken to "become a compagnon." Soon thereafter, an unidentified cleric(s)—possibly the shoemaker's confessor(s)—was troubled enough to bring the confession to the notice of higher church officials, leading to further investigations. The petitioners began their account with the statement that some journeymen shoemakers practice "abominable impieties . . . when they become [*se font passer*] compagnons."[9] The rest of the document fleshes out this accusation.

The *setting* is not described in its particulars, but the initiation is depicted as highly secretive. Evidence from later in the account suggests the initiation took place in the cabaret where monthly assemblies were held. These compagnon shoemakers brought into the initiation chamber bread, wine, salt, and water, which they called the four *aliments* (nourishments). These were placed on a table, either together or separately.

Separation occurred when the novice left his usual routine and came to the place where the ritual was performed, though we do not learn specifically how he was summoned. The novice was also separated in some way from those who were already compagnons.

The phase of *transition* is designated here by the words "se passer compagnon." The words may have been chosen by the chronicler, although it seems more likely that they originated with the compagnons, for they themselves use the phrase in other contexts. The expression aptly conveys what was to happen to the subject during initiation. *Se passer,* "becoming" or "passing over," indicates movement, process, and a crossing from one point to another. During this phase the novice shoemaker was tested by being forced to swear the oath that turned an ordinary journeyman into a compagnon. He swore "on his Faith, his part of Paradise, or, as it is found in one of their writings, on his God, chrism and baptism, not to reveal, to no matter whom, what he has done and seen done, nor the devoir of the Compagnons which he will learn shortly thereafter.[10]

Incorporation consisted of some kind of baptism after the oath. The actual ritual is not described, but on the table were salt and water, elements used in Catholic baptism; the document, moreover, emphasized the presence of a godfather (*parrain*) and an assistant godfather (*sous parrain*), chosen by the subject and charged with the primary responsibility for teaching the new compagnon his devoir. The new compagnon then paid his dues, which were put in a fund used to pay for the monthly assembly at the "usual cabaret." The new compagnon could now attend these meetings, which included festivities but were also used by the compagnons to "pass laws" on work-related issues and the masters' practices.

In this account the central issue of contention was the oath, deemed "irreverent and repugnant to religion," mainly because it placed loyalty to compagnonnage above obedience to any other institutions, religious or social; compagnons could not reveal their oaths even to a confessor.

9. BN, 4° FM 35348, "Compagnons du devoir, cordonniers" (n.p., n.d., [Paris, 21 September 1645]), p. 1.
10. Ibid.

The account enumerated instances when compagnons had lied to religious and secular officials to protect the secret of the devoir. Boldly instructing their interrogators to become compagnons if they wished to learn their secrets, the compagnons held to their oaths and practices "more firmly than to the Gospel" and insisted that their actions were good and holy.[11]

The oath taking occurred during the transition, as a test that forced the novice to choose between old and new lives and allegiances. This transitional, or "liminal," phase, which Van Gennep identified and Turner elaborated, is the most complex and pivotal of the three stages in this and other initiation accounts. In compagnonnage liminality often extended into the period of incorporation because new compagnons were instructed in the devoir not before initiation but only "shortly thereafter." Furthermore, the initiation introduced and mirrored the liminality of being "on the road." The verb "se passer" encodes the passage from town to town as well as the change occurring in the ritual subject.

The shoemakers incorporated members by means of baptism, by bonds of godparenthood, and by having the new member pay dues and participate in meetings. Inasmuch as the baptism itself is not described, we can only speculate on how salt and water, important elements of Catholic baptism, were used. In any event the incorporation was vitally important for drawing new members into an association that itself exemplified transition and liminality in the members' lives. Their liminal social status on the tramp allowed young compagnons a certain leverage and flexibility in dealings with the masters. But such power was dependent on the strength of their fidelity to the association. The new compagnon learned more about the devoir from his "godparents" and the other compagnons after the ceremony. The account of the saddlers' initiation reveals a greater emphasis on this phase of incorporation.

The Compagnon Saddlers, 1654

According to the manuscript account of this initiation, a compagnon saddler who doubted the legitimacy and property of the oath he had been obliged to take to be received as a compagnon, revealed these practices to his confessor.[12] The case shows a link to the rituals of the corps des métiers while also being a source for elements of the compagnons' ceremonies. We might call it a "transitional" account between

11. Ibid., p. 2.
12. BN, Coll. Dupuy, no. 775, 1654, fols. 272–74r and v, "Serment des selliers de la ville de Bordeaux."

those that marked the progression from apprentice to journeyman in trade corporations and those employed by mature sects of compagnonnage.

The saddlers' account states that the officials and senior members (*jurés* and *anciens bacheliers*) of their corporation performed the ceremony, which was obligatory for any apprentice who eventually wished to become a master. It was certainly an anomaly for masters to perform the initiation ceremony in a mid-seventeenth-century compagnonnage. At the same time, other statements in the account do not correspond with the official stage of journeyman prescribed by the saddlers' statutes.

The *setting* was a house with two rooms, hidden from general sight, with a connecting door between them. In one room a banquet was prepared; in the other the "important actions" took place. The time was specified as "late evening."

Separation was accomplished when one or more of those to be received as compagnons arrived at the house. They entered, bareheaded, and found two men holding the gospel (*saintes evangiles*). The door was shut; the shutters and the windows had already been tightly fastened.

Transition began when the two men cautiously opened the gospel as if afraid of being seen. They held *trois carrolus* in their hands, that is, "30 denarii, for which price our Lord was sold." Putting the money in the holy book, one of the men, the "master of the room," put the subject's right hand on the Scriptures. He then made the subject swear never to say or reveal anything of the actions he was about to see and hear to "priest, cleric, father, mother, wife, children, or any other creature whatever." Furthermore, the initiate vowed never to write an account of these actions which anyone other than a compagnon could see or understand.

Incorporation was accomplished when the compagnons entered the adjoining room, where they found an altar, completely and properly outfitted with altar cloth, candles, candlesticks, a font of holy water, chalice, cruet, salt, bread, and wine. The master of the room, now dressed like a priest, wearing an amice, alb, cincture, stole, maniple, and chasuble, performed a ceremony resembling the consecration of the bread and wine in the mass, after which the novice chose a godfather. Everyone kneeled while the master of the room baptized the novice and then gave the bread and wine to the assembly. The new compagnon had to swear his oath once again. Afterward, all those present began the feast and made great merriment for the whole day, presumably in the prepared banquet room, although this is not specified in the account

The most obvious feature of this initiation is its simulation of two key sacraments of the Catholic Church—baptism and communion. Both the participants in the ceremony and the objects they used were to be as authentic as possible. Far from mocking these sacraments, as the author of this document suggests, the compagnons were appropriating the power of the Catholic priesthood and ritual, even though they may have had some Protestant members among them. The participants acted as if they, like the church's agents, had the power to incorporate newcomers into their association by means of baptism and to bind them together through communion rites. Swearing an oath on the gospel invoked a spiritual and a socially recognized test of honesty, and it was reinforced by an additional oath on the "blood" money. The implication was clear: he who betrayed compagnonnage was as doomed as he who betrayed Jesus.

Like the compagnon shoemakers' oath, the saddlers' oath severed the initiate from people and institutions on which he would normally rely and to which he would owe loyalty. This breaking of prior ties left the initiate in a truly liminal state before incorporation into compagnonnage. The liminal phase began in the phase of separation, when the subject was placed in a realm of darkness and secrecy, bereft of real bearings and given no knowledge of what was to occur. The whole process up to swearing the oath was part of the initiate's testing, which culminated in his vowing not to reveal what he was *going* to see and hear.

This liminal phase ended with full integration into the association. Much preparation and care was devoted to the rites of incorporation. The communion was especially symbolic, for all present partook of the bread and wine. Finally, an elaborate and costly feast, a secular communion, reinforced and extended the process of incorporation. That this feast went on for "the whole day"—almost always a workday—reinforced the new compagnon's ties and loyalties to his fellows. The masters associated with this "compagnonnage" generated a certain amount of goodwill among their workers and reinforced vertical ties of solidarity.

STRUCTURAL SIMILARITIES AND OPPOSITIONS

A number of important and recurrent themes emerge in a comparison of the initiation accounts for all five condemned trades of compagnonnage. In all of them the setting was most likely the compagnons' usual inn. Tailors, hatters, and saddlers required two adjoining rooms—one for the ceremony and the other presumably for the postceremonial feast. The cutlers conducted the first part of the ceremony inside and then, some time later, finished the initiation in a deserted place in the countryside. All trades prepared whatever room they used with an altar, readying it as if for a mass.

Many objects were required in each ceremony, and most of them derived their meaning from Christian practice, though compagnons also drew on symbols from popular culture and the world of work. Many of the saddlers' and hatters' ceremonial articles were replicas of those used in the Catholic mass—or were the genuine articles. The saddlers apparently dressed one of their members as a priest in real vestments. Substitutions, however, were acceptable: even the saddlers used a cup or glass for the chalice; the hatters used a chair for the baptismal font. Many of these ceremonial objects drew on aspects of Christian iconography, sometimes simulating them, sometimes representing them metaphorically. Christ's Passion, for example, became the focus of the ritual for the hatters: accordingly, they adorned their altar with three knives representing the three nails of the cross, a piece of wood representing the lance that pierced Christ's side; two ropes tied to this "lance" became the whips that scourged Christ. The hatters also employed non-Christian symbolism: two candles, one said to be the sun, the other the moon, stood on the altar surrounded by all this Christian symbolism. The cutlers, too combined Christian and natural symbolism: in their account fire signified the angel of God, air signified time, the wind was God's wrath, and the four elements (earth, water, fire, and air) were the four evangelists. Thus, the cutlers joined the four elements of Greek science to the four evangelists of Christian theology, creating an eclectic mix of the pagan and Christian which identified and united important material and spiritual forces for these compagnons.

All members of the brotherhood appear to have attended these initiations; some of them played a role in it. The presence of "godparents" is particularly conspicuous in all the trades except cutlery. In the cutlers' account "all the compagnons conduct the one to be received through the ceremony."[13] Hatters had a godfather and godmother (played by a man); shoemakers had a godfather and assistant godfather; saddlers and tailors employed a single godfather for the new compagnon.[14] In all five trades the first part of the ritual is some kind of oath. Saddlers, tailors, cutlers, and hatters swore their oaths on the Bible, specifically the Gospels. The very presence and use of the Bible, even if only to swear an oath, and the mention of the four evangelists in the cutlers' ritual seem

13. Emile Levasseur, *Histoire des classes ouvrières en France, avant 1789*, 2 vols. (Paris, 1900), 1: 703–7, using the account in Pierre Varin, *Archives législatives de la ville de Reims: Collection de pièces inédites pouvant servir à l'histoire des institutions dans l'intérieur de la cité*, part 2, vol. 2: *Statuts, 1514–1699* (Paris, 1847), 249–55.

14. Some eighteenth and nineteenth century initiation accounts refer to *curés* as well as godparent(s), but I have not yet seen the term *curé* used in seventeenth-century archival accounts. It would be quite odd for prosecutors in the seventeenth century to ignore this additional blasphemy were it there, and yet report that the saddlers' "master of the room" performed these ceremonies as if he were a priest.

important indications of some degree of Reformation influence. The saddlers, who used the Bible most, had both Catholic and Huguenot members.

Only the shoemakers used no Bible in their ceremonies. They swore their oaths on the four *aliments*—bread, wine, salt, and water. These natural symbols had important religious meaning as well: salt and water are used in the sacrament of Baptism; bread and wine in the sacrament of Communion. Perhaps the shoemakers used the *aliments* to represent the four Gospels, just as the cutlers state they used the four elements to represent the evangelists. Possibly the compagnons were also joking, punning on *éléments/aliments*. The accounts do not give the content of the tailors' and cutlers' oaths, but the saddlers and hatters, like shoemakers, swore to guard the devoir's secret zealously or forfeit their right to eternal salvation. Saddlers swore never to reveal what they were about to see to "priest, cleric, father, mother, wife, children, or any other creature whatsoever."[15] Hatters promised by their part of paradise that they would never reveal, even in Confession, that which they were to do or the password they were to learn.

After the oath there followed procedures whose order and emphasis varied. All but tailors and hatters had a spiritual communion; all trades had a secular "communion"—a postceremonial feast. In each ceremony, the novice, after being tested (primarily with the oath), gained entry into the new rights and privileges of compagnonnage. The use of baptism as the primary model of transformation in these initiations is significant; only the tailors failed to perform it (and theirs is a truncated account). Baptism, as a sacrament in both Catholic and Protestant liturgy, was a widely recognized ritual of change and regeneration which incorporated new members into a community. Moreover, the terms used in the accounts—"se passer" and "compagnons passé"—forcefully convey a sense of crossing over into a new life.

Van Gennep's rites of passage are readily identified in these accounts. The need for separation is recognized, although not greatly emphasized. The initiation chamber becomes a special place—decorated, darkened, sometimes hidden or secret. Van Gennep notes that a novice may be symbolically separated by being stripped of some of his clothing: the cutlers' novices removed one shoe; novice saddlers were bareheaded; novice hatters' clothes were in "disarray" and their suspenders pulled down.[16] During transition, the novice faced various tests: the hatters ques-

---

15. BN, Coll. Dupuy, no. 775, fol. 274r and v, "Serment des selliers."
16. "Débraillé et desjartelé" (Varin, *Archives législatives*, part 2, 2:252). On the importance of hats in the old regime, see Michael Sonenscher, *The Hatters of Eighteenth-Century France* (Berkeley, 1987), chap. 2.

tioned their novices, as did the cutlers. The most obvious test is the oath, for it asks the novice if he is willing to forsake all else for compagnon-nage. The cutlers excepted, however, no obvious hazing of novices is found in any of the seventeenth-century accounts.

The cutlers' account indicates mild hazing and suggests that more may have escaped the written record. The novice cutler, after swearing on the Gospels, had to swallow a crumb of bread mixed with salt; when he had trouble doing so he was given two or three glasses of wine to wash it down, the drinking of which affirmed that he had become a compag-non. Sometime later, "in a deserted place," a coat was spread on the ground in a circle. The new compagnon was made to take off one shoe, and then, with his bare foot in the center of the coat, he made several circuits around it. More obviously sacrilegious than the other accounts was the compagnons' preparation of this same coat as a communion altar. Both acts might be intended to recall or parody the Passion. Al-though accounts generally presented these initiations as solemn affairs, such elements hint at the possibility of the levity, vulgarity, and parody commonly found in the rituals of other urban workers.[17] Clerics and magistrates found all these rituals extremely disturbing. And, acts per-formed in dead earnest were a potentially more empowering use of Christian ceremonies than mockery.

Finally, the compagnons were incorporated into the devoir by quasi-religious communions and secular feasts, by instruction, and—quite tan-gibly—by paying dues and receiving new privileges of mutual aid and labor defense. The model of the rites of passage is thus a useful construct in the analysis of compagnonnage, but it must be employed carefully and in the context of these particular rituals. The structure and detail of these seventeenth-century rituals of initiation varied: certain elements and features were emphasized or deemphasized; some values were pro-

17. See, for example, printers' confraternities and initiations in Natalie Zemon Davis's sem-inal articles "Strikes and Salvation at Lyon," *Archiv für Reformationsgeschichte* 56 (1965): 48–64, reprinted in Davis, *Society and Culture in Early Modern France* (Stanford, 1975); and "A Trade Union in Sixteenth-Century France," *Economic History Review* 19 (1966): 48–69. William Sewell compares one such initiation to those of the compagnonnages in *Work and Revolution in France: The Language of Labor from the Old Regime to 1848* (Cambridge, 1980), pp. 51–53. Robert Darnton interprets a rowdy performance staged by apprentice and journeyman printers as an organized "joke" against their living and working conditions in *Great Cat Massacre*, pp. 75–104. Early modern German journeymen typographers' initiations were more elaborate, rougher, and cruder than those of compagnonnage. See Christian Gottlob Tübel, *Praktisches Handbuch der Buchdruckerkunst für An-fänger* (Leipzig, 1791); and Johann Christoph Hildebrand, *Handbuch für Buchdrucker-Lehrlinge* (Ei-senbach, 1835). For a popular morality play related to these rites, the *Depositio Cornuti typographici*, see Jacob Redinger, *Neu aufgesetzes Format Büchlein* (Frankfurt-am-Main, 1679). The English ty-pographer, William Blades, edited two accounts of the *Depositio*, a translation of the 1648 version and "the original version" by Paul de Vise (1621). Blades says the 1648 version was performed in the seventeenth and eighteenth centuries. Cf. Darnton on these rites and plays, *Great Cat Massacre*, p. 271 n. 21.

moted over others. The origin of these differences remain unknown but apparently responded to the empirical needs, beliefs, or traditions of a particular trade or of the actual compagnons creating the ritual.

While all five cases shared many common structures, each emphasized one particular element: for the shoemakers, the baptism; for the saddlers, the communion; for the hatters, Christ's Passion and sacrifice; for the tailors, instruction in the devoir; and for the cutlers, hazing or testing. In Van Gennep's terms what was most critical for the tailors, shoemakers, and saddlers was incorporation, whereas for the hatters and cutlers the most importance was placed on separation and transition. For all, however, the ultimate goal was incorporation, which admitted and integrated novices, after a period of testing, into a new society, thereby increasing their status and privileges.[18] In this regard compagnonnage functioned something like many African or American Indian "age groups." Far closer in time and place to the compagnonnages were the official initiations of journeymen and masters into trade corporations and early modern youth groups such as the lords of misrule.[19] All such groups organized young men in a transitional phase of the life cycle and allowed members certain freedoms after subjecting them to some degree of hazing and humiliation.

The rituals varied in their degree of elaboration and complexity and in the closeness with which they simulated Christian sacraments. Saddlers seemed most intent on following the mass as closely as possible; the hatters' account was replete with detailed Catholic symbolism, particularly that of the Passion and Judas's betrayal. Nonetheless, saddlers consorted with Huguenots, and hatters used candles to represent the sun and moon. Examining privileged (or unprivileged) elements in these initiation rituals, helps uncover their particular meanings and functions. Initiation made compagnons into loyal friends, even "brothers." Yet, how could they be brought to trust comrades who were essentially strangers? Compagnonnage had to build on journeymen's common work experience and on Christian and popular beliefs and practices to create a new solidarity. Baptisms, communions, and passions integrated, tamed, and purified the unknown novice. This use and transformation of Christian iconography had important consequences not only for the internal, fraternal solidarity of each devoir and trade but also for their external, fratricidal enmities.

18. Van Gennep, *Rites of Passage*, pp. 21, 26, 96; and Turner, *Ritual Process*, pp. 166–68.

19. On such youth groups, see Philip Hoffman, *Church and Community in the Diocese of Lyon, 1500–1789* (New Haven, 1984), esp. pp. 62–65, 132–36, 145–46; and Darnton, *Great Cat Massacre*, pp. 79–89.

THE LATER SEVENTEENTH CENTURY

The 1655 decision of the faculty of theology of the Sorbonne formally and historically established the existence of associations called the compagnons du devoir and compagnonnage, but this and subsequent condemnations, even when enforced by secular powers, never destroyed these associations. In the later seventeenth century, particularly in Dijon, Lyon, and Nantes, authorities began an energetic surveillance of compagnons and their Mères, looking for illegal conduct and incriminating documents. By the end of that century, their inquiries yielded a wealth of evidence on the consolidation and spread of compagnonnage. Beyond a "transitional" case of 1663, at least ten disputes involving compagnonnage can be documented to the end of the seventeenth century, and these establish the existence of practices and terminology that persisted in some form into the nineteenth century. The joiners' compagnonnage in Dijon dominates the testimony, but incidents in other trades—hatting, turning, bonnet making, and wigmaking—and in other cities—Lyon, Montpellier, and Nantes—began to proliferate in the 1690s. I will present all the cases on the joiners and briefly examine incidents in other trades.

After 1655, the first archival mention of an association closely related to compagnonnage occurs in a 1663 case against joiners. Joiners had long been actively organized, even if not in the devoir. As early as 1626 they kept rolls, practiced the bienvenue, and maintained secrecy; evidence from 1638 and 1639 indicates the persistence of a similar association. In 1663 the activities of compagnon joiners were prosecuted by the town council (*Chambre*) of Dijon. Using the strictest definition of compagnonnage, this association is a transitional case that reveals further articulation, definition, and development. Key terms—*rôle, rôleur, mère, serment,* and *bienvenue*—appear in the evidence, but the workers are still not called (nor do they call themselves) compagnons "du devoir" or "non du devoir." They had, however, sworn an oath, "which has been prohibited and forbidden by this *Chambre*" and on which the prosecutor had requested clerical advice and opinion. Both procedures clearly recall the Sorbonne intervention against compagnonnage.[20] And like compagnons du devoir in Paris, Bordeaux, and Toulouse, these compagnons plagued their masters. A *délibération* of 31 July 1663 included prohibitions against "any scene (*scandal*) or insolence" against the masters. Lest

---

20. Henri Hauser, *Les Compagnonnages d'arts et métiers à Dijon aux XVIIe et XVIIIe siècles* (Paris, 1907), pp. 97–98 (AMD, B 302, fols. 69–70, 2 August 1663, "Extraict des registres des délibérations").

this pronouncement be too vague, the town council issued an ordinance on 7 August 1663 which forbade compagnons from "gathering in the streets, carrying cudgels or other arms, and forming any assembly prejudicial to the masters." The council invoked two earlier court arrêts, dated 7 October 1627 and 28 March 1639, which identified and banned a wide range of illegal activities performed by compagnons and backed by their innkeepers.[21]

Further suspicions led to the seizure of a valuable piece of evidence in 1670—the compagnon joiners' "roolles," a twenty-six-page manuscript, dated 25 August 1667, which contained sixteen articles regulating their organizational and fraternal practices. The last article was followed by a list of twenty-eight "premiers roolleurs," two names on each line. Unfortunately, no detail is given on how or how often the group chose its leaders or the duties and duration of each premier rôleur's tenure. Seventeen other names were listed below the first group: both groups of names indicated the compagnon's place of origin (for example, André le Parisien). These compagnons came from as far west as Nantes, Bordeaux, and Toulouse, as far south and east as the Languedoc and the Dauphiné, as far north and east as Paris and Champagne.[22]

Who took in and lodged these long-distance travelers? Margueritte Joly, widow of Edme Bonvalot, attested that "for the past *40 years* she received the compagnon joiners of this city in her inn, gave them to eat and drink and furnished them with a room."[23] The duration of her tenure cannot be overemphasized. Undoubtedly, she had a financial interest in this organization's continued existence, and the permanent base of operations she provided the compagnons was invaluable. At Joly's inn the compagnons had a well-established and quasi-legitimate foothold in Dijon, where they could conduct their alleged "crime of monopoly and illicit assembly." Although not called the mère in these documents, Joly served that function.

A town council deliberation that led to a ban dated 21 October 1672 strongly suggests that the association banned in 1663 was indeed a compagnonnage. The journeymen joiners were forbidden from "assembling in troops, taking on the quality of *capitaine, lieutenant,* of *mère,* or any other, or to demand any rights from any of the said compagnons on the

---

21. Ibid., pp. 98–99 (AMD, G 10 and B 302, fol. 67, 31 July 1663, "Extraict des registres des délibérations," and AMD, B 302, fol. 72, 7 August 1663, "Extraict des registres des délibérations").

22. Ibid., pp. 99–102 (AMD, G 10, Rôle, beginning with the words: "Jesus Maria, Roolles des compagnons menuisiers de la ville et faubourg de Dijon," seized in a raid on the compagnons' inn on 18 December 1670, AMD, B 309, fol. 149v°).

23. Ibid., p. 102 (AMD, B 309, fol. 139v, 18 December 1670, "Saisie du livre des compagnons menuisiers"); my emphasis.

pretext of the *droit du debvoir* [*sic*] or any other." In later documents terms such as captain (for the compagnons' leader), lieutenant (for his assistant), mère, and most important, devoir differentiate compagnonnage from other journeymen's brotherhoods. Yet, flexibility, mutation, and "disguise" remained operative associational principles: in 1674 compagnon joiners and turners were pursued for exercising both the *droit du devoir* and the claim to be a legitimate religious confraternity.[24]

The compagnons demanding these rights assembled every Sunday for mass at the Cordeliers' convent, indicating that clerics were not always averse to workers' associations, even if they had some sacrilegious elements. Perhaps they hoped to reform any wrongdoing while retaining some control over their parishioners. After mass and assembly, the compagnons went to the inn of the Three Pigeons, the scene of "continual debaucheries and expenditures. They called the inn's hostess their mère."[25] Their *société* (the prosecutor's term) came to light following a fatal brawl, provoked by a remark made by one Jean Dautirac, called Le Bordelais. After having eaten and drunk at the mère's, Bordelais and some other compagnons were sitting around talking when he was "reproached" for having criticized another compagnon, named "Le grand Flamand." Bordelais admitted he had said he was forced to leave a workshop because Flamand was "too quarrelsome." Unfortunately, Flamand overheard this remark and lived up to Bordelais's allegation. He quickly assembled three or four other compagnons and followed Bordelais to the city's outskirts, where they "threw themselves on him and one of them stabbed him in the chest with a tool called a gouge," a chisel with a rounded, troughlike blade. The compagnons' tools could double as deadly weapons, particularly in the hands of young men who prided themselves on their toughness and who were not particularly concerned about modern concepts of fair play. Bordelais tried to pull the gouge out, but succeeded only in pulling off the handle; he died soon afterward.[26]

Such violence was not limited, of course, to workers, organized or unorganized. Anger, verbal abuse, and violence were not as severely stigmatized or condemned in the old regime as they would later be. Quick anger and ready violence were hard to separate from (or were provoked by) a social gathering where eating, drinking, and joking had been in full swing. Nonetheless, Bordelais, having socialized with fellow compag-

24. Ibid., pp. 103–4 (AMD, G 10, 21 October 1672, "Extrait des registres des délibérations de la chambre"), pp. 105–9 (AMD, G 10, "Mémoire de M. l'Avocat Vallet," prepared for presentation to parlement in August 1674).
25. Ibid., p. 106. The mère's name is not given. Because the case concerns joiners *and* turners, this may possibly have been a new, rival compagnonnage.
26. Ibid., p. 107 (AMD, G 10 "Mémoire").

nons at the Mère, was chastised for having spoken against another compagnon. Would it have been possible to resolve this insult without
violence? If Bordelais had made amends by, say, buying a round of
drinks, would matters have calmed down? Once tempers flared, the situation rapidly worsened, and it seems Bordelais's only option would have
been to "beat it" as rapidly as possible. The important links between
sociability and violence in everyday life in the early modern era have
been well explored. Daniel Roche finds that "violent scenes occurred
every day from childhood on, in the home, in the family, in the street,
in the cabaret."[27] Similarly, for the members of compagnonnage disorder and violence were often closely tied to their normal activities of
business or pleasure.

By 1677 the compagnon joiners of Dijon had reestablished their illegal
compagnonnage, while continuing to assert their legitimacy as a confraternity. A police investigation of that year resulted in the seizure of a
considerable cache of papers and correspondence of an association the
compagnons called the "compagnie du devoir," as well as a detailed
interrogation of the compagnons' père, Bénigne Simonnet. These papers included a 1676 register of new arrivals (*livre des arrivées*), a 1676
rôle of compagnon joiners, and correspondence between Dijon, Montpellier, and possibly Nevers. This rich block of evidence adds at least
three new findings to our knowledge of compagnonnage: first, it tells us
something about the "ceremonies" compagnons used to "link themselves in a cabal and monopoly to make themselves masters over the
compagnons arriving in this city." This contemporary recognition of the
functions of these ceremonies is in itself significant. Second, we learn of
the activities of compagnon joiners du devoir in Montpellier. Finally, the
evidence reveals the existence of a rival sect of compagnons called the
"gaveaux."[28]

27. Daniel Roche, "Pleasures and Games: Jokes, Violence, Sexuality," in Jacques-Louis Ménétra, *Journal of My Life*, ed. Roche, trans. Arthur Goldhammer (New York, 1986), pp. 270, 271–
74. See also Natalie Zemon Davis, "The Reasons of Misrule," and "The Rites of Violence," in
her *Society and Culture*, pp. 97–123, 152–87; Daniel Roche, *Le Peuple de Paris* (Paris, 1981), pp.
242–77; Arlette Farge, *La Vie fragile: Violence, pouvoirs, et solidarités à Paris au XVIIIe siècle* (Paris,
1986), esp. pp. 17–30, 123–52, 291–324; and Darnton, *Great Cat Massacre*, pp. 75–104. Roche's
nuanced treatment of the experience and uses of violence is a valuable corrective to older works,
which make aggression an inherent trait of the early modern popular classes. See, for example,
Louis Guéneau, *L'Organisation du travail, industrie, et commerce à Nevers aux XVIIe et XVIIIe siècles
(1660–1790)* (Paris, 1919), p. 421. Guéneau makes a more valid point when he notes that play
and games could turn deadly serious for all classes during festive occasions such as baptisms and
marriages: "All this rough-housing could be dangerous. . . .belligerents were armed with sling-
shots, canes of compagnonnage, tools of the trade, even firearms, pistols and rifles" (p. 431).

28. Hauser, *Compagnonnages*, pp. 109–19 (AMD, G 10, B 316, fols. 74v, 112, 206, July 1677–
March 1678, including a "Procès-verbal contre les compaignons menuisiers contenant saisie des
registres de leur compaignie du debvoir"). Simonnent claimed the compagnons called themselves the "compagnie du devoir." Only police notes of these documents still exist.

The compagnons' père, Simonnet, not only furnished the police with a wealth of detail on the compagnons' entry rite but even showed them the "lofty room" on the third floor of his inn, the Cheval Blanc, where the compagnons had their meetings. They also allegedly met after mass at the Cordeliers convent on the first Sunday of every month and on the feast day of Notre Dame. The père showed the authorities the compagnons' locked trunk, which held their registers and papers and to which only the rôleur and the "cottry," the "company's" main officers, had a key.[29] Brought to the inn, the rôleur, François Dier, called François le Blois, was made to open the trunk; it contained a sack that enclosed, among other papers, several "*lettres missives* . . . written by the compagnons du devoir of each city where the devoir is established." Unfortunately, the prosecutor omitted to give a complete list of those cities and the papers no longer exist. The prosecutor was probably more concerned with an important letter from the compagnons du devoir of Montpellier, which gave "notice to all the other compagnons in the cities where there is the devoir that [the authorities] have broken [the devoir] in the said city of Montpellier, for said reason the said compagnons have banned [*interdit*] the said city for ten years." During the ban, no compagnons would be allowed to work in Montpellier. Whether or not the compagnons could realistically impose this boycott, they reveal a robust belief in their power to oppose police action against the devoir.

Part of that force, the authorities recognized, derived from the ceremonies, which joined compagnons "in a cabal and monopoly to make themselves masters over the compagnons arriving in this city." Under interrogation, Simonnet gave extensive detail of an entry ceremony the compagnons called the *levée du sac*, literally, "the lifting of the [knap] sack." This ceremony was an inquiry into the new arrival's credentials by the "company's" key members. The rôleur and the cottry had to assemble in their meeting room with the new compagnon; usually three or four compagnons and sometimes more were also present. Next the compagnons called for a washbasin and a pitcher of water; the new arrival washed the hands of the other compagnons and paid for a pint of wine, a loaf of bread, and a piece of meat. The compagnons then drank and ate together. Only after the levée du sac was the new compagnon placed in a workshop.[30]

This ceremony has important analogies with the *lavez-pied* practiced by sixteenth-century compagnons; it also recalls the *lavabo*, the washing of

29. Hauser suggests *cottry* is a corruption of *cottiseur* (assessor), meaning treasurer. But the term could also derive from *coterie* (circle, clique). *Coterie*, meaning brother or comrade, was common in compagnonnage from the eighteenth century.

30. Hauser, *Compagnonnages*, pp. 109–19.

the priest's hands before the Eucharist in the Catholic mass. Just as the priest purifies himself before the blessing and taking of the body of Christ, the compagnons seem to be sanctifying themselves before eating together. Because the new compagnon must wash the hands of the others, and pay for the food and drink, however, the levée du sac resonates with the earlier practice of the washing of the feet. The new compagnon not only paid for the expenses of the levée but also contributed another thirty sous to help defray the costs of further celebration. Simonnet reported it was common after the levée for twenty to thirty compagnons to gather at the inn and spend the whole day there until nine or ten o'clock. This large group took four meals together: lunch, a "snack" (*goûter*), dinner, and late supper. The other compagnons contributed to costs over the thirty sous. During these meals, the new arrival was given "the choicest morsels." The ceremony became a lively demonstration of shared substance and mutuality.

Although compagnons du devoir like those described by Simonnet flourished in the late seventeenth century, masters and authorities were not their only opponents. In a council deliberation of 5 November 1677, the prosecutor mentioned "a society or company, which [the joiners] call among themselves the Devoir, different and divided from another company which they call the Gaveaux."[31] Significantly, *gavots* (the usual spelling) is the name given or imposed by the compagnons du devoir on their rivals. The compagnons du devoir, by contrast, "named themselves." I have found no earlier use of *gavots* to name a rival compagnonnage and no seventeenth-century explication of the term. In the nineteenth century, Perdiguier gave two derivations: first, mountain people, with the negative connotation of "hillbillies"; second, Huguenots who fled religious persecution in the Pyrenees gorges, perhaps deriving from *gave,* a torrential gorge in those mountains. The latter explanation would suggest that compagnons du devoir equated the gavots with heretics and schismatics who had broken from the true faith, in this case, the devoir. Fernand Braudel notes that social prejudices against mountain people are long standing and persistent in European culture.[32] In any case, Perdiguier's etymology is not confirmed elsewhere.

That the compagnons du devoir had the upper hand over the gavots in the 1670s is evident from the prosecutor's opinion that their rivalry "gives rise daily not only to criminal proceedings . . . but also to such a monopoly that these compagnons [du devoir], by their mutual understanding, are tolerably bold and seditious." For their audacity, the town

31. Ibid., p. 114 (AMD, G 10 and B 316, fol. 112, 5 November 1677, "Délibération").
32. See Fernand Braudel, *The Mediterranean and the Mediterranean World in the Age of Philip II,* 2 vols. (New York, 1966), 1:46, and see 1:35–38, 44–47.

council in its deliberation of 5 November 1677 banned the assemblies of both sects. Some masters, however, opposed the ban: in March 1678 twenty masters, most of them "les grands," complained that since the ordinance had gone into effect, the number of compagnons in Dijon had dropped from forty to about ten or twelve. The petitioners claimed the compagnons had left town because they "saw themselves as prohibited from frequenting or visiting one another in this city . . . and felt themselves liable to be taken prisoner should they be found together on feast days." Those masters making the original complaints, said "les grands," were few and had very little work; some of them weren't even in business. Again, as in earlier cases, larger, more viable producers found they could work with the compagnons' organizations and opted against municipal and corporation regulation of hiring. The town council was not swayed, and the edict of 5 November 1677 remained in effect, with one slight concession: up to six compagnons were allowed to associate "honestly" as long as they did not form any "society, assembly, or monopoly."[33]

No record of troubles between master and compagnon joiners appears between 1678 and 1693—perhaps reflecting successful enforcement of the city's edicts. Yet, compagnonnage outlived all bans against it, disappearing for a while, but after the mid-seventeenth century, always reappearing. Prohibitions in a specific place might temporarily curtail it locally, but organizational practice and principles were kept alive in other towns, to be brought back again when restrictions eased. Disbanded compagnons may have channeled their energies into popular festivities or religious confraternities, although the latter were often as suspect as compagnonnage.

The compagnon joiners du devoir attempted this confraternal strategy when eight of their number presented a petition to the mayor and aldermen of Dijon in 1693, requesting the right to perform their traditional religious practices. "This year," they said, "several master joiners wish to oppose this celebration, although they have no reasons or grounds." The compagnons "had always celebrated" the feast of Saint Anne, offered a blessed bread, and had a mass said at the Cordeliers' the first Sunday of each month. The official reply depicts raucous celebrations in the past and agrees to permit the petitioners only to celebrate mass on their feast day with "devotion and piety." There was to be none of the usual assembling with violins, oboes, and other instruments, no going to a cabaret, no eating and drinking together, no assembling, and

33. Hauser, *Compagnonnages*, pp. 114, 116, 118 (AMD, G 10 and B 316, fol. 112, 206, 5 November 1677, "Délibération," ca. 29 March 1678, "Supplique de plusieurs maîtres," and 29 March 1678, "Délibération").

no carrying arms by "day and night." Revealingly, the deliberation concluded by prohibiting compagnons "from exacting anything from the
compagnons of the said trade unless by their consent." Clearly, officials
were aware of the tactics used to induct members and to subsidize compagnonnage. Their detailed decision betrays their skepticism of the compagnons' religious motivations and addresses civic concerns about the
revival of the compagnons' association.[34] These concerns were not
groundless, as subsequent events demonstrated.

If the devoir was temporarily suppressed in Dijon, it found a haven in
Lyon. No public complaints about "compagnons du devoir" or "gavots"
survive until 1699, although closely related organizations existed.[35] A
"Livre des Compaignons Menuisiers," dated "ce 6 Septembre 1696"
was found in the papers of compagnon joiners du devoir seized in a
1707 raid on their Mère, indicating that compagnonnage could, at least
for a time, coexist with the official world of production.[36] Absence of
opposition could merely indicate effective clandestinity, but this seems
unlikely: authorities tended to spot the outward signs of compagnonnage
with relative ease. The typical practices of meeting and socializing at the
Mère, job placement, exacting fines and dues could not occur without
some knowledge and tacit consent of masters and townspeople.

Whatever the degree of knowledge and toleration of the joiners' compagnonnage in 1696, however, three years later its existence became
unacceptable. Five *jurés* of the community of joiners and eighty-three
masters (its "largest and soundest part") held a deliberation on their
compagnons' illegal activities on 4 January 1699. On 29 January 1699
the master joiners requested the provost of the merchants and alderman
to investigate and pronounce upon the "assemblies and debaucheries
commonly practiced by the compagnons of the said profession who improperly demand and by monopoly exert rights over the poor compagnons who arrive in this city on the pretext of what they call among
themselves the devoir and other terms." These activities paralleled those
described in Dijon. The Lyonnais compagnons, for example, controlled

34. Ibid., p. 122 (AMD, G 10, 21 July 1693, "Supplique des compagnons menuisiers de-
mandant à célébrer la sainte Anne" and official reply in the margin, same date). The petitioners
had signed only with their nicknames, e.g., "Languedoc." The geographical origins revealed in
the petition again show a wide distribution—from Brittany and Picardy to Languedoc and Provence.

35. See Cynthia M. Truant, "Independent and Insolent: Journeymen and their 'Rites' in the
Old Regime Work Place," in *Work in France: Representations, Meaning, Organization, and Practice*,
ed. Steven Laurence Kaplan and Cynthia J. Koepp (Ithaca, 1986), pp. 131–75.

36. AML, HH 109, 12 September 1707, "rapport de Charles Goujaust, notaire royal et gref-
fier." Goujaust reported this book (no longer in the archives) had a "large number of leaves."
The document states that the "joiners' devoir" had existed prior to 1696 and was being "reestablished."

the hiring and placement of new arrivals, made them contribute money to their association, and were received by religious communities as a confraternity. Lyonnais masters had made quite a study of compagnonnage and the responses to it elsewhere: their petition cited Dijon edicts of 1693 and 1698 against these and related associations. Lyon's *procureur général* wholeheartedly supported the masters, insisting it was crucial to "arrest the progress of the compagnon joiners' efforts to *ræ*establish [my emphasis] the devoir."[37] The *consulat* of Lyon responded with an ordinance banning compagnons' assemblies, violence, and "exactions" on other workers.

The 1698 Dijon edicts were issued, according to Hauser, because the "devoir, once again, was all powerful." But the masters themselves were somewhat divided over whether or not to ban that devoir and its control of placement. In an assembly of master joiners, forty-four of the fifty-four voting on these issues opposed the devoir and its practices. But, the ten dissenting masters, who operated larger shops and had more business than the rest, expressed the opinion that "the devoir of the compagnons should continue."[38] Convinced that the compagnons' management of the labor pool assured them an adequate and steady supply of workers, these larger masters were willing and able to grant the compagnons more favorable working conditions than other masters. By edicts of 29 November and 3 December 1698, however, the majority opinion was upheld: the associations of the compagnons were prohibited; two official *embaucheurs* (recruiters) were established. The ten dissenting masters were criticized for "bad intentions," for "wanting to favor the debaucheries of their compagnons and secretly to ruin the others [masters]." The minority kept up their opposition, nevertheless, and finally won a partial victory. A parlementary decision of 20 March 1699, while upholding the 1698 edicts, granted two important concessions: masters could hire as many workers as they saw fit, and compagnons could serve and live with whichever masters they chose.[39] The debates over compagnonnage and control of placement resumed very early in the following century.

The practices of compagnon joiners organized in the devoir dominate

37. Ibid., 29 January 1699, "Maître menuisiers aux prévôts des marchands et echevins," and "Avis du procureur général."

38. Hauser, *Compagnonnages*, pp. 121, 123 (AMD G 10, 27 November 1698, "Assemblée des maîtres menuisiers pour faire casser le debvoir des compagnons du mestier et establir un embochuer"). This liasse includes a list of the fifty-seven master joiners and the results of the vote (five masters were absent; two opposed the devoir by proxy).

39. Ibid., pp. 124–26, 127 (AMD, G 10 and B 338, fol. 167, 29 November 1698, "Supplique de la majorité des maîtres" and "Homologation de la précédente requête," and 20 March 1699, *Extrait des registres de parlement*, "Opposition de la minorité des maîtres").

the late seventeenth-century archival documentation, but three other trades were also involved in such associations at this time: hatters and bonnet makers in Dijon, and wigmakers in Nantes. In 1664, a year after the city's investigation of the joiners' association, two "foreign" (not Dijon natives) compagnon hatters lodged a complaint against seven others, leading to the disclosure of the devoir's existence in this trade. This case is especially important because it confirms the continued existence of compagnonnage in hatting after the 1655 condemnation by the Sorbonne. The two accusers, a Forézien and an Auvergnat, explained they had dined with the other compagnons at the Petit Suisse, the compagnons' usual inn, and were then forced to pay all expenses, a sum of eight livres. When the two, Antoine Staron and Denis Mouvet, said they couldn't pay, the others first made them turn over their belongings (*sacs*) and swords and then forced them to leave town. Fearing trouble after the complaint was brought, two of the compagnons' leaders had left town; police eventually found and arrested four others. Their interrogations reveal a well-established network of written correspondence between compagnons in the devoir on the tour de France.

The first worker interrogated by the alderman in charge was Germain Moreau, called Printemps bourguignon, who explained the "custom they observed among themselves" that, if arriving compagnons "conducted themselves badly toward the other compagnons and toward their master," they were required to pay for their portion of the common meal "and sometimes to pay the whole bill." Printemps here implies that the compagnons in Dijon had had advance knowledge of the newcomers' conduct. That implication is borne out in the interrogation of Claude Louveau, called Nivernais, who stated: "The comrades [*camarades*] sent us complaints, by letters, about several of their compagnons. Not knowing with certainty whether it was they [Staron and Mouvet], [we] only constrained them to pay their own part of the expenditures."[40] Unfortunately, nothing further is said about these letters; nevertheless, this evidence corroborates earlier testimony from masters and magistrates about such interurban correspondence. That compagnons relied on written communication to conduct their business at this early date is significant both for an understanding of the tactics of compagnonnage and as a striking example of how ordinary people made use of their literacy in secular pursuits.

The interrogation of Sebastien Hurtault, from Champagne, revealed more about the compagnons' practices, including something about the

40. Ibid., p. 94 (AMD, G 18, 19 August 1664, "Interrogatoire des compagnons chapeliers," summary and excerpts).

initiation oath. Hurtault explained that he would not have been constrained to pay for his "welcome" because "he had been on good terms
with the compagnons of his trade in the places where they worked and
where they passed." Next he revealed "it was true that when they passed
[became] compagnons they took an oath," which included the payment
of the welcome by the new arrivals. The examiner then asked Hurtault,
"What constitutes the devoir of the compagnon hatters"? Hurtault
would "speak nothing of all that passed between them by oath; he would
not even inform his father of it."[41] This statement confirms the other
initiation accounts. The alderman remonstrated with Hurtault, warned
him that he owed more to the authorities than to anyone else, and
obliged him to tell them everything about the oath. Given the importance of the matter, the alderman threatened to use any means to force
him to talk, but the compagnon simply replied that "even if [threat-
ened] by death, he would not tell, unless to a compagnon of their
trade." The magistrates discovered nothing more from him or the others. Although not all compagnons held out as staunchly as Hurtault, such
resistance was not uncommon and was at once frustrating and troubling
to local authorities. In the event, the compagnons were fined five livres
each: unable to pay, they were imprisoned. No new ban on the compagnons' activities was issued but the edicts of 1627 and 1663 remained in
force. The earlier edict forbade "foreign compagnon joiners and others
from forming any illegal assembly and monopoly or exacting any sum
of money from one another on the pretext of bienvenue or for any other
reason." The second edict restated these key provisions and prohibited
"compagnons from gathering in the streets, carrying cudgels or other
arms, and forming any assembly prejudicial to the masters."[42]

Bonnet making provides the last seventeenth-century Dijonnias example of compagnonnage. Like the joiners and hatters, compagnon bonnet makers practiced "a certain formality that they call devoir"—placing
arriving compagnons, performing levées du sac, celebrating at cabarets,
and blacklisting masters who displeased them. In a petition of 29 April
1678 master bonnet makers claimed such conduct was "entirely ruining
the trade" and making masters "dependent on the compagnons." This
striking image of reversal, of a topsy-turvy, disordered world is frequently
invoked in protests against the compagnonnages. The masters found the
situation particularly grave because of the critical shortage of workers
due to Louis XIV's war with Holland. The city council issued an edict
the very same day prohibiting the "society" and "assemblies" of com-

---

41. Ibid., p. 95.
42. Ibid., pp. 93–95, 98–99 (AMD, B 302, fol. 72, 7 August 1663, "Extrait des registres des
délibérations").

pagon bonnet makers, which "establish regulations that they call the devoir." Taking no chances, moreover, the council extended the ban to compagnons in all trades.[43]

My archival reconstruction of seventeenth-century incidents of compagnonnage ends with a case involving garçon (here meaning compagnon) wigmakers in Nantes in 1695. The master wigmakers submitted a lengthy accusation chronicling the illegal activities of the garçons and their *syndic*, Douzé, caught distributing seditious handbills to their fellow garçon wigmakers, directing them to assemble the following day at two in the afternoon at the inn of the Bons Enfants to discuss a number of matters concerning their "community." A search of Douzé's effects uncovered other handbills convoking meetings and conduites held earlier in the month. The masters' accusation led to a general prohibition, issued by officials of the corps des métiers, decreeing that the garçons must not form "any convocation, assembly, gathering or any devoir of compagnonnage . . . on pain of . . . a fine of 200 livres."[44]

The ban emphasized that the corps des métiers had always forbidden garçons of all trades from forming such organizations. Significantly, it indicated that officals were familiar with prior incidents of the devoir and other associations, and it referred specifically to both "devoir" and "compagnonnage." The ban identified Douzé and prohibited him from *compagnoner*, bringing compagnons together or, loosely, "organizing." All compagnons were again warned that assembling on any pretext whatsoever was strictly forbidden. Nonetheless, Nantes became a focus for the activities of the compagnonnages in the eighteenth century.

CONTINUITY AND DIFFERENTIATION

Seventeenth-century evidence helps distinguish the lines of continuity and differentiation among compagnonnage, the corps des métiers, and the confraternities. The corps des métiers and confraternities also had codes for conduct, oaths, and Catholic religious practices. Compagnons, like members of corporations and confraternities, tried, insofar as possible, to keep written codes of regulations and account books, rôles and règlements. But among compagnons, probably because their sects were

43. Ibid., pp. 119–20 (AMD, G 33, 29 April 1678, "Délibération contre les compagnons bonnetiers").

44. AMN, HH 102, *Barbiers*, 31 August 1695, "Accusation du nommé Douzé." None of these handbills has survived. There was a rival sect of compagnons called the "bons enfants" (also the name of the wigmakers' inn); the edict, however, explicitly refers to the garçons' devoir.

illegal and persecuted, these documents were treated as sacred and secret books and not only or primarily as bureaucratic tools.

The internal organization of compagnonnage represented an attempt
to balance the conflicting principles inherent in the Christian and familial models. Despite the fact that life in the corporations and the master's family in the sixteenth and seventeenth centuries tended to
subordinate and isolate the journeyman, compagnons did not reject
these models. Instead, they recast them into a brotherhood structured
around principles of solidarity, sentiment, and mutual aid. Compagnonnage created solidarity for its members within a framework of authority
and discipline, with premiers, capitaines, lieutenants, rôleurs, statutes,
fines. The code of the devoir informed the organization and was put
into practice in the workshop and particularly, at the Mère.

Significantly, compagnons called their lodging the Mère and not the
Père and often chose a woman to play the dominant role in their "family." Although pères could be mentors and friends, privileging the maternal over the paternal may have been a strategy to weaken the
culturally accepted authority of fathers. Mothers may have appeared less
threatening and less powerful than fathers for young men wishing to
assert their manhood. At the Mère, compagnons could be the male authorities of the household, brothers who were equal in many ways even
if differentiated by seniority. In reality, problems arose in the fictive
mother-son relationship, and when compagnons ran up large debts at
the Mère, mothers seem to have been only slightly more lenient than
fathers. Both mères and pères could loyally defend and refuse to inform
on their compagnons, and both could also reveal their secrets. Nonetheless, in the life of the compagnonnages, the mother-innkeeper's authority could serve as a structural opposition to that of the father-master.
At the very least the choice of a Mère reveals how compagnons reworked
the patriarchal and parental authority that still loomed large in the lives
of dependent individuals.

The custom of the Mère, so central to compagnonnage, helped distinguish these associations of itinerant compagnons from other workers'
brotherhoods. Compagnons also differentiated themselves by freely borrowing terms from other institutions and applying them to new purposes.
For example, compagnons would call a boycott of masters or shops a
mise en interdit (ban) or *damnation* (literally, damnation), borrowing directly from the legal language of the Catholic Church, appropriating the
power of these terms to enforce their jurisdiction over their members'
social and economic lives. Nevertheless, material interest was generally
expressed in complex, ritualized exchanges. Compagnons demanded

honorable and civil behavior—as they defined it—of all those who
crossed their paths.

Some terms and practices—dévorant, gavot—were specific to compagnonnage in the seventeenth century. Others, such as the use of nicknames, were found among other groups but gained a special importance
in the compagnonnages, in part because of their illegal status. Soldiers
and unorganized journeymen, for example, were certainly known by
nicknames in the old regime and, like compagnons, often based them
on their regions of origin. But compagnons formalized this practice in
their ritual baptism and even made renaming into something of an art.
Compound names such as Printemps bourguignon (the springtime of
Burgundy), came to include some personal attribute of the new compagnon in addition to his region of origin. The process has some parallels to the renaming of monks and nuns in their taking of final vows.
Looking to his or her past life for some special ability, a novice often
chose the name of a saint noted in that field. For example, a woman
skilled in music might choose the name Cecilia, patron saint of musi-
cians, presumably to benefit from the saint's aid and inspiration. Taking
this name conferred grace, sanctifying and enhancing the novice's talent.
Although they did not take the names of saints, compagnons nonetheless
were "reborn" and renamed in their initiation ceremonies, and sometimes they took on the attributes of noted compagnons or of their worthy
baptismal sponsors. After initiation, compagnons avoided using their
birth names on the tour de France. They might commonly use or give
only the regional part of their nicknames, but postinitiation rituals and
documents, particularly in the eighteenth and nineteenth centuries, give
the complete *nom compagnonnique.* Thus, the compagnons' use of nicknames was both more complex and more ritualized than it was for soldiers or other sorts of workers and often posed problems for the
regulation and control of the itinerant work force.

All the institutions from which seventeenth-century compagnons borrowed organizational concepts and practices were fundamentally Christian and corporate. The importance of these influences cannot be
overestimated, particularly with regard to initiation rituals. Whereas the
church condemned them as blasphemous mimicry of Catholic rites, compagnons understood their rituals differently. Their mimicry of Baptism,
Communion, and other rites was meant not to ridicule these sacraments
but to appropriate their sacred and legitimate power. In the seventeenth
century, journeymen's confraternities were limited or strictly monitored,
and membership was usually confined to sedentary workers. And as trade
corporations increasingly became the domain of masters after the sixteenth century, journeymen were excluded from the ceremonial and

festive life of the corporation. The compagnonnages thus replaced the access to legitimate corporate and ceremonial life compagnons may once have had in confraternities or corps des métiers.

Borrowing the ritual practices and common vocabulary of legal, easily recognizable institutions gave the associations of compagnonnage a convincing aura of legitimacy, meaning, and power and conveyed a sense of familiarity and security to compagnons who were far from home and had few, if any, prior social ties with those they met on the tramp. Nonetheless, compagnons clearly transmuted Catholic ritual, adding other sorts of symbolism—pagan, natural, and popular—to it. The religious motivation for the condemnation of compagnonnage thus remained strong in a century concerned with rooting out expressions of popular religiosity.[45] Church authorities also recognized the important economic and social reasons for eliminating compagnonnage. The earliest complaints brought to the Sorbonne had had a dual thrust: compagnons committed sacrilege and deformed sacred rituals but also disrupted the normal economic order and social hierarchy. Compagnons denied that masters had the right to treat them like servants, thus challenging the subservient role of journeymen in trade corporations.

The issue of resistance in the workplace, however, is complex. It would be anachronistic, for example, to suggest that compagnons regarded their labor as a market commodity. Their opposition to placement regulations or to the erosion of wages, working conditions, and certain privileges did not stem from a clear conception of the worth of their labor in a free market. Compagnons saw their labor in terms of its just price in the context of the moral *and* legal community of the corporation.[46] They were not naive about the deficiencies of this "moral community," and they used what legal rights they had to defend their economic needs and their desire to be treated as valued producers. Thus, thinking about the compagnons' resistance primarily in terms of walkouts and boycotts or imagining that they regarded their labor as a commodity makes little sense before the nineteenth century and obscures issues that might help to explain how workers viewed their labor before the "rise of market culture."[47]

45. See Hoffman, *Church and Community*, chaps. 1, 3, 4; James R. Farr, *Hands of Honor: Artisans and Their World in Dijon, 1550–1650* (Ithaca, 1988), chap. 6; Orest Ranum, *Paris in the Age of Absolutism* (Bloomington, 1979), chaps. 7, 11; and John Bossy "Blood and Baptism: Kinship, Community, and Christianity in Western Europe from the Fourteenth to the Seventeenth Centuries," in *Sanctity and Secularity: The Church and the World*, ed. Derek Baker (Oxford, 1973), pp. 129–43.

46. Cf. Michael Sonenscher, *Work and Wages: Natural Law, Politics, and the Eighteenth-Century French Trades* (Cambridge, 1989), chaps. 6 and 8.

47. See especially the work of William Reddy, *The Rise of Market Culture: The Textile Trade and French Society, 1750–1900* (Cambridge, 1984).

Furthermore, compagnonnage was neither strictly egalitarian nor able to contemplate a solidarity reaching beyond individual devoirs, which divided trades into rival unities. A dynamic tension between equality and hierarchy, brotherhood and exclusion, spontaneity and structure encoded in the compagnons' ritual practices was integral to these associations from their origins. Only much later would this tension become a serious impediment to their success and expansion. As compagnonnage entered the eighteenth century its brotherhoods practiced a solidarity that gave its plots and assemblies potentially serious economic and social consequences.

CHAPTER 4

Independent and Organized
in the Old Regime

> Compagnons . . . cannot demand any sum of other [work-
> ers] be it on pretext of *Devoir, Bienvenue, Levée de sac,* chang-
> ing shops . . . or employ any constraint or bad treatment
> against compagnons to oblige them to eat and drink with
> them in taverns and inns.
>
> —Parlement of Bordeaux, 22 June 1709

The compagnonnages gained visibility in the course of the eighteenth century, as they took on a greater role in organizing labor practices and the sociability of their members, easing the transition between
the road and the workshop for itinerant compagnons. Don Quixote
might have said, "The road is always better than the inn," but compagnons knew better. At the Mère they attempted to make daily life and
work at least as good—and as exciting—as life on the road. But what
compagnons recognized as good working conditions, brotherhood, mutual aid, and amusement, masters and officials saw as sedition, conflict,
disorder, and debauchery.[1] Injunctions issued against compagnonnage
in the seventeenth century were renewed in the following century, vastly
extended in number and jurisdiction.

Beginning in the first quarter of the eighteenth century, secular rather
than clerical authorities opened the struggle against compagnonnage.
Although not uninterested in ritual practices, secular authorities viewed
them with little alarm; they focused their police powers on the disruptive
economic role of these brotherhoods. By midcentury, compagnonnage,
divided into two major sects, was fully established and expanding, despite
attempts to contain and repress it. The presence of organized compag-

---

1. See Cynthia M. Truant, "Independent and Insolent: Journeymen and their 'Rites' in the
Old Regime Work Place," in *Work in France: Representations, Meaning, Organization, and Practice,*
ed. Steven Laurence Kaplan and Cynthia J. Koepp (Ithaca, 1986), pp. 131–75.

nons in workshops and on the streets, whether in conflict or at relative peace with their masters and each other, had become a virtually ineradicable part of the old regime economy.

An Overview

It is not possible to estimate with any accuracy the number of men involved in compagnonnage in the eighteenth—or any other—century. In this chapter, nonetheless, I want to provide a more empirical reconstruction of the geography, trades, membership, and labor actions of compagnonnage as far as these can be determined from police and judicial records as well as the compagnons' own written testimony.[2] My research has included a close examination of archival holdings in Paris, Dijon, Mâcon, Lyon, Marseille, Toulouse, Bordeaux, Nantes, Tours, and Troyes.[3] In all these cities except Paris, compagnonnage had a marked eighteenth-century presence. Even in Paris, where confraternities dominated associational life, compagnonnages began to play a more active role in the decade before the Revolution.

Beginning with normative evidence—primarily local, regional, and royal legal prohibitions—I have found at least 140 cases of compagnon-

2. For an exemplary demonstration of how this often anecdotal and disparate empirical evidence has been used to analyze larger economic issues, see Michael Sonenscher, *Work and Wages: Natural Law, Politics, and the Eighteenth-Century French Trades* (Cambridge, 1989). His work provides the context for my more limited focus on the material world of compagnonnage and my more extensive focus on its culture and organization.

3. In addition to research in the Archives nationales, particularly valuable for nineteenth-century compagnonnage, I have examined municipal archive collections in all these cities. For the old regime, I have systematically worked through the papers of almost all the trade corporations (series HH), police records (series FF), and specific dossiers on compagnonnage in Dijon, Mâcon, Lyon, Marseille, Bordeaux, and Nantes. For the post-1789 era, I have examined municipal archive holdings in Dijon, Lyon, Marseille, Toulouse, and Bordeaux. I have found other cases in the departmental archives of the Bourgogne, Sâone-et-Loire, Rhône, Bouches-du-Rhône, Haute-Garonne, Gironde, and Loire-Atlantique (series B, Sénéchausée/Criminel). I have also drawn on the primary sources found in the following works: Georges Bourgin and Hubert Bourgin, eds., *Les Patrons, les ouvriers, et l'état: Le Régime de l'industrie en France de 1814 à 1830*, 3 vols. (Paris, 1912–41); Jean Cavignac, "Le Compagnonnage dans les luttes ouvrières au XVIIIe siècle: L'Exemple de Bordeaux," *Bibliothèque de l'École des chartes* 126, no. 2, 1969 (1968): 377–411; Emile Coornaert, *Les Compagnonnages en France du Moyen Age à nos jours* (Paris, 1966); Maurice Garden, *Lyon et le lyonnais au XVIIIe siècle* (Paris, 1970); Henri Hauser, *Les Compagnonnages d'arts et métiers à Dijon aux XVIIe et XVIIIe siècles* (Paris, 1907); Emile Isnard, *Documents inédits sur l'histoire du compagnonnage à Marseille au XVIIIe siècle*, vol. 4 of *Mémoires pour servir à l'histoire du commerce et de l'industrie*, ed. Julien Hayem, 4th ser., 5 vols. (Paris, 1911–17); Gabriel Jeanton, *Compagnons du devoir et compagnons de liberté à Mâcon au XVIIIe siècle* (Mâcon, 1928); Germain Martin, *Les Associations ouvrières au XVIIIe siècle (1700–1792)* (Geneva, 1974 [Paris, 1900]); Gaston Martin, *Capital et travail à Nantes au cours du XVIIIe siècle* (Nantes, 1932); Etienne Martin Saint-Léon, *Le Compagnonnage: Son histoire, ses coutumes, ses règlements, ses rites* (Paris, 1901).

nage in the period from 1700 to 1791. This evidence consists of bans against existing associations and reports of illegal association or actual master-worker conflict. The estimate is conservative because I have, with very few exceptions, counted only evidence specifically and precisely identifying the workers involved as compagnons "du devoir" or "gavots," or their associations as "du devoir," "gavots," or "compagnonnage." To err on the side of caution, I have excluded cases with general references to assemblies, cabals, or other groups of journeymen, unless compagnonnage was strongly implied because of related incidents.

Almost two-thirds of the identified cases date from the period 1755–1789 (about 90 of 140 cases). From about midcentury, police interrogations, depositions, minutes of the corps des métiers, trials, and compagnons' own papers supplement the legislative evidence. The decades after 1755 witnessed some expansion in artisanal production, particularly the building trades, as many cities began major construction projects. The notable increase in the visibility and activity of compagnonnages is also explained by their wider geographic implantation. Before about midcentury, compagnonnage can be verified in about ten major cities and towns; among the most important were Dijon, Lyon, Marseille, Montpellier, Bordeaux, the cities and towns in the Loire region (Orléans, Angers, and Tours), and Nantes.

After midcentury at least ten other cities and towns reported major problems with compagnonnages, notably Mâcon, Chalon-sur-Saône, Moulins, Nîmes, Toulouse, La Rochelle, Troyes, Chartres, and Paris. The compagnon glazier Jacques-Louis Ménétra worked in a wider circuit of at least thirty places on his two tours de France and visited a great many more (see Maps 2 and 3).[4] In all but two or three places, he found compagnons du devoir or gavots or both in his or other trades. At least nineteen had a Mère—from small towns such as Bourg-en-Bresse to large cities such as Lyon. Compagnons and compagnonnages thus had a far different existence from that of the mid-seventeenth century in Paris, Bordeaux, and Toulouse. Eighteenth-century compagnonnages were strongest in the provinces, particularly south of a line from Saint-Malo to Geneva, similar to the one scholars use to divide southern and western France from the generally more prosperous and more literate north and

4. Jacques-Louis Ménétra, *Journal de ma vie,* ed. Daniel Roche (Paris, 1982), pp. 31–84, 92–110. Ménétra apprenticed in Paris under his father, a master glazier, and returned to work there permanently after completing his second tour de France. I usually list the cities on the tour in clockwise order, beginning in Paris; Perdiguier called this the "ideal" direction, but not all compagnons followed it. Ménétra travelled counterclockwise in his first tour (1757–1763) and clockwise in his shorter second tour (1763–1764). He also frequently backtracked, as Map 2 demonstrates.

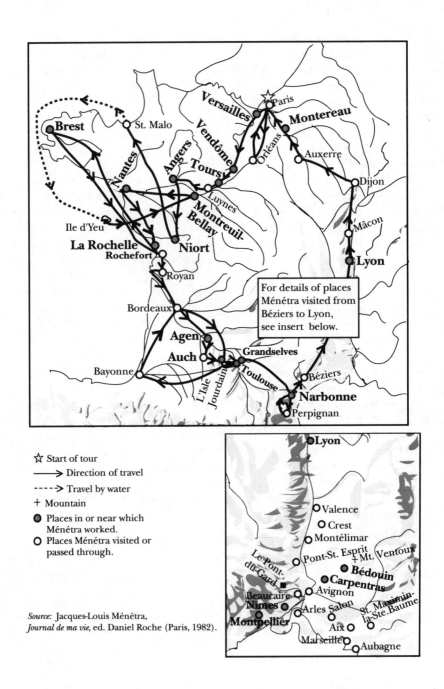

For details of places
Ménétra visited from
Béziers to Lyon,
see insert below.

MAP 2. The first Tour de France of Jacques-Louis Ménétra, 1757–1763

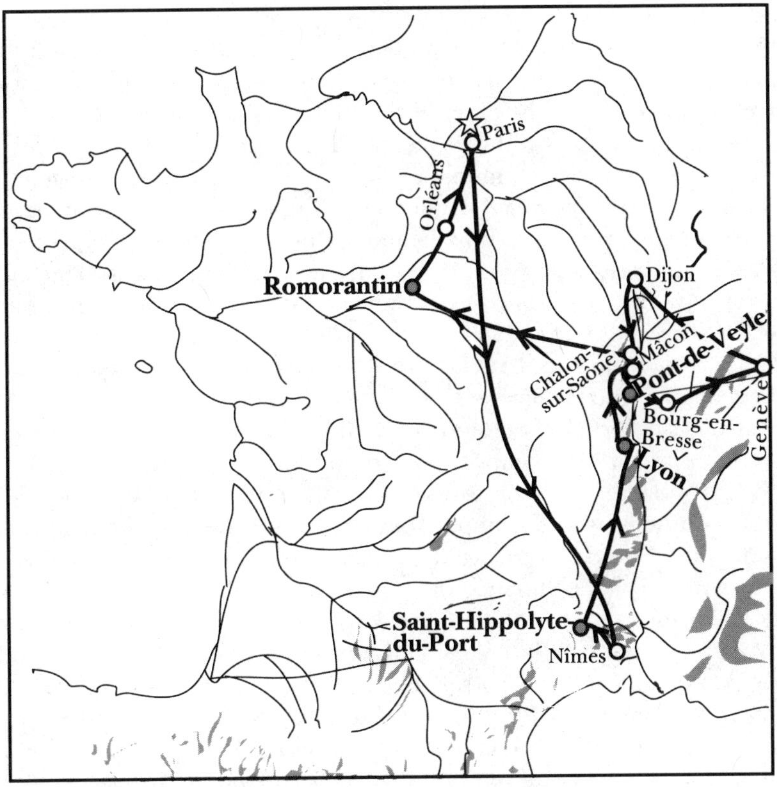
Paris
Orléans
Romorantin
Dijon
Mâcon
Chalon-sur-Saône
Pont-de-Veyle
Bourg-en-Bresse
Genève
Lyon
Saint-Hippolyte-du-Port
Nîmes

☆ Start of tour

⟶ Direction of travel

● Places in or near which Ménétra worked.

○ Places Ménétra visited or passed through.

Source: Jacques-Louis Ménétra, *Journal de ma vie*, ed. Daniel Roche (Paris, 1982).

MAP 3. The second Tour de France of Jacques-Louis Ménétra, 1763–1764

east. These distinctions might have less bearing for compagnons because they often worked in larger urban areas where socioeconomic and literacy levels would have been above the statistical norm.

Compagnons themselves help us chart their presence geographically and by trades. The "Chanson nouvelle" (1757) salutes the courage and reputation of the gavots and mentions two trades (locksmiths and "noble" stonecutters) and their tools (mallets and chisels). Another song, written "to celebrate the glory of the basketmakers, of worthy memory" sang of their troubles with masters in the mid-1760s.[5] In the eighteenth century joiners and locksmiths headed the list of compagnonnages and vigorously pursued control of labor conditions. Many important trades related to construction also had compagnonnages: stonecutters, turners, carpenters, plasterers, roofers, glaziers, and cabinetmakers. The metal trades—cutlers, blacksmiths, nail makers, tool makers, and tinsmiths— were well represented. Then came an eclectic mix of trades—bakers, coopers, basketmakers, hatters, harness makers, saddlers, tailors, weavers, wheelwrights, and wigmakers. From the five trades (shoemaking, hatting, tailoring, saddlery, and cutlery) condemned by the Sorbonne in the mid-seventeenth century, compagnonnage had grown nearly fivefold.

Not all journeymen, of course, were members of these associations, even in trades where compagnonnages flourished. Nonetheless, the numbers of compagnons could be substantial. In Nantes, for example, when a municipal ordinance of 1743 required all compagnons in joining, tailoring, saddlery, and wigmaking to recant their oaths to "the devoir," 162 joiners, 62 tailors, and 22 saddlers appeared before police magistrates to comply.[6] Correlating the numbers of these compagnon joiners and tailors with the numbers of masters in joining and tailoring yields a ratio of about 1 compagnon per master among the tailors to 1.4 compagnons per master among the joiners. Given an average of 3 to 4 journeymen per master in joining and tailoring in Nantes, compagnons in these trades would make up roughly 25 percent to 33 percent of a shop's journeymen. This percentage compares favorably to union membership in more modern eras in France, with the exception of the Popular Front.[7] Moreover, workers would not have to be compagnons to

5. AMM, HH 11/18, 18 January 1757, "Chanson nouvelle" by the "Père Intrepid"; AD Loiret, B 1988, [1764]; song beginning "Pour célébrer la gloire," reproduced in Jules Doinel and Camille Bloch, eds., *Archives du Loiret: Inventaire sommaire des archives départementales,* 10 vols. (Orléans, 1900), 3:45. The documents in this series were destroyed in World War II.

6. AMN, FF, Audiences de police, joiners (1743, 1745, 1750); saddlers (1750); tailors (1743); no record of wigmakers' recantations remains. See Truant, "Independent and Insolent," p. 154.

7. Theodore Zeldin, *France, 1848–1945,* 2 vols. (Oxford, 1973), 1:280. Union membership varied widely in France. During the Popular Front, membership in the Confédération Générale du Travail (C.G.T.) reached just over 50 percent of the work force. On the conflicts and influences that led to a decline in its membership, and the growth of the "union of the unorganized,"

have been encouraged or coerced to walk out of a workshop by those who were. Other reports draw a vivid picture of the distinctive and assertive presence of compagnonnage. In Nantes Ménétra attended a festive Twelfth Night celebration (January 6 of 1759) at the Mère, where "well nigh a hundred and eighty of us," compagnons du devoir of all the trades, gathered. In Lyon in May 1764 more than ninety compagnon joiners and locksmiths du devoir gathered on "Saint" Monday to bury a compagnon joiner at the church of Saint Nizier. And in 1768 a père of the compagnon joiners non du devoir in Marseille claimed the membership in this trade was "roughly 1,000 throughout the cities of France."[8]

We can glean additional evidence from the compagnons' more frequent meetings, gatherings, and disorders, numbering anywhere from a few to two or three dozen workers. In Nantes in 1751, thirty compagnon joiners, after attending mass, returned to their inn "with a band, the captain, and the rôleur" at their head. When Ménétra was premier compagnon in Lyon, twenty-one novices were initiated on the glaziers' patron saint's day in 1764; afterward, he attended a supper with fifteen of the city's premier compagnons. The incessant brawls of compagnon stonecutters in Bordeaux in the 1770s opposed thirty to forty assailants at a time.[9] Sometimes the evidence provides only a rough estimate of numbers, even if it clearly describes the deeds. For example, during a walkout in Lyon in 1764, a "troop" of compagnon locksmiths non du devoir "invaded" their master's shop, and "several" of them were eventually caught and arrested. Even without exact numbers these compagnons appear numerous enough to form a "troop" and mount a threatening "invasion." In the inquest following the arrests a master commented that both gavots and dévorants met regularly in churches or monasteries "as if they were authorized bodies."[10] This testimony demonstrates that whereas compagnons could vanish quickly when trouble broke out, their

see Gordon Wright, *France in Modern Times*, 3d ed. (New York, 1981), pp. 457–58. The rivalries of modern trade unionism are not without parallels to those of compagnonnage.

8. Ménétra, *Journal de ma vie*, p. 64; AD Rhône, Série B, Sénéchausée/Criminel, 23 May 1764, cited in Garden, *Lyon et les lyonnais*, p. 567; and AM Marseille, FF 206, Vernet to Latour, intendant of Provence, n.d. [1768]. Although Ménétra often exaggerates, his numbers here are supported by Garden's sources. Vernet's figure is not inconceivable, although on the high side: estimating 40 compagnons in each of the 10 major towns on the tour de France and 20 in another 20 smaller towns, there could have been at least 800 gavots in this trade in France. Vernet's testimony carries weight for he had been a père for over three years and claimed to have seen the compagnons' records and letters (often signed with the names of all the members in town).

9. AMN, FF 156, 26 July 1751, "Poursuites, rixes, conduites de compagnonnage, 1743–1752"; Ménétra, *Journal de ma vie*, pp. 126, 128; Cavignac, "Compagnonnage," p. 387.

10. AD Rhône, Série B, Sénéchausée/Criminel, 3 November 1764, in Garden, *Lyon et les lyonnais*, pp. 564–65, 567–68.

"corps" also had a solid, continuing, and recognized presence in French society.

Further quantitative evidence emerges from the overview of the legal and economic situation of these associations which follows. I then analyze materials produced by labor conflicts and finally turn to the compagnons' own records of their associations, which lend a comparative perspective to these more "official stories." Two major collections of compagnons' writings, from Mâcon and Bordeaux, allow me to reflect on their modes of organization, formal and informal, and the relationship of compagnonnage to French society in the old regime.

The Official Story: Regulation and Insubordination in the World of Work

Seventeenth-century condemnations of compagnonnage continued in the eighteenth century basically unchanged in form but issued with greater frequency and by secular rather than clerical authorities. The "police" of the world of work was more fully elaborated and centralized in the course of the eighteenth century, but regional variation in policies and laws, written or de facto, continued.[11] Although in theory the concept of strict regulation of the trade corporations had been encouraged from the time of Louis XIV, particularly under Colbert's ministry, trade monopolies were constantly evaded by the opposing interests of large-scale business, illegal producers, and a public that increasingly wanted cheaper and more varied goods.

Yet, although enforcement was often lax or difficult, edicts and ordinances condemning infractions of corporate monopolies were much in evidence in the eighteenth century. One of the earliest documents on the compagnonnages in that century is an arrêt of the parlement of Bordeaux, dated 22 June 1709, revealing that compagnons there had been involved in labor activities comparable to those seen in seventeenth-century Dijon. The judgment, directed against the compagnon locksmiths, reaffirmed an earlier ordinance of 6 July 1651 setting the trade's wages, hours, and provisions for the noon meal ("only bread and wine"). The judgment specifically banned the hiring practices—tantamount, officials said, to extortion—which purportedly gave the compagnons a strong hold over newly arrived locksmiths. The compagnons

---

11. Steven L. Kaplan, "Réflexions sur la police du monde du travail, 1700–1815," *Revue historique* 261 (December 1979): 17–77, is an indispensable examination of this important issue.

defended the bienvenue, the levée de sac, and other practices as essential components of the "devoir."[12]

The judgment of 22 June concluded by prohibiting meetings, gatherings, and work stoppages of compagnons organized in the devoir and established an official placement office. The new arrangement required incoming compagnons to report to city bailiffs, who would maintain a record of masters needing workers and would place them accordingly. The city proposed to substitute public charity for that of the compagnonnages: a small sum of money would be allocated to compagnons who became ill or found no work in Bordeaux and needed funds to move on. But later judgments bear witness to the city's inability to uproot the compagnonnages, even with alternative placement and aid programs. A parlementary arrêt of 1753 reiterated the 1709 decision in greater detail and described persistent conflict between masters and compagnons.[13]

Similar patterns of labor activity and attempts to repress it existed in other major cities of the old regime. For example, an ordinance of 11 May 1730 issued in Montpellier strongly prohibited the compagnon joiners and carpenters du devoir as well as gavots from participating directly or indirectly in the placement of compagnons and forbade masters from hiring any worker presented to them by compagnons du devoir or gavots. This ordinance recapitulated and renewed earlier decisions against compagnons and their illegal activities, including ordinances of 16 September 1688, 16 September 1690, and 27 October 1711. The 1730 ordinance, which imposed new fines and punishments, recounted fights between compagnons and described their activities in a dramatic (but fairly typical) way.

> The compagnon joiners and carpenters, one called du devoir and the other gavots, from time immemorial have been locked in unending contestations which have produced infinite disorders. . . . they gather and go out onto the large thoroughfares and finally abuse those who are not of their sect [parti] with blows of heavy canes (with which they are always armed); moreover, they run around in the night with sabers and drawn swords in hand, eventually led to fight by rage and unparalleled fury so as to kill one another.[14]

12. ADG, 1B, 22 June 1709.
13. ADG, 1A, 18 December 1753. For the texts of this and the 1709 arrêt see Cavignac, "Compagnonnage," pp. 406–10.
14. AD Haute-Garonne, G 150, 11 May 1730, Montpellier. The meaning of gavots is not entirely fixed in this era: some eighteenth- and nineteenth-century officials regarded gavots as unaffiliated journeymen. Others always recognized gavots as a sect of compagnonnage. Whatever gavots were originally (and whatever others thought), by the early eighteenth century there was an association of compagnons who had their own devoir and called themselves gavots.

Lieutenant General Bornier, who wrote the Montpellier ordinance, faithfully recorded the disorders and tried to explain them. He recognized the roots of economic competition between rival compagnons, and he noted how quickly the violence could turn against masters. It was common for compagnons to make deliberations and walk out on a master whose wages or general treatment failed to please them. If necessary, they also used force to prevent other compagnons from working for a master who had been *damné*, condemned, for whatever reason. Both gavots and compagnons du devoir yearly elected a captain who served as their absolute leader. Officials in Montpellier depicted two very well organized groups aligned against each other—and against the masters—and posing a grave threat to the completion of work and to public order in general. Montpellier, however, unlike Bordeaux, established no alternative placement bureau or charitable fund for journeymen.[15]

By midcentury police and trade officials recognized both the power of the compagnonnages and the impossibility of controlling these interurban associations on the local level. Authorities were also aware of the need to deal with the general problem of all itinerant workers and journeymen who never rose to the rank of master. On 31 July 1748 the parlement of Paris issued a judgement requiring traveling workers to register with the police in each town entered. The edict was difficult to enforce and offered little or nothing to replace the mutual aid and fellowship of compagnonnage. The interregional networks of the brotherhoods thus posed serious problems for the crown, which could issue but only partially execute legislation against them.[16]

Additionally, after 1750 opposition to the economic rights of trade corporations and other privileged groups intensified as the public sphere and public debate grew. Opposition to economic monopoly was particularly evident among the physiocratic circle surrounding Louis XVI's controller general Turgot. As the failure of most of Turgot's reforms demonstrates, however, the groups most affected by his measures were still powerful enough to defend their traditional rights. Turgot's most noted attack on these rights, the Six Edicts, included an attempt to sup-

15. See Cavignac, "Compagnonnage," p. 405.
16. BN, Fonds Lamoignon, book 38, fol. 436. On the growing problems of the eighteenth-century trade corporations, particularly the divisions among masters, journeymen, and apprentices, see Steven Kaplan, "The Character and Implications of Strife among the Masters inside the Guilds of Eighteenth-Century Paris," *Journal of Social History* 19 (1986): 631–47; and Kaplan, "Social Classification and Representation in the Corporate World of Eighteenth-Century France: Turgot's 'Carnival,'" in Kaplan and Koepp, *Work in France*, pp. 176–228; Robert Darnton, *The Great Cat Massacre and Other Episodes in French Cultural History* (New York, 1984), pp. 75–104; and Maurice Garden, "Ouvriers et artisans au XVIIIe siècle: L'Exemple lyonnais et les problèmes de classification," *Revue d'histoire économique et sociale* 48 (1970): 45–51; and Garden, *Lyon et les lyonnais*, p. 339.

press the corporations entirely, provoking strong protests from trade officials and heated debate in the royal council prior to the presentation of the edicts for parlementary registration in early February 1776. Remonstrances and complaints ended in outright defiance when the parlement of Paris on 7 February refused to register "a project stemming from an inadmissible system of equality, the first effect of which is to throw all the orders of the State into confusion."[17] Turgot persuaded the king to override the parlementary veto, and the Six Edicts were registered on 22 February 1776, but continuing opposition to the decrees and ministerial intrigue led to Turgot's forced resignation on 12 May 1776 and the revocation of the edicts in August.

The furor over the Six Edicts revealed the growing importance of the public's opinion, for debate was not confined to Paris or to corporation officials. In both Nantes and Lyon, important segments of the population strongly supported Turgot's reforms (or rumors of them). Gaston Martin maintains that in Nantes the "state of public opinion [d'esprit public] had sapped the principle of the corporations even before the law would authorize their demise."[18] Large-scale masters and négotiants (wholesale merchants) and parts of the artisanal work force, including journeymen, welcomed the measure. Small masters and retailers just as strongly opposed it. Their fears that they would be unable to compete with large producers and that they might lose control over the work force were not unfounded. Even when the short-lived edicts had been abrogated, some workers continued to act as if they were still in effect. On 17 December 1776 police in Nantes reported that four sons of master joiners, believing a "rumor that there were no longer any masterships," set themselves up as masters without paying any fees to the corporation. Several other cases of individuals who opened shops without first having been received as masters were recorded on the same date.[19]

Lyon, the reputed "city of free trades," enjoyed certain freedoms from trade regulations. Yet, as in Nantes, Turgot's measures met with stiff opposition from small producers and from older, wealthier masters, firmly ensconced in positions of authority. The most reasonable hope for the success of the reforms lay in the internal divisions in French trade communities promoted by newer, large-scale producers. In 1780 officials

17. Jules Flammeront, ed., *Remonstrances du parlement de Paris au XVIIIe siècle*, 3 vols. (Paris, 1888–98), 3:279. Kaplan presents a stimulating analysis of guild officials' protests against the abolition, which was seen as a "kind of carnivalization of the social order" ("Social Classification and Representation," esp. pp. 180–99). On the debate in the royal council, see Keith Michael Baker, *Condorcet: From Natural Philosophy to Social Mathematics* (Chicago, 1975), p. 72.
18. Gaston Martin, *Capital et travail*, p. 88.
19. AMN, HH 150, 17 December 1776, joiners and other trades, "Procés-verbal, commissaire de police."

of the locksmiths' corporation in Lyon recalled that "several years ago
rumors were being spread about rather publicly which led to the belief
that the communities of arts and crafts of this city had been abolished
as they actually had been in the capital at the beginning of 1776." These
masters linked the illegal and insubordinate behavior of dissenting masters and journeymen to such rumors. The irony, of course, is that the
corporations had been suppressed as much in Lyon as elsewhere in
France. These masters persisted in the misinformation that the abolition
was somehow confined to Paris. Claiming that enforcement of regulations and prosecutions of workers' abuses had been lax since 1776, these
masters insisted on the full reestablishment of the economic and policing functions of the trade communities.[20]

Indeed, enforcement of regulations seems to have suffered after the
reestablishment of the corporations. Promulgation of edicts, ordinances,
and other judgments against workers' labor infractions tapered off
throughout France after 1776. In some cities, corporation records were
kept far less meticulously in the last decade of the old regime than previously. Nonetheless, enough evidence exists to demonstrate that compagnons and other organized workers continued to come into conflict
with their masters and to chafe at trade regulations. Furthermore, some
major edicts against workers' associations emerged after 1776, often extending their force by being promulgated in one region and then reissued in another. One of the most important post-1776 regulations was
issued by the parlement of Paris in 1778 as a homologation of a judgement promulgated the same year in Lyon. This decision prohibited associations under the names: "sans Gêne, Bons-enfants, Gavots, Droguins,
du Devoir, Dévorants, Passés, Gorets, and others."[21] It was an attempt to
suppress all sorts of workingmen's associations, including compagnonnages. Its primary target was private and public meetings, but it also
banned the practice of the Mère. Innkeepers known by the "titles of
mères and pères of compagnons" were threatened with the loss of their
licenses if they continued to permit gatherings of such workers on their
premises. The judgment declared (recalling earlier decisions) that compagnonnages "ruined the workers," who gambled and drank away wages
in taverns where innkeepers extended them too much credit. Whereas
such conduct primarily harmed the individual, other customs affected
public order. This judgment, like previous ones, was intended to restore
that order, but it was no more effective than the others had been.[22]

20. Garden, *Lyon et les lyonnais*, pp. 557–58; AML, HH 184, no. 19, 14 June 1780, "Maîtres
gardes serruriers au prévôt."
    21. François-André Isambert et al., eds., *Recueil général des anciennes lois françaises depuis l'an
420 jusqu'à la révolution de 1789*, 29 vols. (Paris, 1822–33), 25:411.
    22. Truant, "Independent and Insolent," pp. 131–33, 162–73.

VARIETIES OF CONFLICT

In the course of the eighteenth century more capital-intensive modes of production and limitations on masterships created sharper competition for jobs and contributed to increased conflict between compagnons and masters and between rival sects of compagnonnage. Compagnons focused their economic defense on control of hiring, and soon found it necessary to drive out opposing sects and unaffiliated workers or force them to accept their standards. Conflict, therefore, was rarely attributable to simple motives, least of all to straightforward opposition between employers and workers.[23] The large cities where compagnonnage flourished—Lyon, Marseille, Bordeaux, and Nantes—witnessed the beginnings of major socioeconomic transformations. Innovations in production concentrated labor in larger workshops, increased division of labor, and brought about the domination of certain trades by merchant manufacturers who could produce and sell on a much greater scale than previously.[24] Small workshops, run by more independent masters, were gradually superseded by larger production units.

Although compagnonnage could not halt economic reorganization, its presence delayed or contested changes compagnons regarded as disadvantageous, even in more capital-intensive sectors. I have previously demonstrated the strong correlation between compagnonnages and labor conflict in Lyon, where the role of large-scale production and merchant manufacturing was quite marked.[25] Yet, even when artisanal production was not directly affected by the growth of merchant capitalism, rural competition and lower production standards strained workshop relations. Compagnons recognized the need to defend their "rights" in the workshop against changes imposed directly by the smaller masters or indirectly by newer economic forces. For example, in 1680 compagnon and apprentice bakers in Lyon confronted masters who cut wages and frustrated walkouts by hiring rural outworkers (*forains*), less qualified and more poorly paid than urban workers. The compagnons protested this unfair competition to the lieutenant of police and "called on the population" to oppose the masters' "sordid avarice." A "veritable scandal" resulted.[26] And in cities where changes in and pressures on production were less marked, compagnonnages remained an essential

23. In *Work and Wages*, chaps. 3 and 8, Sonenscher examines the problem for the wider world of workers and provides a detailed and nuanced analysis of their conflicts and means of defense.
24. See the important work of Garden, *Lyon et les lyonnais*. On the growth of consumer culture in this era, see Daniel Roche, *The People of Paris: An Essay in Popular Culture in the 18th Century*, trans. Marie Evans in association with Gwynne Lewis (Berkeley, 1987), chaps. 5, 8.
25. Truant, "Independent and Insolent," esp. pp. 133–42, 172–73.
26. Garden, *Lyon et les lyonnais*, p. 564 (AML, HH24, 13 June 1680, "Requête au prévôt des marchands et échevins" and "Supplique addressée au consulat par les garçons boulangers").

factor in the success or failure of workshop production. Finally, even if
smaller workshops were threatened by the growth of capitalism and rural
competition, they remained the rule in the eighteenth century, especially
in the trades in which compagnonnages predominated. My analysis focuses first on conflicts among joiners and locksmiths in two major centers, Nantes and Lyon, and then describes patterns of conflict in other
areas where compagnonnage had a marked presence.[27]

Association and Conflict in Nantes and Lyon

In Nantes I examined the extant papers of twenty-seven corps des
métiers, as well as available police commissioners' reports and other relevant papers for the late seventeenth and eighteenth centuries. Among
the twenty-seven corporations studied, seven—drapers, printers, roofers,
spur makers, pastry makers, restaurateurs, and caterers—left no apparent record of serious conflict between masters and journeymen. Although printers were usually well organized (independent of
compagnonnage) and active in labor disputes, journeymen in the other
six corporations had no significant history of labor organization, although drapers and roofers established compagnonnages after the Revolution. Among the other twenty corps des métiers, six—edge-tool
makers (*taillandiers*), farriers, joiners, locksmiths, tailors, and wigmakers—were strongly organized in compagnonnages with more than half
a dozen incidents of conflict each: walkouts, boycotts of shops, wage
demands, disputes over placement, persistent association, and organization.[28] Three other trades—carpenters, ironsmiths, and plasterers—
experienced labor disputes provoked by their workers' compagnonnages
between 1789 and 1791. All these "active" trades in Nantes were ones
that had associations of compagnonnage in the old regime in other
French cities. The remaining eleven corps—basketmaking, cutlery, nail
making, rope making, rug making, saddlery, shoemaking, stonecutting,
tinsmithing, turning, and weaving—show fewer incidents of organization
or labor conflict, but all the events recorded in these eleven communities
were significant.[29]

---

27. Truant, "Independent and Insolent," pp. 146–67. The following section includes revised
material from this article.

28. AMN, HH 166 and FF 258 (edge-tool makers), HH 145 (farriers); HH 165 and II 147
(locksmiths), FF 68 and HH 168 (tailors), HH 93–95, 101–2, and 104 (wigmakers), and HH
59, 147, 149, 150, FF 67, 69, 256, II 147, and I²137 (joiners).

29. I found no evidence on compagnon glaziers in Nantes in the series HH and little in other
series. Ménétra says Nantes was *défendu* (banned) by the compagnons du devoir when he arrived
there sometime in 1758 or 1759; he nonetheless stayed to work along with three other compag-

In all twenty corporations reporting illegal activities, official intervention was taken only after journeymen had disrupted production over an extended period. A typical example is found in the compagnonnage of edge-tool makers. Despite a prohibition against their labor activities issued as far back as 1732, minutes of the trade officials' meeting of 27 August 1764 reveal that compagnons "disorders" were on-going. Edicts were reissued, without great success, in 1769, 1775, 1776, and 1782 to forbid compagnons from placing workers, controlling the composition of the work force, and demanding changes in wages and working conditions. These edicts emphatically denied compagnons any right to meddle in such issues, contrary to these workers' own claims. Even where only one formal charge against compagnonnage is recorded, a similar pattern emerges. Master turners wished to establish a placement office in 1783 but claimed that their compagnons had "for some time now perpetuated themselves in the devoir of compagnonnage."[30]

In Lyon I examined material similar to that in Nantes, this time in sixteen corporations, all of which experienced some form of master-worker conflict. Six of them—masonry and stonecutting, joining, locksmithing, saddlery, tailoring, and wigmaking—show continued patterns of activity over many years. Joiners, locksmiths, tailors, and wigmakers had all begun their history of association and opposition to the masters in the seventeenth century. There is a similar history of labor activity and protest among journeymen hatters.[31] Among the other nine trades examined—baking, cabinetmaking, carpentry, currying and harness making, cutlery, shoemaking, turning, weaving, and wheel making and repairing—all record at least some incidence of conflict in the eighteenth century. The bakers had also been active in the 1680s and 1690s but seem to have appeared on the record again only in the 1770s, when they openly petitioned for official recognition of their Mère.[32]

Detailed analysis of a selection of relevant examples from Nantes and Lyon demonstrates how association encouraged independence and sparked demands for improved labor conditions among compagnons. I will focus on two corporations whose journeymen were organized in compagnonnage and had a roughly equivalent history of association and labor conflict in Nantes and Lyon: locksmiths (and the related corps of the edge-tool makers in Nantes) and joiners. Each set of cases demon-

nons. Eventually a new agreement was reached with the masters. He and the others then wrote to bring the compagnons du devoir back to Nantes. *Journal de ma vie*, p. 63.

30. AMN, HH 164, HH 166, HH 177, 20 August 1783.

31. For the definitive work on this trade, see Michael Sonenscher, *The Hatters of Eighteenth-Century France* (Berkeley, 1987).

32. It is likely that further research in the records of the Sénéchausée/Criminel in Nantes and Lyon would yield additional cases of master-worker conflict.

strates the important part "major" and "minor" incidents of conflict played in defining the master-worker relationship and establishing the power of associated workers.

Compagnon locksmiths were the most actively organized journeymen in Lyon, although not always in the context of compagnonnage. Their activities and organization were first recorded in 1634; their last conflict in the old regime was reported in 1780. Throughout this long period, compagnon locksmiths were frequently labeled seditious. In 1634 an edict prohibited journeymen from holding assemblies, maintaining a savings chest, demanding money from new journeymen in town, or placing journeymen in workshops. This ordinance also noted the struggle between masters over journeymen and ruled that no master must *débauche* (steal) another master's journeymen or attempt to lure journeymen by advancing them more than thirty sous. This last point illustrates that masters may have depended on advance payment to win journeymen. The edict originally allowed masters to advance a maximum of only sixteen sous to journeymen. This figure was crossed out and replaced by thirty. Masters could still get around this limit if the advance were for "clothing and other necessities" and if corporation officials were informed.[33] It seems clear that journeymen would easily prefer the more generous masters. Such masters might well have made deals with the journeymen's rôleur to send more workers their way. The 1634 ordinance, with some variation, was reissued in 1642, 1661, and 1662. Even the harsh edict of 1661, placing disobedient journeymen under "pain of exemplary punishment," was ineffective in breaking their "monopoly."

Although the law might temporarily thwart the compagnon locksmiths' plans, it never seriously cooled their ardor. New prohibitions, warnings, complaints, or edicts were issued in 1674, 1764, 1767, and 1780. In 1764 compagnon locksmiths in Lyon were organized into rival associations: the compagnons du devoir, or dévorants, and compagnons non du devoir, or gavots. In that year, for example, the gavots called a walkout in Lyon to protest the hiring of a man banned by the compagnonnage. A "troop" of compagnons, led by their captain and rôleur, later returned to "invade" the shop. They threatened, insulted, and struck the master and his wife. Several of them, including the captain and the rôleur, were eventually tracked down and arrested. Three years later, in 1767, a judgment of the criminal court of Lyon forbade compagnons from gathering and meeting in inns, private residences, and even religious communities "to plot the excesses that gave rise to this trial."[34]

33. AML, HH 184, no. 5.
34. AD Rhône, série B, Sénéchausée/Criminel, 3 November 1764, cited in Garden, *Lyon et*

Such illegal behavior had not abated by 1780 when the officials of the locksmiths' corporation petitioned the *prévôt* of Lyon to issue a new ordinance permitting the arrest of insubordinate workers, preventing abuses of the public security, and assuring the masters' tranquility. The ordinance recalled previous attempts "at various times" to bring compagnons back within the "devoir" (obviously that of the corporation) and prior bans of cabals, and associations "under the denominations of confraternities, devoir, gavotage—or others." Rather than the "fidelity and service" they owed their masters, the trade officials wrote, compagnons brought unending disruptions. The officials attributed this neglect of duty and the continued existence of "cabals," to the "independence and insubordination with which the majority of compagnons and workers behave toward their masters."[35] Incidents of a less serious or "secondary" nature connected with major labor conflicts were not less bothersome to masters. In fact Maurice Garden suggests that "secondary conflicts" reveal important underlying antagonisms and problems in the various levels of the eighteenth-century world of work. Compagnon locksmiths frequently insulted or even assaulted masters with an impunity that reinforced their conviction that they were not the necessary and automatic subordinates of their masters or even more highly placed officials.[36]

Evidence of the conflicts of compagnon locksmiths in Nantes appears only in 1733, almost one hundred years after the first recorded case of their fellow artisans in Lyon. Nantais journeymen, however, made up for lost time between 1733 and 1780. An ordinance of 12 September 1733, accused compagnon locksmiths of assembly "under the pretext of the Devoir," which the law wished "to extinguish." These compagnons were said to control the hiring of newly arrived compagnons by meeting in inns and other places. Evidently the devoir was too hardy for this judicial reprimand, reissued in 1737, for troubles continued in 1738. As compagnons of the "so-called Devoir" continued to control the placement of workers, three compagnons were arrested. Fellow compagnons protested these arrests and came to plead for their release. The police court tabled the affair and put it off until the next session; perhaps because compagnons were organized enough to issue a strong protest and to receive a hearing. The years 1755, 1776, 1779, and 1780 witnessed a revival of labor activities under the auspices of the devoir. An incident of 19 July 1776, for example, concerned an illegal assembly that ended

les lyonnais, pp. 564–65, 567–68; AML, impr. 701.414, 6 September 1764; and AML, HH 184, no. 20, 24 September 1767.

35. AML, HH 184, no. 19, 14 June 1780.

36. Garden, *Lyon et les lyonnais*, p. 563; an example of such behavior is found in AML, HH 183, no. 16, "Extrait de sentence."

in a brawl among a large number of compagnons, not only locksmiths
but also joiners and saddlers.[37]

Like the locksmiths, their fellow metalworkers the edge-tool makers,
were first labeled troublemakers in the early 1730s in Nantes. The first
case revealed that the edge-tool makers, again like the locksmiths, had
previously associated in the devoir. The 1730 case emerged after a brawl
between edge-tool makers and wheelwrights, quarreling over adherence
to the devoir. Seven compagnons were sent to prison for three months
and then expelled from Nantes because of the resulting violence. By
1764 the "spirit of sedition" among compagnon edge-tool makers had
reached a high pitch. Masters claimed that they kept wages high by forcing workers who would accept lower pay to leave town. Those who remained had to become compagnons of the devoir, subject to the
authority of the rôleur, whom the masters described as an autocrat: he
"disposed of compagnons at will"; "forced compagnons to leave the
city"; "decided what the compagnons would make the master do."[38]
These exaggerated perceptions of the rôleur's genuine powers are highly
revealing. The masters' fears of their workers, organized under this
strong leadership, reflect the tensions and hostilities present in the trade.

The compagnons' latest demand was for masters to enter the compagnons' association and receive the *accolade* (fraternal salute) as a type
of initiation. As serious as this demand may have been, it also had a
wonderfully comic and ironic force: the compagnons could not have
failed to revel in their masters' consternation at a proposal so at odds
with normal hierarchies. The masters, finding themselves in such "dis-
agreeable circumstances," urged the destruction of this association of
devoir. In 1764 laws were promulgated in Nantes, prohibiting any type
of compagnonnage and setting up a placement office. Yet, these efforts
were in vain. In 1782 a further petition of master edge-tool makers censured their compagnons' "dangerous independence" and called for the
repression of the "society of the compagnons du devoir," while doubting
that it would ever be abolished.[39]

Like the locksmiths, compagnon joiners were among the best-
organized workers in both Nantes and Lyon. In 1704 master joiners in

37. AMN, II 147, 12 September 1733, locksmiths; HH 164, "Procès-verbal, commissaire de
police," 21 June 1738 and 28 November 1780, which referred to a court decree of 3 February
1779 prohibiting gatherings of compagnons calling themselves "du Devoir, Bondrilles [good
fellows], Gavot, etc.", and FF 92, 19 July 1776.
38. AMN, FF 258, 13 November 1732, HH 166, 27 August 1764, "Sentence de police."
39. AMN, HH 166, 27 August 1764, Nantes, petition of master edge-tool makers, 30 August
1764 "Ordonnance de police," 22 September 1767, parlement de Rennes, homologation of
ordonnance of 1764, 12 May 1775, Nantes, homologation of earlier regulations against the
"devoir," and 27 July 1782, Nantes, petition of master edge-tool makers to *siège royal de police* for
renewal of these regulations.

Lyon expressed anger at their inability to control the *associations du devoir*, present in that city since at least 1699. The masters were indignant that religious communities had legitimated these associations by granting them the status of confraternities. Compagnon joiners had drawn up statutes, kept membership rolls, and collected money from members to further the ends of their association. As in other French cities, these compagnons had a mère who lodged them and permitted their assemblies. The location of the inn was quickly made known to compagnons new in town and they soon "came under the devoir's rule," whose force was such, the masters claimed, that the compagnons could deprive them of workers unless they willingly submitted to their demands. The compagnons insisted on the right to control all worker placement, to make incoming workers conform to the terms of the devoir, to assemble in the city or *faubourgs* as they pleased, to "have their rolls and letters and to choose their Mère in order to hold their assemblies." Their demands and activities were a "pure vexation"; masters wanted convicted compagnons to receive harsh prison sentences and corporal punishment.[40] The request was granted, but the resulting edict was difficult to enforce. The compagnon joiners du devoir in Lyon actively pursued this pattern of labor action until at least the 1760s.[41]

In eighteenth-century Nantes compagnon joiners made the same kinds of trouble for their masters. The devoir had been established since at least 1723, when compagnons had "plotted" to "augment their pay" and had continually "refused compagnons to masters." Even though the lieutenant general of police seized their roll and other papers in 1723, the compagnons were still organized a year later, under the leadership of their "captains." On 16 May 1724 the current captain was arrested in the chapel of Saint Gildas, where he was seeking sanctuary; the compagnons joiners du devoir had previously been protected by the religious community associated with this chapel.[42] Even the captain's arrest failed to stop the devoir. By the 1740s, as noted, master joiners, along with master tailors, wigmakers, and saddlers, angry at the inability of edicts to destroy compagnons' associations, demanded that all their compagnons appear before the police magistrates to renounce their oaths to the devoir of compagnonnage. Certainly not all compagnons were found and made to recant (if indeed they had taken such oaths), but officials made a determined effort to compel these workers. In a number of cases, compagnons strenuously resisted, refused to answer questions, evaded trade officials, and ignored police summonses. One recalcitrant com-

40. AML, HH 109, no. 6, 29 January 1699, and no. 8, 31 December 1704.
41. AML, Impr. 701.414, 23 May 1764, joiners.
42. AMN, HH 59, 17 May 1724, corporation minutes (joiners).

pagnon was finally arrested, imprisoned for eight days, and then exiled from Nantes for six months.[43]

Compagnon joiners du devoir remained active in the following decades. In 1781 they met frequently, sometimes daily, at a time when the rival compagnon joiners non du devoir were also present in Nantes. Like compagnon joiners and locksmiths in Lyon and compagnon locksmiths in Nantes, joiners of the gavot sect found a haven in certain churches and monasteries. They often met in rooms provided them by clerics of the Jacobin and Cordelier monasteries in the late 1770s and early 1780s. In these meetings, according to the masters, the compagnons discussed plans to prohibit or blacklist (défendre) certain shops. The compagnons claimed they were meeting only to discuss offering blessed bread on the next feast day. Most likely they had both issues on their agenda. When the police arrived at the monastery, the reverend fathers refused to let them enter the room where police had spied (through the keyhole) on compagnons congregated around a table, examining "a large quantity of papers." One of the clerics, Père Mory, told the police that "he would never allow them to be arrested in the monastery." The reasons for the clerics' defense of the compagnons are not clear, but their position contrasts sharply with the theological faculty's condemnation of compagnonnage in the previous century. Perhaps members of these religious orders were trying to regain spiritual and social ascendancy over urban workingmen; it is also possible that the monks were of the same social stratum as compagnons and were preaching to their "brothers." Ignoring "sacrilegious" rituals and focusing on the charitable and confraternal aspects of compagnonnage, some clerics forged an important bond with compagnons in an age of growing secularization. Those in Nantes also seem to have relished thwarting secular authority and perhaps even the church hierarchy.[44]

The compagnons' reasons for blacklisting shops is much clearer. A new corporate regulation required all workers to be placed in shops by a corporate official. Compagnons adamantly opposed this rule and declared that hiring would take place only under the auspices of compagnonnage. Apparently, they made good on their threat. In 1787 masters described a world of work turned upside down: "The compagnons' liberty has the most dangerous effects [for it] puts the masters in a sort of dependence on the compagnons. . . . The deadly association of Devoir

43. AMN, HH 149 (joiners), "Procès-verbal, commissaire de police," 14 December 1744 and 14 July 1745. For the lists of those who recanted see AMN, FF Audiences de police: joiners (1743, 1745, 1750); saddlers (1750); and tailors (1743).
44. AMN, HH 150, 18 August 1787.

holds the masters under [the compagnons'] empire."[45] Through the years, the "dangerous effects" of the compagnon joiners' "liberty" and "empire" had included continuing control of job placement and enforcement of demands for monetary advances and good treatment. Compagnons kept organizing, reorganizing, and socializing despite obstacles raised by masters, the police, the laws, rival compagnonnages, and nonaligned journeymen. Masters saw a vicious connection between compagnons' labor demands and their sociability: money "extorted" from masters was "squandered" on drunkenness and debauchery, rendering workers unfit to work and ever more likely to threaten masters and their property.

A COMPARATIVE PERSPECTIVE

The link between conflict and compagnonnage is undeniable. The incidence, type, and chronology of conflict recorded for locksmiths and joiners in both Nantes and Lyon are also roughly equivalent, and these patterns are generally repeated in the full sample of trades I have examined. Similarities in the structure, aim, and tactics of compagnonnage in Nantes and Lyon greatly outweigh the differences, although there were some noteworthy regional variations, primarily in three areas: the chronology of the appearance or "disappearance" of conflict; the frequency of conflict; and the degree of complexity or elaboration in organization.

The earliest examples of labor conflict—for example, control of hiring, walkouts, disruptive behavior in the workshop, working independent of the corps des métiers—are found in Lyon, albeit not in associations that are definitely part of compagnonnage. There were serious incidents of conflict among masters and workers in baking, joining, locksmithing, and tailoring in the seventeenth century. Several more minor cases are also recorded for the wigmakers in the late seventeenth century. Among the other trades examined here, only the bakers in Lyon left a record of conflict from before the eighteenth century. If conflict left its record first in Lyonnais trades, it was last recorded in Nantes. Lyon was relatively quiet after 1770—or left little trace of labor conflict. In Nantes, by contrast, major labor disputes occurred in a number of trades after 1770 and even into the early revolutionary period.

Analysis of the frequency of conflict likewise reveals some interesting

45. AMN, HH 150, 18 August 1781, joiners, HH 147, 14 December 1787.

discrepancies between Nantes and Lyon. Judging from complaints, incidents, trials, and edicts generated, the trade most frequently involved in labor disputes in Lyon was locksmithing, whereas in Nantes it was joining. Compagnons in both trades in both cities, however, were very nearly equal in terms of organization and labor activity. In Nantes, moreover, compagnon edge-tool makers were as actively engaged in serious disputes with their masters as compagnon locksmiths. In the records of conflict involving other trades, the incidence of disputes is surprisingly similar in both cities. In both, compagnon tailors and wigmakers were, after locksmiths and joiners, the workers who were most organized and most involved in labor disputes. Even the less active trades reveal an uncanny similarity in frequency of labor activity, although the dates may differ. Compagnon carpenters in Lyon had one major labor dispute in 1782; those in Nantes had one in 1791. Compagnon stonecutters in Lyon provoked two major disputes—one in 1769 and one in 1786; those in Nantes incited one major dispute in 1752.

In almost all the trades where conflict appears, some degree of association is also reported. Both joiners and locksmiths had high levels of master-worker conflict and of organization—for example, evidence of leadership, regular meetings, record keeping, means for the control of placement, and ability to plan for walkouts or boycotts. Yet, some relevant differences in the nature and complexity of organization in each city can also be found. In Lyon, journeymen locksmiths, joiners, and tailors all had very old strong associations that closely followed the model of compagnonnage, although the most common terms of compagnonnage (devoir, mère) are rare or missing in the data until the mideighteenth century. Journeymen wigmakers in Lyon, moreover, though called independent and troublesome by their masters in the seventeenth century, were not very formally organized until 1762.

In Nantes, by contrast, associations among journeymen in these trades emerged later than they did in Lyon, but they emerged "full-blown," with written records—rolls, notebooks (cahiers), lists—and with the distinguishing linguistic markers of compagnonnage. Well before the mideighteenth century, then, the bureaucracy, leadership, tactics, and language of compagnonnage were well elaborated in Nantes. Its ritual and ceremonial aspects among joiners, locksmiths, and many of the other trades studied were also more in evidence in Nantes than in Lyon. It seems possible that ritual played a smaller part in the Lyonnais journeymen's associations than it did in Nantes, but given the difficulties in making definitive pronouncements about such practices, any conclusions on this point must remain tentative.

The most important difference between Nantes and Lyon is the chronological variation in the start and end of labor activities. Master-worker conflict apparently begins and ends earlier in Lyon, for reasons both economic and cultural. Lyon had long been an urban and commercial center. It was a fertile crossroads between France and Italy and between city and countryside, which had developed a strong tradition of popular culture. In Lyon the prerogatives and license of carnival were claimed by organized groups within the urban context, most notably by bands of urban youths, "the lords of misrule," who elected a king and enforced certain moral and social standards while "turning the world upside down." The combinations of pranks, sociability, and social control practiced by such groups provided a rich storehouse of models that young journeymen artisans in Lyon could adapt to their own purposes in the world of work. Journeymen printers, moreover, had been especially active and well organized in Lyon in the early modern period, providing yet another organizational precedent.[46] Lyon, moreover, lies relatively near Dijon, where the earliest records of compagnonnages and their conflicts with masters appear. It is likely that Dijon was a source for early journeymen's associations in Lyon, especially inasmuch as many of the early interurban networks of compagnonnage were somewhat more regionally than nationally based. Finally, local factors such as economic competition from rural and illegal outworkers and from large-scale manufacturing occurred earlier and more fully in Lyon than in Nantes.

The apparent decline in labor activity after 1770 in Lyon is more perplexing. Maurice Garden suggests that the abolition of the corps des métiers in 1776, temporary though it was, dealt a severe blow to the trade communities from which they never really recovered in the last years before the Revolution. Garden thinks that the policing of the trades, although reestablished, was not rigorous after 1776. His supposition is supported by evidence form the officials of the locksmiths' community in Lyon. In 1780 these corporation officials petitioned the provost of Lyon to issue a decree restoring some vigor to the community's regulations, which had been ineffective since 1776.[47] It is possible that master-worker conflict declined in the 1770s and 1780s, although it seems unlikely, given the increase in labor activity before this time. Possibly, labor relations actually worsened in this period without leaving a record. If there was a decrease in labor conflict, it might be tied to an overall decline in the fortunes of the corporations. Yet, labor conflict did not usually correlate strongly with economic prosperity or end dur-

46. Natalie Zemon Davis, "Strikes and Salvation at Lyon," and "The Reasons of Misrule," in her *Society and Culture in Early Modern France* (Stanford, 1975), pp. 1–16, 114–23.

47. Maurice Garden, personal communication, April 1983; AML, HH 184, no. 19, 14 June 1780, "Maîtres gardes serruriers au prévôt."

ing times of economic hardship. Compagnon locksmiths and joiners
seem to have been most active when their trades were prosperous, but
compagnons in other trades, for example, tailors and wigmakers, made
heavy demands on masters when corporate records and other indicators
point to economic decline and debt.[48] The question of labor disputes
after 1770 in Lyon thus remains open.

The continued and vigorous labor conflict in Nantes after 1770 might,
by contrast, have reflected the continuing strength of the trade corporations in that city. Activity among journeymen in the building trades,
in particular, remained high or was first initiated in this period. The
important building boom in Nantes throughout the eighteenth century,
but especially from midcentury on, helps to account for labor activity in
this sector.[49] Another significant economic factor was the growth of the
seaport and related industries, such as shipbuilding and outfitting, which
ensured the continued strength of the artisanal sector.

Perhaps correlated with the persistence of conflict and association in
Nantes and its relative decline in Lyon is the other noteworthy difference
between the two cities: compagnonnages were more prevalent in Nantes
than in Lyon. Gaston Martin called Nantes "truly a city with the reputation of being a sort of school for compagnonnage." The leaders of
confraternities, the heads of the devoir, and the workers' syndics "had
a very precise and much respected authority that presupposed a real
structure within the groups who submitted to their discipline."[50] Martin
gives no explanation for the importance of compagnonnage in Nantes.
One possibility, however, is that the historically strong religious tradition
of western France lent special power to the Catholic ritual and symbolism
the Nantais compagnonnages borrowed and modified. Protection of
compagnonnages by clerics, particularly those associated with the Jacobin and Cordelier monasteries, was especially evident in Nantes. In Lyon
two forces may have weakened journeymen's use of ritual and symbolism.
First, the impact of the Reformation was greater there, and second, the
Catholic Church had responded with a vigorous Counter-Reformation,
which, in largely eradicating Protestantism in the seventeenth and eighteenth centuries, also suppressed many elements of popular religiosity.
Thus, the strong opposition to popular use (or "misuse") of religious
symbols, rituals, and icons, found in both the Protestant and the Catholic

48. For Nantes, see Gaston Martin, *Capital et travail*, pp. 5, 88; AMN, HH 59 (joiners), HH
164 (locksmiths), HH 168 (tailors), and HH 93, 101, and 102 (wigmakers). For Lyon, see
Garden, "Ouvriers et artisans," pp. 45–49; AML, HH 109 (joiners), HH 184 (locksmiths), HH
185 and SM 181 (tailors), and HH 176–77 (wigmakers).

49. Jacques Depauw, "Illicit Sexual Activity and Society in Eighteenth-Century Nantes," in
Family and Society, ed. Robert Forster and Orest Ranum (Baltimore, 1976), p. 167.

50. Gaston Martin, *Capital et travail*, p. 87.

Reformations, may have been reflected in the somewhat lower incidence of fully developed compagnonnages in Lyon.[51]

It would be misleading, in any event, to overemphasize the divergences between Nantes and Lyon. Moreover, similar practices and organizations existed in other major centers of compagnonnage, particularly in Bordeaux and Marseille. In Bordeaux conflict provoked by the compagnonnages was sharpest in the 1760s and 1770s, although compagnon joiners and locksmiths had organizations dating from the 1730s which had often coexisted within the framework of the corps des métiers—at least as long as compagnons controlled placement. In the 1760s and 1770s compagnonnages in other trades—stonecutting, ironworking nail making, and farriery—generated a variety of conflicts beyond placement disputes, including boycotts and walkouts.[52] In Marseille and Aix "uprisings" of compagnons du devoir and gavots in many trades were most significant in the 1770s and 1780s. In 1771 "400 to 500" compagnons "du devoir or gavots" gathered to fight in the plain of Saint Michael. The violent quarrel between sects erupted over control of hiring in various trades. The bakers, who had begun to organize themselves in compagnonnages after midcentury, began a major series of walkouts in the Marseille region in 1786, insisting on an "augmentation of their wages." The masters in Marseille agreed to a raise of three livres per month, which the procureur général of the parlement of Aix hoped would keep the workers who had not walked out at their posts and persuade the "Rebels" to return to the city. By mid-1787 the city's aldermen stated that "public tranquility" had already been "troubled" several times that year by the excesses of the compagnons in various trades, which endangered the citizens and spread "alarm" everywhere.[53] In smaller cities such major disputes were less frequent, but compagnonnages provided a constant base of operations for the control of hiring and retained the potential to organize resistance to economic threats.

The similarities in the labor actions and disputes can be attributed to three interdependent sets of factors. First, given the ever-present and relatively uniform institutions of the church, the trade corporations, and the confraternities, a certain degree of conformity among journeymen's associations, which borrowed elements from these institutions, was in-

51. Philip Hoffman concludes that "both the Catholic and Protestant reformations sought to discipline the populace, to rob it of worldly diversions, joy and levity." Although the Protestants were far more opposed to popular celebrations and rituals than were the Catholics, he maintains that both "waged war on popular culture" and tried to " 'disenchant' the world." See *Church and Community in the Diocese of Lyon, 1500–1789* (New Haven, 1984), pp. 169–70.

52. Cavignac, "Compagnonnage," esp. pp. 396–404, annexe II.

53. AM Marseille, AA 69, 23 July 1771, BB 287, 18 and 19 July 1786, procureur général to intendant, Aix, and AA 70, 21 and 22 May 1787.

evitable. Next, similarities in conflict and association in these old regime cities originated in the major and parallel economic changes occurring throughout much of eighteenth-century France. The trade communities in these cities were under common pressures, and labor conflict reflected shared economic and social conditions. Finally, members of compagnonnages transmitted and diffused their ideas and methods as they traveled on the tour de France. The labor disputes of compagnonnage thus reveal a very consistent pattern of tactics and objectives.

In most cases, master-worker conflict occurred within the framework of rights and privileges established by the corps des métiers. Thus, compagnons' attitudes toward trade corporations were somewhat ambiguous. In Paris, where compagnonnages were not particularly prominent, workers were reported to be "delirious" over the idea of the abolition of the corporations and manifested many signs of disorder in late 1775 and 1776. Yet, most workers had little clear sense of what economic "liberty" meant. Compagnonnages, like other old regime institutions and *corps,* "hedged liberty within a system of constraints, subordinating individual interests to the needs and values of the community."[54] The compagnons' own record books, papers, and letters support the impression that they pursued certain liberties but always within the context of the existing corporate order.

THE COMPAGNONS' STORY: BUILDING BROTHERHOODS AFTER 1750

After midcentury, more varied and complete evidence comes increasingly from the compagnons' own records. These suggest that their associations had been present in many places before 1750 without provoking serious disturbances.[55] The evidence also attests to compagnons' attempts to regulate their brotherhoods more closely. In 1753, for example, compagnon glaziers in Tours returned a letter from their counterparts in Orléans because it had not "at all been written in the accustomed manner" and reprimanded them on several other points of protocol.[56] The example indicates that compagnons were intent on establishing common standards throughout France and took them seriously enough to correct others' mistakes. Although compagnons were

54. Keith M. Baker, "State, Society, and Subsistence in Eighteenth-Century France," *Journal of Modern History* 50 (December 1978): 703.
55. Such papers and registers, which are currently held in public archives, were usually seized in police raids, but the data themselves were recorded under everyday conditions. Unlike interrogations, thus, this evidence was not produced under duress.
56. AD Loiret, B 1988, 16 June 1753, compagnon glaziers, Tours, to compagnon glaziers, Orléans, cited in Germain Martin, *Associations ouvrières,* p. 109.

not always so exacting, ideally they adhered to form, whether they were writing a letter or performing a ritual. With compagnonnages in more and more cities, communication needed to be regular, and practice had to be codified. Major collections of documentary evidence from Mâcon and Bordeaux further illustrate the growing organization and increased labor activity of the compagnonnages in the eighteenth century.

The decade of the 1750s was an active one for compagnons in the Mâconnais. In 1753 an ordinance of the *bailliage et prévôté royale* of Mâcon condemned the "daily disorders" caused by the rivalries of compagnons du devoir and gavots. The ordinance blamed the compagnons du devoir of all trades and ordered their expulsion from Mâcon and environs, giving them three days to leave and forbidding their return. The ruling also forbade innkeepers who called themselves pères and mères of compagnons du devoir from lodging them or permitting their assemblies. Officials exempted gavots, considering them simply "ordinary journeymen who were not part of any association."[57] But documents captured by the police in 1758 at the inn of their père and mère reveal that the gavots were indeed solidly organized. In songs, letters, and formal papers, they express a well-developed sense of group identity, growing out of, but far exceeding, their work. One of the songs depicts them fighting with the tools of their various trades (and ever-present canes) to defend their honor against dèvorants; vaunting their exploits and many charms, the gavots damn the dèvorants' perfidy and fury. Letters record respect for and attachment to their mères and pères, who often served them for long years. Finally, the gavots' *rôle* (statutes) documents their practices in thirty-eight articles, demonstrating their clear sense of the nature and purpose of their union.[58] Although the police raid did not yield the joiners' *registres* (account books), which normally would have included membership and placement records, the rôle nonetheless provides a normative picture of the practices in this trade and sect throughout France.

The gavots' purpose was stated at the outset:

> In the name of the father and the son and the Holy ghost— amen—jesus maria joseph joachim anna

57. AMM, HH 11/11, 2 June 1753.

58. AMM, HH 11/17, 18 January 1757, "Chanson nouvelle," HH 11/20, "Rolle des compagnons menuisiers non du devoir de la ville et faubourg de——," n.d., HH 11/21, 3 July 1758, "Procès verbal de la perquisition chez le nommé Vinçenot, cabaretist dit le père des garçons gavots." This rôle was in use from at least the early 1750s; other papers, including an important cache of letters, date from 1756. The locksmiths non du devoir also lodged chez Vinçenot (a not uncommon practice), but their rôle was not among these papers. For the complete text of the joiners' rôle, see Cynthia M. Truant, "Compagnonnage: Symbolic Action and the Defense of Workers' Rights in France, 1700–1848" (Ph.D. diss., University of Chicago, 1978), appendix 5, pp. 328–34.

> We compagnon joiners all being assembled in the dwelling of
> the père to carry on the good custom that our predecessors have
> left us for the well-being of the masters as well as for that of the
> compagnons.[59]

Like their seventeenth-century counterparts, compagnons continued to
profess concern for the masters' well-being, even though in practice their
own well-being was paramount. Their welfare depended heavily on the
leaders of the *chambre* (local branch) of compagnonnage—the capitaine
and the rôleur—as well as the mère and père. For these gavots, however,
the rôleur, even more than the captain, carried out the most important
business of the local compagnonnage.

The compagnon joiners' rôle devoted the majority of its articles to
defining the rules and rituals of job placement and the rôleur's functions. Fines, usually ten sols, were assessed for any infraction of regulations. The chambre required the new arrival to find the rôleur by going
to various workshops in town and looking for compagnons' names inscribed on the masters' ledgers (article 1). This requirement reveals how
openly compagnonnage could operate in French society and indicates
that minimal literacy was expected, although newcomers may also have
asked if compagnons were present. If other members spotted a new arrival, they were "obliged" to bring him to the rôleur who presented him
to the captain. The captain questioned the new compagnon and examined his papers to determine if he was a member in good standing or a
renégat (a turncoat) and deadbeat. In some sects this meeting was followed by a more formal ceremony of *entrée*, which, in ritualized form,
communicated the expectations of reciprocal hospitality among compagnons and established the new man's right to work in that town. If no
work was available, however, the new compagnon had to leave (Article
2). If he was in need, the captain and four senior compagnons provided
him with enough money to travel to the next town. The rôleur was
obliged to give the departing compagnon a *conduite*—and pay for it himself.[60] It was this sort of good fellowship and interregional network that
authorities found it impossible to supplant, even with placement bureaus
and charity.

The compagnon joiners' rôle carefully described how the rôleur was
to place those workers who remained in town. Once a compagnon was
placed, the rôleur relinquished his post to the next designated compag-

---

59. AMM, HH 11/20, "Rolle," fol. 1. The copyist left a blank on the title page of the rôle
where the name of the city would be. This practice implies standardization and use of the statutes
by this sect's local branches. The rôle, moreover, says nothing specific about conditions in Mâcon.
60. Ibid., fols. 3r and v.

non (articles 2 and 4); compagnons who refused their *tour de rôle* (article 5) were fined. The rôleur's position was short-term, passed on by "turn of the roll" (the membership list), often as frequently as every month or every week. If, however, there were few incoming compagnons or few capable of serving as rôleurs, the position might change hands only every three months.[61] These regulations were intended to ensure that all members had an opportunity to familiarize themselves with the economic and ritual life of compagnonnage, and to guarantee that no one was unfairly burdened or became too powerful, for the rôleur's functions were many and varied. For example, he had to make sure that workers did not change shops without prior notification (Article 22). If a compagnon changed masters, the rôleur certified that he had fulfilled his obligations toward the former master, and if he left town, toward the mère and père (Article 26). The rôleur was to take scrupulous care of the rôle, announce the chambre's annual feast days and monthly masses (compagnons were required to attend mass together on the first Sunday of the month), notify compagnons of meetings, distribute correspondence (after notifying the premier of its arrival), collect fines, and help keep the accounts. Finally, the rôleur's participation at burial ceremonies and conduites (the initiation is not discussed) was crucial. In theory, the frequency with which this post changed hands denotes a strong egalitarian component in the association. Such compagnons would be active and direct participants in exercising authority. Furthermore, the rôleur's multiple functions demonstrate that the social and fraternal support bound up in ritual was not dissociated from or less privileged than economic support.

The most pressing concern of the chambre, outside of placement, was regulating and "civilizing" its members' behavior: there was to be no fighting, excessive drinking, or swearing in the presence of other compagnons, the père and mère, and masters (Article 16).[62] Nor were compagnons to bring shame on their fellow compagnons (Article 17). Compagnons were to observe the utmost loyalty and discretion in the matter of their secrets (Article 20) and be honest and prompt in paying their debts (Article 19). Another rôle, that of compagnon turners in Toulouse, was even more adamant about etiquette: talking out of turn, using the familiar *tu* form, laughing, spitting, sleeping, not being properly dressed, and "breaking wind" during assemblies were deemed un-

---

61. Coornaert, *Compagnonnages*, "Livre de règles," p. 364.

62. This evidence tends to confirm Norbert Elias's argument about the spread of the "civilizing process," although he focuses on the spread of manners and courtesy from aristocratic to bourgeois elites. Here we see the process occurring among artisans. *The Civilizing Process* (New York, 1978), vol. 1: *The History of Manners,* esp. pp. xi–xviii, 35–50, 70–152.

acceptable and liable to fines. This compagnonnage drove the point home by having a member called "Bourguignon le poli."[63] Finally, compagnons' rôles detailed the manner in which members visited the sick, buried the dead, and performed the conduite.

Evidence in Bordeaux confirms and broadens my analysis of prescriptive regulations like those found in Mâcon.[64] By the mid-eighteenth century Bordeaux was an active center of compagnonnage, and archival records there can be used to reconstruct the actual practices of one local brotherhood, the compagnon locksmiths du devoir. Their account books (*registres*) of 1741–1742 and 1757–1761 are divided into tables of various activities, each listing the names of compagnons. For example, the *table d'arrivant* (table of arriving compagnons) records the newcomers' names and places of origin. Other tables listed visits and contributions to sick members, attendance at mass, workshop changes, placement, and serious fines. Records were kept for six-month intervals: from 30 June (the feast of Saint Pierre, the locksmiths' patron) to 5 January; and from 6 January (Epiphany) to 29 June. A new premier compagnon was elected on the first day of each term.

Jean Cavignac discusses these registers in a major article on compagnonnage in Bordeaux, describing it as an "institution created by and for workers to defend their material situation, their salaries, and standard of living" and conclusively demonstrating its socioeconomic importance.[65] As I have noted, Cavignac felt the need to dispel the image of compagnonnage as marginal and esoteric, and therefore, he downplayed the significance of its ritual and social practices. By ignoring such practices, however, he somewhat underestimated the size of the locksmiths' organization. Rather than derive my census from the table d'arrivant, as Cavignac did, I used the more complete and consistent listings in the tables of masses and hospital visitation. Only arriving compagnons had to be registered in the Table d'arrivant, but all members were required to attend mass together and to visit or contribute to the aid of sick compagnons. My estimate of numbers of compagnon locksmiths du devoir in Bordeaux is therefore somewhat larger than Cavignac's. In the final analysis, however, numbers are less significant than the fact that the very nature of these brotherhoods often hides their strength and presence from modern scholars.

Certain features of the registers need clarification. First, the names of compagnons appear to have been written into the table d'arrivant as they arrived in Bordeaux in each six-month period, but the entries are

63. Coornaert, *Compagnonnages*, "Livre de règles," p. 359.
64. ADG, 12 B 280, register for 1741–42, and C 3708, register for 1757–61.
65. Cavignac, "Compagnonnage," p. 377.

not individually dated. Thus, some compagnons may have been in the city almost six months more than others. Second, a number of the same names are repeated for the period 1757–1761. It is impossible to determine whether four usages of "Pierre le bourguignon" represent one man or four. Pierre is obviously a common name, and many compagnons came from the Bourgogne. Furthermore, a compagnon may have left and returned to Bordeaux any time within a six-month period. I counted repeated names as only one case. Thus, from thirty-three repeated registrations, I counted thirteen names, perhaps underestimating the number of compagnons present.[66]

Comparing the table d'arrivant to the *table des messes*, I found that the number of incoming compagnons was always significantly less than the number of compagnons already resident in Bordeaux. None were natives of that city. Residents outnumbered arriving compagnons by roughly 3 to 1 in the first period (1741–1742) and roughly 1.5 to 1 in the second (1757–1761). These ratios suggest that most compagnons stayed in Bordeaux longer than six months. With at least six major cities on the tour for this trade at this time—Dijon, Lyon, Marseille, Toulouse, Bordeaux, and Nantes—if a compagnon stayed six months or more in each location, he would remain in compagnonnage three to four years. And as the possibility of mastership moved beyond the reach of most compagnons by the eighteenth century, the tour may often have lasted even longer.

The sample from the Bordeaux registers permits some further observations. These figures present a pattern of fluctuation rather than sustained growth or decline. Such fluctuation, responding to economic conditions in the region of Bordeaux, indicates that local brotherhoods of compagnonnage were flexible enough to regulate the flow of workers, sending on or calling in compagnons as the situation dictated. On the whole, however, judging from the six-month breakdowns, there tended to be more compagnon locksmiths du devoir passing through and working in Bordeaux from 1758 to 1761 than from 1741 to 1742. Other evidence corroborates the view that by midcentury the compagnonnages had expanded their presence in this region. In 1751 an assembly of compagnon joiners was reported to number 55; another gathering in 1788 numbered 150. In 1765 there were roughly 50 compagnon locksmiths and joiners lodging or meeting at their Mère in Bordeaux. A combined total of 180 compagnon locksmiths, joiners, and stonecutters non du devoir can be counted in 1768. In the same period 250 shoe-

---

66. More extensive data on this question appears in Truant, "Symbolic Action," appendix 6, p. 336.

makers in Bordeaux claimed to be compagnons, even if not officially recognized by other compagnonnages. Reports on brawls reveal that, particularly after 1750, more trades were involved—from locksmiths, joiners, and stonecutters to blacksmiths, nail makers, turners, carpenters, shoemakers, and roofers.[67] Compagnonnages in this era seem to have been relatively open, not elitist, associations.

Another set of data supports this characterization. Local chambres of compagnonnage represented a wide geographical membership (see Map 4). These regions have been identified using the name given to the initiated compagnon, for example, Pierre le maloin. The registers of compagnon locksmiths du devoir do not list the more complex *noms compagnonniques* indicating both the compagnon's origin and something of his character, although such names existed at the time (Ménétra was Parisien le bienvenue). These names nonetheless demonstrate that the compagnons' tour was solidly established and drew on workers throughout France and sometimes even from beyond its borders.[68] The most significant conclusion to be drawn from the Bordeaux registers is that geographical recruitment was very wide-ranging for all periods. If anything, Gascony, the area around Bordeaux, is the least represented in the compagnonnage of the locksmiths du devoir in that city, which indicates that the tour was functioning as it was intended. Data in the table des messes parallel those in the table d'arrivant (see Maps 5 and 6). The north of France as a whole, with the northwest predominating, supplied the largest number of compagnons. The stability of the recruitment pattern in each six-month period, even during periods of expansion, is particularly interesting. Generally, the largest number of compagnons would come from the northwest, followed by the northeast, the southeast, and finally the southwest. Map 6 also illustrates the point made earlier that the table des messes is a better indicator than the table d'arrivant of the number of compagnon locksmiths du devoir in Bordeaux during any six-month period.

Clearly, the members of this compagnonnage pursued the aim of working in other regions of France to learn techniques and trade secrets. And compagnonnages obviously played a central role in easing the tensions generated by the presence of so many workers who were strangers to each other and the region. Ritual practice—in and out of the workplace—became an important factor in creating a sense of community

67. Cavignac, "Compagnonnage," pp. 386–87, 411.

68. Additionally, primarily in Nantes, I have come across about a dozen cases of compagnons from other European countries as well as a few compagnons called "l'Américain," presumably because they had spent time in the Americas or had been born there. Michael Sonenscher has also found a small number of black compagnons in mid-eighteenth-century Bordeaux. *Work and Wages*, pp. 302–3. Such cases reveal the heterogeneity possible in compagnonnage.

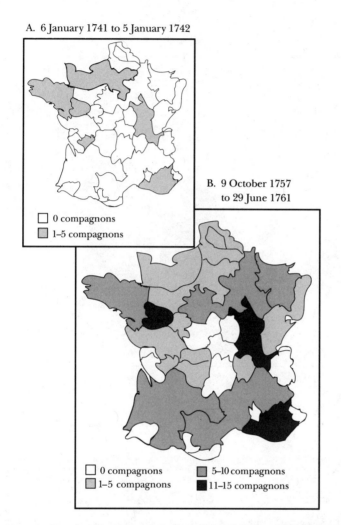

A. 6 January 1741 to 5 January 1742

B. 9 October 1757
   to 29 June 1761

☐ 0 compagnons
▨ 1–5 compagnons

☐ 0 compagnons   ▨ 5–10 compagnons
▨ 1–5 compagnons   ■ 11–15 compagnons

Source: AD Gironde, 12 B 280, register for the period 1741–1742, and C 3708, register for the period 1757–1761. I have classified the origin of the compagnons into provinces based on the geographical indicator in their nicknames (province, subregion, city or town). For example. Pierre le maloin is presumed to come from St. Malo or its environs and is thus counted as coming from the province of Britanny. The origins of six compagnons do not appear on this map: one is unidentified; one is from Germany; one is from Luxembourg; and three are from Piedmont.

MAP 4. Compagnon locksmiths du devoir in Bordeaux: Origin of compagnons by province, based on the *Table d'arrivant*

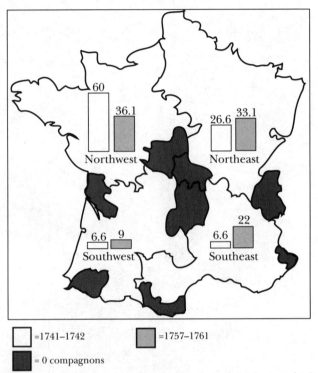

□ =1741–1742   ■ =1757–1761

■ = 0 compagnons

Source: AD Gironde, 12 B 280, register for the period 1741-1742, and C 3708, register for the period 1757–1761.

Note: I have grouped the compagnons' provinces into the following regions: northwest—Anjou, Bretagne, Maine, Orléanais, Poitou, and Touraine: northeast—Alsace, Artois, Bourgogne, Champagne, Comté, Flandre, Ile de France, Lorraine, Nivernais, and Picardie; southwest—Angoumois, Gascogne, Guyenne, Limousin, and Marche; southeast—Dauphiné, Languedoc, Lyonnais, and Provence. These somewhat arbitrary divisions give a rough idea of variations in membership by major region. I am here omitting all foreign compagnons as well as those from unidentified areas (6 in all).

Numbers of compagnons for January 1741 to January 1742: northwest, 9; northeast, 4; southwest, 1; southeast, 1 (total, 15); and for 9 October 1757 to 29 June 1761: northwest, 48; northeast, 44; southwest, 12; southeast, 29 (total, 133, with 1 case unidentified and 5 non-French cases).

MAP 5. Compagnon locksmiths du devoir in Bordeaux: Origin of compagnons by major regions of France, based on the *Table d'arrivant* (percent of total)

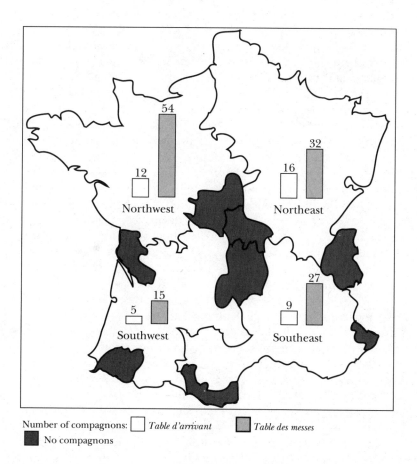

Number of compagnons: ☐ *Table d'arrivant* ▨ *Table des messes*
■ No compagnons

Source: AD Gironde, C 3708, register for two periods: 30 June 1758 to 5 January 1759 and 30 June 1759 to 5 January 1760.

Note: Numbers for the two periods based on the *table d'arrivant* total 42. Those based on the *table des messes* total 128. The names on the *table d'arrivant* are duplicated on the *table des messes* in each six-month period; the names of the compagnons who had remained in Bordeaux longer than six months account for the larger number on the *table des messes*.

MAP 6. Compagnon locksmiths du devoir in Bordeaux: Origin and numbers of compagnons by major regions of France for two six-month periods (comparison of the *Table d'arrivant* and the *Table des messes*)

for these disparate workers. Although the devoir mitigated regional differences for its own members, however, it exacerbated tensions between native and "foreign" compagnons, between married and unmarried compagnons, and between compagnons of different sects.

That we can examine how these compagnons constructed their community is largely due to their own efficient and painstaking record keeping, proof of a marked degree of bureaucratic organization. The registers confirm that the locksmiths du devoir regularly attended their assemblies and the initiations of new members, went to mass together, visited the sick and contributed to their welfare, and buried their dead properly. From the *table des grosses amendes* (major fines), which listed the names of those who failed to perform their duties, we can gain an idea of the range of misdeeds and the concerns and priorities of the compagnons. The infractions recorded in the table des grosses amendes from 30 June 1760 to 5 January 1761 (Table 4.1) can be subsumed under two basic categories: first, offenses against rules regulating work and economic obligations; and second, offenses against rules regulating ritual and social practice. In the first category compagnons were fined, for example, for working twice in the same workshop, unless they first obtained the premier's permission. Although the aim of the compagnonnage was probably to keep its members circulating throughout France, a number of compagnons apparently left town briefly and then returned to work in a shop where they had been employed, without incurring an offense. Another offense against prescribed work practice occurred if the rôleur failed to inform the premier compagnon of a worker's placement; if another compagnon besides the rôleur placed a worker, the offense was far more serious. Because control of hiring was the compagnonnages' primary and most effective economic weapon, premiers and rôleurs tried to adhere closely to the required procedures. The compagnons' economic responsibilities toward compagnonnage were also scrutinized. Many cases of compagnons who failed to bring the money they owed the *chambre* appear in Table 4.1, and in other six-month periods in the table des grosses amendes. None of these registers gives the chambre's total debits and credits, but frequent cases of non-payment or late payment of dues clearly weakened its ability to provide aid to needy members. Despite the problem of indebtedness, nonetheless, compagnonnages generally remained solvent enough to establish and extend credit to their members. For many compagnons, the brotherhood was their only resource.

Compagnonnages raised some of these funds for loans, charity, and sociability by levying fines for (apparently) minor as well as major infractions of the rules, but fines unquestionably had cultural as well as

TABLE 4.1. Table des grosses amendes, 30 June 1760 to 5 January 1761

Name	Reason for fine	Fine (livres)
Claude le bourguignon	Worked twice in the same shop	1
Jacques le comtois	Did not attend a baptism	2
Jean-Pierre le comtois	Did not bring the money he owed	1
Philippe le brie	Missed assembly	1
Mathieu le provençal	Missed assembly	1
Joseph l'avignon	Worked twice in the same shop	1
Joseph l'allemand	Ate before the premier compagnon	1
Pierre le bayonnais	Reported on the compagnons' papers	2
Jean-Pierre le comtois	Did not do his part at a baptism	2
Jean-Bpt. le flamand	Did not bring the money he owed	1
Joseph l'avignon	Worked twice in the same shop	1
Claude le bourguignon	Fought with a compagnon	2
Jean-Bpt. le flamand	Took the holy name of God in vain[a]	2
François l'angevin	Did not bring the money he owed	1
Jacques le guépin	Missed assembly	1
Abraham saintonge	Missed assembly	1
François le languedoc	Consorted with renegades	2
Louis le picard	Did not bring the money he owed	1
Louis le picard	Did not bring the money he owed (second infraction)	1
Joseph l'allemand	Sang out of turn at a baptism	1
Jean-Bpt. le champagne	Acted shamefully at the baptism of an aspirant[b]	2
Philippe le brie	Missed assembly	1
Bertrand le bayonnais	Forgot to call the assembly	1
Jean le languedoc	Forgot to call the assembly	1
François l'angevin	Fought with a compagnon	2
Antoine le provençal	Hit a compagnon	2
Antoine le languedoc	Placed a compagnon without informing the premier compagnon	1
Jean-Bpt. le flamand	Took advantage of Maître Jacques for his profit[c]	2
Bertrand le bayonnais	Talked about the compagnons' papers	2
Jacques le guépin	Ate dinner with the renegades	2
Thomas le flamand	Consorted with the renegades	2
Jean-Pierre le comtois	Did not bring the money he owed	1
Pierre le bordelais	Arrived within the fortnight[d]	2
Claude le bourguignon	Fought with a compagnon	2
Jacques le guépin	Worked twice in the same shop	1

Source: AD Gironde, C 3708, register for 1757–61.

Note: "Baptism" is the term used for initiation.

[a]This entry covers an entire folio-sized page in the register.

[b]This entry covers nearly a quarter of a folio-sized page.

[c]This entry covers one-half of a folio-sized page. The French is, "pour faire du profit à Maître Jacques."

[d]"Pour avoir arriver en quinzaine" means the compagnon arrived at the wrong time during the two-week pay period.

economic functions. Significantly, fines for infractions of duties having to do with ceremonial life were usually double those for other offenses. There were misdeeds, too, that cannot be radically divided into either of my categories. For example, although it was not an "economic" offense, compagnons who consorted with renegades or revealed the chambre's secrets jeopardized the well-being of the whole association. Likewise, compagnons who consistently missed meetings or acted improperly during solemn ceremonies weakened the organization's authority and meaning. One of the most serious crimes reported in the Table des grosses amendes occurred when Jean-Baptiste le champagne "acted shamefully" during an initiation. His offense was recorded in dramatically large script that covered one quarter of the folio page, and he was assessed a heavy, two-livre fine. Two other major offenses were both committed by one Jean-Baptiste le flamand who took God's name in vain and made "profit" from Maître Jacques in some unspecified way. The meaning of "Maître Jacques" here is not defined: the term could stand for the founder of the devoir, but it was also a name given to the rôle or even the chambre's strongbox. Le flamand may have disclosed the devoir's secrets for money or misused its funds; he was further cited for failing to pay his debts. This compagnon clearly flouted serious conventions; his disobedience could eventually erode discipline and unity. Yet, fines also enforced restraint and civility in apparently far less important cases. Joseph l'allemand was fined for singing out of turn at an initiation and for beginning to eat before the premier compagnon. *Politesse*, self-control, and discipline were thus not only elite concerns in the eighteenth century.

Judging from the repeated offenses of Jean-Baptiste le flamand and other compagnons, fines did not always check improper behavior. Like all institutions, compagnonnages had some problems controlling their members, especially since they simultaneously encouraged these young, often high-spirited men to be tough and ready to fight outsiders. When, for example, a local dandy came looking for a fight with the compagnons, Ménétra gave him a pounding with his cane and noted with satisfaction, "That taught him not to mess with and insult the compagnons."[69] Sometimes the compagnons chafed at the devoir's discipline, and they might well talk to renegades, perhaps natives of their region, workers simply regarded as companions. Compagnons also relished "a good joke" on solemn occasions or boasting about secret practices. Yet, as seen in Bordeaux, such transgressions never seriously

69. Ménétra, *Journal de ma vie*, p. 68.

undermined a compagnonnage's abilities to protect its members' interests, place them in jobs, and control the price of their labor.[70]

THE history of the compagnonnages in the eighteenth century reveals a healthy and expanding organization. By at least midcentury, members openly fought for what they called their rights, provoking anxiety and hostility among masters, townspeople, and authorities. The institutional growth and development of the compagnonnages in this era continued to draw on the complex interrelationship of ritual practice and practical considerations. Compagnons codified and implemented principles expressed in their initiation rituals, and compagnonnages became powerful as an early form of labor organization. Through walkouts, control of hiring, and assertion of territorial rights by means of public displays of bravado, ceremonial, and especially brawls, compagnons defended their honor and empowered themselves. Compagnonnage enabled them to maintain and sometimes improve their work conditions.

The possibility of sacrilege no longer greatly concerned officials, who were much more worried about the visible socioeconomic consequences of rituals and other practices. Thus, eighteenth-century authorities acted primarily to curtail the external manifestations of compagnonnage, monitoring and suppressing any public disorder and workshop disruption occasioned by conduites, burial rites, initiations, and the brawling, attacks on authority, and general "debauchery" that followed in their wake. The apparent lack of interest in their content may stem partially from the fact that eighteenth-century police learned little new about the rituals. What they did discover no longer seemed "shocking" or "blasphemous" as it had in the previous century, for secular power and concerns had gained the ascendancy. The operations of compagnonnages in the secular realm, undoubtedly effective, were inextricably bound up in their identity as culturally constructed communities built on laboring and living together, ritual practice, and a shared, mythic past.

70. Cavignac, "Compagnonnage," pp. 404–5.

CHAPTER 5

Eighteenth-Century Rituals
of Daily Life

I was received [a] compagnon du Devoir and the compagnons made me recopy, in its entirety, the rôle or that
which was called Maître Jacques, or, better yet, the Devoir,
and [I] was named Parisian the Welcome.
> —Jacques-Louis Ménétra, *Journal de ma vie*

Jacques-Louis Ménétra's words provide some of the most direct evidence about ritual in the daily life of compagnonnage in the eighteenth
century. Yet, as valuable as his long autobiographical account is, it does
not stand alone. In this chapter I examine it along with the written
testimony of many other compagnons. Ménétra may have hoped to publish his journal, but it remained a private account, virtually unknown
until its fortuitous discovery and publication in 1982. Other accounts
written by eighteenth-century compagnons survived and became known
because they were seized in police raids and later placed in state archives.
Although not as detailed as Ménétra's account on some questions, certain of these archival records—letters, registers, and statutes—are
equally personal and revealing about the daily concerns and practices of
compagnons and their brotherhoods. Despite the silences and omissions
they share with all texts, they form one of the best collections to date
for examining the uses and potential of the written word by workers in
the old regime.

FORMS OF RITUAL PRACTICE

Becoming a Compagnon

Studying the eighteenth-century initiations of compagnons poses major challenges: unlike either the seventeenth or the nineteenth century,

this century yields relatively few complete initiation accounts. (See Appendix III). Generally, the verifiable accounts are sketchy, and the authenticity of the more detailed accounts must be treated with more reservation.[1] The relatively more complete accounts of seventeenth and nineteenth-century initiations tempt one to assume these rituals remained largely unchanged. Such, however, was not necessarily the case.[2] One of the most authentic accounts, found by Michael Sonenscher in the municipal archives of Troyes, is that of a 1782 initiation of compagnon leather dressers (*mégisseurs*): this relatively brief and uncomplicated account lacks a number of elements found in earlier initiations.[3] I thus begin by assuming little, starting with smaller pieces, and building toward

1. Three of the most elaborate accounts were edited by Joseph Pradelle, an early twentieth-century compagnon turner who wrote extensively on compagnonnage and edited two of its journals, the *Union compagnonnique* and the *Ralliement de Tours*. Pradelle does not explain why he was allowed to publish such sensitive material, nor does he provide a context for his accounts, and internal evidence casts doubt on his dating. See Joseph Pradelle, "Legendes, initiations, règlements, moeurs, et coutumes de compagnonnage" (c. 1700), and "Moeurs et coutumes—compagnonnage" (1743), both in Musée du Vieux Toulouse, mss. cahiers 13 (dated May 1941) and 7 (n.d.); Pradelle, "Réception des compagnons menuisiers et serruriers de devoir de liberté sous l'ancien régime à Toulouse," *Mémoires de l'Académie des sciences, inscriptions, et belles-lettres de Toulouse*, ser. 13, 3 (1941): 135–53. Two other accounts, though not without problems, permit comparisons that help to establish their authenticity. The first, consisting of two articles from the 1731 "Livre de règles" of the turners du devoir in Bordeaux, art. 41, "Concernant la Réception," and art. 42, "Concernant le serment de fidélité au Devoir," is reproduced in Emile Coornaert, *Les Compagnonnages en France du Moyen Age à nos jours* (Paris, 1966), from the Archives de l'Association ouvrière. The statutes are far longer than any I have discovered in public archives (55 articles) and also exceptional in having two articles on initiation, but they are otherwise similar to others I have looked at. I believe this document to be genuine, but it seems likely that some articles were added or revised after 1731. The other document—BN, mss. Collection Joly de Fleury, 421, fols. 366–74, "Lettre en form de dénonciation au ministre publique, d'une compagnie ou association formée dans les villes de Châlons, Angers, et Le Mans, sous le nom de compagnons blanchers ou chamoiseurs du devoir," edited and published by Paul-M. Bondois as "Un Compagnonnage au XVIIIe siècle," *Annales historiques de la Révolution française* 6 (1929): 588–99—raises the fewest doubts as to its authenticity. This text, the product of an anonymous denunciation, can be read in much the same way as the seventeenth-century initiation accounts and can be corroborated by contemporary archival data. It also appears consistent with the eighteenth-century archival account in the AM Troyes, FF Supplément, police investigation of initiations and activities of compagnon leather dressers du devoir, 1782.

2. Germain Martin, for example, concluded, based on extensive archival work, that eighteenth-century practices "reveal a less complex and rigorous formalism" than they had earlier. Arguing that compagnons' ritual practices varied by city and sect and were kept orally until the nineteenth century, Martin posits a strong link between the growing complexity of nineteenth-century ritual and the increased influence of Freemasonry on compagnonnage. *Les Associations ouvrières au XVIIIe siècle (1700–1792)* (Geneva, 1974 [Paris, 1900]). This view has some merit. Nevertheless, while the complexity of some aspects of ritual and symbolism increased in the nineteenth century (as did Masonic influence), other factors played key roles in this trend, as subsequent chapters will demonstrate. Furthermore, there is eighteenth-century evidence that compagnons in at least some trades had recorded and standardized many of their (complex) ritual practices.

3. AM Troyes, FF Supplément, 30 August 1782. Michael Sonenscher found these documents (in an unclassified series) during research in the communal archives in June 1982 and has generously shared his notes with me. Unfortunately, the papers were not reclassified. I was unable to locate them during research in Troyes in January 1989.

a more complete picture of eighteenth-century initiations. But the initiation was only the beginning of a worker's life as a compagnon. As will be seen in the rest of this chapter, one really became a compagnon by the practice of the "rituals of daily life," those more public and more frequent practices of solidarity and sociability.

Ménétra's memoirs permit unusual access to such practices. This wily compagnon glazier is a self-styled anticlerical freethinker and dashing libertine. He tells us a great deal about the *vacations* ("vocations" or trades) of compagnonnage, as he calls them, but says very little about his own initiation in the summer of 1758, well before the more usual date of the feast of the glazier's patron, Saint Luke (18 October). Ménétra's complete statement about his initiation bears repeating:

> I was received [a] compagnon du Devoir and the compagnons made me recopy, in its entirety, the rôle or that which was called Maître Jacques, or, better yet, the Devoir, and [I] was named Parisian the Welcome.[4]

This brief passage nonetheless says some important things: Ménétra was "received" and he recopied the written rôle (yielding an extra copy). Furthermore, he makes a link between this "Maître Jacques" and the "Devoir." Finally, he is renamed.

Ménétra tells us nothing about the ceremony itself, unless the ceremony *was* the recopying of the "Maître Jacques"—unlikely in an age when not all compagnons were able to read and write. Ménétra does not even mention whether other novices were initiated with him or if a celebration followed. His very next words are "My boss worked for the abbey of Beaumont-lès-Tours." He then tells about work at the abbey and an accident he sustained there. The allusion to initiation is casual— almost a throwaway. We can tease out more information: Ménétra's renaming suggests the reception included some sort of baptism. Other eighteenth-century accounts refer to baptism—without the detail of the seventeenth-century accounts—and state that the other compagnons chose the new name.[5] Ménétra also mentions becoming a *compagnon fini*, or "full-fledged" compagnon—revealing levels of seniority above that of novice and compagnon. Finally, he provides a few other fleeting references to initiations, mentioning that when he was premier compagnon in Lyon "21 compagnons were received at the Mère between midnight

---

4. Jacques-Louis Ménétra, *Journal de ma vie*, ed. Daniel Roche (Paris, 1982), pp. 50–51.
5. Nineteenth-century accounts explain that the new name derived from the other compagnons' assessment of the initiate's character.

and 1 A.M." on the feast of Saint Luke.[6] The time is clearly significant, and it recalls evidence from much earlier initiations. Also typical are the date and the initiation of a group rather than an individual.

Whether Ménétra chose not to discuss initiations more fully because they were ceremonies he regarded (or took an oath to regard) as sacred and secret or whether he minimizes commentary because he found the process itself of slight importance is harder to determine. Ménétra lavished detail on the feasting, parading, and finery (ribbons, dress, coiffure) associated with the initiation he presided over during the feast of Saint Luke. His own initiation *may* have been simple and straightforward—like filling out a union card today—but it seems more likely that it was accompanied by many of the usual details and festivities. I will return to the possible motives for Ménétra's taciturnity after an investigation of other eighteenth-century initiations which helps illuminate what Ménétra leaves obscure.

The table des grosses amendes (Table 4.1) of the compagnon locksmiths of Bordeaux, which lists compagnons who had been fined for committing offenses against the devoir, is a valuable reference.[7] Among the thirty-five infractions recorded the six months from 30 June 1760 to 5 January 1761, four relate to initiation, or "baptism," as it was called: Jacques le comtois, did not attend a baptism; Jean-Pierre le comtois, did not do his part at a baptism; Joseph l'allemand, sang out of turn at a baptism; and Jean-Baptiste le champagne, acted shamefully at the baptism of an aspirant. This compagnonnage, thus, practiced baptism of their *aspirants* (a term Ménétra uses), and its members had a formalized set of expectations about this performance. Compagnons who failed to attend, failed to do their part, or acted shamefully were fined the large sum of two livres, the compagnons' highest penalty, about equal to a week's pay. Even not knowing when to begin singing merited a fairly stiff fine of one livre.

One wonders particularly about Jean-Baptiste le champagne. Had he begun postinitiation merriment and drinking just a bit too soon? Was he playing tricks, even mocking the ceremony? We know Ménétra always enjoyed a good joke. Once on his tour he made up a "pseudo-devoir," the "compagnons of the loaf" (*compagnons de la croûte*). He and his buddies "received" innumerable compagnons in the next three months. The joke caught on famously, and with his usual bravado, Ménétra claimed that "everywhere in France, everyone wanted to be [part] of the

---

6. Ménétra, *Journal de ma vie*, pp. 52, 125–26. Roche says compagnonnage had three degrees of membership: *aspirant* (novice), *compagnon initié* or *reçu* (initiate), and *compagnon fini* or *ancien*, but I question how widespread the use of *compagnon fini* was before the nineteenth century.

7. ADG, C 3708, register for 1757–61.

loaf." Its *réception* consisted primarily in buying a bottle of wine, drinking it and eating the loaf of bread. That Ménétra's compagnons "took communion" to become members of "the loaf" suggests that his own initiation into compagnonnage included a form of communion as well. Furthermore, just as the Sorbonne condemned the compagnonnages for blaspheming *church* practices, the compagnons du devoir quickly chastised what they indicated was all too obvious mockery of *their* practices. Ménétra received an extremely formal letter, signed by "all the premier compagnons of all the trades on the tour de France," requiring him to put an end to the "Devoir de la croûte." Ménétra had hit too close to home. What he laughed off as a prank and a bit of "pure amusement," the devoir's officials took seriously.[8] Such dangerous play struck at their concept of the honor and mystery of compagnonnage—which Ménétra himself ardently defended on other occasions.

The compagnon basketmakers du devoir in Orléans in the 1760s left records that deepen our knowledge of eighteenth-century initiations. Among these records was a song glorifying the compagnon basketmakers and recounting their recent history: the masters had "broken" their devoir in 1764, but the compagnons quickly reestablished themselves. Perhaps it was continuing conflict with the masters which made it necessary to "baptize" a fairly sizable group of nine novices in 1765.[9] An example of the baptismal record follows: "Chartrain received baptism. He was named 'ready to drink' by Bethune the merry and Valencienne the torment, godfather and godmother. Thus was he named."[10] The basketmakers' initiations apparently occurred under less than ideal conditions. Evidence indicates that the only two previously initiated compagnons present during the ceremony were the godfather and "godmother" for four of the novices; these four served in turn as godparents to the remaining novices. It was not typical practice to use new initiates as godparents but, apparently, an act of necessity to build up membership. This case is significant in documenting how an actual initiation could vary from ideal procedure. It is also rare among eighteenth-century initiations in mentioning godfathers and godmothers, a link to seventeenth-century ceremonies. Compagnons were already fictive "brothers," living and sharing food at the "Mère." Baptism, a common,

8. Ménétra, *Journal de ma vie*, p. 132.

9. Jules Doinel and Camille Bloch, eds., *Archives du Loiret: Inventaire sommaire des archives départementales*, 10 vols. (Orléans, 1900), 3:45, citing AD Loiret, B 1988; 25 November 1765, commissaire de police, supplique du procureur du roi [1765], and song of the compagnons vanniers du devoir [1764].

10. Germain Martin, *Associations ouvrières*, pp. 106–8, citing AD Loiret, B 1988, 1767 [events of 1765]. Some discrepancies exist between Martin's account and the archival record reported in Doinel and Bloch, *Archives du Loiret*, pp. 45–46.

unambiguous religious practice, further enlarged the network of fictive kin who could presumably aid and protect them as could real godparents.

These documents place the novice's renaming in relief. Like the *noms companonniques* found in other eighteenth-century evidence, the basket-makers' nicknames or surnames fell into two fairly distinct categories. The most common and popular names conveyed a sense of the spirited, fraternal, and sometimes rowdy life of compagnons who were "welcome," "merry," "diverting," "ready to drink," or the "ruin of the girls." Other names proclaimed a compagnon's prowess and audacity as the "conqueror" or "ruin" of rival sects. With similar bravado, compagnons sometimes refused to give any name or tossed off an insolent rejoinder in official encounters. In a dispute over the distribution of compagnons in workshops in Nantes in 1762 guild officials asked a compagnon tailor his names. He replied, " 'I don't give a damn about it'—those are the names that I bear on my tour de France.'"[11] Thus, beyond confirming their new status and expressing certain character traits, compagnons names' could be used to deflect and resist official inquiries.

Evidence of the further requirements for proper initiation, called the *réception,* is revealed in a letter of 1751 from compagnon glaziers near Paris to those in Orleans: aspirants had to buy colored ribbons and pay for a mass and a feast (with most of the money going for the last item). In an interesting (and early) tie to Freemasonry novices also paid a fee for white gloves. In 1753 glaziers in Tours announced the reception of a new member to their fellow compagnons in Orléans. They asked, "Are we not all *enfants de* Maître Jacques? We think it better to fight than suffer any insult."[12] Once initiated, the compagnons passed over from one state into another, gained a new status, entered a new family, and were pledged to defend this common family against all affronts. Thus, while details could vary, compagnons had certain requirements and set practices, including celebrations, which were integral to the process.

One wonders, however, about what seems to be missing in eighteenth-century accounts: symbolic communions and passions. Postinitiation feasts, of course, are amply documented, but with few symbolic counterparts. The testing of novices, with its parallels to the Passion, is minimized or nonexistent. Was the same true of the infamous oaths and secrecy that played such a role in the previous century? Apparently, those

11. René Blanchard, ed., *Ville de Nantes: Inventaire sommaire des archives communales antérieures à 1790,* vol. 3, série GG (suite), HH, II et supplément (Nantes, 1919), p. 119, quoting AMN, HH 169. One of the most interesting examples of the name *vainquer* was "Américain le vainquer," perhaps suggesting that this compagnon had fought in the French and Indian wars. AM Marseille, FF 206, "Copie des trois billets," 1766–67.

12. Germain Martin, *Associations ouvrières,* pp. 107–8, letters to compagnon glaziers in Orléans.

wishing to join continued to take oaths. As seen in Chapter 4, authorities in Nantes in the 1740s and 1750s issued and enforced an edict requiring all workers in joining, saddlery, tailoring, and wigmaking to appear before police magistrates and renounce "their oaths to the devoir of compagnonnage."[13] How could the roughly 162 joiners, 22 saddlers, and 62 tailors who came forward forswear their oaths? Of course, coerced renunciations are suspect: compagnons may have acted expediently, to survive and establish associations elsewhere. But the number of compagnons and the speed with which they recanted is interesting. Seventeenth-century compagnons were threatened with dire consequences if they revealed their oaths, although some of them broke under questioning or the pangs of conscience. Did eighteenth-century compagnons take their oaths less seriously, or were their oaths now not so solemn?

Evidence from an initiation of compagnon leather dressers in Troyes reveals the continuing importance of the oath to the "making" of compagnonnage. It also demonstrates that some journeymen were (or felt) coerced into taking the oath and were willing to go to the authorities with their objections. One such compagnon, twenty-one-year-old Jean-Baptiste Pirey (called Mâconnais) testified against those he said had forced him to join the devoir. The ceremony he described "consisted in making the *récipiendaire* kneel on a napkin, in pouring wine on his head while saying, child I baptize you in the name of the Father, and the Son and the Holy Spirit, and in making the *récipiendaire* swear that he will always hold to his compagnonnage and . . . say nothing of that which has happened." Jacques Minder, a newly initiated compagnon of nineteen, corroborated Pirey's version; he recalled "kneeling and being baptized with wine and swearing on one's blood that one will never reveal anything of that which went on in the assemblies of the *associés;* after which one was given a name; they gave the depositioner the name of *aimable.*"[14] Both considered the oath a central aspect of the ceremony. Minder brought a complaint against the compagnonnage for compelling him to this agreement while he was drunk, and he further objected to being forced to pay fifteen livres before his initiation and another fifteen livres later. Not much else is learned about the ceremony itself, although de-

13. AMN, FF Audiences de police: joiners (1743, 1745, 1750); saddlers (1750); tailors (1743). See also Cynthia M. Truant, "Independent and Insolent: Journeymen and Their 'Rites' in the Old Regime Work Place," in *Work in France: Representations, Meaning, Organization, and Practice,* ed. Steven Laurence Kaplan and Cynthia J. Koepp (Ithaca, 1986), p. 154.

14. AM Troyes, FF Supplément, 9 March 1782 and 28 August 1782. Pirey, who came from Cluny, worked for Pierre Berthier; Minder worked for Louis Berthier. This incident is one of the few archival cases specifically related to this trade; it is not clear how active the leather dressers were in compagnonnage at this time.

tails emerge about preparations for it and subsequent celebrations, as well as their effects on compagnonnage and the outside world.

Officials did all they could to contain the rowdy celebrations that usually followed initiations, and they continued to prohibit the illegal oaths, but eighteenth-century authorities appear to have been almost indifferent to the content of the rituals. Whether these practices were sacrilegious or Freemasonic hardly mattered; what mattered was what compagnons did in public. In 1767 the procureur général of the parlement of Paris, Guillaume-François-Louis Joly de Fleury, received a lengthy and detailed denunciation of the initiation and other ritual practices of the compagnons *blanchers-chamoiseurs* (dressers of soft leathers such as chamois) du devoir but seemed quite uninterested. He failed to pursue the case even though the manuscript may well have been the work of a police informant, who warned that the devoirs of the compagnons were not just pernicious and libertine from a religious standpoint but a threat to production and public tranquility in a number of cities in the kingdom. At the top of the informer's cover letter was a notation, presumably written by Joly de Fleury: "Only the oath deserves condemnation. The rest seems merely common *[de la misère]* and puerile!"[15]

For the scholar, however, this account is far from banal, despite the problems of its source.[16] The author, for example, reveals that the initiated compagnon received a detailed *lettre patente,* a certificate to carry with him while on the road; the letter was deposited in a coffer at the Mère while the bearer was working in a particular town. The chamois dressers' certificates provided far more extensive information on the initiate's origins (for example, names of his father and mother, specific place of birth) than did, for example, the basketmakers' letters. These certificates also made some references to parts of the initiation ceremony, were signed by all the compagnons present, and were "sealed" with a *pavillion,* a paper cutout shaped like a key, with something like a fleur-de-lis at the top.

Like the leather dressers, these chamois dressers had no objection to

15. BN, Coll. Joly de Fleury, 421, mss. fol. 372. For additional information, see the published edition of this manuscript, "Un Compagnonnage au XVIIIe siècle," ed. Bondois. On fol. 366 there is a note, possibly written by Joly de Fleury, stating that the chamois dressers' oath imitated that of the Freemasons, but this is really not the case. The practices in this document tend to imitate Christian or older popular beliefs and practices and are much closer to the compagnons' seventeenth-century rituals than to those of Freemasonry. Revisions made in the chamois dressers' practices in the nineteenth century, however, were clearly influenced by Masonry.

16. Further research in the cities of Châlons, Angers, and Le Mans might well confirm these data. Discovery of a set of certificates such as those described in this paragraph would be invaluable for a more definitive knowledge of initiation procedures and membership in this devoir of compagnonnage.

conducting their ceremonies during the day. The ceremony in the complaint took place on a Sunday afternoon at the Mère. The room used,
however, was to have no communicating doors, and it was completely
darkened—all chinks, apertures, and windows closed up. A compagnon
stood guard outside the door to the room. The kneeling aspirant was
asked: "Comrade, do you desire to be Received?" If the answer was yes,
the aspirant was than asked if he had ten écus to give them. Once the
money was paid, the compagnon was asked if he "truly promised not to
Reveal to anyone—father, mother, relatives, friends or anyone else—that
which one will tell you." If he so promised, he took the oath with one
hand raised and the other on Le Livre, that is, the Bible. The oath had
a sort of codicil, for the new compagnon had to promise to help any
(fellow) compagnon who found himself in a fight, "to the best of his
ability" and even "at all cost," as if he were defending himself.[17]

The baptism of the new compagnon took place next. The compagnons
undid his hair and left it all disheveled. After the aspirant took the oath
a second time, four tapers were lit. A compagnon holding a bottle of
wine in one hand and a jug of water in the other poured these liquids
equally over the head of the aspirant (the account does not indicate if
he is kneeling). The compagnon officiating was to make a cross and say
"in the name of the father, the son, and the holy spirit I Baptize you."
The wine and water that had poured over the aspirant's head were
caught in a basin and given to him to drink with the words "Comrade,
you must indeed drink this, because this is the pure blood of the Compagnons." In the final part of the ceremony the aspirant was asked what
name he wished to take "in consideration of his baptism" and was to
choose by lot one of three names selected for him.[18]

One of the most important aspects of this document is its indication
that the new compagnon was given some instruction in the other ceremonies of the compagnons, or as the document put it, "that which must
be known, and praticed having been Received Compagnon in order to
travel [as a member]."[19] Thus, the rest of the text revealed details of
ceremonies such as those of the entry and the leave-taking, the first meal
the compagnon took with those in a new town, and the procedures at

17. BN, Coll. Joly, 421, fol. 367.
18. Ibid., fol. 367v.
19. Ibid., fol. 368. In French this reads, "Ce qu'il faut scavoir, et pratiquer etant Reçeu
Compagnon pour pouvoir Roulleur." That the word roulleur is used rather than, for example,
"faire son tour de France" suggests a link with the office of the rôleur. Each compagnon would
certainly have to know these practices in order to fulfill this key role. If compagnons were given
these instructions early on in their membership, as this document suggests, it is more likely that
the post of rôleur could be passed around in a fairly regular and equitable manner among all
members.

the monthly meeting. These details included the intricate toasts, the gestures, the "secret words," and some of the songs, which all compagnons had to know to perform their ceremonial duties.

Some aspects of the chamois dressers' initiation are mirrored in one of the most complete eighteenth-century initiation accounts, articles 41 and 42 of the "Livre des règles" of the compagnon turners du devoir in Bordeaux. The turners put far more stress on elements of rank, hierarchy, and Catholic symbolism than did the chamois dressers. Yet, while demanding that their members be Catholics and even recite some prayers, the compagnon turners had no compunction in substituting, for example, Maître Jacques for the Trinity in their appropriation of Catholic language and practice. On the feast of their patron, Saint Michael, all the compagnons gathered for the reception (no specific time or place is stated); the compagnons stood according to their "turn [on the membership roll] and rank." Anyone knowing of anything to be said against any aspirant had to speak then; candidates had to be Catholic and in good health. The rôleur brought the first aspirant forward: he was left at the door and had to request entry three times. After the second request he was blindfolded and remained so throughout the rest of the ceremony, until swearing his oath. The aspirant removed his hat and gave any personal objects, such as "firearms [!], knives", to the rôleur, who put them in the hat. Each candidate was thoroughly examined, mostly in the form of chanted questions and responses, first by the rôleur and then by the premier compagnon.[20]

The aspirant was told early on that the reception would cost twenty-five francs and was warned of the "great tests" and "great dangers" to which he would soon be exposed. Kneeling, the aspirant made the sign of the cross, recited the Our Father and Hail Mary, and crossed himself again. After his prayers, he had to make a circuit of the initiation chamber on his knees, guided by the rôleur and coterie. After this the "accustomed tests" took place, but the text gives no details on them and their dangers. Next, the rôleur and coterie took off the aspirant's frock coat (habit), put it on the table, and laid the aspirant down on top of it. All this was to proceed in dead earnest; the attendant compagnons were to keep silent under pain of fine—perhaps implying that some levity occasionally broke out. The premier next named all the compagnons present and the aspirant chose a godfather. Then came the baptism. The premier held his right hand above the aspirant's face, saying "On my honor and conscience, before God and the Compagnons, Child! I baptize you in the name of Maître Jacques! in the name of the Compag-

20. "Livre des règles," in Coornaert, Compagnonnages, pp. 375–77.

nons!" After the aspirant received his new name, his godfather made him drink a cup of water and salt.

When all the aspirants had finished this part of the ceremony, they were brought into another room, where each "newly received" compagnon swore an "oath of fidelity to the devoir." Holding his right hand over a cup containing bread and wine, he vowed "not to reveal the Devoir to Father, mother, brothers, sisters, relatives, friends or confessors, or to anyone in this world on pain of mortal sin or damnation of my soul!" The new compagnons repeated the oath twice more before they drank the wine, ate the bread, and paid their fees. All the compagnons then embraced, addressing each other by the familiar *tu*. The most senior compagnons instructed new members in the devoir but told them nothing about becoming a *compagnon fini*, which would occur in another *Ville de Devoir*. Elaborate celebrations, held in conjunction with Saint Michael's day, followed the réception.[21]

These examples of eighteenth-century initiations depict a relatively wide range of variation. Within a fairly consistent framework, actual initiations might be more spontaneous or more formal as circumstances and desires permitted. In the seventeenth century, according to the accounts, initiations were carried out by properly designated individuals acting according to specific scripts, using precise words, gestures, and objects. Judging by the accounts of the turners and the chamois dressers, such detailed prescriptions could have been carried over into the next century, presumably in written form. The other eighteenth-century cases, however, reveal less elaborate Christian (or pseudo-Christian) symbolism, language, and trappings. Even the turners' intricate communion does not mention the use of religious or mock-religious objects. Moreover, both the chamois dressers' and the turners' accounts, with communions in which the initiate drinks wine or eats bread or both, provide no record of a dramatic reenactment of the Passion like those of the seventeenth century. Some of these changes may have resulted from the Sorbonne's prosecution of compagnonnage. The very imitation of Catholic Communion, of course, invokes the Passion. And the chamois dressers' transformation of "baptismal" wine (and water) into "the pure blood of the Compagnons" created a vivid image of a secular "passion" by which compagnons had died (and should be ready to die) for their beliefs.

---

21. Ibid., pp. 376, 377. Note the sorts of retribution threatened for betrayal of the oath (mortal sin, eternal damnation). This attribution of divine powers to compagnonnage was ironic, considering that its secrets were not to be revealed even to one's confessor, quite contrary to the church's tenets. Other trades tended to menace initiates with human punishments (expulsion, beatings, death) for betrayal of the oath.

The oath and some type of baptism remained centrally important. The text of the oaths and the procedure for taking them were also quite similar to those found in the seventeenth century. Like the seventeenth-century saddlers, the turners demanded that the new compagnon reveal nothing to a list of persons which includes a cleric. Whereas the saddlers began their list with "priest, cleric," however, the turners put the confessor at the end, after parents, relatives, and friends. Perhaps saddlers were more concerned about priests because of their Huguenot members. As to the manner of swearing, the seventeenth-century shoemaker swore "on his Faith, his part of Paradise, or . . . his God, chrism and baptism"; the saddler swore on the New Testament and the "30 denarii." In the eighteenth century the turner swore on the bread and wine; the chamois dresser swore on the Bible; the leather dresser swore on his blood. The chamois dressers, like all of the five trades condemned for compagnonnage in the seventeenth century, baptized their aspirants only after they took the oath. In an important twist, the turners and the leather dressers baptized their aspirants *before* the oath. One could argue that the "great tests" to which the aspirant turner was subjected were equivalent to the trial of the oath. Moreover, in other accounts, the oath was usually repeated again after the baptism. In the case of the leather dressers, the brevity of the account, along with the circumstances (prior drinking and coercion), may indicate that the performance was rushed or jumbled.

Although it is crucial to know that detailed initiation accounts existed in the eighteenth century, the growth of the devoirs of compagnonnage—in numbers, trades, and cities—in that era meant that compagnons might be initiated without meeting all the criteria outlined. Initiation nonetheless continued to serve the function of changing the young worker's status and assimilating him into a new corporate body. Even Ménétra was undeniably caught up in the spirit of compagnonnage: he was skeptical and critical of clerical hypocrisy and superstition, not of his devoir's regulations and code of honor. Coupled with other evidence, Ménétra's story demonstrates that when compagnons could conduct their rituals more formally, they did; but when circumstances did not permit adherence to set practice, performance was much freer—perhaps even carefree.

Compagnons applied this same pragmatism to their oaths and secrets. An air of mystery remained part of the identity of compagnonnage even if its "secret" was never absolute. If threatened by the law, some compagnons recanted, but others refused to submit to interrogations, skipping town or joining the army to avoid surrendering to authorities.[22]

22. Truant, "Independent and Insolent," pp. 170–71.

This code of secrecy created divisions and distinctions among compagnons, between compagnons and masters, and between compagnons and agents of church and state, but these divisions were not permanent or impermeable. Some masters had themselves been compagnons; clerics sometimes sheltered compagnons; compagnons recanted or stopped being members of their compagnonnage. Secrecy, whatever its limits, reinforced the solidarity of each devoir. The aura of mystery surrounding the initiation allowed compagnons to perceive their new status as special, shared only with chosen "brothers." Through initiation they created an important place for themselves in French society.

Entrées and Conduites: Off and On the Road Again

Once initiated, compagnons assimilated the devoir's basic values and rules in various ritualized practices, of which welcoming and leave-taking ceremonies (entrées and conduites) were among the most frequent and important. An example of the entée is found in the rôle of the compagnon turners du devoir of Bordeaux, dated 1731. After the new arrival had greeted the premier compagnon, the rôleur performed the ceremony. The exchange began with the singing of three phrases (not stated). Then the rôleur and the new compagnon performed the *guillebrette,* a ritual embrace, and the ceremony proper began:

> *L'arrivant* [the new arrival]: My *Pays,* I come here from ——. I bear many greetings for you, from the père, the mère, and from all the *jolis* compagnon turners of the City and environs of ——, passing as much from here as to there; and if there is work in the City, you will allow me to participate in it.
> *Le Rôleur:* My *Pays,* may God bless the père, the mère, and all the *jolis* compagnon turners of . . . ——, passing as much from here as to there without forgetting the messenger who brings the news!
>
> . . . . .
>
> *Le Rôleur:* My *Pays,* do you know the secret words?
> *L'arrivant:* Yes, my *Pays!*
> *Le Rôleur:* How many are there?
> *L'arrivant:* There are eight; three above, and five below.
> *Le Rôleur:* My *Pays,* repeat them!
> *L'arrivant:* Jésu (1), Maria (2), Joseph (3), et sanctoe [*sic*] (4) Michaele (5) ora (6) pro (7) nobis (8).

The arrivant sang these words and then embraced the rôleur again in "a joyful welcome."[23] This ceremony verified his credentials and integrated him into the new community. It emphasized the mobility, continuity, and brotherhood of compagnonnage. The phrase "passing as much from here as to there" (or "there to here") invoked the connection among the cities on the tour. Rites of hospitality and the formal exchange of greetings were common practices of the compagnons, reinforcing bonds among members and with mères and pères on the tour.

The term *pays* (country or region), like "brother" in a monastic order, evoked the compagnons' bonds. Although compagnons sometimes used the term brother, it is far less common than *pays* or *coterie* (set, or circle). The use of *pays* articulated the fact that compagnons came from all over France. A fixed component of compagnons' new names was their place of origin, underlining the ability of compagnonnages to unite workers from diverse areas without denying regional attributes. One of the principal goals of the tour was to educate workers by exposing them to regional variation in customs, values, and skills. The use of "secret words" in the turners' entrée reveals continuing Catholic influence and also how open this secrecy could be; the use of such common Christian formulas was a convenient way of linking wider networks of compagnons throughout France.

As much or more attention was devoted to the conduite, the elaborate and fraternal leave-taking that assured departing compagnons of the loyalty of those present while anticipating the hospitality of those awaiting him. The conduite reinforced solidarity and trust among highly mobile workers and mitigated the potential dangers and hostilities of the road for the itinerant worker. The compagnons' attitudes toward the conduite and its importance may be reconstructed from evidence in the mid-eighteenth-century statutes of compagnon joiners non du devoir of Mâcon. Whereas the rôle gave minimal attention to the entrée, six of the thirty-eight articles dealt with the proper performance of the conduite, and several other articles referred to the ceremony indirectly. In a show of solidarity, all the compagnons were to attend the ceremony and contribute at least thirty sols (article 29), primarily for the wine, a vital ceremonial element. The order and language of the toasts (*santés*) were carefully recorded. Once the compagnons assembled, probably near the edge of town, the toasts began.

23. "Livre des règles," in Coornaert, *Compagnonnages*, pp. 360–61. In Figures 1 and 2 compagnons perform the *guillebrette*. *Joli*, literally "handsome," meant "hail fellow" and like *brave* was a favorite title among compagnons.

Article 32

For the first toast . . . one will say, to the health of the compagnon who is the *battant aux champs* [literally the one "hitting the road"], without forgetting those who are still working in the city, and the *battant aux champs* will toast [those] who are still working in the city without forgetting those who are departing.

Article 33

For the second, the toast will be for the compagnons of the place to which one is going without forgetting those of the place one is leaving, and the departing compagnon will toast the health of the compagnons of the place he is leaving, without forgetting . . . those in the place he is going.

Article 34

For the third toast, the captain will drink with the departing compagnon, the right foot in front and the right arm crossed [over his chest]; he will say, to our health, to the health of you all, and then to the health of everyone there; all the compagnons say the same thing in their turn.[24]

These involved and repetitive toasts, seen earlier in the entrée, firmly established the connections among compagnons throughout France, which were far from obvious in the early modern era. As in other ceremonies, inclusiveness and courtesy were stressed: no one in the brotherhood was to be neglected in the toast. One can only speculate on how much the resultant drinking raised the level of sentiment and enthusiasm.

On completing these initial toasts, the rôleur formally presented the battant aux champs to the captain, who instructed the compagnon to give his regards to the compagnons, mère, and père in the next town, "as much from here as from there," again stressing interurban ties. Finally, the captain and departing compagnon began a dialogue establishing his relationships—to God, king, himself, and his enemies.

Article 36

Captain, handing the compagnon his cane: How do you know your cane, my Pays?
Departing compagnon: I know it by the sight and the light God has given me. The hilt is [dedicated] to the King, the ribbon to myself, and the end to those blustering big mouths, the dévorants.

24. AMM, HH 11/20, "Rolle," fols. 10–11.

This passage includes one of the rare references to king or state in old regime compagnonnage. Whatever the nature of this bond, it never stopped compagnons from defying royal edicts or crown officials. More questions followed a brief interlude in which the captain and the departing compagnon performed a *guillebrette*.

Article 37

Captain: How do you know your bag [*sac*], my Pays?
Departing compagnon: I know it by the sight and the light God has given me, by the size of my shoulder. It is in the hands of the *jolis* compagnons, it will be disposed of according to their wishes.[25]

The compagnon's belongings—his knapsack and *affaire* or *trait carré* (a sort of passport of compagnonnage)—were thus not his own unless the other compagnons acknowledged he had fulfilled his obligations. These practices were means of ensuring that members wouldn't leave without paying their debts. In principle a compagnon was not allowed full acceptance into a new town without his *affaire;* he usually could not attend meetings, and until he was "cleared" by the compagnons in his last town, part of his wages might be withheld. The conduite's final phase marked the separation of the compagnon from the city, after a round of final festivities.

Captain (turning toward the city): Look at this lovely and very agreeable city, it will miss you, my Pays.
Departing compagnon: I will miss the *jolis* compagnons, the père and the mère, and his good wine.
Captain (crying out in a loud voice): My Pays, do you know that this compagnon will miss the *jolis* compagnons, the père and the mère, and his good wine?
All Compagnons (loudly): Then he must drink some of it![26]

The conduite recognized the loss departure entails for those who leave and those who stay while creating one last good time and stressing the welcome waiting in the next town.

25. Ibid., fols. 12v–13.
26. Ibid., fol. 14. This passage also reveals that the ceremony was to be held near the edge of town.

Care of the Sick and Burial of the Dead

For compagnons the care of the sick or needy and the burial of the dead were solemn obligations, linking their associations to the traditions of trade corporations, confraternities, and Christian charity in general. The Mâcon rôle required that "if a compagnon is in need of anything or falls sick and if he is obliged to go to the hospital, the compagnons will be responsible to go visit him, each in his turn, and to bring him (according to his taste and appetite) something worth five sols at [the visitor's] expense" (article 12). Any who neglected this visit were fined ten sols. Some ailments were not legitimate cases for aid and comfort: however much they united the brethren, bouts of venereal disease and drunkenness were exempted from support. Visits to hospitalized members were faithfully recorded, as the Bordeaux registers of the compagnon locksmiths demonstrate.[27] Thus, even if far from family or friends, compagnons could rely on fellow comrades in times of need—at least morally correct need.

Care of the body extended to care of the soul. Provision for burial of deceased members suggests that former compagnons remained linked to their associations after their *remerciement* (literally, "thanks giving") or retirement from active membership, although the Mâcon rôle gives no details on the status of retired compagnons. Former compagnons received elaborate burial ceremonies in the nineteenth century, and some earlier cases suggest that one never completely retired from compagnonnage. Ménétra mentions at least two compagnons' funerals (both apparently of active members), attended by compagnons of various trades. Unlike conduites, funerals were quasi-legitimate public affairs, and although police tried to contain them, such events attracted large numbers of compagnons.[28] Funerals could be publicized by means of printed notices posted in central areas of the city. For example, in eighteenth-century Marseille a police agent observed fifteen to twenty people gathered around a small printed notice posted near a main thoroughfare, which announced the funeral procession of M. Montescaux, a premier compagnon of the stonecutters, joiners, and locksmiths "du Devoir

27. Ibid., fol. 5; "Livre des règles," in Coornaert, *Compagnonnages*, p. 368; ADG, C 3708, register, 1757–61, "Table de l'hôpital."

28. For the nineteenth century, see Agricol Perdiguier, *Mémoires d'un compagnon*, ed. Alain Faure (Paris, 1977), pp. 144–45; Arnold Van Gennep, *Manuel de folklore français contemporain* (Paris, 1946), vol. 1, book 2, pp. 817–18; and AM Marseille, I², dos. 137, 3 June 1835. Even if these retired compagnons joined mutual aid or burial societies, their former sect of compagnonnage often participated in the final rites. Ménétra, *Journal de ma vie*, pp. 87, 124. As seen in Chapter 4, more than 90 compagnon joiners and locksmiths du devoir attended a compagnon's funeral in 1764.

de Liberté." The officer ripped down this "provocation," which, in a handwritten addendum, informed the public that "Montescaux had been assassinated by the militia *(sabreurs de ville).*" But he failed to learn more: the people's lively commentary escaped him for he was "not accustomed to listening"—whether in general or to common folks we are not told.[29]

The Mâcon rôle prescribed a proper burial in article 13, stating that "if God calls a compagnon from this world here to the other, the compagnons will be responsible for his burial and for attendance at the burial ceremony, and to pray to God for the repose of his soul . . . [and] for writing from city to city to have [the compagnons] pray to God for him."[30] No further details are provided, but what is said can be correlated with the rituals of greeting and farewell. Passing from one place to another is again emphasized in the phrase "from this world here to the other" rather than the simpler possibility, "from this world." Life and death are depicted as a continuous journey, with various stops along the way. In this final journey compagnons eased the passage of a deceased *pays* much as they had during his lifetime, but instead of toasts, they now helped his soul to heaven with their prayers and those of all the compagnons on the tour. Here the influence of traditional Catholic practice remains strong.

All compagnons in the chamber were strictly required to attend and participate in the *enterrement;* supporting evidence indicates that compagnons in other trades in the same devoir might attend as well. The compagnon turners' burial practices have much in common with those of the compagnon joiners, but the Bordeaux rôle provides more detail. If a compagnon turner died, the premier called on the rôleur (who immediately put black crepe on his cane) to convoke a general meeting to decide specific details of the burial. The steps taken during the ceremony itself, however, were stated in article 31 of the rôle: "When a compagnon dies one must place a compass and a square (crossed) on top of the bier, as well as the colors and the cane of the compagnon, before leaving the Mère. When the priests arrive to remove the body, the rôleur places himself at the head of the deceased, and behind him must form a line of all the compagnons according to their turn and their rank, and their seniority in the devoir." The rôleur asked the compagnons if they knew the deceased and asked them about any outstand-

29. AM Marseille, FF 206, "Compagnons du devoir [and non du devoir], 1740–1786," Marseille, n.d., letter of agent Rave to mayor [unnamed], announcement is dated only 15 July. The notice, bordered in black, is about five inches by three inches and decorated with a small engraving of a funerary urn on an inscribed pedestal under a willow tree.

30. AMM, HH 11/20, "Rolle," fol., 5v. The compagnons' letters confirm that deaths were announced as prescribed in the rôle.

ing obligations they had to him or he to them. After saying the *Pater* and the *Ave* for the repose of the deceased's soul, the rôleur carried, in his left arm, a sealed bottle of wine and a loaf of white bread, "with no imperfections," to the church. Before entering, he performed the same procedures required before leaving the mère and gave holy water to all the compagnons. At the cemetery, with all the compagnons gathered around and the deceased in his grave, the rôleur climbed down into the tomb to place the bread and wine inside the bier. Ascending from the grave, he faced the compagnons and led them in individually renewing their reception oath, in turn according to rank and seniority. Each sang his oath three times "in a mournful voice," turning each time to the other side of the grave. The rôleur then gave each compagnon (again by rank) a spadeful of earth to throw on the bier. Each compagnon said three *Paters* and three *Aves* for the repose of the deceased's soul.[31]

The combination of the Christian and the "compagnonnique" is striking. Squares, compasses, and canes appear together with the mass, priests, holy water, and consecrated bread. And despite this eclectic mix, the church presumably accommodated itself, at least sometimes, to compagnonnage.[32] Compagnons established a highly individual relationship to the church, believing themselves to be good Catholics but keeping their secrets and carrying out their own rites as well. As in the seventeenth-century initiations, compagnons did not consider themselves blasphemers; their solemn cermonies merely transformed and complemented those of the church. The compagnons' burial rites ensured that the dead compagnon was properly mourned, prayed for, and sent off on his last journey. Simultaneously and forcefully, the living were reminded of their own mortality and obligations. The rôleur's descent into the grave to leave the deceased with nourishment for his longest voyage reminded compagnons that they must not fear death. Reciprocally, they learned that if they followed the devoir faithfully, they would not find themselves facing the unknown alone and helpless.

The effect of this ceremony, including the triple repetition of the initiation oath, was to strengthen the solidarity among compagnons and between them and their departed brethren while invoking the hierarchical nature of this solidarity. The complex triple hierarchy of turn, rank, and seniority suggests layers of distinction, in which seniority in the devoir seems particularly important. This concern with order, hierarchy, and discipline is placed in tension with other values, such as the egalitarian rotation of the office of rôleur. Emphasizing rank dur-

31. "Livre des règles," in Coornaert, *Compagnonnages*, pp. 368–69.
32. See examples in Nantes where Cordelier and Jacobin monks sheltered compagnonnages, Chapter 4, p. 128.

ing funerals tended to elevate the hierarchical features of this compagnonnage over its egalitarian ones. These compagnon turners du devoir were more concerned with rank than were the compagnon joiners non du devoir, although this distinction between dévorants and gavots is not uniform.

OTHER WAYS OF BEING BROTHERS

Chains of Alliance: Corresponding Compagnons

The ceremonies of initiation I have examined are primarily normative or prescriptive accounts, with some supporting evidence of practice. These accounts can be enhanced by moving closer to compagnons' voices and experiences. For compagnons, far more than for other members of the "popular classes," direct testimony survived because practicing the devoir involved writing letters. We can "hear" compagnons speaking to one another once again:

> Mother Vinçenot it's Bourguignon the demoiselle who was at your place about 10 days ago. . . . [Along] with the amount I owe you, I am sending my honor and respect. . . . Bassigny says hello. . . . we'll leave [Cluny] by the feast of St. Anne and dine at your place. . . . maybe you'll make a nice suckling pig [for us].[33]

and:

> I tell you my friend that since I've been here I've already taken a mistress, all fresh. . . . I [saw her] while dancing a *sautouse*. She came and took me by the hand. My faith! It was so beautiful. What has given me so much pleasure is that she is really pretty.[34]

and:

> Our very dear fellows . . . some sad news about our mère, whom God has called from this world to the other, who died as a good Christian after having received all the sacraments of our holy mother Church, Catholic, apostolic and roman. And her name was

33. AMM, HH 11/17, Cluny, 11 July [1760?], Bourguignon to Madame Vinçenot, innkeeper; Bourguignon is a compagnon non du devoir. Unless otherwise indicated, I have modernized the spelling, punctuation, and grammar in this sample.

34. AD Saône et Loire, B 1309/69, Burgundy [city name illegible] to Mâcon, 28 October 1760, Le Cadet de St. Pierre (le Corbillion) to an unnamed compagnon.

Claudine Dubul, called Widow Vorriol, aged 60. For 24 years the
Compagnons have been at her place and she has always been on
the side of the Compagnons. We have buried her with great Ceremony.[35]

These excerpts are taken from a sample of forty-one letters all written
by compagnons—joiners, locksmiths, or carpenters—eighteen of them
by compagnons du devoir and twenty-three by compagnons non du devoir.[36] Four letters date from between 1756 and 1759; the rest were
written in 1760. Forty were addressed to other compagnons in Mâcon
or to their mères and pères. One was written to a metalworker (perhaps
a master) by a compagnon on a business matter. Mâconnais police confiscated the letters—together with twenty pages of business accounts,
three *traits carrés,* one letter from a mère, one from a master joiner, and
one from the agent (perhaps an attorney) of a master—in raids on their
Mères in 1761, following a wild Christmas brawl between rival sects. All
these papers establish the wider context of the compagnons' literacy and
reflect the routine business, the struggles, and the pleasures of the life
of compagnonnage. They remain as the rather extraordinary written testimony of a rather typical group of workers, whose *use* of literacy has
remained little known.

The literacy of journeymen varied greatly by trade: for example,
whereas carpenters might have a literacy rate of about 20 to 30 percent,
the rate for locksmiths could be 35 to 50 percent, and almost 50 percent
of joiners were literate.[37] The compagnons' letters cannot be used to
determine literacy percentages, primarily because twenty-five of them
concerned official business and were written by premier compagnons.[38]

35. ADSL, B 1309/44, Chalon-sur-Saône to Mâcon, 19 August 1760, compagnon joiners and
locksmiths non du devoir to the same.

36. See Gabriel Jeanton, *Compagnons du devoir et compagnons de liberté au XVIIIe siècle à Mâcon*
(Chalon-sur-Saône, 1928). Jeanton's work, an invaluable source for my own, was based on these
and related documents now held in the ADSL, B 1309, and the AMM, HH 11. Jeanton focuses
primarily on the compagnons' rivalries and the proceedings against them but devotes some
attention to the letters.

37. Jean Quéniart, *Culture et société urbaines dans la France de l'ouest au XVIIIe siècle* (Paris, 1978),
pp. 103–4. Quéniart's figures, drawn from cities in western France, do not apply directly to
compagnons but serve as a rough guide. The compagnons represented in the sample of forty-
one letters came from various regions of France and not necessarily from larger cities, where
literacy rates were higher.

38. To be most successful, premier compagnons needed more than basic literacy and such
men may have been at a premium. Ménétra, for example, was a premier three times (in Rochefort, Bordeaux, and Lyon). He recounts an incident in Bordeaux involving a dispute with authorities over militia recruitment where his literacy again raised him to prominence. More than
four thousand compagnons had walked out of the city and had chosen a council of thirty compagnons, men "with brains and resolve." Ménétra says the council "needed someone who could
write"; he became the thirty-first member and wrote up the regulations. Given the circumstances,
it seems extremely unlikely that *none* of the other thirty men could write. Ménétra's statement

Nonetheless, the remaining sixteen letters were written by other compagnons. Because of the need to maintain an interurban network and to keep the business relatively secret, the more literate the members, the more successful the association. Moreover, most letters of the compagnons non du devoir were also "signed by the four most senior compagnons" as well as the premier and usually by all members present, the premier signing for those who could not (the compagnons du devoir did not sign their names unless they were writing a personal letter, perhaps for security reasons). It seems clear that literacy or ready access to literate intermediaries was simply assumed.

If the letters cannot tell us how many compagnons were literate, they can reveal much about the nature of this literacy. Varying from one to three pages in length, all the letters in this sample were written in French except for one in a mixture of French and Burgundian dialect. The majority came to Mâcon from cities and towns relatively nearby, eleven from Chalon-sur-Saône (ten to compagnons non du devoir) and ten from Lyon (seven to compagnons non du devoir). We might be led to conclude that compagnonnage was more regional than national, except that many of these were chain letters, which provided vital links to cities far beyond the region. For example, compagnon joiners and locksmiths non du devoir in Chalon-sur-Saône wrote (6 May 1760) to inform compagnons in Mâcon that those in Troyes had changed their père and asked them to begin "circulating the letter." The news was to travel from city to city until it reached its final destination, "Nîmes in Languedoc." Indeed, four of the letters came from the distant cities of Bordeaux, Paris, Nîmes, and Orléans. Regional letters tend to predominate in this sample partly because most of the letters were meant to report on compagnons who left without paying their debts and would usually be going to the nearest town on the tour. Letters were sometimes sent by coach in hopes of reaching that town before the delinquent. Even if the majority of these letters came from closer to home, moreover, the compagnons themselves did not. They hailed from Provence, Normandy, Flanders, and even from Switzerland, Brussels, and Germany. The mere fact that this widely diverse group could communicate in a French transcending regional dialects is impressive. This doesn't mean compagnons wrote like Voltaire—or even Ménétra. Their spelling and grammar were often unique. Nonetheless, the letters are quite legible and usually comprehensible.[39]

---

implies that he was chosen because he could write the most effectively. *Journal de ma vie*, pp. 69–70.

39. Although handwriting yields only a rough indication of levels of literacy (as notaries' draft copies attest), Quéniart attempts to establish six intermediate categories of literacy based on

The format is relatively standardized: all forty-one have very similar greetings, opening phrases and closings.[40] The compagnons du devoir often began their letters with the invocation "Jesus Maria Joseph" (nine cases), followed by the terse greeting, "Les compagnons."[41] The compagnons non du devoir usually began with a flourish: "Salutations be given to all the compagnon joiners and locksmiths non du Devoir of the city and faubourgs of Mâcon, without forgetting the father and the mother." And then: "Our very dear pays." Almost all the letters next asked about the addressees' health, assuring the recipients that the senders were "fort bonne, Dieu merci," or "Grâce à Dieu."[42] The closings were distinctive. Compagnons du devoir gave the number of workers present and made up for their blunt opening: "We are . . . 30 compagnons who drink to your health. Drink, if you please, to ours. Compliments to the père, to the mère, brothers and sisters, if there are any. If there aren't, make some."[43] Compagnons non du devoir usually closed more simply: "We are your faithful fellows, Compagnons de liberté," although this phrase could be preceded by "we embrace you with all our hearts."[44]

Convention was a hallmark of such writing, even in jokes: "if there aren't any [brothers and sisters], make some." Sixteen letters use the phrase "humble respects" or "respects," as in "we beg you humbly to accept our respects." Compagnons always addressed letters to their inn-

---

signatures: from A1, "excellent signatures, embellished . . . above average instruction," to B1, totally illiterate. Following this model, many compagnons would fall into the higher categories such as A3, "careful, applied signatures, not facile . . . elementary instruction," and even A2, "fluent signatures, evidence of practice, more than simple literacy" (*Culture et société urbaines*, pp. 36–37). This rare sample of lengthier writings reveals the difficulties even people with "more than simple literacy" had writing brief letters. Evidently much more time was spent in practicing one's signature than in actually writing. Nonetheless, that compagnons could be highly functional, if not polished, literates, greatly enhances our knowledge of popular literacy in this era. For the nineteenth century, see Jean Hébrard, "La Lettre représentée: Les Pratiques épistolaires populaires dans les récits de vie ouvriers et paysans," in *La Correspondence: Les Usages de la lettre au XIXe siècle*, ed. Roger Chartier (Paris, 1991), pp. 279–365.

40. One letter's greeting is torn. ADSL, B 1309/60, n.d.

41. Jesus and Dieu are among the few words almost never misspelled, probably reflecting the content of school primers. Compagnons would have had few, if any, guides to letter writing before the Revolution other than those compagnonnage provided. Daniel Roche assumes eighteenth-century letter-writing treatises existed for the popular classes. "Les Pratiques de l'écrit dans les villes françaises du XVIIIe siècle," in *Pratiques de la lecture*, ed. Roger Chartier (Paris, 1985), p. 167. But Janet Altman's extensive research does not confirm this view. "Teaching the 'People' to Write: The Formation of a Popular Civic Identity in the French Letter Manual," in *Studies in Eighteenth-Century Culture*, 22 (1992): 147–80.

42. The phrase "Dieu merci" or "grâce à Dieu" appears in twenty-eight of the thirty-nine complete letters and is almost proportionally divided between compagnons du devoir and non du devoir.

43. ADSL, B 1309/17, Orléans to Mâcon, 14 December 1760. This last phrase was one of the few jokes found in the sample.

44. ADSL, B 1309/20, Lyon to Mâcon, 26 May 1760.

keepers as "Madame" or "Monsieur", when "dame" or "sieur" would have sufficed. In oral testimony such as interrogations compagnons were rarely obsequious, and frequently insolent and insulting. The consistent *politesse* in their letters toward comrades and supporters is a sharp contrast, revealing a very different side to these men.[45]

All the greetings and closings stressed some element of equality and, more specifically, brotherhood. A rough draft of a letter reveals how various endings could signal differences in status and relationships. A premier compagnon, Champagne le tranquille, first ended a letter to other compagnons with "Your most humble and obedient servant"; realizing his error, Champagne crossed this out and substituted "We are always waiting for your news. Your faithful fellows, compagnons de liberté." Compagnons had developed a separate language of brotherhood and association in place of "standard" polite forms. Whatever models had been learned in schoolbooks were transformed. Like their ceremonies of greeting, farewell, and burial, the letters employ the compagnons' own standard, often repeated phrases. It is easy to appreciate the significance of the change Champagne le tranquille made, but even a common invocation such as "Dieu merci" cannot automatically be dismissed as an empty formality or superstitious catch phrase. Whatever their particular meaning, formulas provided elements of continuity, consistency, definition, and discipline, particularly valuable in a semiclandestine association.

The formulas, moreover, created the necessary skeleton of each letter for people who were literate but perhaps barely so. The rote aspects of the letter were handles and aids, an outline for the difficult task of writing. Repetition also reflects less a lack of interesting subject matter than the function of these particular letters. In order of frequency, compagnons wrote to one another about delinquent compagnons; money owed by compagnons in good standing; death of compagnons, mères, or pères; employment; the devoir; and finally, personal business—ordering new tools or revealing one's amorous conquests. The letters' most important function was to track compagnons who left town secretly without settling

45. Gabriel Jeanton lauded the compagnons' "exquise politesse" and complete lack of "vulgarité," behavior which confirmed his biases about high and low culture in the eighteenth century. He contended that upper-class gentility in that age permeated society in a sort of "trickle down" effect and found courtesy greatly diminished in his own day—the twentieth century where "la grossièreté des bas fonds et la vulgarité du ruisseau s'acclimatent peu à peu les classes qui se pretendent raffinées." Jeanton, *Compagnons du devoir,* p. 34. Cf. Norbert Elias, who interprets the spread of the "civilizing process" as the creation of distinctions closely connected to elites' social power and status. *The Civilizing Process,* vol. 1: *The History of Manners* (New York, 1978). Also see Mark Motley, *Becoming a French Aristocrat: The Education of the Court Nobility, 1580–1715* (Princeton, 1990), pp. 64–65, on the rules of *politesse* used to curb the rowdiness of young seventeenth-century aristocrats.

their debts or leaving their belongings as security.[46] In a typical example, the association wrote to a compagnon locksmith non du devoir in Mâcon: "This is to warn you that having been informed that you left this city with debts from one end of town to another, and persisting until now without honoring them, you can be assured if you do not promptly send the money to the père des compagnons to satisfy those whom you owe, your knapsack [and possessions] will be sold."[47] The compagnon was further reproached for neglecting his duty and putting others in difficult and embarrassing circumstances.

Deadbeat compagnons, called *coquins* (scoundrels, rogues) and *affronteurs* (cheats, deceivers), received opprobrium: Rochelais tête de mouton's fifty-livre debt "wrong[ed] all the good [*jolis*] Compagnons who are out of work [as well as] the mère. . . . the Compagnons are really badly off compared to such a cheat."[48] Such scoundrels were treated as part of the normal, albeit dishonorable and disabling, facts of compagnonnage. Yet, although the associational life itself added to their debts, most compagnons were not eager to escape its demands. Recognizing how precarious their finances could be, compagnons gave debtors some leeway before labeling them coquins. Many compagnons owed money but were still "good fellows," leaving their belongings as security until they paid their debts. The letters present no unrelieved picture of dishonorable or destitute workers; rather, they underscore how many compagnons wrote to say that they had found work and money would follow, or wrote when they actually sent the money. Compagnons du devoir in Bordeaux gratefully acknowledged the receipt of money from a compagnon in Mâcon and sent his belongings to him by coach.[49] The letter cordially added the interesting note that three compagnons had gone on a pilgrimage from Bordeaux to Santiago de Compostela. One mère wrote an apologetic reminder to compagnon carpenters du devoir in Mâcon about a member who owed her money. Only one clearly dunning letter stressed "dishonorable" and "disgraceful" conduct, and it was

46. Compagnons provided detailed descriptions of these delinquents, e.g., a compagnon joiner non du devoir Allemand le beau danseur, whose debts amounted to 42 livres, 6 sous, 6 pence, was "44 to 45 years old, height 5 feet 7 inches, chestnut hair, ruddy complexion, cinnamon colored coat and vest, black knee-britches, trouble with his legs, even limps a bit." Quite a bit older than most compagnons, it seems that Allemand's dancing days were over. Those in Mâcon were asked to "treat him according to merit" (ADSL, B 1309/31, Chalon-sur-Saône, 13 August 1760).

47. AMM, HH 11/16, 15 March 1758, signed "Bailly"; internal evidence confirms he is a compagnon.

48. ADSL, B 1309/17, Orléans to Mâcon, 14 December 1760, compagnons du devoir. Letters had tracked Rochelais from Orléans to Dijon to Mâcon and finally to the town of Pont-de-Veyle (Ain).

49. ADSL, B 1309/66, 16 June 1760.

written only after this *coquin* had repeatedly failed to respond to earlier letters.[50]

The six letters reporting deaths of compagnons, mères, or pères also followed a rather set formula: "We have learned" or "must tell you the very sad news that —— has left [or, "God has called —— from"] this world for the other." Letters gave particulars about the death and the deceased, who in all six cases, had "received all the sacraments of our Holy mother the Church." The letter announcing the death of the mère (Figure 4) also asked "all the compagnons on the tour de France" to say "a *pater* and an *ave* for the repose of her soul." Genuine sorrow emerges through the formula to express the great loss of a woman who had been their mère for twenty-four years and had "always been on the side of the compagnons."[51]

Letters announced other aspects of the devoir's business, including news of the reception of new compagnons: the 1765 baptism of nine compagnon basketmakers in Orléans, mentioned at the beginning of this chapter, was announced by letter.[52] Although the letter gives no details of the ceremony, it provides pertinent information about the new compagnons and their "godparents." When a letter announced a reception, the local brotherhood was required to note the names of the initiates and godparents in its own records. Three letters received in Mâcon departed from more usual announcements and discussed run-ins with the police, linking them directly to bans against their devoir. The compagnons non du devoir complained of five renegades "who [had] cost us a lot because of the word devoir"—including the arrest and imprisonment of two compagnons. Another letter told how a group of compagnons non du devoir had to go before the magistrates in Nîmes: "We defended ourselves as best as possible." The third case shared the "sad news" not of death but of a compagnon, Picard the vainquer, whom "we thought was an *honnête homme* [but] was a coquin." The compagnons' "misfortune" was to entrust Picard with their precious papers. Attempting to flaunt his importance, Picard had shown these papers around to "all the whores of the city."[53]

Telling an honorable from a dishonorable man was sometimes diffi-

50. ADSL, B 1309/71, 21 November 1760, mère of compagnon carpenters, Dijon; AMM, HH 11/16, 19 March 1758, Mâcon.
51. ADSL, B 1309/44, Chalon-sur-Saône to Mâcon, 19 August 1760, compagnons non du devoir.
52. AD Loiret, B 1988, cited in Germain Martin, *Associations ouvrières*, pp. 107–8.
53. ADSL, B 1309/28, Chalon-sur-Saône to Mâcon, 5 July 1760, and B 1309/29, Nîmes to Mâcon, 23 May 1759 (both compagnons non du devoir), B 1309/43, unidentified to Mâcon, 13 May 1760, compagnons non du devoir.

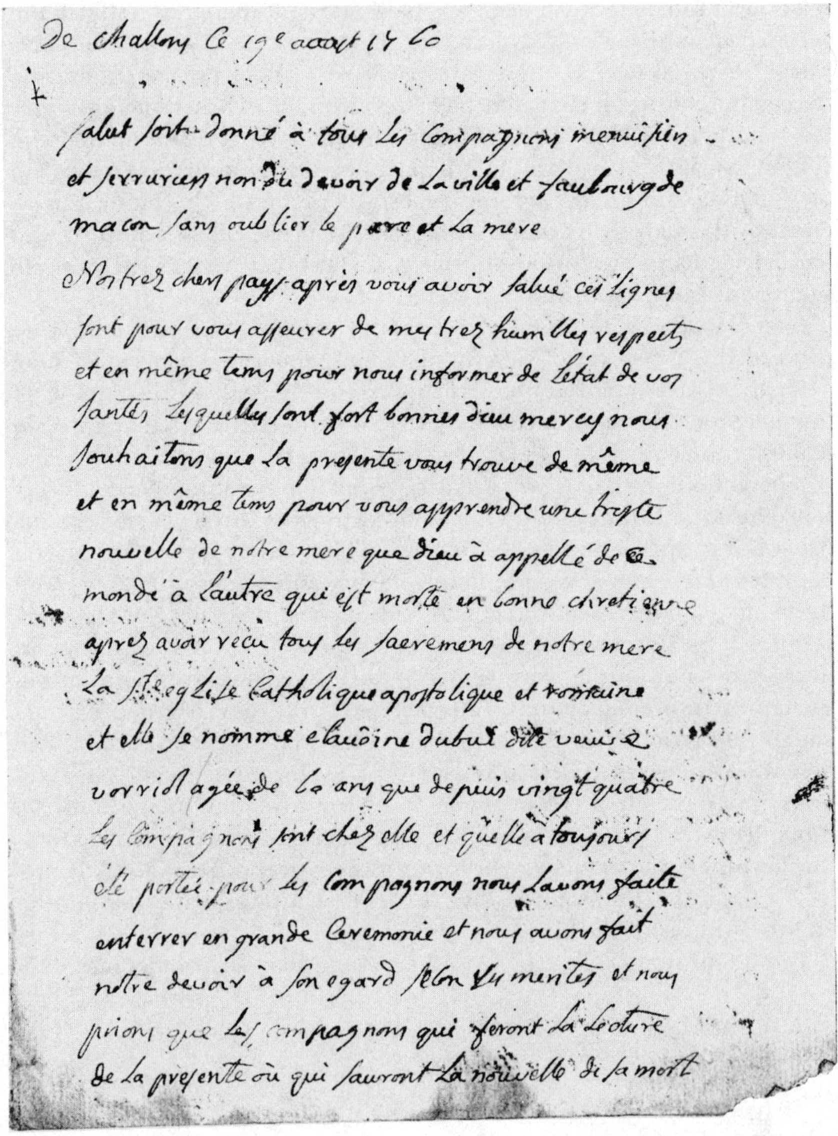

De Challon Ce 19e aoust 1760

Salut soit donné à tous les Compagnons menuisiers
et serruriers non du devoir de La ville et faubourg de
macon Sans oublier le père et La mere

Nostrez chers pays après vous avoir salué cés lignes
sont pour vous asseurer de mes trez humbles respects
et en même tems pour nous informer de l'état de vos
santés lesquelles sont fort bonnes dieu mercy nous
souhaitons que La presente vous trouve de même
et en même tems pour vous apprendre une triste
nouvelle de notre mere que dieu à appellé de ce
monde à l'autre qui est morte en bonne chretienne
après avoir reçu tous les sacremens de notre mere
La ste eglise catholique apostolique et romaine
et elle se nomme clauvine dubut dite veuve
vorriel agée de 60 ans que depuis vingt quatre
les compagnons sont chez elle et qu'elle a toujours
été portée pour les compagnons nous l'avons faite
enterrer en grande Ceremonie et nous avons fait
notre devoir à son egard selon ses merites et nous
prions que les compagnons qui feront la lecture
de la presente où qui sauront La nouvelle de sa mort

Figure 4. Letter announcing the death of a mère. Compagnon joiners and locksmiths non
du devoir, Chalon-sur-Saône, to compagnon joiners and locksmiths non du devoir, Mâcon,
19 August 1760. Source: AD Saône et Loire, B 1309, no. 44, p. 1 of 3.

cult. In 1756 even the premier compagnon in Mâcon turned out to be a coquin who mishandled the devoir's funds. His replacement was Normand la douceur, "known by many Compagnons for [being] an *honnête* Compagnon everywhere he goes. . . .please set him up in a good workshop."[54] Compagnons did not always lose to coquins or the police. One letter relayed news of a triumph over police and corporation regulations controlling hiring in Marseille. As seen in earlier chapters, masters often fought compagnons over the "right" to control hiring and labor conditions. In 1759 placement offices were established in Marseille for joiners and locksmiths and compagnons were obliged to register there. On 2 June 1760, however, compagnons non du devoir in Lyon wrote to pass on the "agreeable news" from Marseille that these regulations had been "entirely abolished." The compagnons wrote: "We don't know how to express the joy that this news causes us. We hope that it will be the same for you."[55]

I have described numerous examples of defiance of masters, drawn from police and judicial records, but the Lyon letter brings us behind the scenes to witness how the joy of the triumph in Marseille was shared by the whole brotherhood. Brotherhood, however, had a darker side. Compagnons also shared pranks, sometimes vicious ones, against a wide range of outsiders—masters, rival compagnons, those who were younger, weaker, and fewer. Fraternal bonding might also include rape, sharing prostitutes, or at least boasting and bragging about sexual violence and prowess. As Robert Darnton comments, "Ménétra's jokes are usually cruel, and they often suggest that he expressed the brotherhood of man through the spoliation of women."[56] Jacques Rossiaud's pathbreaking study of sexual violence and prostitution in early modern Dijon reveals that gang rapes by young men—usually journeymen, servants, or sons of masters aged eighteen to twenty-four—were a common occurrence.[57] In the fifteenth century there were about twenty of these premeditated gang rapes, implicating almost a hundred young men, every year in Dijon. Rossiaud estimates that perhaps half the young males in the city were involved in such rapes before reaching adulthood.

Given such numbers, members of compagnonnages may have been

---

54. AMM, HH 11/15, Lyon to Mâcon, 22 February 1756, compagnons non du devoir. The *coquin* premier was dismissed and made to "give an account of himself." Compagnons often told police and masters they did "not have to give an account of themselves," but they were strictly accountable to their pays.

55. ADSL, B 1309/40, Lyon to Mâcon, 2 June 1760; again note the chain letter's importance.

56. Robert Darnton, foreword to Jacques-Louis Ménétra, *Journal of My Life*, ed. Daniel Roche, trans. Arthur Goldhammer (New York, 1986), p. xii.

57. Jacques Rossiaud, "Prostitution, jeunesse, et société dans les villes du sud-est de la France au 15e siècle," *Annales: E.S.C.* 31 (1978): 289–325.

involved in these assaults, although I have found no corroborating evidence. Moreover, because compagnons were accused of so many public disorders, it seems unlikely they would have escaped the historical record had they been a major element in gang rapes. Itinerant compagnons were not necessarily the most likely perpetrators of such acts, despite their relative anonymity and mobility. Rossiaud maintains that the great majority of gang rapes, at least in the fifteenth century, were deliberate acts by members of the community in good standing, young men who were frustrated and deprived of the ability to marry. Many cities responded by establishing public and semipublic brothels, and gang rape subsequently declined. Nonetheless, more extensive studies remain to be done for later periods.

Ménétra's autobiography provides some anecdotal evidence on this subject. He described having "amused [himself] with [a] girl half willingly the rest by force" in a situation the late twentieth century would classify as rape. Ménétra and a companion came upon a "little shepherd and a young shepherd girl in action." As Ménétra sneaked up on the couple, the boy fled and the girl tried to cover herself. While Ménétra's comrade went after the shepherd, Ménétra "amused" himself. He initially regarded the incident as a prank but began to have "second thoughts because [his] comrade didn't try to take advantage of the situation." Ménétra does not indicate if the second thoughts arose because the prank was no fun if his friend did not want to join in or because his comrade was disapproving. There is no indication that Ménétra saw *his* fun as a violation of the body and honor of the shepherd girl, let alone her companion's honor, but he was briefly troubled by the incident. "I retraced my steps . . . and as I was a good Christian and had heard that a sin paid for was half pardoned," gave the shepherdess a few sous. Although it may be that Ménétra was simply soothing his conscience by putting the girl in a category he understood—that of the willing prostitute—his tone may be ironic but his payment seems more in line with the paying of a penance or a fine. The event, however, apparently had no profound impact as he "continued on [his] way."[58]

This sense is confirmed by an incident that occurred several years later. After completing his tour de France, Ménétra writes, he committed virtually the same act with no compunction. The most likely explanation for the difference in this case seems to be that he and his companion had exactly the same thing in mind. Walking in the forest of Vincennes with a good friend, Gombeaut, Ménétra came across a couple "really

---

58. Ménétra, *Journal of My Life*, pp. 37–38.

going at it." They took turns holding the young man at bay as they
"hopped on the body of the young girl whom we didn't give any time
to get herself together." Far from feeling the need to do penance Ménétra and Gombeaut mockingly "thanked the young lady for her cooperation." A few days earlier, feeling the desire to be even more than
friends, the pair sold their silver shoe buckles to get the money to share
a prostitute and become brothers—"twins in the same family."[59] Ménétra had shared a whore with fellow compagnons on several other occasions as well. Generally, however, he describes his sexual conquests as
the result of his charm, not of force or money.

In trying to understand Ménétra and his world, Darnton writes per-
ceptively of the historical distance between our ancestors and ourselves,
which often seems to surpass our common humanity. He notes that this
disjuncture remains "irreducibly strange" no matter what gloss—class
rivalry, social mobility, or peer group solidarity—is applied. The old regime was so "saturated with violence and death," he writes, "that we
can barely imagine it."[60] Yet, the modern imagination can run rampant
without much experience of violence, and daily life in the inner city may
be even more hostile and lethal than that of the old regime.

Many, for example, might find in Ménétra's attitudes toward rape,
sexual coercion, and boasting not an irreducible strangeness but a troubling familiarity. The sexual beliefs and practices of Ménétra and his
friends were generally legitimated in their culture: few eighteenth-
century Frenchmen would categorize Ménétra's "amusement" with a
girl already engaged in sexual intercourse as rape, and many would share
his belief that "a sin paid for was half forgiven," even if the payment
was not true penance. Nonetheless, the acts of Ménétra and his friends
are not without their counterparts in our own time, even if our explanations derive from a twentieth-century context. His recurring discourse
on sexuality as a marker of virility and fraternal bonding, for example,
has certain modern counterparts in gang or even youth culture. Much
of our understanding, however, depends who the "we" is and on the
various contexts we privilege. Some persistent patterns of violence, par-

59. Ibid., p. 141.
60. Darnton, foreword, ibid., pp. xii–xiii. See also Robert Darnton, "Reading a Riot," *New
York Review of Books*, October 22, 1992, pp. 44–46, a review of *The Vanishing Children of Paris:
Rumor and Politics before the French Revolution* by Arlette Farge and Jacques Revel, trans. Claudia
Miéville (Cambridge, Mass., 1991). Comparing the Los Angeles riots of 1992 and the Parisian
uprising of 1750 of the poor against the police, Darnton concludes that the events are parallel
but not truly comparable because the mental world of 1750 "differed completely from that of
the rioters in Los Angeles." The historical meanings of riots must be discovered in "all their
specificity" (p. 46). I generally accept this position but offer some qualifications, as will be seen.

ticularly sexual violence, both strange *and* familiar, appear across centuries at the transition to manhood and in the context of associations that promote male bonding.

Ménétra's account should not, in any case, stand (or lie) as our only witness, for in contrast to his incessant talk of sexual conquest and sweethearts, the compagnons' letters, with one clear exception, were silent on such subjects. Their letters, of course, were about the devoir's business. Yet, they could involve the discussion of women, and these women generally fell into categories similar to Ménétra's—"mother" or "whore." Compagnons wrote about or to their mères with genuine respect and affection; they discussed whores much as they did coquins. Their overriding feelings toward the *putains* who saw their papers may have been fear—of the whores' power to harm them and the devoir. Their chief worry was that their papers had been seen by outsiders, whether female or male made less difference. Linking whores to scoundrels defined them as dishonorable, which designation may have borne a stigma of immorality, but the incident is best seen as a betrayal whose consequences "honorable" compagnons feared they could not control.

The only letter in this correspondence to speak of women other than mères and whores is a three-page personal letter written in Seurre for a compagnon carpenter du devoir, Le Corbillon, by a compagnon named Bourguignon. The letter, sent to Le Corbillon's "dear pays," a compagnon in Mâcon, recounts Le Corbillon's delight in his "mistress" and mentions another woman he admired and respected, Pierrette, a friend of the addressee. The letter—one of the longest in my sample—tries to be a verbatim account. Le Corbillon wants to tell his friend the very words he spoke to his mistress: he first asked her to excuse him for not speaking "good Bourguignon" and added, "Perhaps, [if] I could once sleep with you, my mistress, perhaps I will speak better Bourguignon."[61] Le Corbillon encouraged his pays to come to Seurre, emphasizing the wine cost only three sous a pint (two sous if bought at a *cave*). He wished to share the good times in Seurre (if not his mistress) with his friend and the other compagnons—to whom he sent warm greetings. Perhaps the compagnons du devoir kept this letter among their official papers as a diversion, a pleasant change from reading and writing about their usual business.

The absence of some subjects is striking. Little is said about the trade, quarrels with masters, or "plots" and opposition to authorities, so common in other evidence. In fact, it is not likely that subjects requiring secrecy would be discussed in these letters. They were almost always sent

61. ADSL, B 1309/69, 28 October 1760.

through public mails, openly addressed to "mères" and "pères" of compagnons du devoir or non du devoir. Strictly illegal matters or very important ones would thus not be communicated by this means. Moreover, the compagnons may have lacked the time or ability to discuss more complex issues in their letters. The several that mention the devoir are among the most confused and difficult to read in the whole sample. It is equally possible that compagnons did not perceive it as the proper function of a letter to include lengthy or explicit communications on these matters.

If the compagnons who wrote the letters in this sample do not demonstrate Ménétra's literary flair, they shared his concerns and pleasures in many ways. They even expressed some things in the same ways. Like Ménétra, individual compagnons were loyal to the devoir but at times wanted to keep it at arm's length. The coquin who showed the compagnons' secret papers to "all the whores in town" echoes Ménétra's sometimes nonchalant treatment of the devoir and spirited jesting and bragging. Overall, however, the Mâcon letters were concerned with the harsh realities and routines of daily life. The compagnons in these letters appear more respectful of (or concerned with) God and religious practice than Ménétra. Of course, even the freethinking Ménétra was not above attending the compagnons' monthly mass and a high mass on a patron saint's day.

The sharpest difference between these compagnons and Ménétra emerges in the fluency of the writing.[62] When the letters move beyond formulas, logic sometimes breaks down and the reader gropes for meaning. Many "sound" more like spoken than written speech; key bits of sentences frequently seem to have been left out, and reading aloud aids comprehension—not surprising in an era when an oral popular culture was rapidly becoming literate.[63] Whereas we stretch to understand the "sous-entendu," the correspondents probably knew what the letters meant. Lacunae reflect less a desire for complete secrecy than the knowledge that their communications were addressed to an audience with common problems and concerns as well as a shared devoir. Their letters could thus assume a common base of knowledge and leave some things unsaid.

The growing utility, even necessity, of both reading and writing in compagnonnage made it worth the effort to take pen in hand, put pen

62. Obviously, when Ménétra edited his journal, he was much older and better read than any of the compagnons in my sample would have been. Yet, even with his wit and instruction, Ménétra's logic and organization can be unclear.

63. For example, "Mother Vinçenot it's Bourguignon the demoiselle"; "Perhaps I could once sleep with you my mistress." For some useful ideas on this subject, see Walter J. Ong, *Orality and Literacy* (London, 1982), esp. pp. 7–10, 115–23, 139–47.

to paper, and move beyond orality. As François Furet and Jacques Ozouf concluded, literacy flourishes best in contexts where it is perceived as functional and desirable for the individual or group.[64] For men with shared goals and interests (not to mention serious debts), separated by distance, written correspondence was essential. But as essential as such communication was, it was not a rote exercise, even if the level of literacy conspired against complex prose. The compagnons' writings bear witness to a language of solidarity encoded in a usually straightforward content. Their written communications employ a language of "honor and opposition" not unlike that they used with the police and officials. Scoundrels and cheats were tracked down, blackballed, and differentiated from *braves, jolis,* or *honnêtes* compagnons. Those who paid their debts and were loyal to the devoir earned the respect and consideration of honest men, sometimes including masters. One master wrote that the "compagnons non du devoir would not wish the dishonor of one to reflect upon them."[65] But sometimes maintaining their honor meant defying authority and insisting on their "rights" to control hiring and other facets of production.

The tone of these letters is markedly unlike that "heard" in other evidence. In the letters compagnons speak as equals with presumably common goals and interests; they have little need to defy social "superiors," although they express anger, disappointment, and worry over those who defied the devoir. Generally the accent is on courteous equality. When compagnons were well or their plans were successful, letters expressed joy rather than arrogant declarations of rights. The letters present them essentially as good friends and good fellows—even polite fellows—ready to carry out the business of the devoir and to share their joys and sorrows.

The letters recall neither the Rabelaisian carnival of Ménétra nor the cocky and insolent repartee of the police record, but both of those worlds were a backdrop and a complement to the more usual practice of daily life evoked by the letters. The writing is gripping prose in its own way. Letters reveal sentiments both commonplace and unexpected, in language that was both part of and foreign to everyday life in old regime France. The letters are most extraordinary simply as signals that other literate working men and women may have written more than has hitherto been suspected. Would they have written, like the compagnons, not only about their troubles but also about loyalty, friendship, honor, the pleasure of a pretty mistress, a handsome beau, and the joy of cheap

64. François Furet and Jacques Ozouf, eds., *Lire et écrire: L'Alphabétisation des français de Calvin à Jules Ferry,* 2 vols. (Paris, 1977), 1:351–52.
65. ADSL, B 1309/42, Auxonne to Mâcon, 13 May 1760.

wine? Perhaps. More likely, the institutionalized networks of compagnonnage were a major impetus for such literary creations. Within compagnonnage, men objectively low on the social scale reworked prevailing views of nobility and status into their own code of *honnêteté* and brotherhood.

Origin Narratives and Songs

This code of compagnonnage was expressed in other aspects of the devoir, particularly in origin narratives and songs. Song often conveys information or articulates beliefs quite directly, although events may be invented, exaggerated, or transformed. Origin narratives make statements about a society or group's origin, conceptual organization, and purpose, albeit in nonliteral ways: such narratives may be fanciful, but embedded in them is a particular understanding of their cultural and material context. These narratives or "legends," as compagnons often called them, became a vitally important vehicle of self-definition and redefinition for nineteenth-century compagnons. In the eighteenth century, however, origin narratives were either not fully worked out or so fiercely guarded that only traces have survived. Given the amount known about other symbolic practices, my sense is that these narratives were relatively fragmentary before the nineteenth century. Thus in the eighteenth-century one finds only fleeting references to origins and founders, which are incorporated into full-blown accounts in the nineteenth century. Among the most important clues for any "prehistory" of these origin narratives are the roughly half dozen appearances of the name Maître Jacques.

Several uses of "Maître Jacques" were seen earlier in this chapter. The most important appears in a 1753 letter in which compagnon glaziers demand, "Are we not all *enfants de* Maître Jacques? We think it better to fight than suffer any insult."[66] This example lends some credence to the existence of a narrative connected to Maître Jacques: these compagnons knew they had become his "children" and were willing to defend his (and, thus, their) name. Other cases reveal Maître Jacques's importance, without telling us much about him.[67] Recall, for example, that the compagnon turners du devoir in Bordeaux (1731) baptized aspirants in the "name of Maître Jacques!" They also displayed an image of him at the start of assemblies. Only then could the compagnons speak, in order of

66. AD Loiret, B 1988, cited in Germain Martin, *Associations ouvrières*, p. 109.
67. E.g., Ménétra recopied "le rôle ou ce que l'on nomme Maître Jacques" (*Journal de ma vie*, p. 51). He mentions Maître Jacques several other times but tells no stories about him.

their seniority in the devoir.[68] Compagnon locksmiths du devoir, also in Bordeaux, record the fine and chastisement (1760) of a compagnon who had somehow "made profit from Maître Jacques."[69] Finally, the compagnon tanners in Troyes kept their papers in a trunk on (or in) which was a "figure called Maître Jacques." Their debts made it necessary to change mères, but their new candidate, femme Briey seemed reluctant and questioned whether they really "were compagnons du devoir because they had no Maître Jacques." A police search at their former Mère in 1782 uncovered the trunk with a figure representing Saint Jacques Pellerin, "which the said compagnons called maître Jacques."[70] In a related way the term could represent the compagnons' funds or treasury: Ménétra talks about being in "debt to Maître Jacques."[71] As seen, Ménétra also uses Maître Jacques as a synonym for the rôle. Despite the significance of these cases, Maître Jacques was used far less commonly in eighteenth-century compagnonnages than were religious names (especially Jesus and saints' names) and terms such as devoir, non du devoir, and gavots.

More important, we learn almost nothing of any stories connected to these terms. Is this Maître Jacques linked to stories of the Templars and their ill-fated leader, Jacques de Molay? Or is there a connection between Maître Jacques and the master mason Hiram in the Freemasons' account of their origins?[72] The Troyes case suggests a connection between Maître Jacques and "Saint Jacques de Compostelle," as the compagnons called him. The link is not unlikely. Saint Jacques was a very popular religious figure in France from the Middle Ages and also a favored patron of travelers. As seen, some eighteenth-century compagnons made the pilgrimage to Santiago de Compostela.[73]

Even less evidence exists on the early origin narratives of compagnons non du devoir (also called gavots or du devoir de liberté). The term

68. "Livre des règles," in Coornaert, Compagnonnages, pp. 358, 376.
69. AD Gironde, C 3708, "Table des grosses amendes," 30 June 1760 to 5 January 1761, only appearance of Maître Jacques.
70. AM Troyes, FF Supplément, 9 March 1782, depositions of Marie Sama (?), femme Briey, and Marie Maître, femme Boyau. Briey also sensibly noted that these compagnons still owed their former mère 80 livres (Boyau said 60).
71. Ménétra, Journal de ma vie, p. 128.
72. Hiram plays the same role for Masonry that Maître Jacques plays for the compagnons du devoir. For detailed accounts of Masonic legends and possible links between masonry and the Templars, see Douglas Knoop et al., The Early Masonic Catechisms (Manchester, 1943); Albert G. Mackey, The Principles of Masonic Law: A Treatise on the Constitutional Laws, Usages, and Landmarks of Freemasonry (New York, 1859); Robert Ingham Clegg, The New Revised Edition of Mackey's History of Freemasonry (New York, 1921); and René Le Forestier, La Franc-maçonnerie templière et occultiste aux XVIIIe et XIXe siècles (Paris, 1970).
73. Ménétra wanted to make this pilgrimage but changed his mind after meeting two compagnons who had been badly beaten while traveling that route. Journal de ma vie, p. 78.

"compagnons de liberté" is used in the correspondence of the compagnon joiners and locksmiths in Mâcon.[74] The term *gavots* was quite common in the eighteenth century, and Perdiguier's commentary on this term figures prominently in later elaboration of this sect's narratives. As noted, Perdiguier, himself a gavot, drew a connection between *gave* (gorges) and "mountain people," and linked gavots to Huguenots seeking refuge in such gorges in the Pyrenees. I have found, however, no confirmation of his etymology in other source materials. No mention of Solomon, the gavots' founder, appears in prerevolutionary archival records; its presence would supply a definite eighteenth-century link between compagnons non du devoir and Freemasonry. Nonetheless, compagnons could have known something about Masonry in this era. Mary Ann Clawson's valuable work on fraternal orders illuminates the relationship between Masons and craftsmen in eighteenth-century England and demonstrates how deeply Masons "affirmed the basic worth of productive activity." Masonry was thus "a venture in boundary-crossing" and not a theory and practice limited to the most elite members of eighteenth-century society. Although Clawson argues that its range of "social inclusiveness proved startling to many who inhabited the hierarchical and circumscribed social worlds of the eighteenth century," her focus is primarily on the British case.[75] Moreover, this boundary crossing was relative. Margaret Jacob's extensive research on European Freemasonry in the eighteenth century reveals that the social range of British lodges was generally limited to the middle and upper classes, a tendency even more common in Masonic lodges on the continent. French lodges, for example, stressed an exclusivity based on merit which in practice would exclude members below the level of the prosperous bourgeoisie.[76]

Elements of Masonic *practice*, however, had become a matter of public knowledge well before a popular production like Mozart's *Magic Flute* (1791), with Schikaneder's libretto constructed around stock Masonic stereotypes. French Masonry was formally established in 1725 (England's

74. E.g., AMM, HH 11/15, Lyon, 22 February 1756: "greatly obliging their faithful Pays compagnons de liberté."

75. Mary Ann Clawson, *Constructing Brotherhood: Class, Gender, and Fraternalism* (Princeton, 1989), pp. 72, 73. For example, a satiric speech in 1688 depicted Masons as "gentlemen, mechanics, porters, parsons, ragmen, hucksters, divines, tinkers, knights" (quoting Douglas Knoop and G. P. Jones, *The Genesis of Freemasonry: An Account of the Rise and Development of Freemasonry in Its Operative, Accepted, and Early Speculative Phases* [Manchester, 1947], p. 152). Clawson thinks it unlikely, but not impossible, for even ragmen to have become Masons. The evidence, however, is anecdotal, and even ragmen were "independent" entrepreneurs in a way that French journeymen were not.

76. Margaret C. Jacob, *Living the Enlightenment: Freemasonry and Politics in Eighteenth-Century Europe* (Oxford, 1991), especially pp. 64–65, 204–5, and the conclusion. Even crossing the boundary between noble and bourgeois in French lodges could nonetheless offer important challenges to the hierarchies and tensions present in old regime society (p. 179).

Grand Lodge was founded in 1717). In 1737 the lieutenant general of
police circulated copies of the Masons' secret words, signs, and rituals
to his subordinates.[77] In the same year the abbé Le Camus could write
to a brother Mason that Masonry's "secret life" was known in the
"streets of Paris. . . .there is not a shop boy who does not greet us by
boasting of his knowledge of our signs."[78] Thereafter followed plays,
vaudeville-type comedies, songs, and poems that employed Masonic
themes, practices, and terminology. Connections between old regime
French artisans and Masons remain to be fully explored, but it is suggestive that Le Camus singles out a group linked to artisanal communities ("shop boys") as having knowledge of Masonic practice. Although
it is uncertain how developed the origin narratives of compagnonnage
were in the eighteenth century, the brotherhoods were probably exposed
to some Masonic constructions in this era. Whatever new cultural material compagnons incorporated from this source, it was not fully assimilated or commonly utilized until the nineteenth century.

Song, rather than origin narratives, seems to be the vehicle eighteenth-
century compagnons chose to articulate their conceptions about and
sentiments for their brotherhoods. While singing and writing songs remained a strong tradition in nineteenth-century compagnonnages (and
all French workers' organizations), other forms of written expression
gained favor among workers. This shift is another marker of the transition from oral to written culture. That a few songs were written down by
compagnons in the eighteenth century, providing material for thinking,
imagining, and acting, draws attention to the importance of literacy to
compagnonnage. The few extant songs usually relate the joys of the road
and the inn in the company of fine companions. They also define and
establish opposition between the two major devoirs. The theme of opposition is worked out, for example, in the "Chanson nouvelle," dated
18 January 1757, composed by the père "Intrepid" of the compagnons
non du devoir in Mâcon. The song began by evoking the traveling man's
pleasures and pains.

> You who traverse the world
> to enrich yourselves in vain
> Instead of wandering o'er the waves
> Wander 'midst the waves of wine.
> In the devoir one meets
> but danger, sighs, and fears,

77. George Henri Luquet, *La France-maçonnerie et l'état en France au XVIIIe siècle* (Paris, 1963),
p. 43.
78. Ibid., letter to Rocheret, 23 December 1737.

And with the gavots one finds
the source of all pleasures.

Vous qui parcourre Le monde
    pour vous enrichis en vain
    aulieu devoguer sur Londe
    vogués sur Les Flos duvin
    Sur Le devoir Lon éprouve
    que danger Crainte et soupirs
    et Sur Les gavots Lon trouve
    La source de tous plaisirs

These gavots, among whom all that is good in compagnonnage is
found, are a noble brotherhood pitted against fanatic dévorants:

I take my mallet in hand
and my cane in the other
against the mutinous dévorants.
Everyone sound the drums and trumpets
    make our songs fill the air
    and gavots take courage
    being all joined together
    to lead away the fanatic
    the renegade . . .
    and give him the conduite[79]
    he so justly deserves.
And you, o noble tour de France
    you must never forget
    our royal [men] so valiant
    [who] have never wavered.
    And on the field of battle
    they are always transported
    waiting with courage
    for its enraged dévorants.

je prend mon mallet en main
epuis ma canne de lautre
pour les devorans mutins
A Tous tambours et trompettes
    faites ressentir nos airs
    et gavots prenés courrages
    etaents tous aux consort

79. That is, the "conduite of Grenoble," running the gauntlet.

> pour conduire la phanatique
> ce renegat . . .
> et luy donner La Conduite
> Comme il La Bien merite
> et vous noble tour de france
> ne faut jamais oblié
> nos royal plien devailliance
> nont jamais Laché Lepied
> et sur Le champ de Bataille
> ce sont toujour transporte
> attandant avec courrage
> ses devorans enflamés.[80]

I have not found such songs in the seventeenth century, although quite possibly some did exist. These songs are powerful expressions of the compagnons' values. Although père Intrepid's song does not duplicate the content of gavots' nineteenth-century origin narratives, it similarly establishes a code and history for each devoir and, like later narratives, largely bases definition on opposition. This song, moreover, contains elements that are elaborated in nineteenth-century narratives, and in an interesting twist on narratives in which gavots were the dissidents, the "Chanson nouvelle" relegates dévorants to the status of rebels. In the gavots' song dévorants are "mutinous" and "renegades," workers who had betrayed the devoir. But gavots do not only condemn dévorants; they also express their love for the tour de France, asking those on the tour to remember the "royal" gavots who, throughout their history, have "never wavered." The use of the word *royal* may be a veiled reference to King Solomon as their founder.

Martial overtones are evident: drums, trumpets, fields of battle, and warlike ardor abound. The "war" here is a defense of economic and social position; the weapons, mallet and cane, are symbols of work and compagnonnage. The song urges gavots to battle to defend their place on the tour and uphold its principles against the dévorants' fanaticism. The song implies economic as well as moral prerogatives. When the dévorant is "led away," gavots will control the workshops. Rixes that might follow or accompany the singing of such songs could sometimes be traced to a struggle between rivals to gain a monopoly on placement. Economic rivalries were thus reinforced by the ideology of membership.

80. AMM, HH 11/18.

Brawls, Brotherhood, Motherhood

The records of compagnonnage in eighteenth-century French cities reveal a high degree of organization reinforced by ritual practices. But rituals such as the conduite, which became an integral part of these brotherhoods, generated a capacity to disrupt production and to spawn more general disorder. During the period 1784–1789, for example, many petitions from master cabinetmakers, turners, joiners, coopers, box makers, and other woodworking trades in Le Mans claimed that journeymen frequently left work without notice to *battre aux champs* (perform conduites).[81] Whether or not these workers were members of the compagnonnages, the ubiquity of this custom is significant. The disruptions arising from conduites were persistently troublesome, whether conducted by compagnons or other journeymen, but the involvement of compagnonnage made matters worse. Masters in Le Mans also complained bitterly about being forced to hire through the compagnonnages, for workers refused to register at the official placement bureau.

Conduites often led to fights and further work stoppages, but there were many other ways to trigger a brawl. In Mâcon the 1753 ban on compagnons du devoir calmed open discord for several years, and also allowed the gavots to build up their forces. Then renewed violence in 1760 between compagnons du devoir and gavots (now also called dévorants and compagnons de liberté by the police) demonstrated that the dévorants had returned in force. The brawl that erupted "out into the open, in broad daylight, in front of the peaceable bourgeoisie of Mâcon," began on 27 December, when four drunken compagnon joiners du devoir serenaded the gavots in insulting terms right under the windows of their Mère.[82] Twenty-five angry gavots armed themselves and dashed out of the Mère. As the wily dévorants slipped away, the gavots spied what they thought were two compagnon carpenters du devoir (actually innocent bystanders) and gave chase from the Palais de Justice through the cour au Prévôt in the center of Mâcon. In this melee, which "seriously troubled the public order" (beginning near the residences of many judicial magistrates), one carpenter was badly injured. The triumphant gavots put their victim's bloodied hat on a pike and paraded it through the city streets and home to their Mère.

Their victory was short-lived. The very next day the *procureur du roi*, on the basis of the 1753 ordinance, imprisoned four of the compagnon

81. AD Sarthe, E 255, "Communauté des arts et métiers: Ouvriers ébénistes, tourneurs, et autres ouvriers en bois," 1784–89.
82. Jeanton, *Compagnons du devoir*, p. 3, based on material in ADSL, B 1309/3–190.

gavots (caught "en flagrant délit") and their mère. The procureur ordered a full investigation and another seizure of their papers. Interrogation proved fruitless. Those arrested denied having any association among them: no mutual obligations, no mère, no père, no special inns for any such association in the city. Both the mère of the compagnons non du devoir and the mère and père of the compagnons du devoir adamantly agreed. Perhaps because of their staunch and unanimous denials, the compagnons' sentences were fairly lenient; most received a twenty-five-franc fine. The innkeepers who had ("inadvertently") lodged either sect of compagnons "in numbers greater than three" were similarly fined. Three of the worst offenders were banished from Mâcon.[83]

Two key issues are raised by this case: the socioeconomic aspect of brawls and the role of mères and pères in defending compagnonnage. The Mâcon brawl was apparently generated not by conflict with the masters but by friction between two closely related trades—joining and carpentry—whose boundaries may have been weakening. The brawl could well have been the attempt of one devoir to eliminate potential competition. The almost religious fervor of the clash, however, can be attributed to each group's social and cultural bonds to its own devoir. The compagnons themselves may have realized a successful fight could effectively ward off competitors, but they fought to defend the honor and prowess of their brotherhoods.

Honor did not require compagnons to fight "fair." Sometimes, however, competition could take a distinctly "civilized" form, in challenges of skill. In 1773, for example, the stonecutters of opposing sects in Bordeaux proposed such a competition.[84] Each sect's honor would be defended by its most skilled member, who would execute a model of his own design and also his opponent's model according to the submitted specifications. The written challenge was drawn up on 28 November and each competitor handed over 360 livres to be held by a M. Mazarin until delivered to the winner. Each man set to work in a locked and guarded room. When La Réjouissance emerged after three months claiming victory for the compagnon stonecutters non du devoir (*étrangers*), however, the "jury" (two men of each devoir) couldn't or (wisely) wouldn't pass judgment.

La Réjouissance's opponent, La Pensée, a compagnon du devoir (*pas-*

83. Ibid., pp. 10, 14, 18.
84. Charles Braquehaye, "Défi des compagnons 'passants' et des compagnons 'étrangers' jugé par l'Académie de peinture, de sculpture, et d'architecture de Bordeaux le 27 mars 1771 [misprint for 1774]," *Bulletin historique et philologique*, nos. 3–4 (1901): 493–503. This is a rare documented study of such a challenge, based on the procès-verbaux of the academy.

sant), declared that the so-called victor had not executed the second model and began to take legal steps against the compagnons du devoir. La Pensée also addressed a petition to the city council, and in a city where compagnonnage's conflicts and work stoppages were on-going and serious, the aldermen paid attention. The stonecutters' brawls were notorious and "almost perpetual" between 1770 and 1776.[85] With discord growing and compagnons threatening to come to blows, the aldermen decided the pieces should be judged by nine members of the Académie de peinture, de sculpture, et d'architecture. The nine men of the jury took their assignment seriously, even assigning additional tasks to the competitors, who were clearly both very talented. Eventually, the jury rendered a dimplomatic (if ultimately unsatisfactory) judgment that distributed honors between the two compagnonnages almost equally and returned each side's deposit. The decision began by separating the competitors' individual talents from the talent of and respect due to each compagnonnage. The jury lavished praise on both La Réjouissance and La Pensée, who won overall by a slight edge, but the superior quality of La Réjouissance's designs was recognized. On the academy's advice, the city awarded each man a fifty-livre prize and a medal, the only difference being that La Pensé's medal was a bit heavier and bigger. Although the two devoirs were not entirely content, this high-level public attention to their artistry succeeded in calming the two camps—at least for a time.

Such peaceful resolutions were rare. The compagnon stonecutters' internecine brawls continued while they simultaneously mounted "a decided resistance against the masters, and quickly declared an absolute independence from them [and] aren't even afraid to assault them."[86] It is, moreover, unlikely that the compagnons accepted the jury's premise that their champions' talents reflected only on the individual and not on the group. We can find a more applicable model in the feud as John Bossy defines it. Bossy has explored how marriage alliances and godparenthood relations in early modern Europe created a formal system of "artificial" kin, which strengthened natural kin ties and extended social support networks. In the process, those outside the network were proscribed. Thus, "the system of formal friendship implied a system of formal hostility, of what one may loosely describe as a feud." Bossy and other scholars stress that in the early modern era neither the lineage nor the nuclear family formed the most significant set of social relations. The most significant group was a "mainly horizontal body of relations

without much depth in time . . . composed of two main elements, the
consanguini and the *amici.*" Friendship tended to be a "formal relation,
rather than a purely emotional or sentimental one."[87]

Similarly, compagnons refashioned themselves as kin, temporarily replacing or supplementing natural kin and local friendship networks. Anyone not a part of the compagnons' artificial kin group was a potential
enemy. Nonetheless, just as ties of blood, marriage, and baptism could
break down, the ties of compagnonnage were also subject to vicissitudes.
Compagnons sometimes failed to act as brothers and to meet the requirements of their devoir. And although mères and pères ideally regarded
compagnons as sons, they sometimes betrayed their trust. We are thus
led to examine the second major question raised by the Mâcon brawl:
what was the extent of the power of compagnonnage to command its
members' and supporters' allegiance? In the 1760 case the compagnons
and their mères and pères resolutely protected the devoir's secrets. The
relationship between compagnons and their innkeepers was a delicate
one: the inn itself was essential to the chambre's welfare; yet mères and
pères were usually not (at least before the nineteenth century) ritually
initiated into the kinship network as were the "brothers." The Mâcon
correspondence demonstrates how well the system could work: innkeepers often treated compagnons with affection and maintained enduring
relationships with them, even when owed money. Compagnons in turn
respected and honored their "mothers" and "fathers." Sometimes there
were more tangible bonds of fidelity and affection. Even if not initiated,
mères and pères had formal "titles" that sealed their relationships with
the devoir and permitted them to hold the compagnons' papers.

But bonds of fidelity were almost always reinforced by written contracts, making the relationship between compagnons and their innkeepers both familial and financial, companionate and instrumental.[88]
Although the importance of emotional ties in family relationships, at
least as an *ideal*, was increasingly recognized in the eighteenth century,
this trend must not be exaggerated, even among elites. Most old regime
mothers and fathers were still far from pursuing, even as an ideal, the
parental behavior Rousseau celebrated in *Emile* and *La Nouvelle Héloïse—*

87. John Bossy, "Blood and Baptism: Kinship, Community, and Christianity in Western Europe from the Fourteenth to the Seventeenth Centuries," in *Sanctity and Secularity: The Church
and the World,* ed. Derek Baker (Oxford, 1973), pp. 129–43, 136.
88. See Lawrence Stone, *The Family, Sex, and Marriage in England, 1500–1800* (New York,
1977), on the socioeconomic and emotional components of the gradual shift from a more
patriarchal to a more egalitarian family. In the nineteenth century, Agricol Perdiguier depicted
the emotional bond as an essential part of compagnons' relationships with their innkeepers.
Arriving at a Mère with a fellow compagnon, he noted: "We were well received. . . .[We] embraced the plump père and mère Bertrand. It is not necessary to know the pères and mères to
embrace them" (*Mémoires,* p. 133); he later criticized an "unmotherly" mère in Nantes (p. 181).

maternal nurturing, tenderness, and individualized care. Nevertheless, scholars may underestimate the extent to which these sentiments existed and how their absence could be censured: Ménétra writes warmly of his close relationship with his grandmother (whom he usually calls Mother) and depicts his father as physically and emotionally abusive.[89] Yet, while both portraits may accurately reflect Ménétra's experience and feelings, his recollections, written at the end of the eighteenth century, could have been reshaped, sharpened, or even transformed. Love and brutality were probably both present in Ménétra's childhood, but the popularization of Rousseauean views may have helped him recast these memories in more dichotomous and gendered terms—maternal affection and paternal authority.[90]

Thus, it is not odd for mères and pères to care for their compagnons *and* make contracts with them. Long-lasting relationships between innkeepers and compagnons deepened the emotional links in these fictive families. If major financial disputes arose, however, as they might well where mobile, often insolvent workers were involved, prior bonds could be cut, as in a complaint brought against compagnon joiners non du devoir in Avignon by Jean Vernet, their père. Vernet held three notes of debt signed by these compagnons between July 1766 and September 1767, totalling 1,933 livres, 4 sols.[91] Sometime in late 1767 or 1768, most of the compagnons skipped town without paying up. When Vernet discovered that six of these compagnons (including two former premiers) were in Marseille, he sought them out personally. They promised payment but gave him nothing. Finally, Vernet wrote to the intendant of Provence. To strengthen his case and perhaps in retaliation against his debtors, he informed on their operations, no doubt to the delight of the authorities, for the Marseille region was rife with labor conflict provoked by compagnons of both devoirs.[92]

89. We know Rousseau did not extend the model of parental care he advocated to his own children, nor did he allow his partner, Thérèse Levasseur to do so despite her wishes and his insistence on the critical role of maternal care. Children abandoned to the state, if they survived, would have been fortunate to receive the care Ménétra had.

90. Changing ideals of love also worked to transform the marital relationship, but more slowly. Marriages remained much more business than sentimental affairs well into the nineteenth century. Ménétra portrays his marriage as one of good sense, not great love. Love and sexual desire were very important to Ménétra but had little to do with marriage.

91. AM Marseille, FF 206, Jean Vernet to Latour, intendant of Provence [1768], and "Copie des trois billets."

92. E.g., in 1759 an edict of the parlement of Provence banned placement by compagnons of whatever devoir and ordered each trade corporation to name a placement officer. In May 1765 a master joiner, Laurent Ripert of Marseille, submitted a complaint to the parlement which enumerated the compagnons' violations of the 1759 edict: a month later the edict was reissued. AM Marseille, FF 206, 21 May, 3 and 5 June 1765. These conflicts continued and became particularly acute in Marseille and Aix in 1771 and again in 1786–87.

Vernet explained that the compagnon joiners had chosen him as their
père; he served under a "sort of contract" which could be terminated
by either party for just cause after payment of all debts. He also revealed
the compagnons kept a large bound book, used during the reception
ceremony of new compagnons, which contained the "secrets of their
devoir gavotal, which they highly value." They guarded their secrets well:
when the compagnons absconded, they "fraudulently ripped out and
took away" this book's most confidential pages. Vernet claimed the right
to collect the debt owed him "as a body and jointly" (*en corps et solidai-
rement*) by all joiners non du devoir, who "numbered about 1,000
throughout France." Although Vernet was technically guilty of harboring
an illegal association, the intendant made no mention of it. Rather, he
supported Vernet and wrote to Marseille's mayor and aldermen on 9
August 1768, requesting that they track down the compagnon joiners
who had fled there and threaten them with arrest if they failed to satisfy
their obligations promptly.[93]

The compagnons' credit-debt situation is closely linked to wage structures and payments in the artisanal trades. Payment was irregular, often
coming at the end of particular job, which could last for weeks. Moreover, food, drink, and lodging, advances by masters, and irregular payment all meant that a money wage rate was not fixed and inviolable.[94]
Compagnonnages added to the equation with credit extended by premiers, mères, and pères. Compagnons would and could accumulate large
debts at the Mère, reflecting not only the importance of this institution
in compagnonnage but also the generally high degree of trust between
mères and pères, and their compagnons. Mères believed, as had Vernet,
that compagnons throughout France would remain responsible for all
debts. Because compagnons had many long-term associations with
particular Mères, their belief was probably right. The Mâcon correspondence demonstrates that deadbeat compagnons plagued compagnonnages as much as they did mères and pères. Yet, despite the sometimes
precarious finances of local chambres, compagnonnages functioned as
a serious impediment to the official organization of labor in France.

93. AM Marseille, FF 206, Vernet to Latour; Latour to mayor and aldermen. I found no
further reference to the case after August 1768; perhaps the compagnons paid up.
94. See Michael Sonenscher, "Work and Wages in Eighteenth-Century Paris," in *Manufacture
in Town and Country before the Factory,* ed. Maxine Berg, Pat Hudson, and Michael Sonenscher
(Cambridge, 1983), p. 152; and Sonenscher, *Work and Wages: Natural Law, Politics, and the Eighteenth-Century French Trades* (Cambridge, 1989), esp. chaps. 5 and 6. As a rough guideline, skilled
workers such as carpenters were paid between 40 and 50 sous a day in Paris toward the end of
the old regime; joiners and locksmiths there might be paid somewhat more.

RITUAL AND THE PRACTICE OF EVERYDAY LIFE

The examples analyzed in this chapter reveal eighteenth-century associations in which ritual was woven into members' lives on almost a
daily basis. Friendship, harmony, and unity, even within a sect, might
not always prevail. Fines were assessed; deadbeats were pursued. Nonetheless, the rituals continued to integrate compagnons into the local
brotherhood. These rituals, which interrupted work routine, were perhaps necessary breaks, helping the workshop to function by granting
workers some independence and control over their time. Masters often
tolerated these disruptions to keep a full complement of workers.[95]

The compagnons' rituals of daily life were thus not dark, esoteric cor-
ners of their brotherhoods but vital and meaningful organizational practices. Rituals served utilitarian needs while investing labor with value;
their associations enabled and encouraged compagnons to undermine
their masters' power and gain a mastery of their own. Whether or not
insubordinate compagnons welcomed the Revolution, they could well
herald the abolition of the guilds in March 1791 without imagining that
the Revolution would also prove far more effective than the old regime
in silencing their own associations. They would be forced underground
for a time, only to spring up again on the other side of the Revolution.

95. Cf. Michael Sonenscher, "Journeymen's Migrations and Workshop Organization in Eighteenth-Century France," in Kaplan and Koepp, *Work in France,* pp. 74–96.

CHAPTER 6

From Revolution to Restoration

Our cities du devoir had but a few compagnons who met as
secretly as possible. . . .no one dared admit who he was.

—Compagnon joiners du devoir,
"Mauvais souvenirs de la Révolution"

The very success of revolutionary governments in outlawing the compagnonnages and other forms of organized labor, coupled with general
social and political upheaval, has left little evidence on these associations
from about 1792 to the start of the Empire. Like almost all French men
and women, compagnons found prior loyalties and beliefs challenged
and were caught up in the vast changes of this period. Some may have
served in revolutionary armies and gloried in the experience. Others
claimed their willingness to give up their own "colors" and "take on
those of the nation."[1] But during the Empire the compagnonnages enjoyed a rapid resurgence, suggesting that many members wished to continue or revive their past traditions, dormant during the Revolution, but
not destroyed. The brotherhoods had been preserved; after the Revolution they were reconstructed.

THE REVOLUTION AND ITS RHETORIC

A valuable unpublished manuscript of the compagnon joiners du devoir of Toulouse titled "Unpleasant Memories of the Revolution" depicted the First Republic as a "time of troubles." It was "a Pandora's
box opened for the compagnons who left our cities to seek peace in
more isolated areas, a peace which seemed to have escaped them as soon
as they found it. Our cities du devoir had but a few compagnons, who

1. AMN, I² 137, no. 3, 25 June 1792, "Procès-verbal, commissaire de police," compagnons
forgerons.

met as secretly as possible; their correspondence was intercepted; finally no one dared admit who he was."[2] The attitudes of compagnonnages and other workers' associations toward the Revolution, however, were complex at best. Initially, workers heralded the new government, which recognized their importance to the nation. Between 1789 and 1791 labor remained organized and relatively active. Analysis of these activities for the compagnonnages is, however, frequently impossible, because the records of labor disputes often fail to discriminate between types of associations or to define the participants' allegiances. In any event, after the Le Chapelier Law (14 June 1791) prohibited workers' "coalitions" on pain of fine and imprisonment, there are only scattered references to compagnonnages (or other labor organizations). The Le Chapelier Law completed the abolition of the corporations begun in March with the Allarde Law. With the end of the legal system of privilege, whereby rights such as masterships were property, a new system of property relations emerged. Moreover, as William Sewell writes, the Le Chapelier Law "implied not only the reduction of all citizens to an equal submission to the law common to all Frenchmen, but the annihilation of any sense of common interest intermediate between the individual and the nation."[3] Compagnons probably tried, as their words suggest, simply to exist quietly, concealing or obscuring their enduring corporate ties.

Germain Martin's classic study of workers' associations maintains that compagnonnage must have been engaged in the major labor disputes of the early revolutionary era in Paris, particularly those in carpentry, and the recent work of Michael Sibalis lends some weight to this view. Martin links compagnonnage to the important Union de la charpente, a Parisian mutual aid society that played an important role in early revolutionary labor agitation and was the focus of attention in the drafting of the Le Chapelier Law against associations. Martin says that the Union claimed to be a successor to the societies "des devoirs," and Sibalis, on the basis of a painstaking analysis of available sources, calls the Union a likely cover organization for the compagnonnage du devoir.[4] Confrater-

2. "Livres d'antiquités des compagnons menuisiers du devoir destinées pour Toulouse," three ms. booklets [Lyon, 1839], cited in Louis Claays, "Le Compagnonnage à Toulouse de 1800 à 1848" (Maîtrise, Université de Toulouse, 1969), p. 28.

3. William H. Sewell, Jr., *Work and Revolution in France: The Language of Labor from the Old Regime to 1848* (Cambridge, 1980), p. 89. Cf. Michael Sonenscher, *Work and Wages: Natural Law, Politics, and the Eighteenth-Century French Trades* (Cambridge, 1989), pp. 68, 346–51. "Only when master artisans were divested of *their* collective identities," Sonenscher writes, "were journeymen collectively unable to challenge their claims to legal entitlements in the courts" (p. 68). Members of the compagnonnages, however, were already less actively engaged in legal redress of rights before the Revolution than other journeymen's associations or unaffiliated workers.

4. Germain Martin, *Les Associations ouvrières au XVIIIe siècle (1700–1792)* (Geneva, 1974 [Paris, 1900]), p. 244; Michael David Sibalis, "The Carpenters of Paris, 1789–1848," revised version of

nal associations, however, were generally more active and common than
compagnonnages in Parisian labor disputes on the eve of the Revolution.
Moreover, these confraternities were more flexible and broadly based
than compagnonnages: they accepted married workers, those who had
finished their tours de France, and workers from more diverse trades.[5]

Nonetheless, there are compelling references to compagnonnages' labor activities in various trades, including carpentry, in this era. One of
the earliest dates from 12 June 1789, when a merchant hatter in Paris
brought a complaint before Alexandre Ferrand, king's counselor, concerning a dispute between compagnon hatters du devoir and those calling themselves *bons enfants*.[6] The *bons enfants* were organized similarly to
a compagnonnage and opposed themselves to compagnons non du devoir. The plaintiff claimed organized hatters were plotting to increase
their membership; moreover, other hatters had joined the work stop-
page begun by the original disputants on 4 June.

While hatters fought over which of their organizations should dominate the labor force, other workers appear to have opposed all labor
organizations, but particularly compagnonnage. A petition, addressed to
the new government by "journeymen of all professions, skills, and
trades" demanded the complete abolition of compagnonnage. The petitioners denounced the compagnons du devoir and "other groups" who
disrupted society. Members of compagnonnage were accused of forming
a corporation with "signs" and words known only to its initiates, who
bore fictitious names, taken to avoid discovery by authorities. This petition further detailed how compagnons extorted placement fees from
workers, attacked innocent workers on the road if they couldn't give the
proper signs, and created an association existing throughout France.[7]
The petitioners concluded by reminding the authorities that compagnonnage had been illegal even in the old regime: the principles of the
Revolution demanded its permanent suppression.

Dupont de Nemours, who recalled violent encounters in the provinces
between compagnon joiners du devoir and those of "another corporation whose name he had forgotten," gave the petition a favorable reading. He sent it to the constitutional committee with a recommendation
for serious consideration. At least two other similar petitions were pre-

a paper originally given at the annual meeting of the Society for French Historical Studies,
Minneapolis, Minnesota, March 1987, pp. 9–10, 51.
  5. Sonenscher, *Work and Wages*, chap. 9.
  6. AN, Y 13016, "Cabale des chapeliers," 12 June 1789.
  7. AN, D IV 51, dos. 1488, 31 March 1790, "Pétitions, adresses, adhésions, et suppliques des
corps administratif et des particuliers," ms. notation, Dupont de Nemours, as cited by Germain
Martin, *Associations ouvrières*, pp. 225–27. Martin provides an extended discussion of this document (which is missing in the Archives nationales).

sented to the authorities before the passage of the Le Chapelier Law. One of them, dated May 12 1790, was a list of grievances submitted to the National Assembly by the *renards*, "compagnon carpenters, outside the devoir," who "dare to present [themselves] at the feet of the august representatives of the nation."[8] They complained that the powerful monopoly of the compagnon carpenters du devoir, called *drilles*, made it impossible for the renards to find work in the capital and its environs: "Your glorious works, our lords, have guaranteed the liberty of all the individuals who have the fortune to make up France, and yet all are not free. The petitioners, who form a large part of this vast empire, are perhaps the only ones who do not enjoy this right so dear to all the French."[9] Liberty was thus recognized as a sacred individual right, closely linked, in the renards' view, to the economic freedom to work where and for whom they chose, without adherence to any organization, even those directed by workers. But, who were the renards? Their petition explicitly stressed their being *outside* of the devoir and thus *not* a workers' coalition. Nonetheless, although not a compagnonnage, neither were they always an amorphous gathering of "individuals."

Evidence, from Nantes, for example, reveals that the renards themselves formed a loose sort of organization. The *sécretaire-caissier* of the artillery works and of the National Guard at Richebourg wrote to the public prosecutor to defend two compagnon carpenters du devoir, Painparé and Saintonge, accused of being the leaders of a "cabal of compagnonnage." The author, Bouffet, portrayed the mutual aid practices of the compagnons du devoir in a most sympathetic light and passionately argued that if these compagnons monopolized work, it was because they were "true artists" and highly trained. Masters generally preferred them, even though the renards were willing to work for less, in contradiction of the "fraternity and mutual aid reigning among [compagnons du devoir] whom I have almost always known to be good citizens." In fact, Bouffet stressed the compagnons' probity and their fidelity to the new laws of assembly. By contrast, the renards, disorderly men who "did not know their trade," led by the "dangerous" Tourangeau le rampart, had been "assembl[ing] in groups of 20 to 25" to harrass and insult the compagnons du devoir for the past several months. These efforts had redoubled after the renards came to believe that the National Assembly had suppressed the "compagnonnage du devoir."[10]

8. AN, D IV 57, 1488, as cited by Germain Martin, *Associations ouvrières*, p. 227.
9. Germain Martin, *Associations ouvrières*, p. 227.
10. AMN, I² 137, no. 3, dos. 4, 6 August 1791, Nantes, Bouffet to the procureur de la commune. Bouffet's wife had previously interceded on behalf of the two, but we are not told more about her association with the case. Saintonge had worked for Bouffet for the prior three months.

Generally, however, as Sibalis contends, the renards in Paris were un-affiliated workers who believed that the revolutionary society would up-hold their rights. In 1790, having never fully experienced the potential ramifications of the free market, the renards seemed to think workers' associations were not necessary, for the new regime "makes all individ-uals free and abolishes all assemblies in general." The renards outlined the practices of the compagnons du devoir for the lawmakers. They held "meetings three times a year in the cities at what they call their Mère . . . under pretext of visits to learn the whereabouts of the compagnons they call renards; there they renew the oath to devour [*gruger*] and ex-terminate all those of the [same] class as the petitioners, and these abuses persist in spite of the decrees of the august National Assembly."[11] The renards' language presents the drilles in the worst possible light, as violent men whose corporate allegiance runs counter to the will of the nation. The renards, by contrast, wished only to live in accord with the decrees of the "august" *National* Assembly, not the *particular* assemblies of compagnons du devoir.

Almost a year later, on 5 May 1791, an address was given in the Na-tional Assembly on behalf of "the great majority of the working class in the trade of hatting [and] of the entrepreneurs and manufacturers of all the professions, and of the greatest part of the journeymen of the *arts et métiers*." This broad spectrum of workers, entrepreneurs, and man-ufacturers urgently requested the assembly to "destroy the institution of the compagnons du devoir," which they claimed was the best known and most powerful of all the sects of compagnonnage.[12] Many journey-men, particularly in hatting, found its domination as onerous as that of the masters. Nonetheless, their ties to the entrepreneurs and manufac-turers is intriguing, for the growth of large-scale manufacture was a ma-jor threat to skilled journeymen. Yet, it is likely that the unskilled workers without formal apprenticeships flooding into the capital were eager to evade controls imposed by both trade corporations and compagnon-nages.

The compagnonnages' role in labor disputes in the Revolution can be most concretely documented toward the end of April 1791. On 3 April 1791, Jean-Sylvain Bailly, mayor of Paris, wrote to the Comité des re-

---

Dissatisfied with the official response to his wife's plea, Bouffet wrote to tell "the truth" of the matter. He says he learned about the compagnons du devoir from traveling on his own tour de France but does not admit to having been a member. While his level of literacy and position put him in a different social class from most compagnons du devoir, Bouffet may have been in the association. He may also have been a Freemason with some links to compagnonnage.

11. Germain Martin, *Associations ouvrières*, p. 228.

12. Jérôme Mavidal and Emile Laurent, eds., *Archives parlementaires de 1787 à 1860, 1st ser.*, 2d ed., 82 vols. (Paris, 1879–1913), 25:609. Only a brief report of this address still exists.

cherches of the National Assembly, warning them about the expected arrival of a number of compagnons du devoir in Paris. Bailly had received information from the municipal officers of Arnay le Duc on 27 March 1791 that "compagnons called du devoir, of various trades, have received the order of their confrères to come to Paris on the fourth [of April]. The greatest secrecy surrounds the subject of this trip, those of our town left yesterday, we know that they will be followed by others from neighboring towns to whom they sent a circular letter."[13] The letter provides striking evidence of the strong organizational and communication network developed by the compagnonnages in the course of the eighteenth-century. Although surveillance had led to the interception of some of the compagnons' correspondence, it had not been soon enough or complete enough to thwart their designs. The meeting may have had the broader aim of discussing the problems facing compagnonnage under the new regime, but it seems likely that the call to Paris was tied to proposed labor agitation, perhaps linked to the strike of Parisian carpenters which began on 19 April.

The main demand was higher wages, although no exact figure was stated. The carpenters also called for a uniform wage for a day's work. Nothing in the evidence specifically identifies the participation of the compagnons du devoir, but there was a "total coalition of the compagnon carpenters who refused to work." Thus, it is more than likely that compagnons du devoir were involved in the strike. Germain Martin is more affirmative about a link, citing "a gathering of compagnons du devoir near Notre Dame," but provides no archival reference for this assertion.[14]

By 21 April the strike was spreading and strikers were actively threatening workers who would not join their cause. The carpenters met frequently and appointed deputations to make the rounds of all workshops and sites to ascertain that all work had been stopped. On 26 April, Bailly, fearing compagnons might "forcibly remove the apprentices and stop work," asked the marquis de Lafayette, commander of the National Guard, to provide special surveillance of carpentry workshops in the Archêvé district. Finally, on 29 April 1791, in an attempt to resolve the strike, a proclamation and edict were promulgated stating that "by virtue of the idea of liberty, it is impossible to impose any decision on the masters." Not similarly limited in their liberty, masters unilaterally set the minimum wage in carpentry at two and a half francs per day and

13. AN, D XXIX bis 18, dos. 196.
14. Archives de la Préfecture de police (hereafter APP), Paris, Actes et délibérations des sections, AA/83, Buttes-des-Moulins, 19 April 1791, and AA/98, Observatoire, 21 April 1791; Germain Martin, *Associations ouvrières*, pp. 231–32.

requested the commune's aid in breaking the strike.[15] The National Assembly countered that the authorities must first be legally empowered. The Le Chapelier Law, voted on 14 June 1791, provided the necessary authority.

That this law was essential seemed obvious to those who were increasingly concerned about workers actively pursuing their rights to petition and assembly, even if such workers opposed compagnonnage. A group of Parisian masters and entrepreneurs revealed their worries in a petition of early June sent to the constitutional committee. They claimed that there was a "general coalition of 80,000 workers in the capital," led by *compagnons* who believed themselves to be "divided in interests and principles from the rest of their fellow citizens." They greatly feared that the disorders in carpentry were now spreading to workers in other trades: farriers (*maréchaux*) had already joined the carpenters. These employers predicted that similar demands from locksmiths, shoemakers, and joiners would soon follow.[16] Martin sees this document as evidence of compagnonnage. Rhetorically, it is close to those of 31 March and 12 May 1790, and 5 May 1791, which specifically mention compagnons du devoir. There is no direct proof, however, that the petitioners were only or primarily referring to compagnons du devoir.

A group of workers, calling themselves *ouvriers* and not compagnons, responded to this attack in a *réfutation* of 2 June 1791, signed by at least 120 carpenters. The authors warned their fellow citizens that there were several "entrepreneurs in carpentry, still attached to those consuming and arbitrary laws of the trade corporations, still stubbornly clinging to those revolting privileges which gave them the power to dispose of the labor of the Workers they employ." The workers described their working conditions—including hours and pay—and found much fault with the status quo. They demanded to be protected from the "ambition" of their employers and asked if fifty sols was really an exorbitant sum to pay a man who did such difficult and dangerous tasks. Whether the carpenters who wrote the refutation had links to compagnonnage is less important than the fact that these *workers* wanted to take their chances as individuals in the new order of things, even while recognizing the power the masters' unity gave them: "We know well that the corporation was our misfortune, we will never allow ourselves to form one, because we know that it is illegal and prohibited by the laws of the French em-

15. APP, Paris, AA/98, Observatoire, 21 April 1791; Germain Martin, *Associations ouvrières*, pp. 231, 232. Previous wages were generally thirty to forty sols per day.

16. Germain Martin, *Associations ouvrières*, p. 233, June 1791, addressed to "Monsieur le Président du Comité de constitution."

pire.''[17] The power granted by such unity was not a positive but a negative force, allowing elites to exploit others and fragment virtue.

The farriers, who had supported the carpenters' strike, took a different stance and maintained their rights to association in a dispute of their own. This strike ended in the workers' favor. Salaries were increased and the workday was shortened. The masters blamed the workers' success on the weakness of the assembly, but the farriers' strike was the last major victory for organized workers before the Le Chapelier Law.[18] Once it was in effect, the very act of association became a crime. Agreements between employers and workers were henceforth to be made on an individual basis without pressure from workers' coalitions. By 1791, however, some workers recognized that, while their associations were condemned, masters and entrepreneurs still acted together to defend their interests, albeit outside the framework of trade corporations.

The dearth of evidence on workers' coalitions during most of the 1790s indicates that the Le Chapelier Law, assisted by revolutionary upheaval and war, did what it was intended to do. Yet, its effects may have been delayed in the provinces. There is evidence of strike activity in Nantes among organized plasterers, carpenters, farriers, and joiners before and for some months after the law was enacted. The carpenters, joiners, and plasterers in these cases were definitely involved in compagnonnage; the farriers probably were as well. Ironsmiths (*forgerons*) remained openly dedicated to compagnonnage until the following year. On 25 June 1792, on the "pretext" of celebrating the feast of their patron, Saint Eloi, a "troop" of about thirty to forty workers openly promenaded in the streets of Nantes, displaying signs of compagnonnage (canes, ribbons). One compagnon, a member of the National Guard, marched at their head, saber in hand. The police commissioner condemned "a display which only upholds compagnonnage and all those associations and corporations abolished by law." But ironsmiths demonstrated their loyalty to compagnonnage several days later at a meeting at the inn of a femme Mesnard. On being told that their assembly was illegal, the ironsmiths wrote a letter to the municipal officers stating they were all "good citizens." Some of them were even enrolled in the National Guard, willing to offer their services to the nation at all times. They added, "If we carried some ribbons suspect by the new constitution, we were ignorant of the infraction [and] we are ready to take on those of the nation."[19] Perhaps these workers were again recanting

---

17. AN, AD XI 65, dos. "Rapports, opinions, discours, et écrits divers, publiés depuis 1789," *Réfutation des ouvriers en l'art de charpente à la réponse des entrepreneurs* (Paris, [1791]), pp. 1, 2, 3.
18. AN, AD XI 65, dos. Maréchaux, *Précis pour les maréchaux de Paris* (Paris, [1791]).
19. AMN, I² 137, no. 3, dos. 4, March (plasterers), July–August (carpenters), November (far-

in public only to resume the ways of compagnonnage in private. It is also possible, as Gaston Martin suggests, that something remained of such workers' associations in the democratic clubs in the provinces in 1792 and 1793. It would be harder to reconcile the culture of independent, defiant compagnons with the political culture of Parisian sans-culottes, even though some compagnons may have become sans-culottes.[20] Furthermore, inasmuch as the major force of compagnonnage remained in the provinces rather than Paris, compagnons were far less likely than workers in the capital to experience and practice a republican and activist political education.

A salient example from Montpellier in 1798 demonstrates that the Revolution had neither completely rooted out compagnonnage nor completely changed it. The relative stability after the coup d'état of Fructidor may have encouraged the compagnons to come out into the open again. The commissioner of the Executive Directory assigned to Montpellier was informed that the outlawed associations of dévorants and gavots were attempting a revival and had already held several assemblies in the house of two women called the "mères des compagnons." The case involved an association of shoemakers agitating for an augmentation in the price of their work. This trade, not officially recognized by compagnonnage, perhaps took advantage of the association's disarray in the Revolution to begin reorganization and renewal as a brotherhood of compagnonnage. Eventually, six compagnons—including one Jean de Montbasin, "dit le Parisien"—were arrested and brought to trial. Simultaneously, local authorities took the opportunity to issue an edict forbidding "lodges" of compagnons and their mères, the use of passwords, and other "antics" (singeries) practiced in the streets by associations such as dévorants and gavots. Clearly, the edict was responding to more than a single recurrence of these associations. Other trades organized as compagnonnages were seeking to raise prices and keep workers willing to accept less out of the workshops.[21]

Two pen-and-ink drawings, dated "year VII of the Republic, One and Indivisible" (1799), tend to confirm this reemergence of compagnon-

---

riers), August (joiners), 1791, 25 June 1792, "Procès-verbal, commissaire de police" and an undated letter [late June or early July 1792]. The procès-verbal also included an order for the widow Mesnard to appear before the police on 29 June 1792 and a letter from her doctor, 3 July 1792, declaring her too ill to do so.

20. Gaston Martin, *Capital et travail à Nantes au cours du XVIIIe siècle* (Nantes, 1932), p. 87; Sonenscher, *Work and Wages*, chap. 10, esp. pp. 330–33.

21. AN, F[12] 1560, dos. Manufactures: Montpellier, 17 floréal an VI [7 May 1798], Report, commissioner, Executive Directory to minister of the interior; and 17 floréal an VI [7 May 1798], minutes, meeting of the departmental administration, Hérault. These are the most complete of the few references to compagnonnage after 1792 and before 1804.

Figure 5. Compagnon stonecutters passant du devoir, Bordeaux (1799). Left: fraternal accolade. Right: meeting of two compagnons. Pen-and-ink drawings. Source: Musée du Compagnonnage, Tours.

nage (see Figure 5).[22] Set in Bordeaux, these sketches depict the compagnon stonecutters passant du devoir performing the fraternal accolade and a meeting between two compagnon stonecutters, La Fidelité of Angoulême and La Sincerité of Beaufort (Anjou). Some of the symbolism—decorated canes, ribbons, the names, the square and compass, the accolade—is familiar. The interlinked hearts and the rose designs

22. The drawings and text were apparently mounted together sometime after the sketches were completed. In part the text reads "9 Prairial and VII [28 May 1799] de la République Une et Indivisible," and "Rencontre compagnonnique de la Fidélité d'Angoulême et de la Sincerité de Beaufort en Anjou sur leur Tour de France. Bordeaux 9 Prairial an VII." See also Roger Lecotté, *Les Archives historiques du compagnonnage* (Paris, 1956), pp. 41, 128.

(*rosaces*) in the right panel, the classical arch and starlike symbols in the
left panel, and the Republican date reveal adaptations or personaliza-
tions. Both drawings give evidence that compagnonnage, dispersed and
silenced in the 1790s, had not died or abandoned its customs, even if
some novel elements had been introduced. By the first decade of the
nineteenth century, the revival of compagnonnage seemed assured. But,
this return marked a critical juncture in its history as both compagnons
and their observers became increasingly aware of the distinction between
the values, beliefs, and practices of compagnonnage and those of the
postrevolutionary society.

REEMERGENCE IN THE EMPIRE

Many trades organized as compagnonnages in the old regime reestablished their local organizations and interurban networks in rapid suc-
cession in the early years of the nineteenth century. These brotherhoods
of compagnons, increasingly called chambres or *sociétés,* reemerged in
the Napoleonic era as institutions with some stature as more men and
new trades sought admission to them. By the end of the first decade of
the nineteenth century, Napoleonic police recognized that the compagnonnages would be as much trouble for the Empire as they had been
for the old regime. Some officials thought their interference in the workplace would be worse, for they appeared more disciplined and better
organized than previously. Yet, in most trades, these early signs of
strength did not continue past the 1820s, when sects of compagnonnage
faced severe challenges to their authority from internal dissidents and
external critics and from changes in the organization of economic production.

Despite their internal strife and eventual decline, in the first half of
the nineteenth century compagnonnages displayed remarkable vigor
and a stubborn refusal to die, particularly in the building trades. The
revival was marked by an increased tendency for each sect and trade to
differentiate itself from all others. This propensity for differentiation had
existed from the very beginning, of course, but it was increasingly formalized. Nineteenth-century compagnons wished to enforce stricter adherence to their devoir and statutes, to keep more accurate and detailed
written records, and to increase control over members, particularly novices. Moreover, nineteenth-century compagnons put greater emphasis on
the value of their traditions, including correct performance of their rituals and the proper narration, preservation, and even publication of

their legends.[23] Official reports provide crucial information on the successes and failures of compagnonnage in the postrevolutionary era, and more direct testimony from correspondence and the work of compagnons with a literary turn, such as Perdiguier, Jean-François Piron (Vendôme la clef des coeurs), and Toussaint Guillaumou, announces the degree to which compagnons wished to define, redefine, and reinforce their beliefs and practices.

As early as 1804 an ordinance of the prefect of the department of Maine-et-Loire provides compelling evidence of widespread revival.[24] The prefect considered the threat sufficient to ban compagnonnages and establish placement offices to register all incoming workers and assign them to workshops. He condemned the associations on two counts: its sects provoked many bloody brawls, and more serious, it created a "system of insubordination and license contrary to the intentions of the government, to the interests of the heads of workshops, and to the execution of their work." Fouché, minister of police, approved this decree on 6 fructidor an XII (23 August 1804) and thought it could serve as a model for other provinces. Indeed, in 1805 prefects of the nearby departments of the Loiret and the Eure-et-Loire issued similar rulings.[25]

These prefects echoed their colleagues' views on compagnonnage and attempted to give an account of its activities in their own departments. The mayor of Orléans (Loiret), had a rather successful informant who discovered, among other things, that compagnonnage already existed among cutlers, wheelwrights, blacksmiths, locksmiths, saddle makers, hatters, wrought-iron workers, harness makers, cloth shearers, roofers, carpenters, tanners and curriers, dyers, shoemakers, and bakers (although he noted that these last two trades were not accepted by the others). This was all in early 1805. Reading this report, the prefect of the Loiret commented: "Although the associations known under the names of compagnons du Devoir and Gavaux [sic] do not have a visible organization, nonetheless they have a real existence in various trades.

23. These developments correlate with certain of Norbert Elias's observations about written documents, etiquette, and ceremony. For example, "apart from their other functions," written documents "have the function of control," and etiquette and ceremony are "important instruments of rule and the distribution of power" (*The Court Society* [New York, 1983], pp. 29, 140).

24. As seen, there is sporadic earlier evidence of reemergence, but by 1804 reports on the associations became much more regular and reached police officials in Paris from almost all parts of France. For an earlier report on compagnonnage among Parisian carpenters see AN F[7] 3830, police report, 30 messidor an X [18 July 1802], cited by Sibalis, "Carpenters of Paris," p. 6. For the wider context of labor and politics, see also Michael D. Sibalis, "The Workers of Napoleonic Paris, 1800–1815" (Ph.D. diss., Concordia University, 1979).

25. AN, F[7] 4236, 18 thermidor an XII [5 August 1804], minutes, arrêts, dos. Maine-et-Loire, 19 thermidor an XII [6 August 1804], "Arrêt sur les Compagnons du devoir et les gavots," dos. Loiret, 9 fructidor an XIII [26 August 1805], "Extrait du registre des arrêts du Préfet," dos. Eure-et-Loire, 14 thermidor an XIII [1 August 1805], arrêt.

The workers assemble at the inns of women called mères to deliberate on their interests . . . and to perpetuate adherence to their alleged statutes." A report, titled "Sur le compagnonnage," commissioned by the central police administration in Paris, revealed the same—or worse—problems in 1811.[26]

Probably written for or by the councillor of state of the First Arrondissement, "Sur le compagnonnage" examined the nature and activities of the associations and tried to analyze the effects of the Revolution on them.[27] At first, the author contends, the Revolution caused disruption; all thought the compagnons were in disarray and had forgotten about their old forms of organization. In the end, however, the Revolution actually furthered the cause of compagnonnage. These "corps," since the reestablishment of order, "have been replaced and resettled, the workers have gone back to their former habits. . . . the license of the Revolution has accustomed them to independence [providing] a favorable situation that allows them to work when and at the price they choose."[28] The report concludes that this return of compagnonnage had made itself felt in a number of large cities. Nor were these societies abberations found in one or two departments: compagnonnage formed an interurban organization that made it a potentially dangerous social and economic force.

With regard to the rival sects, the author of "Sur le compagnonnage" found that although compagnons du devoir and compagnons du devoir de liberté (gavots) generally violently opposed each other, the two groups had worked together on at least one occasion. In Chalon-sur-Saône on 13 October 1808 about a hundred compagnons du devoir and gavots in unspecified trades had formed a united coalition against the masters. They planned to join forces, desert Chalon-sur-Saône, ban (interdire) the town, and leave the masters without workers, thereby forcing them to raise wages and improve working conditions. Rapid police intervention scuttled the plan, but departmental authorities considered the coalition an extremely dangerous precedent. The unity of dévorants and gavots might thus be rare, but was not impossible. Rival allegiances could sometimes be put aside to pursue common goals.

In his 1810 "Observations" on associations known as compagnons du devoir, the prefect of the Haute-Garonne had stated that isolated meas-

26. Ibid., dos. Loiret, 19 messidor an XIII [7 July 1805], mayor to prefect of the Loire, and 9 fructidor an XIII [26 August 1805], "Extrait du registre des arrêts du Préfet," dos. 538/R, 17 July 1811, Police générale.
27. Napoleon reorganized the Ministry of the Police générale on 10 July 1804 into four arrondissments: (1) west, north and parts of eastern France; (2) south and parts of eastern France; (3) Parisian region; and (4) Italy. Each district was under the jurisdiction of a councillor of state.
28. AN, F⁷ 4236, dos. 538/R, 17 July 1818.

ures were of no avail "against compagnons who form essentially only
one association throughout the whole Empire, whose members are
linked together by the strongest ties and who correspond with each
other, from city to city, by means impenetrable to those not initiated
into their secrets."[29] The prefect's observation reveals important official
perceptions about compagnonnage: it is dangerous not only because of
its use of secrecy but because it cannot be localized; it unites workers
throughout France. In later decades compagnons would again act in
concert to achieve their goals. Although coalitions between sects were
usually short-lived, they encouraged those wishing to reform compagnonnage and alarmed the authorities.

Officials also recognized that compagnonnage need not be fully
united to gain a certain degree of control over labor conditions. Compagnons within a trade often eliminated or curtailed the effectiveness of
their rivals. In Nantes, for example, in the fall of 1809 compagnon shoemakers there wrote to fellow compagnons on the tour de France of their
victory over "the heads of the workshops and over the police." By with-
holding their labor, these workers had forced the majority of masters in
Nantes to increase the price of a pair of boots from Fr 4.10 to Fr 6.30.
The letters told compagnon shoemakers not to leave for Nantes until all
masters had agreed to the price increase. One master who had refused
to submit and insulted some of the compagnons, called *braves,* found his
shop promptly blacklisted.[30] Thus, the interurban organization and ability to communicate effectively along that network—whether to spread
news, request reinforcements, or control the influx of workers during a
strike—helped the compagnons to achieve their goals and gave compagnonnage both the reality and the appearance of a threat to production and the employers' prerogatives.

Again and again police recognized—and denounced—the efficiency
and organizational abilities of compagnonnage. In 1809 one official
pointed out that its strength resulted from a close-knit organization with
similarities to the military. Shortly thereafter the police commissioner of
the Rhône issued a general report describing compagnonnage as "very
well organized." Administered by well-established laws and statutes, the
brotherhoods exercised a "revolting despotism" over the masters. The
councillor of state, Second Arrondissement, warned his counterpart in

29. Ibid., dos. Saône-et-Loire, report, lieutenant, Imperial Gendarmerie (for the subprefect),
dos. Haute-Garonne, 29 April 1810, "Observations sur les associations d'ouvriers connues sous
la denomination de Compagnons du devoir" and proposed edict forwarded to councillor of
state, Second Arrondissement, Toulouse.
30. Ibid., dos. Gironde, 8 November 1809, attorney general to minister of police, Bordeaux.
The police had made inquiries after intercepting correspondence among Nantes, Bordeaux, and
La Rochelle which gave the compagnons further instructions.

the First Arrondissement in 1813 that the compagnons only disguised themselves as a mutual aid society. Their real goal was "to impose their will on the masters and on those workers who are not of their sect."[31] Police officials in the First Arrondissement, of course, had already learned much from the 1811 report "Sur le compagnonnage."

Although the prefect of the Haute-Garonne had called for a far-reaching law specifically banning compagnonnage and many senior officials shared his qualms and his views, no such law was ever passed. The police had to contend with the confusion over which anticoalition laws actually applied and with varied ministerial and judicial interpretations of them. The absence of a consistent policy or a specific legal prohibition with regard to compagnonnage persisted into the Restoration era. The law of April 1803, outlawing all combinations of workers, could not always or simply be used to disband societies of compagnonnage. Evidently, its range of activities and chameleonlike nature made compagnonnage hard to define under such laws.[32]

Despite these legal difficulties, Napoleonic police and judiciary did not tacitly condone compagnonnage: the compagnons themselves stressed that the "bad times" of the Revolution did not end when the Empire began. The police were more centralized than ever before, and the law held out the threat of conscription and the dangers of war as punishment for the misdemeanor of illegal association. The compagnon joiners du devoir of Toulouse, describe these menaces—sometimes melodramatically—in their "Livres d'antiquités":

> With the advent of the Empire, the compagnons thought they
> could breathe a little easier—but this notion did not last long. On
> the contrary things were always going from bad to worse; it came
> to the point where they were sought in their lodgings, their inns
> and even in their workshops. . . .Once arrested, if they were known
> to belong to the society, they were obliged to leave their workshops
> where they were commanded gently and peacefully by Maître
> Jacques and go into our arsenals to associate with the disciples of
> Vulcan or scale the mountains and cross the seas to steep Napo-
> leon in the blood of the peoples of all the nations.[33]

These flamboyant allusions express the author's knowledge of contemporary events and his unfavorable view of them in the self-conscious tone

31. Ibid., dos. Rhône, Lyon, 3 and 14 May 1809, two letters from Maillocheau (subprefect?) to councillor of state, First Arrondissement, dos. Haute-Garonne, 29 April 1810, "Observations sur les associations," dos. 538/R, Paris, 11 February 1813.
32. See Chap. 1, p. 28, for more on the ambiguities of these laws.
33. "Livres d'antiquités," cited in Claays, "Compagnonnage," p. 44.

that became common in compagnons' writings after 1789. Poetic license allowed him to ignore contradictions between his portrait of Maître Jacques's "peaceful commands" and the actual tendency of compagnons to attack their rivals, often violently, whenever possible.

The passage is nonetheless right in noting that conscription was prescribed as an antidote for the ills of compagnonnage. In 1808 the prefect of the Saône-et-Loire approved a police decree banning compagnonnage, forbidding its meetings, and prohibiting compagnons' use of "any distinctions" whatsoever. Article 4 further stated that anyone arrested for defying the decree would be "conducted to one of the corps of the army"; article 8 stated that anyone seen taking part in an assembly would be sent off as a conscript.[34] In general, however, members of societies of compagnonnage do not appear to have been rigorously prosecuted or severely punished (or conscripted) simply for belonging to these associations.

REGULATION, STANDARDIZATION, AND HIERARCHY

Uniform regulations for all cities of a trade on the tour de France facilitated standardization of local practices; correspondence between cities ensured proper adherence to the devoir; and increased literacy and improved postal services expedited this interurban communication. Compagnons' nineteenth-century correspondence stresses the importance of conformity in behavior and procedure. In 1805 two compagnon wheelwrights in Lusont, for example, felt it their duty to write to fellow compagnons in La Rochelle to criticize them for neglecting certain aspects of the devoir. They further complained that the chambre in La Rochelle had not written to tell them if the money sent to settle their account with the mère had been credited. Compagnon shoemakers in Nantes wrote to those in Paris in 1813 to ask them to send the regulations on the burial ceremony, presumably so as to carry out the practice correctly.[35] These shoemakers also duly noted the receipt of the *affaires* of two compagnons.

Compagnons continued to keep detailed records on initiation of novices, again implying concern with correct implementation of the devoir. In the nineteenth century, close attention to such details seems to have provoked speculation about the meaning and purpose of the ceremo-

34. AN, F⁷ 4236, dos. Saône-et-Loire, Mâcon, 9 October 1808, confirmation of decree issued 9 May 1808 in Chalon-sur-Saône.
35. Ibid., dos. 9897, 15 September 1805, "Interrogations," letter from Bordelais sans peur and Angevin la fidélité, dos. 538/R, 3 January 1813, Police générale.

nies. For example, as early as 1806, the premier compagnon of the compagnon wheelwrights in Bordeaux announced a new regulation on initiations in a letter to the chambre in La Rochelle. Henceforth, he stated, initiations were to be prohibited in *villes bâtardes,* that is, cities or towns of secondary importance on the tour de France. The *villes de devoir* (or *villes de boîte*), that is, major cities, for these compagnons were designated as Marseille, Lyon, Bordeaux, Nantes, and Orléans.[36]

Records of an initiation held a year earlier in La Rochelle (a *ville bâtarde*) may reveal why this regulation was established. In the letter announcing the initiation of four novices, the premier, Provençal le bien décidé, informed the "tour de France that Tourangeau l'aimable, Tourangeau le plaisir de fille, Bordelais sans peur, and Tourangeau la douceur had been received and baptized between the hours of 11:00 P.M. and 12:00 P.M" and that each had a "Curate, Godmother, and Godfather." The premier compagnon requested that these four men now be recognized as "fine compagnon wheelwrights for life." Besides the premier, however, only two other initiated compagnons—Poitevin la prudence and Comtois san chagrin—had served as sponsors; they had to keep switching roles for each novice. A fourth compagnon, Lyonnais le résolu, was present, but only as a witness.[37] In the eighteenth century a similar case had provoked no change, and using one compagnon to sponsor several novices seems to have been used to swell the ranks. By the nineteenth century, apparently, the compagnons had come to believe that initiations should be more formal affairs, with a full complement in attendance, and that smaller cities and towns might not be able to provide the requisite numbers. Elaborate "furnishings" noted in seventeenth-century rituals, moreover, are again common in nineteenth-century evidence. An 1825 search at the compagnon bakers' lodgings in Marseille, for example, yielded quite a haul: ribbons of various colors, emblems, registers and objects used for initiation, including candles, a square, a compass, two crosses, a rope, a roll of black paper, seven pieces of crêpe, and a black veil.[38] It may not have been practical to keep all these materials in every town on the tour.

As the major sects of compagnonnage became more efficient, disciplined, and uniform throughout France, the structure of each trade unit underwent some change. Internal hierarchy increased as new ranks were

36. Ibid., dos. 9897, letter dated 27 July 1806.
37. Ibid., dos. 9897, 6 July 1805, "Interrogations," signed also by the "second" and "third" *en ville*—Comtois sans chagrin and Poitevin la prudence. This is one of the earliest archival uses of the term *curé* I have found.
38. AN, F⁷ 9896, dos. 4, Marseille, October 1825, prefect, Bouches-du-Rhône to minister of the interior.

introduced and ranks that had been rare in the eighteenth century were now widely adopted. The relationship between trades and their ranking within a sect or devoir, moreover, became an issue of central concern early in the nineteenth century. Compagnons may have thought that prescribing rules of hierarchy and precedence could protect them from increased competition for jobs and the decline of skilled work. Changes in these areas may also reflect compagnons' desires to rationalize and centralize their associations in accordance with their perceptions of a more bureaucratic postrevolutionary social order.

The primary division continued to be that between initiated and un-initiated, but the increasing and eventually destructive tensions between these two groups was further exacerbated by the new emphasis on "grades" within compagnonnage. In his *Mémoires* Perdiguier criticized an 1803 assembly of compagnons du devoir de liberté which created a "third order" of initiated compagnons. I have found no prerevolution-ary use of the term *third order* and no agreement on the length of time or the qualifications necessary to pass from one rank to the next at this time. Perdiguier does not describe this 1803 assembly or its participants in detail but states that before that time his *société* used a "very old code" (replacing an even older set of "fundamental laws") which divided com-pagnons into two grades, "received" and "finished."[39] Similarly, al-though precisely when is not clear, by the early 1830s the compagnons du devoir had instituted a third order of initiates.[40]

Generally a staunch champion of even obscure or esoteric customs of compagnonnage, Perdiguier apparently accepted the division into two grades of initiates but condemned the third order as aristocratic, trivial, and unnecessary. He implied that this order was not indigenous to com-pagnonnage but a Masonic borrowing. Perdiguier respected Masons as freethinkers and men of standing, but he was unenthusiastic about Ma-sonic influence in compagnonnage and particularly objected to the re-placement of its "ancient" practices with those of the Masons. Despite such objections, Masonic ideas, symbols, and practice became increas-ingly diffused through compagnonnage in the nineteenth century. Ma-

---

39. Agricol Perdiguier, *Mémoires d'un compagnon,* ed. Alain Faure (Paris, 1977), p. 253. I have found no other reference to this meeting. Little prerevolutionary evidence exists on these ranks or the term *pigeonneau* (little pigeon), equivalent to "received" in some trades (e.g., joining). Nineteenth-century examples of its use are found among compagnons du devoir in Nantes (AN, F⁷ 4236, dos. 538R, 12 January 1810) and Toulouse (AN, F⁷ 4236, dos. 9897, "Association de compagnons menuisiers [du devoir] à Toulouse," September 1811).

40. See, for example, Carpentras le coeur fidèle, "Discours pour l'installation d'un premier compagnon serrurier [du devoir] à Chartres, 1833," ed. Maurice Jusselin, *Compagnonnage* (June 1950): 5.

sonry was a powerful model for compagnons disposed to elaborate their hierarchy, and its influence was particularly visible in certificates (see Figure 6) and souvenirs.[41]

Evidence of direct contact between groups of Masons and compagnons is harder to discover, but a rare early nineteenth-century case confirms their occurrence. In a statement to the police the père of the compagnon shoemakers du devoir in La Rochelle, a Sieur Caniès, reported that the compagnons told him they were constantly on guard against police raids and thus "quite pleased that their strong box in Bordeaux had been placed in the hands of the Freemasons." They wished their own papers could be so well secured, but their hopes were not realized. In 1810 La Rochelle police seized their papers, including a long Masonic booklet with details on the grades of apprentice, compagnon, and master.[42]

Perdiguier supplied another important piece of evidence about personal interaction between compagnons and Masons. He described the temple legend of the compagnons du devoir de liberté as a recent and "completely Masonic invention introduced by men . . . initiated into both of these secret Societies." Perdiguier criticized the introduction of such "Masonic inventions" into compagnonnage by commenting on the "deadly results" of a narrative in which Hiram, the master Mason named by Solomon, is murdered by false compagnons, that is, compagnons du devoir.[43] While this myth might be suitable for Masons, Perdiguier said, it was not acceptable for compagnons du devoir de liberté, who were only too eager to justify their enmity against compagnons du devoir. He thus vividly illustrated potential danger in borrowing from outside sources and encouraged the preservation of the compagnons' own customs.

These, however, were his views as expressed in the *Livre du compagnonnage* (1839) and his *Mémoires* (1854–1855). As a young compagnon, Perdiguier had accepted initiation into this "third order" in Lyon in 1828,

41. Examples of Masonic symbolism in compagnonnage include the image of an eye in a triangle, the Hebrew word for Jehovah in a triangle, the phrase "A la gloire du grand architecte de l'univers." AN F⁷ 4236, dos. 9897, 19 January 1810, "Interrogations".

42. AN F⁷ 4236, dos. 9897, 19 January 1810, "Interrogations." The shoemakers were not yet officially recognized by any sect of compagnonnage at this time. Thus the link with and acceptance by Freemasons is of even greater consequence.

43. Agricol Perdiguier, *Le Livre du compagnonnage, contenant des chansons de compagnons, un dialogue sur l'architecture, un raisonnement sur le trait, une notice sur le compagnonnage, la rencontre de deux frères, et un grand nombre de notes*, 2d ed., 2 vols. (Paris, 1841), pp. 79–80. Perdiguier raised this discussion of the Hiram legend in response to a letter of 11 October 1840 from a compagnon nail maker du devoir, Varnier, called Beau désir le gascon, who praised many aspects of the first edition of the *Livre du compagnonnage* but took issue with Perdiguier on several points. Perdiguier's letter, published in the second edition of the *Livre du compagnonnage* was dated 14 October 1840.

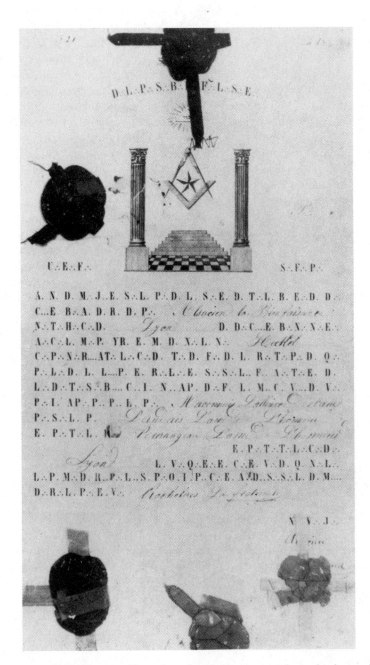

Figure 6. Lettre de course, or certificate, in code, of a compagnon shoemaker-bootmaker du devoir, ca. 1840–1860. Source: Emile Coornaert, *Les Compagnonnages en France du moyen âge à nos jours* (Paris, 1966), fig. 16.

toward the end of his tour. In his *Mémoires* he would write that "this initiation aroused no enthusiasm at all in me: I knew it to be an empty and meaningless order."[44] His reconstruction of the event is that he accepted the rank rather than cause trouble over what he then perceived to be a minor issue. He regretted his decision in the 1840s, however, when he began to champion the complaints novice compagnons and other workers had voiced since the 1830s about the inequalities in compagnonnage. Perdiguier now spoke of the cumulative effects of such "minor" issues in creating an overly hierarchical and authoritarian association. Thus, although he had apparently recognized the emphasis on rank and grades as a flaw in Masonry in the 1830s, he had been slow to object to a similar tendency in compagnonnage.

Further complicating the question of Perdiguier's attitudes toward hierarchy and toward Masonry itself, was the fact that he became a Freemason in December 1845 and rose to the rank of master Mason in October 1849. Never a "zealous Freemason," Perdiguier spoke little of his reasons for joining. His biographer, Jean Briquet, notes that his membership "certainly served his political career."[45] It may well have reflected his growing attachment to wider social and political "orders" as well as the real obstacles to a united compagnonnage. As he suggests in his analysis of the Hiram legend, beliefs and practices that were essentially intellectual exercises in Freemasony could exacerbate rivalries in compagnonnage. Thus, in the 1840s Perdiguier could have had less resistance to Masonic hierarchies, while becoming more openly critical of compagnonnage's rigid caste system. He recognized that excessive inequality and division blocked reform efforts and weakened the devoirs' potential to ameliorate the social and economic conditions of their members.

Increased emphasis on members' ranks did not necessarily extend to changes in the status and responsibilities of the leadership. The premier compagnon and the rôleur were still the principal officers of the local trade associations. The premier oversaw all accounts and ensured that members upheld the devoir; he was usually elected once a year (twice a year in branches with over sixty members).[46] The rôleur remained in control of placement and the organization and direction of rituals. Pediguier states that the rôleur was replaced weekly, but this may not have been the case in all compagnonnages. Some changes in officers' titles may signal changes in *mentalités*. After 1803 Perdiguier claims his sect

44. Perdiguier, *Mémoires*, p. 254.

45. Jean Briquet, *Agricol Perdiguier: Compagnon du tour de France et représentant du peuple (1805–1875)* (Paris, 1955), p. 214.

46. Claays, "Compagnonnage," p. 129.

officially changed the title *capitaine* to *premier compagnon* without explaining why. He personally regretted the change, believing that *capitaine* "admirably and succinctly expressed the fact that the leader of the société was its head." Perdiguier may have preferred *capitaine* because it evoked the metaphor of the body, privileging the organic over the hierarchical relationship implied in *premier compagnon*. Yet, although he stresses that *capus* is the Latin root of *capitaine*, he ignores the equally striking hierarchical and military implications of this term. Gavots also differentiated between types of premier compagnons: compagnons finis elected to this post became premier compagnons, but compagnons third order were called "dignitaries" (*dignitaires*). Perdiguier criticized this artificial inequality created between two men fulfilling the same function.[47]

Although Perdiguier does not comment on it, the use of the term *premier* created the logical possibility of numbering or ranking compagnons from lowest to highest. Such ranking is evident in the nineteenth-century correspondence and papers. Compagnon wheelwrights in La Rochelle signed an order banning a workshop as follows: "First in town, Provençal la douceur; . . . second in town, Tourangeau la gaîté (not knowing how to sign has made a cross); third in town, Versailles l'ami du devoir; fourth in town, Provençal frappe d'abord; fifth and last in town, Provençal l'île d'amour." Seniority became important and could determine what role a compagnon would play in the local organization's business. In Toulouse, for example, after the premier compagnon of the joiners du devoir was arrested, the chambre's records and effects were divided for safekeeping among five compagnons:

> The first compagnon fini, Jean François le toulousain, to guard the Great Roll and the Great Seal, the record of debt, the note of silence [*billet de silence*], and the pen of the premier compagnon. The second compagnon fini, Gabriel l'angevin, to guard the book of incoming compagnons. The third compagnon fini, Joseph l'angevin, to guard the book of chicanery [*livre de chicane*]. The fourth compagnon fini, Jean-Baptiste le genevois, to guard the book of judgments [*livre de voix*] of the tour de France and the book of particular judgments [*livre de voix particulières*]. The fifth compagnon, a *pigeonneau*, to guard the book of town judgments [*livre de voix de ville*], the book of the countryside, and the seal.[48]

47. Agricol Perdiguier, *Livre du compagnonnage*, 2d ed., 1:51. Perdiguier, *Mémoires*, pp. 253–54.
48. AN, F⁷ 4236, dos. 9897, 13 August 1809, "Interrogations," title page, account book, and 30 November 1811, minister of justice to minister of police general, "Association" (a rich source of compagnons' papers), report on a letter from compagnons in Toulouse to same in Bordeaux and Montpellier, 23 September 1811. The great roll contained the statutes of a compagnonnage du devoir; the note of silence "[kept] the world respectful" of the devoir; the book of chicanery

The importance and scope of each task was correlated with the compagnon's rank. Delegation of responsibility was crucial given the sheer amount of paperwork generated by these compagnon joiners du devoir, anxious to record accurately their chambre's practices and business. Because they had so many important records, it follows that they would need to develop a system to safeguard them when the local chambre—or the compagnonnage as a whole—was threatened. Assigning such materials on the basis of seniority was efficient in that it allowed a chambre to regroup quickly after the loss of its "head" without dispute over who would perform what function. Of course, such assignments could yield unfortunate results should seniority not correspond with ability and could reinforce tensions between younger and older compagnons.

Rank order often dictated the role to be played in rituals as well. The compagnon chamois dressers of Paris, for example, wanted members to stand according to rank during their initiations. The first compagnon sat at the center of the table laid out for the initiation; the second compagnon stood at his right; and the last compagnon to his left. Such ranking may indeed have given all the more weight to the "first place" of the premier compagnon. In this instance, however, two novel features are introduced: the "last," as opposed to the third, compagnon plays a key role, and among these chamois dressers, rank was determined by lot, not seniority.[49]

Although the premier compagnon's role was not formally redefined in the postrevolutionary era, in practice his functions expanded. The position may have been more difficult to fill well in the nineteenth century as societies of compagnonnage sought to become better organized, adhere more closely to the devoir, keep closer accounts, and correspond with other societies more regularly. To direct this development the premier compagnon required varied talents. Perdiguier says the premier had to be "a president, a captain, an arbitrator, a judge, a brother, a father." In 1833 the retiring premier of a society of compagnon locksmiths told his successor: "The important place that you are about to fill demands serious attention and vigilant care; be prudent, judicious, impartial. . . . I hope that you will enjoy security, peace, and happiness

---

listed the names of those the devoir excluded. The book of judgments of the tour de France recorded errors reported from all over France, and the book of particular judgments recorded decisions made by all chambres of a trade. Although *particulière* can mean "private," the contrast here is between judgments made by the whole devoir and those made by a particular trade. The book of town judgments recorded errors committed inside the local chambre, and the book of the countryside recorded the names of those who worked outside the city. See Claays, "Le Compagnonnage," p. 129.

49. AD Seine, 4 AZ 1068, register 2, "Devoir des Compagnons blanchers et chamoiseurs réunis," pp. 70, 71.

in governing a society so worthy of being well administered." The responsibility as well as the honor in being a premier compagnon was great, as were the financial burdens. This officer was expected to make up any deficits, especially defaults on payments to the Mère, as the records of a premier of the wheelwrights in La Rochelle show.[50] Moreover, the majority of the accounts I have examined show deficits at the end of a premier's term of office—debts usually left to his successor.

Thus, the office could provide its holder with valuable experience and real power, but it could also ruin him financially or lead him to abuse his power. Although Perdiguier was quite a successful premier, who profited greatly from his experiences, he recognized the dangers: "The first function is heavy, ruinous, it is too much to demand [more than once] from the same man: sometimes his future or his honor perished under the charge." Such seems to have been the case for Comtois la fleur d'orange, premier of the wheelwrights in La Rochelle from 24 November 1806 until expelled from that office on 8 February 1807 for a period of three months. Apparently Comtois had not taken his duties seriously enough: he missed assembly once, was late another time, and on a third occasion failed to announce an assembly to the members.[51] Compagnons who performed successfully as premier were often asked to serve again. At least three wheelwrights—Provençal la fleur d'orange, La Brie la prudence, and Mâconnais le bien decidé—served as premier compagnon in La Rochelle and in at least one other city. Mâconnais le bien decidé may even have been premier a third time, in Orléans. Comtois sans chagrin held the office of premier compagnon twice in La Rochelle.[52]

If the premier's power and functions gradually expanded to accommodate the needs of the nineteenth-century compagnonnages, the rôleur's functions—at least as chief placement officer—may have diminished somewhat. In the nineteenth century, the premier often dealt directly with masters, subcontractors, or employers and played a growing part in negotiating general hiring arrangements. The rôleur, nevertheless, still kept the placement records, and no member, whether novice or compagnon, could work at a shop without the rôleur's sanction. He also continued to receive the customary token of thanks—usually a drink—from each worker placed. According to the testimony of

50. Perdiguier, *Mémoires*, p. 270; Carpentras le coeur fidèle, "Discours pour l'installation d'un premier compagnon," ed. Maurice Jusselin, in *Compagnonnage* (June 1950): 5; AN, F[7] 4236, dos. 9897, 19 January 1810, "Interrogations," account book.

51. Perdiguier, *Mémoires*, p. 254; AN, F[7] 4236, dos. 9897, account book, entries 25, 31, and 32.

52. AN, F[7] 4236, dos. 9897, account book (Provençal and La Brie also served in Bordeaux and Mâconnais served in Angoulême): For Comtois sans chagrin, see entries 9 bis, 23, and 25, Orléans, 23 October 1808, letter, Mâconnais to Libourne la tendresse.

the père, given at the trial of a premier compagnon in Toulouse for *délit de coalition,* anyone who disobeyed the rôleur was driven out of the society, written into the book of chicanery, and forever discredited.[53] Furthermore, the rôleur's influence in ritual must have risen as compagnons became more concerned with the correct performance of their ceremonies in the nineteenth century. Finally, the rôleur's office remained a rotating, not an elective, position, whose privileges all compagnons would presumably share in turn without undue emphasis on rank or seniority—once initiated.

Redefinition of relationships occurred not only within but also between the trades and devoirs. The devoir, or "rite," as compagnons increasingly called the major divisions in compagnonnage, began to mirror the codification of behavior evident on the local level. Perdiguier provided some detail on an assembly of all trades of compagnons du devoir (enfants de Maître Jacques and enfants de Père Soubise) held in Lyon in 1807. Emerging from the meeting was a list, by order of seniority, of the devoir's officially recognized trades (see Table 6.1). According to Perdiguier, this ranking of trades was accepted by the compagnons du devoir on 16 May 1807, after "correction" by the principal trades— stonecutters, carpenters of the *hautes futaies* (timberlands), joiners, and locksmiths.[54] The list was generally accepted for more than a decade, but by the early 1820s some compagnons du devoir began to question and even refute the 1807 classification.

This ranking attempted to establish the status of existing bodies of compagnons du devoir before examining petitions for official recognition submitted by bakers, shoemakers, and weavers in the early nineteenth century. In the eighteenth century compagnonnages seem to have expanded in number and trades without much debate. In the changing nineteenth-century economy, however, compagnons in general may have felt threatened by the influx of too many new trades whose ability to adapt to the old traditions and values was uncertain. The enfants de Salomon, for example, apparently accepted no new trades in the first half of the nineteenth century and very few before that time.[55] Because this sect comprised so few trades (albeit important ones), it may have seemed easier to maintain their traditional ranking: stonecutters, joiners, locksmiths, and carpenters.

---

53. Perdiguier, *Mémoires,* p. 270; AN, F⁷ 4236, dos. 9897, "Association," 30 November 1811, minister of justice to minister of police general, trial of François le bourguignon.

54. Perdiguier, *Livre du compagnonnage,* 3d ed., 2 vols. (Paris, 1857), 1:258–59.

55. Perdiguier, *Livre du compagnonnage,* 2d ed., 1:43. The compagnons du devoir de liberté had accepted the carpenters in the eighteenth century. According to Perdiguier, a group of novice carpenters of the enfants de Père Soubise, called renards, had broken away to join the gavots, who nicknamed them the renards de liberté.

TABLE 6.1. Dates of foundation, trade, and rank order of the Compagnons du devoir, enfants de Maître Jacques and enfants de Père Soubise, 1807

Established in:	Trade	Rank
558 B.C.	Stonecutters[a]	1
560 A.D.	Carpenters of the timberlands (*hautes futaies*)	2
570	Joiners	3
570	Locksmiths	4
1330	Tanners	5
1330	Dyers	6
1407	Rope makers	7
1409	Basketmakers	8
1440	Hatters	9
1500	Chamois dressers	10
1601	Smelters	11
1603	Pin makers	12
1609	Ironsmiths	13
1700	Cloth shearers	14
1700	Turners	15
1701	Glaziers	16
1702	Saddle makers	17
1702	Stove makers	18
1702	Coopers	19
1703	Cutlers	20
1703	Tinsmiths	21
1706	Harness makers	22
1706	Wheelwrights	23
1758	Nail makers	24
1759	Roofers	25
1797	Plasterers	26

Source: Agricol Perdiguier, *Le Livre du compagnonnage*, 3d ed., 2 vols. (Paris, 1857), 1:258–59.
[a]Perdiguier says the trade of stonecutting "disappeared for some time and reasserted its rights and rank in the time of Jacques de Molay of Orléans, the founder of the beaux-arts" (ibid., p. 258).

In the event, the major codification within the ranks of compagnons du devoir increased the rivalry with compagnons du devoir de liberté without fully uniting the dévorants. Compagnons were more closely identified with the belief systems of their devoir and demonstrated these affiliations by wearing—on hats, canes, or coats—color-coded ribbons, sashes, and cockades corresponding to their trade's rank within the devoir. Certain hand signals were also used to identify compagnons or "enemies." Improper attire or recognition of rivals could be enough to provoke quarrels, which frequently escalated to brawls.

All the compagnonnages hardened their position toward renegades (*rénégats*), those expelled for serious violations of the devoir. If a renegade's crime were heinous enough, he would never be free from the compagnons' hostility. Compagnon joiners in Toulouse, for example, instructed fellow compagnons on the tour de France that three members of their chambre had just been branded renegades because of the "atrocities" they had committed. The chambre struck these men from its rolls and those of all the cities of the tour de France in perpetuity and inscribed their names in the book of chicanery. The compagnons notified their brothers in Bordeaux, Montpellier, Nantes, Marseille, Lyon, and Tours of the decision and enclosed detailed descriptions of each man (much like police identification sheets) to assist in bringing the renegades to justice. The three had opposed the chambre's call for a series of walkouts against master joiners in Toulouse who had rejected demands for better pay and working conditions. These men were also held responsible for the premier compagnon's arrest. Unwillingness to pledge solidarity in a labor dispute and overt treachery were to be severely punished.[56] As the nineteenth century progressed, the definition of renegade grew to include those who had never taken any direct action against the devoir, the chambre, or other compagnons. Novices or compagnons who simply left or broke with compagnonnage could be designated renegades. Violence against such "renegades" may have derived from compagnons' growing consciousness of their associations' boundaries and the need to assert their "rights" to control the work force.

Although most of this violence seemed incomprehensible to outside observers, brawls between compagnons and between compagnons and renegades expressed a complex of economic and cultural rationales. Few were motivated purely by clear-cut economic rivalries; most had socioeconomic rationales complicated and intensified by the ritual practices and the belief system of each sect. Compagnons acted on the premise that their optimum situation would be achieved when they had driven their enemies out of town—in the name of Maître Jacques, Solomon, or Père Soubise—and had won a monopoly on all its shops. If complete victory was impossible, a major brawl might at least intimidate one's enemies into keeping their economic and ritual influence within circumscribed limits. One chambre might dissuade a rival group from accepting lower prices for their work by parading their compagnons in full regalia. Brawls among different trades in a devoir, however, are not as readily understandable in these terms. Perhaps, a particular devoir worked to reject trades regarded as "polluting" its strength or desired image. In this sense discipline and hierarchy were as necessary for the devoir as a whole as they were for the local branches.

56. AN, F⁷ 4236, dos. 9897, "Association," letters dated 23 September 1811.

ORGANIZATION, RITUAL, AND ICONOGRAPHY

The basic organizational structures of the local branches did not change essentially from old regime to new. Continuing one of their oldest and most distinctive customs, compagnons still lodged together or, at the very least, ate meals together at the Mère. Mères and pères continued to play a central role in maintaining the framework of mutual aid and care for members' well-being. Compagnons continued to express the need for affective bonds with mères and pères: the very first article of the 1835 statutes of the compagnon tanners and curriers of Lyon was to "respect the père and the mère above all"; only then came the second article, "honor to the devoir."[57] Article 8 defined polite behavior "chez la Mère": compagnons must not call the père monsieur or the mère madame; these titles would have distanced them from their surrogate mothers and fathers.

Mères and pères often aided the rôleur in his task of placement by informing him of compagnons' arrivals and departures. They received prospective employers who came to the Mère seeking workers and relayed notices of job openings to the rôleur.[58] Such services had always been performed, but there is some indication that mères and pères were taking on greater responsibility than they had had earlier, both in socializing compagnons and in furthering relationships between compagnons and the wider society. For example, in Marseille, mères and pères often interceded with the authorities on behalf of their compagnons. They submitted petitions to officials, for example, when compagnons wished to celebrate their patron saint's day or other feast days. The rôleur or premier compagnon might undertake this task but presumably realized requests might look better coming from licensed innkeepers.

In one case the père of the compagnon joiners du devoir wrote to the mayor of Marseille requesting that the gavots not be allowed to celebrate the feast of Saint Anne at a particular inn. It was too close to the one where the compagnons du devoir had celebrated their patron's day for the last ten years, and the père feared hostilities would quickly erupt between the rivals once the drinking began. He further claimed that the gavots had chosen the inn in question with the express intent of provoking a fight with the compagnons du devoir. The père thus defended his sect's interests and prerogatives by enlisting official help. The police in Marseille also received correspondence from men and women who

57. Musée historique de vieux Lyon, "Règlement des compagnons tanneurs et corroyeurs," 14 articles, approved 1 February 1835, 57 signatures.
58. Claays, "Compagnonnage," p. 122.

wished official recognition as mères and pères of sects of compagnonnage, suggesting that these associations enjoyed a semilegal status in Marseille in the 1820s.[59]

Within the Mère, rituals seem to have begun an evolution toward greater complexity. Perhaps the compagnons elaborated their rituals both to define their identity more precisely and to protect themselves from detection during the dangerous revolutionary era. Perdiguier and other compagnons attest that ritual practice, rank, and hierarchy had become more prominent in compagnonnage by the early nineteenth century. Perdiguier urged moderation; others encouraged their societies of compagnonnage to "modernize" and simplify their rituals. Even such revised rituals, however, remained heavily symbolic and complex.

Even if ceremonies remained, in essence, similar to the earlier practices, the desire for proper performance intensified after the Revolution. "Public" rituals—conduites and funerals—were ever more frequent and involved great display. We know about them partly because of more efficient policing and partly because they were both disruptive and newsworthy. Conduites and funerals, at least in urban areas, may also have appeared more noticeable than in the old regime, when large-scale religious and royal rites were more common. The manner of celebrating such rituals and feast days demonstrates the importance compagnons attached to a public show of force. As in the old regime, large numbers of compagnons turned out for these demonstrations. The police of Marseille, for example, reported on an assembly of roughly one hundred compagnons gathered "under the pretext of performing their ceremonies."[60]

During the Restoration era, however, the compagnons developed the desire to capture these public displays in more permanent forms. Several large watercolors of conduites or "retirement" (remerciement) ceremonies still exist as testimony to pride in compagnonnage (see Figures 1 and 2). It is impossible to know how many compagnons commissioned these large and presumably expensive, watercolor paintings, but at least six of them still exist, in addition to many smaller works.[61] They yield important

59. AC Marseille, I², dos. 137, "Compagnons du devoir," 20 June 1827, no response noted (joiners of both devoirs honored the same patron, Anne), "Compagnons du devoir," 1826–27.

60. AN, F⁷ 4236, dos. Bouches-du-Rhône, 14 June 1809, police report.

61. Maurice Jusselin, "Vues de Bordeaux sous la restauration d'après les tableaux de compagnonnage," Revue philomatique de Bordeaux et du sud-ouest, no. 3 (1938): 114–27. Jusselin's valuable article does not, however, discuss the painting's cost. See also Roger Lecotté, "Essai pour une iconographie compagnonnique: 'Champs de conduite' et 'Souvenirs' du Tour de France," in Artisans et paysans de France (Strasbourg, 1948), pp. 135–55, and his catalogs of two major exhibitions on compagnonnage, Archives historiques and Le Compagnonnage vivant (Paris, 1973), which provide impressive evidence of its rich nineteenth-century iconography.

iconographic insights into compagnons' self-image in the 1820s and 1830s, when most of these colorful and elaborate scenes were painted.

The artists who painted the examples in Figures 1 and 2 specialized in this kind of souvenir production. In a style sometimes labeled "naive" or, perhaps more properly, vernacular art, Etienne Leclair, Auguste LeMoine, and others worked "outside the canons of taste established by the elite culture."[62] Although they were not of the academy, however, they were professionals, commissioned to capture the uncommon experiences of "common" people. Compagnons must have been permitted a certain amount of collaboration, for the paintings amplify details significant to them. Had Leclair and LeMoine been noted artists we might have learned far less about the compagnonnages. Nevertheless, much of the presentation in these paintings was standardized. Leclair, about whose techniques we know a certain amount, painted these souvenir watercolors "in series."[63] He prepared much of the painting in advance by reproducing the many repeated elements (ritual objects, ceremonial stances) and then varied only the most essential features (the skyline of the city in question). Leclair's "mass" productions satisfied compagnons eager to purchase a much-desired remembrance.

All the extant paintings depict cherubs floating high above the assembled artisans. In one hand each cherub holds a tool of the departing compagnon's trade and in the other, the edge of a banner identifying and glorifying the particular sect of compagnonnage. Work and ritual, the real and the ideal, are fully integrated. The compagnons assembled in the foreground are larger than life in comparison to the surrounding passersby. In Figure 1, painted in 1825, most passersby continue with their own work, apparently unconcerned with the compagnons' activities even though these well-dressed and colorfully beribboned workers are out in force. The painting centers on the departing compagnon, who is performing the *guillebrette,* the ritual embrace, crossing arms and toasting with each of the compagnons present. The one exception to the general lack of concern over the leave-taking is the young woman to the left of the long building on the right. Holding a handkerchief to her eyes, she watches the departure of (in this case) De Blois l'aimable. The bereft woman is a standard motif in most of these paintings, symbolizing not only the sorrow of parting but also the compagnon's virility and conquests. So, the tears were ignored, for he was the ultimate traveling man, who always moved on.[64] Another common feature in these works was the

62. James Ayres, *English Naive Painting, 1750–1900* (London, 1980), pp. 9–10.
63. Jusselin, "Vues de Bordeaux," pp. 115, 116.
64. Both Ménétra and Perdiguier, in different contexts and with different sensibilities, reveal that compagnons did not always treat women so cavalierly, even if they still left them behind.

faithful dog, sitting near the departing compagnon: a symbol of loyalty to compagnonnage.

Figure 2, set in 1839 Orléans, positions the compagnons even more fully in the foreground, but also, symbolically, outside the city limits, across the Loire. This painting shows a stronger sense of proportion than does the previous example. Nonetheless, the compagnons are still somewhat larger than the passersby. Even more than in Figure 1 the line of compagnons, marching two by two, seems to stretch on forever. Again compagnons are depicted as elegant and well-dressed, distinguished from ordinary men by the colorful ribbons that stream from their top hats. In this painting a few of the passersby are interested enough to stop and watch the ceremony. These observers, moreover, are not other workers but rather the local bourgeoisie, especially two well-dressed ladies. Even the requisite tearful young woman is depicted more as a *bourgeoise* than a working-class woman.

The paintings create a powerful ideal and aesthetic. Figurative exaggeration and emphasis on imagination and ideals are especially important. Both paintings confront us with large numbers of prosperous and sober artisans, linked together fraternally in the serious practice of the devoir amid the symbols of their sects and their work—squares, compasses, and other tools. No opposing sects of compagnons mar the harmony of the moment as angelic cherubs proclaim the glory of these particular compagnons. These images of more successful artisans dressing well and commissioning paintings may represent a growing elitism within compagnonnage rather than the actual practice of the conduite in the early nineteenth century. Nonetheless, such paintings are valuable evidence of the self-image to which many compagnons aspired. They also helped inform compagnons' construction of their practices and associations.

It is worth reemphasizing the most telling difference between Figures 1 and 2: the stance of the noncompagnons, which may bear indirect testimony to the changes I have detected in public perceptions of compagnonnage from the 1820s (Figure 1) to the late 1830s (Figure 2). While other workers appear uninterested in the compagnons' activities in both paintings, in Figure 2 the bourgeois public, particularly its female members, is quite curious about the unfolding ceremony. They do not hurry away or express fear of the workers, who appear neither "dangerous" nor "barbaric." Whether the painting displayed reality or whether the compagnons commissioned this particular representation, the depiction reflects the view that a middle-class public could have a positive interest in compagnonnage and its practices.

Although these paintings are among the richest iconographic sources for nineteenth-century compagnonnages, they are not the only ones. Many other objects chronicle and give iconographic permanence to symbols and practices: decorated canes, ribbons, cockades, sashes, gourds, and prints, which cost far less than paintings and were therefore far more common. Public archives also yield examples of reception certificates, diplomas, and seals of compagnonnage.[65] Reception certificates included such vital information as the date and place of initiation and the godparents' names. These certificates were relatively secret papers which protected the initiate and his sponsors. Most were written in code as in Figure 6—capital letters followed by three triangular dots.[66] I have found no archival copies of coded certificates before the nineteenth century. Roger Lecotté cites one example of an eighteenth-century seal (the private possession of a group of compagnon carpenters) bearing the letters UVGT (*Union Vertu Gloire Travail*) as well as a square and compass held up by two angels. He says that the seal, bearing the words "Compagnons passants charpentiers bon drilles—de Tours" and the roller were used to ink ribbons and sashes in the eighteenth century.[67] This evidence indicates that some groups of compagnons may have employed more formal seals, certificates, and quasi-Masonic symbolism in the old regime. Nonetheless, the use and elaboration of these materials became common only in the nineteenth century.

The compagnons' dress was another means of creating identity. The eighteenth century yields little direct evidence of elaborate costume, although Lecotté's seal provides evidence of imprinted designs on ribbons and sashes in the prerevolutionary era. In any event, male dress was generally more colorful and elaborate in the eighteenth than in the nineteenth century. Compagnons preserved some of its more flamboyant aspects into the nineteenth century: police reports note, and paintings,

65. E.g., AN, F⁷ 4236, dos. Gironde, 12 January 1810, report, councillor of state, First Arrondissement, to councillor of state, Second Arrondissement, dos. Carcassonne, 18 June 1810, Procès-verbal, mayor to the magistrate of the Sûreté, dos. Gironde, 8 November 1809, attorney general to minister of police, dos. Gironde, Bordeaux, 23 February 1810, inventory of papers seized by the police commissioner (including 94 certificates of compagnon bakers) and 8 November 1809, attorney general to minister of police (seizure of a hundred diplomas of compagnon shoemakers), dos. 9897, subprefect to councillor of state, First Arrondissement, La Rochelle, 22 January 1810 (including a copy of an *affaire* of compagnon wheelwrights), dos. Rhône, prefect to director general of the police, Lyon, 12 December 1821 (seizure of papers and statutes of ironsmiths and blacksmiths, with insignias of compagnonnage), dos. 4, Marseille, October 1825, perfect, Bouches-du-Rhône to minister of the interior (ritual objects seized at the compagnon bakers' lodgings).

66. Emile Coornaert, *Les Compagnonnages en France du Moyen Age à nos jours* (Paris, 1966), pp. 433–34, gives a transcription by a twentieth-century compagnon baker du devoir, René Edeline. Contemporary compagnon shoemakers contest his rendering at some points without specifying their objections. The transcription begins: "Union Et Force. Au Nom de M.·.aître Jacques Et Sous La Protection De l'Etre Suprême. . . ."

67. Lecotté, *Archives historiques*, pp. 25, 18.

drawings, and eventually, photographs, verify that compagnons affected a precise and complicated symbolic dress. Whereas the appearance of eighteenth-century compagnons probably did not attract a great deal of attention, nineteenth-century compagnons began publicly and proudly to mark themselves off from the wider society.

Some of the art forms nineteenth-century compagnons created to commemorate important moments of their tour de France reveal growing interest in their traditions, particularly their origins. This artwork frequently included scenes from the life of the founder of a sect or symbolism adapted from origin narratives. At the top of one "souvenir of passage," an engraving dated 1845, Père Soubise directs a master, compagnon, and apprentice working at the temple site. A quatrain honoring Père Soubise appears at the bottom:

> Three times honor to you, Noble Soubise
> May your shade, leaving its deathly abode,
> Look down upon your children,
> Giving them for a motto
> Order and activity in their prudent labors.[68]

Such focus on origin legends was rare in the eighteenth century; no similar iconographic materials are found in public archives. Even terms linked to these legends can be traced back only to the mid- to late eighteenth century. By contrast, the profusion of these symbolic materials after the Revolution reflects the need to institutionalize procedures and practices. All these objects—canes, sashes, seals, certificates, engraved souvenirs, gourds—identified compagnons and their status in these trade associations. Such documents and objects were functional but also deeply invested with symbolic meaning, created and used in accordance with the devoir's principles. Together with the other modifications I have noted, this preoccupation with symbols reestablished compagnonnages as viable organizations of mutual aid and labor resistance, but at the same time, changes emphasizing discipline, hierarchy, and subgroup definition, undermined fraternal sentiment and strained relations between compagnons and novices.

NOVICES AND COMPAGNONS: A GROWING DIVIDE

As the nineteenth century progressed, some novices complained about an extended novitiate and more stringent qualifications for initiation.

68. Lecotté, "Essai pour une iconographie compagnonnique," p. 15, "Souvenir du passage à Lyon."

Contemporary officials agreed. The minister of justice, for example, commented: "*Aspirants* do not easily become compagnons. Not only must they have proven their entire devotion to the society but, furthermore, they must have acquired a certain degree of skill in their trade. . . . only after their [masterpieces] have been verified are they admitted as compagnons."[69] This increasing subordination was intended to help the compagnons control the labor market more closely and gain concessions from employers. The novitiate might be prolonged further because of high initiation fees. The records of income, expenditure, and fees kept by the premier compagnons of the wheelwrights in La Rochelle records that each novice was charged forty-two francs for his reception, generally payable within a month of the ceremony. In one case, of the four aspirants initiated, all but one settled their accounts roughly one month later and the fourth paid all but six francs of the fee. Novices had to save most of their reception money before proceeding with the ceremony, for credit was rarely extended in this case. Considering that they earned little more than three francs a day (usually one to two francs less than compagnons) and paid twice as much as compagnons for placement (six francs instead of three), it was not easy to save such a large sum.[70] The fee, moreover, did not cover all costs: the novice also had to pay for materials used in his masterpiece, an expensive and labor-intensive obligation.

Nonetheless, there is little hard evidence that it was more difficult to enter compagnonnage in the nineteenth century than before, although many compagnons argued that workers now needed more training to retain a competitive edge. This argument, of course, worked best in building and related trades, where less deskilling had taken place. Yet, even in the construction industry the practice of subcontracting encouraged the use of less-skilled workers and undermined the compagnons' advantage. Nevertheless in building and woodworking trades skilled workers were sometimes in short supply. Master joiners and cabinetmakers in Toulouse, for example, complained of difficulties in finding qualified workers and were often forced to meet the compagnons' demands in order to keep a steady supply.[71] Compagnons might, thus, believe themselves justified in insisting novices demonstrate advanced skills before initiation.

Although the compagnonnages might promote this ideal, however, in reality nineteenth-century novices were hardly better treated or in-

69. AN, F⁷ 4236, dos. 9897, 30 November 1811, "Association," minister of justice to the minister of police general.

70. Ibid., account book.

71. Ibid., 30 November 1811, "Association," minister of justice to minister of police general, reporting on the testimony of Jacoby, master cabinetmaker.

structed than in earlier centuries. And by the late 1820s, many novices expressed resentment at what they believed was their increasing exclusion from full participation in the life of compagnonnage. Whether because of their own experiences or as a more general legacy of the Revolution, some rejected this second-class status. Many novices were no longer willing to endure a long waiting period to become full members. Young workers began to recognize that changes in the labor market and the general decline in skill necessary in many trades made it possible for them to find work without the mediation of a hierarchical and strictly disciplined compagnonnage. In the early nineteenth century, more and more workers saw the need to associate, but the new associations were not compagnonnages. The Revolution of 1830 and the growth of workers' consciousness in the following decades split compagnons, novices, and other workers on many levels.

In the nineteenth century the trade organizations of compagnonnage defined their nature and purpose in more systematic and structured ways than they had previously. These changes were generated by the revolutionary experience and by the social, economic, and cultural context of postrevolutionary society itself. Compagnons were forced to "go underground" during the Revolution and to guard their secrets closely. Bands of compagnons who upheld the devoirs may have become more self-conscious about their practices. In the event, the compagnonnages vigorously reemerged in the early Empire with apparently more developed and elaborated bureaucratic forms and a greater insistence on proper ritual practice.

Economic and social realities such as the decline of skilled trades, the destruction of the trade corporations, and a more laissez-faire economy in nineteenth-century France also forced compagnons to reorganize their associations to some extent.[72] They continued to believe, however, that their skills and control of the labor supply were crucial to their success. Compagnons found themselves not only working in new eco-

---

72. Edward Berenson provides a valuable overview and analysis of the French agricultural and industrial situation from about 1815 to 1848 in his *Populist Religion and Left-Wing Politics in France, 1830–1852* (Princeton, 1984), chap. 1. See also, on the theme of the French economic change and its relation to the world of work in this era, Sewell, *Work and Revolution in France*, esp. chaps. 7–9; William Reddy, *The Rise of Market Culture: The Textile Trade and French Society, 1750–1900* (Cambridge, 1984), esp. chaps. 4–7; George J. Sheridan, Jr., "Household and Craft in an Industrializing Economy: The Case of the Silk Weavers of Lyons," in *Consciousness and Class Experience in Nineteenth-Century Europe*, ed. John M. Merriman (New York, 1979), pp. 107–27; Christopher H. Johnson, "Patterns of Proletarianization: Parisian Tailors and Lodève Woolens Workers," in Merriman, *Consciousness and Class*, pp. 65–84; and John Rule, "The Property of Skill in the Period of Manufacture," in *The Historical Meanings of Work*, ed. Patrick Joyce (Cambridge, 1987), pp. 99–118.

nomic conditions but also dealing with new forms of social control, particularly the centralized and expanded police of the Empire. Workers who had themselves perhaps served in Napoleonic armies seem to have recognized the advantages to be gained from a more disciplined and bureaucratic administration. Finally, and perhaps most important, confronted with the destruction of the corporate structures on which they had been based, compagnonnages had to evaluate and more clearly define the value and meaning of their beliefs and practices.

This self-examination did not make compagnonnages into more corporate institutions, at least not in the traditional sense. The brotherhoods did not simply preserve their corporate legacy intact; they were also greatly influenced by the economic, social, and cultural world of nineteenth-century France. Long-standing tensions between hierarchy and equality and between solidarity and schism tended to be exacerbated. Some of these changes may have made the compagnonnages more efficient and effective vehicles for the defense of the workers' interests. By the Restoration era the compagnonnages were more strictly ordered, better organized, and more self-conscious associations than they had been in the old regime. But at the very same time, a growing number of compagnons began to object to the direction in which their compagnonnages were moving.

CHAPTER 7

Reconstructing Brotherhoods

Of compagnonnage I sing today
And this my friends I say
Let progress pass us by.

—Albigeois le bien aimé, *Les Bêtises
de la régénération du compagnonnage*

The development of more formal institutional structures was accompanied by continued growth in the compagnonnages during the Empire and Restoration. The associations continued to provide hospitality, fellowship, and practical material aid to many traveling artisans. As they more explicitly defined (or redefined) their boundaries and practices, however, the incorporation of new trades and members became correspondingly more difficult. The enfants de Maître Jacques had officially recognized twenty-four trades in the course of their history; the great majority were "adopted" as "children" of an original trade of this rite.[1] Glaziers, coopers, cloth shearers, tinsmiths, harness makers, wheelwrights, and nail makers were all sponsored this way in the eighteenth century. Before the Revolution, the enfants de Père Soubise recognized two new trades (roofers and plasterers); the enfants de Salomon officially recognized only the carpenters. In the nineteenth century, the process of admission became long, expensive, and rigorous. Indeed, the compagnons du devoir did not fully accept any new trades into their ranks between 1800 and 1848. This hardening of beliefs and position brought increased criticism from compagnons and outsiders.

Despite great obstacles, a number of trades made the attempt to gain official acceptance in the early nineteenth century. Of all these trades, the bakers and the shoemakers endured the worst treatment: they were ambushed, beaten, even assassinated by gangs of "real" compagnons in

1. See Table 6.1. Carpenters and roofers are omitted from the total. Although they were du devoir, they were also enfants de Père Soubise.

innumerable brawls in the 1820s and 1830s. Shoemakers, already looked
down upon by other workers and those in the wider culture, were especially vulnerable to attack. The Wandering Jew of Eugène Sue's epon-
ymous novel is a shoemaker.[2] Ofttimes, hatred of so-called usurpers was
the only issue on which compagnons du devoir could agree.

These quests for recognition, however, reveal much more. The bakers'
case helps define structural constructs within existing compagnonnages
as well as their relationships with other labor associations emerging in
the early nineteenth century. The shoemakers' struggle for acceptance
perpetuated and mirrored the internal schisms of compagnonnage and
may have accelerated the movement for reform and reconciliation which
culminated in 1848.

THE BAKERS

Although bakers had grouped themselves in organizations very similar
to compagnonnages in the old regime, they were not recognized as "legitimate" until accepted as compagnons du devoir by the enfants de
Maître Jacques in 1860. Acceptance came only after many bakers risked
grave injury and even death to learn the rituals and secrets of compagnonnage, and their prying only confirmed some compagnons' view that
bakers had never really been members of compagnonnage.[3] The bakers,
however, insisted they were received as compagnons by Maître Jacques
and had "founded themselves." They thus refused, as was required, to
seek an adoptive "father" among the established trades. Although the
bakers' prerevolutionary associations were very similar to compagnonnage, they had a number of original features. For example, bakers permitted married men to be active members.[4] Such unorthodoxies
infuriated other compagnons and fueled their intransigence.

Yet, bakers remained attached to compagnonnage, finding this form
of association (if not its members) highly adaptable and suited to their
needs. Maurice Agulhon argues that for many trades there was, in practice, little distinction between compagnonnages and mutual aid societies.
Nonetheless, "the model of compagnonnage exercised an undeniable

2. Jacques Rancière, "The Myth of the Artisan: Critical Reflections on a Category of Social
History," in *Work in France: Representations, Meaning, Organization, and Practice*, ed. Steven Laurence
Kaplan and Cynthia J. Koepp (Ithaca, 1986), pp. 318–19.

3. Emile Coornaert, *Les Compagnonnages en France du Moyen Age à nos jours* (Paris, 1966), p.
198.

4. William H. Sewell, Jr., "The Structure of the Working Class of Marseilles in the Middle of
the Nineteenth Century" (Ph.D. diss., University of California, Berkeley, 1971), p. 202. See also
Sewell, *Structure and Mobility: The Men and Women of Marseille, 1820–1870* (Cambridge, 1985).

attraction [for the bakers] by reason of its secret and interregional nature.''[5] William Sewell's data on the bakers in Marseille confirm many of Agulhon's conclusions. In 1823 bakers there formed a mutual aid society, which was disbanded after a strike later that year. Two years later the same group reorganized into a society of compagnonnage. Sewell further discovered that a compagnonnage could simultaneously be a mutual aid society, revealing not only structural similarities and flexibility but also that many workers had no absolute aversion or attachment to one form of association over the other.[6]

In Bordeaux, for example, where bakers' labor disputes were rife, a police raid of their lodgings yielded papers including a set of regulations dated 24 November 1809 which convinced the prefect of the Gironde that these workers had constituted a compagnonnage. The bakers adamantly denied this charge, claimed to be a simple mutual aid society, and demanded their papers back. These documents (not returned to them) exemplify the mutability of compagnonnage. Members called themselves *sociétaires,* as in a mutual aid society, rather than *pays,* as they might in a compagnonnage. Yet, they were initiated after swearing an oath of allegiance and receiving a *nom compagnonnique* to be used in lieu of given names. The initiation certificate of one Sablais la bonne conduite, dated 1810, is analogous to those given in compagnonnage, though somewhat less elaborate.[7] Finally, the bakers' society, like compagnonnage, required members to have a mère (or père) and a rôleur. The regulations instructed members never to insult or scorn those bakers outside the society, though this passage may have been inserted to pacify officials.

Despite these parallels to compagnonnage, the bakers insisted "that there never were any compagnons among the bakers." The prefect and the councillor of state did not believe them; they pointed to clandestine activities and to the damning evidence in the first article of their regulations: "The novice [*récipiendaire*] will take an oath to maintain, until death, that which had been entrusted to him." The councillor of state particularly distrusted secret oaths in light of the concurrent development of similar associations among bakers and other workers in Lyon and Marseille.[8] He was convinced that all these new mutual aid societies

5. Maurice Agulhon, "Aperçus sur le mouvement ouvrier à Toulon," *Provence historique* 7 (1957): 147; Agulhon, *Une Ville ouvrière au temps du socialisme utopique: Toulon de 1815 à 1851* (Paris, 1970), pp. 117–19, 118.

6. Sewell, "Structure of the Working Class," p. 202.

7. AN, F⁷ 4236, dos. Gironde, Bordeaux, 16, 22, 23, and 24 February 1810, police commissioner reports, 1 May 1810, general counsel, Prefecture, to councillor of state, Second Arrondissement.

8. Ibid., Bordeaux, 1 May 1810, general counsel, Prefecture, to councillor of state, Second Arrondissement, Bordeaux, 1 May 1810 bakers' testimony, and Paris, 20 April 1810, councillor of state to the prefect.

requesting authorization were merely thinly disguised compagnonnages. Whatever they called themselves, he felt sure they would generate continual labor unrest and opposition to authority.

THE SHOEMAKERS

While the bakers generally accommodated compagnonnage to their own needs, the shoemakers tended to pursue orthodoxy. Although there were dissidents and multiple schisms in their protocompagnonnage, most compagnon shoemakers wanted official recognition. The lengths to which they went to achieve it might have stemmed from the belief or knowledge that shoemaking had been one of the original trades of compagnonnage. There are two surviving explanations of how shoemakers discovered they had once been compagnons. The first claims a dusty old manuscript—a copy of the shoemakers' rituals mentioning the 1655 Sorbonne condemnation—was found in the effects of a dead shoemaker and somehow fell into the hands of a tanner. He quickly initiated three shoemakers on 25 January 1808; these three initiated other shoemakers. Branded a traitor by his compagnonnage, the tanner escaped its wrath only by joining the army. The second version has it that a drunken tanner revealed his own society's secrets to three shoemakers in Angoulême in 1807 or 1808.[9] Whichever version was accepted, the tanners received the blame for initiating shoemakers into the devoir.

Whether either version is true, by the first decade of the nineteenth century, groups of shoemakers formed organizations very similar to compagnonnages. Of many references from this time, a collection of documents in La Rochelle provides the most detail about their activities from about 1808 to 1813. Probably by 1811, and certainly by 1813, shoemakers had societies, all following the same regulations, in Angoulême, La Rochelle, Angers, Paris, Marseille, Bordeaux, Orléans, Autun, Nantes, Rochefort, Toulouse, and Chalon-sur-Saône. According to the customs of compagnonnage, there was no chief administrative city for the society: establishing a new branch required written approval of its statutes by all the other chambres on the tour de France. A song written on the founding of the Bordeaux chambre reveals that compagnons traveled to the new city to confirm the proud event:

> We are leaving La Rochelle
> And going straight on to Bordeaux

9. Coornaert, *Compagnonnages,* pp. 196, 197.

> To announce to all our *braves* [good fellows]
> In the devoir so very fine
> That we're going to name a mère there
> And establish the devoir
> So we can all be known
> As compagnons du devoir.

> Nous partons de La Rochelle
>   Pour aller droit à Bordeaux
>   Pour faire part à tous nos braves
>   Dans le devoir aussi bon
>   Pour y nommer une mère
>   Et établir le devoir
>   Et pour nous faire reconnaître
>   Compagnons du devoir.[10]

The statutes paralleled those of other societies of compagnonnage and covered a wide range of behavior. Their correspondence indicates that shoemakers, like other compagnons, closely monitored their activities on the tour: each city's chambre served as a check on the others, ensuring uniform performance of the devoir. Evidence confirms that such supervision was necessary: compagnons in the Paris chambre seem to have followed the devoir somewhat less rigorously than those in the provinces and were admonished at least twice (by chambres in Angers and Nantes) for neglecting prescribed duties.[11]

The record of labor actions demonstrates the efficacy of the organization. In early 1813, for example, compagnon shoemakers in Paris formed a coalition against their masters and unaffiliated workers. The police arrested six coalition leaders during a meeting and confiscated their papers, diplomas, seal, stamps, and strongbox. The councillor of state, Second Arrondissement, warned a colleague about this organization whose "apparent aim . . . is mutual aid, but [whose] real aim is to impose their will on the masters and those workers who are not part of their society." Interrogated after the raid, the compagnons insisted their society's sole purpose was mutual aid. Pressed further, they admitted they were obliged to take an oath and had secrets, but nothing could per-

10. AN, F⁷ 4236, dos. 9897, "Interrogations," songbook, no. 3, v. 3. The oldest document in this group is the songbook of a compagnon shoemaker named Benoît Droint, dit bien aimé, received in Angoulême, 25 September 1808. The Bordeaux chambre's existence can be confirmed by 1812.

11. Ibid., dos. 538/R, compagnon shoemakers, letters, 20 December 1812, Angers to Paris, and 1813, Nantes to Paris.

suade them to disclose the nature of either.[12] This case triggered the
arrests of other compagnon shoemakers throughout France. Yet, despite
police surveillance and the hostility of other compagnons, the shoemakers' compagnonnage was not suppressed in the nineteenth century as it
had been in the seventeenth.

It was, however, undermined by factionalism. As early as 1811 a serious
dispute arose in Bordeaux over the novices' outspoken objections to
"hierarchy and inequality."[13] Whereas the revolutionary legacy may have
informed their clear articulation of these issues, a growing experience
of subjection generated their complaints. The novices broke from compagnonnage and formed a mutual aid society, whereupon the compagnons condemned these *margageats* (good-for-nothings, tramps), expressing their anger and disdain in song:

> In our most lovely city
>> Those insolent tramps—and so clumsy too,
>> Want to do their evil deeds.
>> We'll let them see our dazzling ardor,
>> And out the window those jokers will jump.
> In our assemblies so very dear
>> Lucifer calls for those tramps
>> Who are his vile minions.
>> May the fires blaze up and consume them,
>> May they be swallowed up eternally.

> Dans nos plus belle ville
>> Margageats insolents
>> Si mal habile
>> Veuille faire leur méchanceté
>> Nous leur ferons connaître notre brilliante ardeur
>> Et par la fenêtre sauterons les railleurs.
> Dans nos assemblées si cher
>> Des margageats Lucifer demande
>> Qui sont ses scélérats
>> Que les feux s'allument
>> Pour les consommer
>> Qu'on les englouti dans l'éternité.[14]

12. Ibid., dos. 5, "Arrestation à Paris de six ouvriers cordonniers, 1813," including the "Règlement de la chambre d'Angoulême approuvé . . . à Bordeaux de 25 juillet 1812," and 11
February 1813, councillor of state, Second Arrondissement, to councillor of state, First Arrondissement.

13. Toussaint Guillaumou (called Carcassonne le bien aimé du tour de France), *Les Confessions
d'un compagnon* (Paris, 1864), p. 51.

14. AN, F⁷ 4236, dos. 9897, "Interrogations," songbook, no. 2.

Stung by this betrayal, the compagnon shoemakers considered it essential to oppose the dissidents lest their own bona fides be tarnished. Thus, they accused the novices of lacking skill and called them heretics in league with the devil. Yet, dissent and schism continued to plague the shoemakers. In 1827 a group of novices in Marseille revolted; they called themselves the "independents" and took William Tell as their patron.[15]

As well founded as the complaints were, senior compagnons generally failed to heed them. The compagnon shoemaker Toussaint Guillaumou (Carcasonne le bien aimé) was a rare exception. He admitted that compagnonnage, and his own society, urgently needed reform and, from the mid-1830s on, worked actively for this cause. Guillaumou thought that the Marseille schism could have been avoided had it not been for the vanity and selfishness of certain individual compagnons: "Always ready to block progress, men of limited intelligence who were fanatic about their title of compagnon and, above all, their threatened authority, they draped themselves in their mysteries as the ancient Romans did in their togas."[16] Guillaumou noted, however, that the new societies recapitulated many features the novices had strenuously objected to in compagnonnage: hierarchy, inequality, ranks. The independents, for example, "wore colors" (ribbons) that easily identified them and fed into longstanding patterns of provocation and brawling. Evidently, many workers still felt the need or desire to establish their territorial identity and dominance by means of symbolic dress and ritual practice.

Guillaumou wanted reform but thought it would not be possible in a compagnonnage that had not yet accepted the shoemakers. In the course of his 1864 memoirs, he told the story of the their crusade for recognition (*reconnaissance*), beginning with their unofficial acceptance by several trades of compagnons du devoir in 1807–1808. The first steps toward formal recognition began only in 1831–1832, spurred by the political activity following the Revolution of 1830: "In 1831 and 1832, our society was given some respite [from the compagnons' constant attacks]: 1830 bore its fruits; something of a truce was made on the tomb of Bourguignon coeur de lion, hero of July, who died bravely while fighting for liberty" (p. 54). As in the revolutionary period, some compagnons were attracted by and willing to fight for political liberty.

The post-1830 discourse, moreover, fully launched the debate on the nature of liberty, association, and their potential relationships. The shoemakers took advantage of the moment. Other trades of compagnonnage were impressed with their bravery on the barricades of July, and oppo-

15. Guillaumou, *Confessions*, p. 52.
16. Ibid., hereafter cited in text.

sition softened. Their society was strong and well organized, initiating between sixty and eighty men a year in Lyon alone (p. 200). Thus, when the shoemakers sent official representatives to negotiate with compagnonnage, they met with some success. Even so, "the official recognition did not take place; the time was not yet right" (p. 54). Meanwhile, the shoemakers made their masterpiece, one of their (expensive) admission requirements. In this and in other regards their initiation into compagnonnage would mirror the initiation of an individual compagnon, though its trials far outweighed the ordinary.

The shoemakers made no new progress toward acceptance for over ten years, a period of declining membership. The number of novices initiated in Lyon plunged dramatically from a maximum of sixty to eighty in the 1820s and 1830s to a minimum of twenty in 1846 (p. 200). There were, nonetheless, some hopeful signs. Brawls between compagnons and shoemakers were on the decline, and Perdiguier's message of reform was beginning to take effect. The Parisian carpenters' strike of 1845, led by united sects of compagnons, had made the possibility of reconciliation seem more realistic. The shoemakers were further encouraged that their greatest strength was in Lyon, a city witnessing some of the most advanced and active programs of association and worker consciousness in the 1830s and 1840s. Compagnonnage was healthy and well represented there, with twenty-eight Mères in the region, twelve of which had recently recognized the weavers as compagnons du devoir. Nonetheless, compagnon shoemakers in Nantes took the lead in 1846, when the most serious and successful bid for acceptance was made. They sent letters of intent to all trades of compagnonnage in their region. Each chambre of shoemakers on the tour followed this model with the exception of the Paris chambre, which had hoped to lead the endeavor itself. Thwarted, the Parisian shoemakers proved sullen and unresponsive, an example of the strength of regional allegiances, which might sometimes outweigh interurban loyalties. Apparently, more married and retired compagnons in all trades were actively participating in compagnonnage, marking a distinct change in traditional regulations. These more settled compagnons gave individual chambres more localized voices and aims.

As momentum picked up in the movement for recognition, the Lyon chambre became its driving force. It established a committee of twenty-five members—twelve retired (*anciens*) compagnons and thirteen active members. Guillaumou, a married man, was still an active member, and the society throughout France prevailed upon him to lead the committee and arrange a general assembly. Only "thirteen *corps*"—the weavers and their supporters—agreed to meet with the shoemakers, for the weavers' recognition had created a "separate family" in compagnonnage. Some trades that had not recognized the weavers refused to meet and further pollute compagnonnage by discussing the shoemakers' petition. In the meeting of these thirteen trades, three shoemakers, including Guillaumou, were initiated. Led into the "terrible enclosure," as in an individual initiation, the three found themselves surrounded by compagnons. Guillaumou read a prepared speech, exhorting unity. While admitting the shoemakers' faults, Guillaumou stressed those of compagnonnages' other trades and urged them to end their "hideous scenes" and "incessant and antisocial discord." Much like Perdiguier, Guillaumou called upon the compagnons' "progressive spirit" to reform compagnonnage into a harmonious union based on the "the first principles of its organization" (p. 206).

Despite Guillaumou's sharp criticism, the shoemakers were favorably received—but not to the point of actual admission. The assembly's president, a hatter, declared that all major branches (*cayennes*) of compagnonnage must ratify any decision, and the shoemakers must bear the time and expense of the necessary paperwork. Shoemakers were also expected to expend fairly large sums of money to entertain the other trades, enabling at least one unscrupulous committee member to defraud them of a sizable sum during this campaign. Distressingly, the embezzler had been a premier compagnon in Lyon for two years. Compagnonnage, meanwhile, continued to block the shoemakers' progress. Guillaumou blamed the delays on "the *raison de compagnonnage* that no one understood and because of this alone was elevated into a great mystery" (p. 218). The other trades now insisted that the shoemakers submit to a time of testing and find a trade of compagnonnage to sponsor them as their "father."

The general assembly, now seventeen trades strong, proposed as the first test that the shoemakers give up all their insignias, especially their canes and colors, for five to ten years. Most shoemakers violently opposed this demand; they would never give up their insignias, said Gillaumou, "even for one minute." Such a test would strip the shoemakers of their prestige, dishonoring them in their own eyes and those of the other trades. Whereas humbling and loss of dignity are one of the purposes of ritual testing, Guillaumou clearly thought that the shoemakers had suffered indignity enough. They had endured more than forty years of ostracism and hatred, which should be considered test enough of their devotion to compagnonnage. These answers presumably satisfied the general assembly; no further talk of tests was heard.

On the second issue, however, the general assembly was unyielding: the shoemakers must find a trade to serve as their father and recognize them as its children; if they could not, they would never be accepted into compagnonnage. None of the seventeen trades present would consent to sponsor the shoemakers. Guillaumou must have known that many new trades in the eighteenth century were adopted in this way. Nevertheless, he insisted that the shoemakers needed no father, for they were already children of Maître Jacques: "One cannot be a child of Maître Jacques and of the saddle makers, or a child of Solomon and of the locksmiths or another *corps d'état*" (p. 216).

Guillaumou knew all too well from the weavers' example that adoptive fathers frequently exploited their children, demanding large payments and requiring the new society to modify its regulations and customs to conform with the parent's. The weavers' sponsor, the saddle makers, had forced them to change some precepts of a "devoir that had suited them admirably." When the general assembly remained adamant, Guillaumou acquiesced and began to pursue "whatever kind of paternity we could find" (p. 214). The metaphors of paternity and bastardy which run through the shoemakers' story evoke the model of the family rather than membership in a political or economic community. Yet, this familial language remained typical not only in compagnonnage but in the wider contemporary cultural and political discourse. The assembly strongly hinted that the shoemakers should persuade the tanners to adopt them: one way or another the tanners would be held responsible for bringing the shoemakers back into compagnonnage. The tanners, however, wanted no part of this scheme, having enough trouble with their original transgression.

The cloth shearers of Vienne were the first chambre to show any interest in "giving their name" to the shoemakers. Before promising paternity, however, they had to consult their three other major chambres. After some deliberation, the Paris chambre joined the one in Vienne in agreeing to adopt the shoemakers as their children, without any tests or trials. The general assembly accepted this split decision as a "majority," accorded official recognition and scheduled a ceremony confirming the recognition in Lyon, a site approved over the vocal objections of the Parisian shoemakers' chambre, which long continued to resent this "insult."

Nonetheless, in June 1846 the Lyon chambre prepared an elaborate initiation "to dazzle the other corps with [their] wealth and size" (p. 224). The compagnons constructed a "temple" and spared no expense to adorn it properly. Then, at the last moment, the compagnon cloth shearers of Paris withdrew their support, perhaps, as Guillaumou believed, encouraged by his own society in that city. The day of the ceremony found only thirteen cloth shearers (nine from Vienne and four from Lyon) present to greet the sixteen corps accepting the shoemakers' invitation. The session was stormy; eventually all the representatives left, refusing to regard the support of thirteen cloth shearers as acceptable for a true recognition. Guillaumou begged the remaining cloth shearers to go through with the reception, further dividing them. Finally, only seven men remained to recognize the shoemakers and sign their constitution. These men worked to persuade the other corps to accept the shoemakers.

Two months later, in August, another city on the cloth shearers' tour recognized the shoemakers, and another ceremony took place. Although the ceremony was simple (for the shoemakers could afford no more), it was the official one and charged with significance. Guillaumou, the shoemakers' chief representative, stood in the middle of the seventeen trades present, wearing a chain around his neck, symbolizing the shoemakers' former slavery and their isolation from compagnonnage. After he walked around a simulated tomb, perhaps in memory of the shoemakers' wanderings and wish to be reborn into compagnonnage, the chain was ripped violently from his neck and replaced by a rope of green silk which had been passed around the circle of compagnons. Each representative tied a knot in the rope linking all these "knots" of compagnonnage in a chain of alliance. After the compagnons broke bread and drank wine together and gave Guillaumou the fraternal embrace, a great feast celebrated this new union. The shoemakers' long struggle was apparently over. But problems remained: only the cloth shearers had signed the shoemakers' constitution. And this incomplete recognition had cost the shoemakers five thousand francs (p. 231).

In 1847 another five thousand francs were spent to persuade more trades to accept the recognition, but most compagnons continued to ostracize the shoemakers. A discouraged Guillaumou left Lyon in December 1847 "full of bitterness" and sought work in Paris (p. 232). Although nothing came of their charges, compagnon shoemakers in the capital blamed Guillaumou for failing to achieve full recognition and for improper use of the society's funds. The events of 1848 quickly focused the compagnons' attentions elsewhere. Guillaumou became very active in revolutionary politics and played a central role in the attempted 1848 reconciliation of the compagnonnages.

The whole complicated saga of the shoemakers' attempts to become "real" compagnons has important parallels to the social integration and exclusion of the old regime. Orders, estates, and corporate bodies before the Revolution absorbed new members, but rates of acceptance and continued resistance to or avoidance of new members varied greatly over time and within particular social strata. Like elements of the aristocracy at the end of the old regime, compagnonnage continued to find a compelling aspect of their identity in the principles of privilege, hierarchy, and exclusion. Nevertheless, we should not assume from the shoemakers' inability to win full acceptance until 1865 that many in compagnonnage did not cherish the revolutionary ideals of liberty, equality, and brotherhood. While compagnon shoemakers pursued official recognition, compagnons in other societies worked to reform the organization itself. Some members would now try to make compagnonnage "fit" the times.

THE MOVEMENT FOR REFORM

Even before Perdiguier's *Livre du compagnonnage* appeared in 1839, other compagnons and even entire societies had attempted to solve the most pressing problems of compagnonnage. Despite growing awareness of the need for reform, however, most compagnons still believed the worst abuses could be corrected without fundamental reorganization. I have already described the efforts of assemblies in 1803 and 1807 to codify and reorganize the two major devoirs. Apparently, no other large-scale meetings transpired until early November 1821, when a general assembly of the various societies du devoir met in Bordeaux to discuss the "reestablishment of the compagnonnage du devoir"—to "put [the compagnons'] affairs in order," settle all questions of precedence and legitimacy, and end the widespread violence between societies.[17] The assembly chose Bordeaux as their venue to focus on the alarming number of violent brawls that had taken place in that city among the various trades within the devoir. The compagnons themselves were eager to end this endemic fighting, for they now realized their internecine quarrels weakened the whole organization. Although their aims did not include proposals for the general reconciliation of all the rites, they called for a renewal of "true" spirit, a major theme in later reform projects.

The planning behind the assembly appears to have been thorough. In September police learned of circular letters summoning compagnons in Orléans, Nantes, Paris, and Lyon, and perhaps other cities to Bordeaux.[18] The prefect of police of the Seine noted that a group of compagnons in Lyon left for Bordeaux as early as 18 September. On 5 November 1821, roughly 80 delegates (150 according to some witnesses) gathered for the first meeting, empowered by their societies to "consent to all the measures that could lead to the proposed goal [of reconciliation]." Some representatives wished to recommend emendations to the socie-

17. AN, F⁷ 9786, dos. "Compagnons du devoir," Paris, 25 September 1821, prefect of police, Seine, to director general of police and departmental administration.
18. Ibid.

ties' statutes and regulations which would "maintain among them the principles of perfect honor and probity." The tanners and curriers of Paris, unable to attend, wrote an open letter to the assembly, defining some of their objectives.[19] In sophisticated and legalistic language they expressed great concern over disunity among compagnons du devoir, which they attributed to inability to agree on a common code of regulations. Stricter adherence to all precepts of a standardized devoir would lead to a harmonious and, more important, stronger association, which could assert its prerogatives more effectively.

The tanners and curriers went beyond formal proposals to appeal to sentiment; they described themselves as "deeply filled with the desire to see a general reconciliation . . . [and a] perfect accord." They claimed that the current quarrels arose from the loss or destruction of compagnons' "genealogical acts" and other historical documents in the Revolution, which left few reliable means of verifying opposing claims. They proposed a thorough and systematic examination of existing papers and the minutes of assemblies held immediately following the Revolution. They urged that the most enlightened and trusted of the retired compagnons who had lived through the revolutionary era be questioned and asked to help clarify areas of disagreement, in the hope of achieving definitive—or at least mutually acceptable—settlements of disputed issues.[20] Cleverly, the tanners and curriers suggested that it was likely that trades claiming the most seniority would have best preserved their documents, and they urged these trades to present their verification to the assembly. This proposal is a fascinating and eminently reasonable brief for historical reconstruction using existing documents and oral history.

In the event, however, the tanners and curriers' plans were never presented and long-standing rivalries tended to assert themselves. Officials had "received information" that "the blacksmiths are in agreement with the ironsmiths and the hatters, but the carpenters are, it is said, enemies of the leather curriers. The distinctions established by each trade are often the cause of the quarrels among them."[21] The carpenters' opposition to most of the reforms proposed in the 1820s may suggest how much their views had had to change by the 1845 strike, when they were acclaimed for breaking down the barriers between the devoirs. Yet, with the exception of the 1840s—and even then with reservations—the car-

19. Ibid., prefect of police, Gironde, to director general, Bordeaux, 9 and 14 November 1821, and a letter addressed to "Les Pays et coteries" (n.d. [before 5 November 1821]).
20. Ibid.
21. Georges Bourgin and Hubert Bourgin, Les Patrons, les ouvriers, et l'état: Le Régime de l'industrie en France de 1814 à 1830, 3 vols. (Paris, 1912–41), 2:20, citing AN, F⁷ 9786, letter from prefect of police, Paris, to the general director of departmental administration and police, 25 September 1821.

penters generally insisted on their privileges and seniority within compagnonnage throughout the nineteenth century. Priding themselves on their strength and skill, the carpenters claimed to be the most orthodox, most senior, and largest trade in compagnonnage. Indeed, they were a dominant trade and had organized many successful labor disputes, but other trades—stonecutters, joiners, locksmiths—could make roughly equal claims. Nonetheless, the carpenters' ability to persuade the other trades of their "rights" enabled them to impede reform. Interestingly enough, they based these claims to privilege on the origin narratives of the compagnons du devoir and not the historical record as the tanners and curriers would have liked. Carpenters, for example, were *not* among the trades the Sorbonne condemned in 1655; they began to appear in archival records only in the late seventeenth century, and their ranks made significant gains only after the mid-eighteenth century.

Despite the resistance to reform, hopes for resolving the devoir's problems ran high at the outset of the Bordeaux assembly. About twenty compagnons—carpenters, hatters, curriers, and members of the "quatre corps" (cutlers, tinsmiths, smelters, and coppersmiths)—convened separately to try and resolve the most thorny problems facing the devoir. A currier proposed that their small group come to some kind of agreement and use their prestige and influence as the "oldest" of the compagnons to persuade the delegates to adopt their measures. Almost immediately, the carpenters refused to support any reform measures, and their obstinacy effectively blocked the proceedings.

> The carpenters continued to maintain, as they always had, that they were the oldest of the compagnons and had existed since the era of Solomon and the building of the temple. The hatters who had passed for the oldest for centuries, stonecutters for the second oldest, and the leather curriers for the fourth oldest asked that all these primacies now be forgotten and that all the compagnons of the various corps d'état be equal to one another.[22]

Significantly, a solid coalition of compagnons and even entire trades was convinced that the system of rank and privilege must be abolished. The hatters, stonecutters, and curriers appear to have realized that compagnonnage had always been based on privilege to some extent. Yet, they deplored the growing tendency of many trades to overemphasize these organizational features. Some at this "Congrès compagnonnique" (as the police called it) believed the insistence on prerogatives and privileges

22. AN, F⁷ 9896, dos. "Compagnons du devoir," 14 November 1821, prefect of police, Gironde, to director general, including a report of a former compagnon attending the meeting.

was gradually eroding the spirit of brotherhood and mutual aid which they perceived as the cornerstone of compagnonnage. I attribute this rejection of privilege and hierarchy based on "ancient titles" both to the cultural changes brought about by the Revolution and to the reorganizations of postrevolutionary societies of compagnonnage which reinforced inequalities. Eventually most delegates proved unwilling to compromise, and the future unity and strength of the compagnons du devoir was left in doubt. It is noteworthy that these problems were articulated as early as 1821; although the assembly was not successful, it made a beginning and helped influence reforms later proposed by Perdiguier and others.

Most compagnons and the most powerful societies were not yet convinced that reform was desirable, let alone essential for survival. We have no record of any subsequent meetings on the Bordeaux scale. In general, the impetus for change returned to the local and individual level until the 1840s, with some exceptions. The shoemakers' struggle for recognition, after all, was an effort to make the compagnons du devoir less exclusive and more willing to accept new "brothers." And in Toulon in the mid-1820s, Provençal la fleur d'amour (né Jaume), a compagnon joiner du devoir de liberté, was one of the first to voice the idea that all trades and devoirs could be joined into one association. Jaume was also interested in ridding compagnonnage of what outsiders labeled unnecessary features, for example, their "folkloric ostentation—canes, colors, secrets."[23] Jaume knew how radical his proposal was and made no attempts to convert the compagnons directly. Instead, hoping that reform could come from above, he brought his ideas to Baron Charles Dupin, a highly placed administrator in the department of the Navy.

Dupin had met Jaume during an inspection tour of various port cities in 1821 and listened to his evaluation of the potential and actual benefits of compagnonnage for workers. Dupin was convinced and made a report to the National Assembly in 1829. Eventually, with Jaume's help, he developed the idea of placing this new, unified compagnonnage under official patronage, arguing that the association "could do no better than to continue to improve the moral conduct of the working class."[24] The Dupin-Jaume project, however, went no farther. Hopes of government support, crucial to the project, vanished with the Revolution of 1830. In any event, it is unlikely the compagnons would ever have submitted to state regulation and direction.

23. Agulhon, *Ville ouvrière*, p. 123.
24. *Le Moniteur universel*, 23 February 1829 (Jaume was not mentioned in Dupin's report); Agulhon, *Ville ouvrière*, p. 123.

The Reforms of the Blanchers-Chamoiseurs

Other reform efforts before 1840 tended to begin in a major urban center of a particular trade. For example, the society of compagnon chamois dressers du devoir began their reforms in Paris under the leadership of Jean-François Piron, called Vendôme la clef des coeurs (1796–1841). The chamois dressers took the radical step of writing down, standardizing, and revising their language and even their ritual practices. Later, as the principal editor and moving force of this reform movement, Piron wanted to share some of Perdiguier's public acclaim. "You would be wrong," he wrote Perdiguier, "if you were to suppose that your ideas are entirely new.... I myself have known of many, and notably [the corps] to which I have the honor of belonging, which have professed these ideas for quite a long time now, and which march along with the progress of this century." He claimed that most of the chamois dressers' changes had been enacted in the 1820s and 1830s, long before publication of the *Livre du compagnonnage*.[25]

Some doubt, however, remains on the date of the chamois dressers' reforms and, more critically, on how widely known or fully adopted these changes were in the 1820s and 1830s, or even later. Piron claims they had begun in his society as early as 1816, the year he became a compagnon. The fruit of this reform was five manuscript booklets or registers, but Piron's "introduction" to the devoir (register 1) is dated 1840, by which time he was already a retired compagnon.[26] The language of these revisions and the sentiments they embodied may well have emerged in 1816; his society could have chosen the end of the Napoleonic era to reflect on the state of their association. The revision process itself may then have occurred over several years. The entire revolutionary era had engendered severe repression of the compagnonnages. According to Piron, their customs had fallen into disuse and much of their oral tradition had become confused. Piron seems painfully aware that these traditions were "no longer suited to the times," and the changes he proposed tended to focus on modernization. Nonetheless, the language of the introduction is consistent with and informed by the debate on the "social question," which emerged after the Revolution of 1830.

25. Agricol Perdiguier, *Le Livre du compagnonnage, contenant des chansons de compagnons, un dialogue sur l'architecture, un raisonnement sur le trait, une notice sur le compagnonnage, la rencontre de deux frères, et un grand nombre de notes*, 2d ed., 2 vols. (Paris, 1841), 2:18–19, Vendôme to Perdiguier.

26. AD Seine, 4 AZ 1068, five ms. registers, "Devoir des compagnons blanchers et chamoiseurs réunis," Introduction. These registers are now in print: J[ean]-F[rançois] Piron, *Devoir des compagnons blanchers et chamoiseurs réunis* (Paris, 1990).

Whether or not Piron predated the reforms, his analysis is valuable, for he recognized a dissonance between the culture of compagnonnage and that of contemporary French society, an incompatibility that could be overcome, he believed, only in terms of language. Compagnonnage must be made to "speak" the new language of the nineteenth-century. Its organization and practice must be put into the "new words" introduced and implanted in French culture by the revolutionary experience. The Revolution had made the allegorical language of the devoir incomprehensible. The new age, he said, had engendered new interpretations of words and phrases common in the old regime. Revolutionary upheavals, changes in the social order and in modes of production had disrupted the traditional configuration of compagnonnage, provoking an unhealthy emphasis on hierarchy, exclusivity, and order.[27] One might say that compagnonnage was reconstructing itself in response to a postcorporate world grounded in the model of an often chaotic and alienating individualism. Compagnons responded by attempting to incorporate some of the power and efficiency of the new bureaucratic structures.

Although Piron's reform included a substitution of new words for old, he also worked for a redefinition of the meaning and use of familiar words. He attempted to explicate symbols, practices, and particularly the devoir and its "fundamental rules." This redefinition and clarification was not, however, based on strictly egalitarian principles. Use of rank continued in many situations: the registers employ the titles "first, second, third . . . in town," usually corresponding to the compagnon's seniority. Thus, the chamois dressers' reforms never meant to do away with hierarchy entirely or to institute absolute equality, and their "new" language was not intended to be a complete break with the past. Their primary concern was to transmit their traditions and beliefs to their descendants accurately and securely. Piron edited and preserved the compagnons' regulations and customs in writing in what he called their "sacred book." He compared this book to the Jews' Talmud and the Christians' Bible, a "sacred text," which all chamois dressers could read for themselves. No longer would only a small number of privileged compagnons know the meaning of their customs.[28]

Furthermore, although hierarchy remained an organizing principle, Piron sought to moderate its influence, to mitigate the role of distinction in certain performances and activities. For example, the new statutes expressly stated that "young" and "old" compagnons should be seated

27. AD Seine, 4 AZ 1068, register 1, "Devoir," introduction.
28. Ibid., introduction.

side by side, not segregated, at society banquets.[29] Undoubtedly, Piron's reforms, if fully implemented, would have had some egalitarian consequences, but his rhetoric is religious rather than political. The reform might be characterized as "Protestant," with the compagnons as a "priesthood of all believers." Simultaneously, however, Piron draws on an Enlightenment belief in the power of language to change the common way of thinking. He was convinced that words and what they represented were no longer in harmony.

We can see how Piron worked out his ideas in the revision of the chamois dressers' initiation, dated 1816. In his introduction to this text Piron notes that from the beginning of compagnonnage only oral transmission of ritual practices had been permitted.[30] In fact, the extant text of the chamois dressers' rituals from the eighteenth century is the work of an informer and not found in a set of the association's written statues. Now, however, tradition must be broken because of the urgent need for reform and because the wars and dislocations of the Revolution and Empire had decreased membership to the point that the practices of compagnonnage had fallen into disuse, leading to misunderstandings and to inaccuracies in form and content. "All these causes together," said Piron, "have so contributed to change the sense of the figurative language of our devoir, that a reform has become necessary, at least as far as concerns the use of dialect, the old and outmoded style of which is no longer that of our times."[31] His perception of the cultural changes wrought by the Revolution strikingly reinforces what contemporary scholars such as Lynn Hunt have said about the transformation of French culture at all levels during that era. Piron's revisions attempted to make the society's language and practices more meaningful to present and future members.

Because the initiation of a "brother" is the most solemn ceremony, said Piron, it must be imposing and performed with order and propriety. The *setting,* a room in the Mère (probably the attic), is to be decorated according to the taste and ability of the compagnons in that city. Certain elements, however, must be standard: windows are to be hung with white cloth (symbolizing purity), and the room is to be furnished with a rug and a table set like an altar with six tapers and a crucifix in its center. A Bible or the Gospels replace the crucifix when the aspirant is a member of a "reformed Catholic" religion. In the center of the altar, near the edge, lies a dagger or knife with a red ribbon fastened to one end.

29. Ibid., register 2, "Devoir," pp. 99–100.
30. Ibid., pp. 69–85. If Piron is correct, we might question the authenticity of accounts supposedly written by members of compagnonnage prior to the nineteenth century.
31. AD Seine, 4 AZ 1068, register 1, "Devoir," introduction.

In front of the altar, at a prescribed distance, is the "quadrangle" (representing the temple's four points—east, west, north, and south). In the middle of the quadrangle is a table with a bowl holding the future compagnon's "colors." Another bowl, covered by a cloth, holds three names, one of which the aspirant will choose. Each angle of the quadrangle is lit by a candle; a container of baptismal wine is placed toward the southern angle. The premier compagnon is seated at the center of the table with the *second en ville* (second senior) to his right and the *dernier en ville* (least senior) or secretary to his left. When the aspirant enters, all the compagnons form a circle from the right to the left of the altar so the aspirant can see them all in one glance. The compagnons are ranked according to the numbers drawn during their own initiations. An equal number of men must stand to the premier compagnon's left and right.

The *separation* phase begins after the aspirant has completed a chef-d'oeuvre, approved by the other compagnons, and has saved up his admission fee. He is told the day and hour he is to report to the Mère. The ceremony itself takes place at midnight. Before midnight, each aspirant "goes up" to the initiation room three times, accompanied by the rôleur (who knocks three times on the door). Each aspirant is brought up in turn. His name as well as those of his parents, his age, place of birth, department, and province are written down, and he pays his admission fee. Next, all the aspirants come up to the room together, and they draw lots to determine their future rank in the society. In that order, "without any consideration of age or any other factor," they go up to the room once more. Each is asked the name he wishes to have as a compagnon; it must conform to his character and natural inclinations. Piron specifically rejected the custom of giving new compagnons ridiculous or undignified names. To the aspirant's choice the compagnons themselves add two names. All three are written on slips of paper and put in a cup. Each time the aspirant goes up to the room, he is plainly informed of the gravity of this undertaking and told the society accepts only men of goodwill.

The *transition* phase begins for each candidate when he is brought up to the room for a fourth and last time. While all the compagnons sing a low, prolonged chant, the aspirant is blindfolded and brought "toward the east" of the quadrangle to be questioned by the premier. The aspirant's commitment to the society is examined, and he is informed of the society's nature and purpose:

Q. Our devoir is ruled by honor and virtue. Do you believe yourself capable of following it?

A. Yes, I believe myself capable and I wish to pledge myself to it.

Q. Our society is a society of charity and mutual aid. Do you consent to share in this?

A. Yes, my Pays, I consent to it with all my heart.

Q. Our secrets are inviolable. Do you believe yourself to have the force and courage to guard that which will be confided to you inviolably?

A. Yes, my Pays.

The premier compagnon reads the oath:

> I swear and promise in front of God to guard inviolably the secrets which will be confided to me by the society of the C. [Compagnons] du devoir, chamois dressers. . . .I commit myself without coercion, but rather by the spirit of my own free will and promise to observe [its] statutes and regulations . . . faithfully, certain as I am that they contain nothing opposed to honor or a good conscience.[32]

Again the aspirant is questioned on his commitment and asked if he has the strength and courage to uphold the oath. If he agrees, he raises his left hand, and with his right hand over his heart, repeats the oath after the premier compagnon. The aspirant is asked what he seeks. He responds, "The light," and his blindfold is removed. He repeats the oath. The taper at the eastern angle of the quadrangle is removed; kneeling there, the aspirant swears the oath a third time.

The aspirant next approaches the altar by the southern angle and, kneeling in front of it, holds the dagger in his right hand with the point pressed against his heart. His left hand, from which the red ribbon hangs, is raised; the rôleur holds his cane over the aspirant's head. The aspirant says: "I confess to God and to the compagnons that I am ready to shed my blood and to give myself over to death, rather than betray the oath that I have just sworn." Finally, the aspirant is brought back by the northern angle (the "septentrion") and, kneeling on the quadrangle, says: "I give up all other, bad Societies to attach myself wholly to that of the chamois dressers to which I promise fidelity unto death."[33]

The *incorporation* phase of the ceremony is called the baptism and begins when the aspirant draws one of the three possible names out of the cup. The names not chosen are burned. The aspirant then chooses

32. Ibid., register 2, "Devoir," pp. 75–76, 76–77.
33. Ibid., p. 79.

a godfather, a godmother, and a third witness from the assembled compagnons. These three stand close to the premier compagnon. The godfather adjusts a napkin under the aspirant's collar and holds a basin under his chin. The premier then pours the baptismal wine over the aspirant's head three times, saying each time: "In the name of the S. [society] in front of God and the compagnons, [new name], I Baptize you, in the name of the Father, Son, and Holy Spirit, so be it."[34] The new compagnon drinks the wine in three sips, saying: "May this name be engraved on my heart and may the wine give me the strength and the courage to uphold [my new name] unto death." He swallows the slip of paper bearing his name. Next the premier compagnon gives him his colors and the *attouchement* (special handshake), saying, "In the name of the S., C. and F. [Society, Compagnons and Frères], you are recognized as a brother and compagnon du devoir"; the other compagnons reply, "Yes," three times. After the premier gives the new compagnon the *accolade fraternelle*, the other compagnons, in turn, do likewise. The ceremony ends when all the aspirants have been initiated and brought into the room. There all the newly received are presented to the mère.

This text of the chamois dressers' initiation is structurally consistent with most of the accounts I have previously examined. Yet, it also introduces a number of forms and symbols that move it away from the eighteenth-century account of their own initiation and in the direction of Masonic practice. The transitional stage of the initiation differs not only in degree but also in kind from all the previous examples. For this "reformed" society, the point is to enable compagnons to understand their commitment to the devoir in a rational way. The aspirant is told something of the society before he is allowed to take the oath; he is warned it takes "strength and courage" to proceed. Coercion is specifically abjured, and nothing is demanded which members may not do with honor and good conscience. The oath remains sacred and "inviolable," but the aspirants make a firm and binding commitment to the society without physical harassment. It is the aspirant himself, not the other compagnons, who had to play out this representation by pointing the dagger at his heart. He voluntarily swears his readiness to shed his blood or lose his life rather than betray his oath. Thus Piron's presentation of the initiation followed his general plan of reform: to make symbolic acts more meaningful and less esoteric and to inform novices of their future duties.

Other aspects of the ceremony also reveal transformations in the nature of this fraternal organization. The aspirants' names are no longer

34. Ibid., pp. 81–82.

to be "ridiculous," making them or compagnonnage itself a target for mockery. The compagnon's past is not to be negated (his place of origin is still an integral part of his new name); instead, its worthy aspects are to be dedicated to compagnonnage. Names such as Comtois la fidélité (the faithful), Provençal la sagesse (the wise), Sommière l'ami des arts (friend of the arts), and Parisien le bien aimé (beloved) are only a small sample of the virtues that compagnons such as Piron and Perdiguier wished to promote.[35] These positive traits are substituted for those no longer favored, which expressed aggressive and amorous exploits—for example, "the terror," "the girl's pleasure." This apparently minor decision to reject certain names as "inappropriate" reflects an important shift in the perception of compagnonnage's place in contemporary society.

Piron's account aims to impress the members with "seriousness of purpose" and to provide a practical demonstration of the organizational capabilities of compagnonnage. The initiation, furthermore, deemphasizes rank and order, not casting them aside but assigning them on a somewhat more equitable basis, by chance rather than by seniority. Nonetheless, because a compagnon kept his randomly assigned rank throughout his membership, this formulation was a less than perfect solution to the problem of inequality. Piron's reform, moreover, remained ambiguous on this point. He never clearly stated how—or whether—the new compagnons' "numbers" were integrated with those of the previously initiated. If these ranks were operative just during the ritual itself, the reform would have been only a partial step toward easing the tensions of a seniority-based hierarchy on a day-to-day basis.

In addition, despite the rationalist and bureaucratic elements of the initiation, symbolism and tradition remain central in this account. Reforming compagnons such as Piron and Perdiguier generally admired the basic principles of compagnonnage and felt the need to change only their outer forms (and language). Ritual and symbol were part of the fundamental nature of compagnonnage, to be modified, not abandoned. Piron, for example, considered number symbolism and temple imagery meaningful, and unlike earlier compagnons, he provided an exegesis of this symbolism. The ceremony as a whole, however, remained deeply Catholic, with certain concessions to Protestant and Masonic practices. Baptism was still the central focus of incorporation. The initiation thus remained a mandatory rite of passage, deeply permeated with symbolism.

In his reforms Piron worked to recapture what he believed were the

---

35. These names appear among those of the hundreds of compagnons who subscribed to Perdiguier's *Livre du compagnonnage*, 2d ed., 2:220–30.

original and most powerful characteristics of compagnonnage—spontaneity, brotherhood, and openness. His proposed semantic changes, he hoped, would keep the figurative language of compagnonnage intact while making it, in his terms, more technical, precise, and comprehensible to nineteenth-century men. Whether or not this new language was really more accessible is questionable, since it borrowed heavily from the often esoteric language of Masonry. Perhaps the chamois dressers hoped to elevate their own status and to counteract some of the most pernicious aspects of their own rigid hierarchy by adopting what they may have considered Masonry's more "enlightened" and elite form of social organization. As noted in the last chapter, Agricol Perdiguier's views on the relationship between Masonry and compagnonnage were less enthusiastic. He wanted to protect the integrity of compagnonnage by highlighting its most socially constructive values and practices.

AGRICOL PERDIGUIER AND REFORM

The compagnons du devoir who met in Bordeaux in 1821 and men such as Jaume and Piron made some important contributions to reform, but it was Agricol Perdiguier who finally succeeded in generating widespread enthusiasm and energy for this cause. Perdiguier's ideas had been evolving since the 1820s, beginning with his first, four-year tour de France (20 April 1824—24 August 1828) during which he not only sang the traditional songs of compagnonnage but also, like many workers of his generation, began to write his own. He composed songs about his experiences and about the enfants de Salomon, and he also wrote "songs of regeneration," based on his growing rejection of rivalries and violence among compagnons. By the mid-1830s Perdiguier was firmly convinced that the warring factions could be united. A true son of the nineteenth century, he hoped compagnonnage could "follow the progress of our era and march along with civilization."[36]

Publishing songs that celebrated the peaceful and constructive rather than the aggressive and competitive features of compagnonnage, Perdiguier hoped to speed this progress. In 1834 he published, by means of subscriptions raised among compagnons, the first part of a songbook titled *Devoir de liberté: Chansons de compagnons et autres*, containing six of his own songs. The songbook was so popular that part 2 came out in 1836; five hundred copies of the first songbook and thirteen hundred

36. Agricol Perdiguier, *Devoir de liberté: Chansons de compagnons et autres*, part 1 (Paris, 1834), p. 5.

copies of the second were printed.[37] Perdiguier's own songs were quite unlike the traditional war chants and satires of gavots or dévorants sung to provoke fights between rivals. Nevertheless, he included such songs in his book as examples of the "revolting abuses, the blind prejudices ... which must be put to rest."[38]

By printing songs he characterized as "insulting, gross, barbarous, and prejudiced," Perdiguier hoped to shame and shock compagnons into rejecting them. No sensible man could hear the "satirical song of the gavots" without "shrugging his shoulders with a smile of pity":

> When blind fortune made itself ruler of the universe,
>   A time one often calls the iron age,
>   Maître Jacques lived on the earth,
>   Not knowing how or where to earn his wage,
>   To make his living only one thing he knew,
>   He founded a devoir and called it new. (Repeat)
> With old Soubise the two tramping founders
>   Peddled their wares in the city of Orléans. . . .
>   As soon as they hit town
>   The simpering scheming pair,
>   Exposed their mysteries and secrets
>   In all the public squares.
> Since then hordes of imbeciles, called dévorants,
>   Multiply all over Orléans. (Repeat)

> Lorsque l'aveugle fortune
>   S'empara de l'univers,
>   Qu'une expression plus commune
>   Fit nommer l'âge de fer,
>   Maître Jacques sur la terre,
>   Sans argent ni savoir,
>   Pour vivre ne sachant que faire,
>   Fonda un nouveau devoir. (bis)
> Associé au vieux Soubise,
>   Ces fondateurs ambulants
>   Pour vendre leur marchandise
>   Partirent pour Orléans. . . .
>   Nos deux faiseurs de grimaces
>   Sitôt dans cette cité,

37. Ibid.; Jean Briquet, *Agricol Perdiguier: Compagnon du tour de France et représentant du peuple (1805–1875)* (Paris, 1955), pp. 133, 137.

38. Agricol Perdiguier, *Devoir de liberté: Chansons de compagnons et autres,* part 2 (Paris, 1836), title page, v.

> Exposèrent sur les places
> Leur mystère et leur secret
> Depuis ce temps-là fourmille
> Dans la ville d'Orléans
> Quantité des imbeciles
> Que l'on nomme dévorants. (bis)[39]

Despite his opposition to such songs, even Perdiguier was not free from partiality in 1834. "Le Départ," for example, enjoins the children of Solomon to be tolerant of compagnons du devoir, but only if possible. The song does not hesitate to condone reprisals if the dévorants' arrogance becomes insupportable. Another of Perdiguier's compositions, the "Hymn to Solomon," went well beyond celebrating and expressing love for the founder of his rite and exhorted gavots to defend the noble name of Solomon until death.

> Worthy children of a king
> Whose wisdom created in days of old
> Our equitable laws,
> On this beautiful day
> With hearts full of cheer,
> With ardor sing with me. (Repeat)
> . . . . .
> Son of David, from the eternal vaults,
> Cast your eyes down on your pious children,
> Lend an ear to their solemn voices
> Receive, receive their generous vows. (Repeat)
> . . . . .
> Great founder, sage full of glory, (Repeat)
> Your sons know how to live and die for you.

> Dignes enfants du roi dont la sagesse
> Créa jadis nos équitables lois,
> En ce beau jour, le coeur plein d'allégresse,
> Avec ardeur accompagnez ma voix. (bis)
> . . . . .
> Fils de David, des voûtes éternelles
> Jette les yeux sur tes pieux enfants,
> Prête l'oreille à leurs voix solennelles,
> Reçois leurs généreux serments. (bis)

39. Perdiguier, *Devoir de liberté*, part 1, p. 4, reprinted in the *Livre du compagnonnage*, 2d ed., 1:80–81.

. . . . .
Grand fondateur, sage éclatant de gloire, (bis)
Tes fils pour toi savent vivre et mourir.[40]

The hymn is still far from Perdiguier's stated message of peace and harmony between rites.

In the 1836 songbook Perdiguier felt ready to take a more decisive
step toward unity and included not only songs by compagnons gavots
but also those by a compagnon du devoir, Bordelais va sans crainte. No
songs proposed a radical fusion of the two sects, but all proclaimed the
message that, at least within each rite, compagnons should love each
other as brothers. One song expressed the children of Solomon's "loyalty, the joy of union and fraternity, the familial spirit of the gavots,
respect for tradition and gratitude toward [compagnonnage]."[41] Perdiguier's songbooks demonstrate the power of this medium in working-
class culture. If songs could arouse hostility and aggressive, Perdiguier
reasoned, they could also engender brotherhood and, eventually, a spirit
of reconciliation. Many compagnons apparently agreed with him; they
eagerly contributed their compositions and bought the books.

Perdiguier's next work, *Compagnonnage: La Rencontre de deux frères*
(1836), condemned the ritual of *topage,* a challenge to fight issued by
compagnons of rival sects when they met on the road. Perdiguier told
of a battle he supposedly witnessed between compagnons of opposing
rites who, unbeknownst to them, were long lost brothers; the two nearly
killed each other before discovering their true identities. Greatly chas-
tened, they accompanied Perdiguier to an inn where compagnons of
different devoirs were assembled. There followed a lively exchange, in
which, though he proposed no formal plan for reconciliation, Perdiguier
outlined his moral sentiments and convictions that these attacks were
unworthy: "No one profits from these encounters: everyone loses. . . .our
intellect is clouded, our soul is degraded; our thoughts are no longer
lofty or charitable; our understanding becomes troubled and confused."[42] Brawls and challenges dishonored compagnons and compagnonnage and rendered them impotent. He ended with a plea for
tolerance among all workers, regardless of rite or devoir, which reflected
his own optimistic view of human nature. He believed that compagnon-

40. Perdiguier, *Livre du compagnonnage,* 2d ed., 1:128–29, 123–24. Despite its message, Perdiguier reprinted the hymn in the *Livre du compagnonnage,* perhaps to reassure his fellow gavots
of his ultimate loyalties. See also "Le Champ de conduite" with the refrain: "Du grand Salomon
intrépides enfans, / Faisons, faisons un noble effort, / Nous serons triomphans" (Perdiguier,
Devoir de liberté, pt. 1, n.p.).

41. Perdiguier, *Livre du compagnonnage,* 2d ed., 1:145, 144.

42. Agricol Perdiguier, *Compagnonnage: La Rencontre de deux frères,* reprinted in his *Livre du
compagnonnage,* 2d ed., 1:91.

nage gave its members a unique opportunity to develop their talents and skills, an opportunity denied most workers. Utilizing and extending this potential for good, compagnons would make a major contribution to the working classes. Perdiguier thus exhorted them to recognize their own importance, to "rid themselves of their errors and vices" and develop their virtues.

La Rencontre de deux frères included a dramatic statement of all (male) workers' need for solidarity and association: "He who travels alone, without ties to other workers, has little hope of avoiding the blows of poverty and oppression; . . . nothing encourages or facilitates his opportunities to instruct himself. . . . isolated and forced to rely totally on himself as an individual, he becomes cold and self-centered, lucky indeed if these are the worst vices he acquires."[43] Perdiguier explained how a reformed compagnonnage could lead them out of a precarious, limited, and alienating existence. He spoke, moreover, not as an observer from another social class but as one who had experienced the benefits of association.

Thus, Perdiguier's drive to reform compagnonnage developed in the much larger context of opening up the benefits of association to more men and trades and from his realization that compagnonnage would soon decay if its societies simply submitted workers to new forms of oppression. Isolation and individuality, Perdiguier contended, were just as dangerous on the level of the trade or local society. A divided compagnonnage, like unorganized workers, would be powerless. Intransigent compagnons and societies would be unable to control their fate in the changing economic and social conditions of nineteenth-century France. The fictional workers in *La Rencontre de deux frères* left their debate eager to work for reconciliation. But among real compagnons, Perdiguier's resolve to speak "the good truth and effect some good" faced many obstacles.[44]

In 1839 Perdiguier published the *Livre du compagnonnage* and put the brotherhoods into the public forum. Throughout this book he maintained two basic premises: first, it was the members and not the institution of compagnonnage itself that needed reform; and second, compagnonnage could "reform itself" without outside assistance.[45] To reform the membership Perdiguier spent much of the 1840s on a new tour de France, exhorting compagnons to live up to his vision of the devoir's essential principles—fraternity and unity. If the spirit of compagnonnage was to be regenerated, change would have to be wrought in the "compagnons' hearts."

By 1848 Perdiguier reluctantly conceded that his original premises

43. Ibid., 1:95–96.
44. Ibid., 1:96, 109.
45. Cf. Briquet, *Agricol Perdiguier,* p. 183.

were flawed and his reform project too limited. Changing the compagnons' spirit would require a more fundamental change in compagnonnage itself. Warring devoirs, rites, and trades would have to renounce their privileges and accept each other as equals. Many divisions, however, were inherent in the institutional structure of compagnonnage, perhaps even part of its raison d'être. Distinctions were legitimated and reinforced in its ritual practice and origin narratives, and even the limited kind of change Perdiguier proposed would entail major structural modifications. Nevertheless, Perdiguier's approach was compelling, for compagnons would never be willing to change their institution at all unless they examined their relationships to one another as workers and recognized the need for the organization of all labor. Finally, had Perdiguier directly attacked the practices and beliefs of compagnonnage, he undoubtedly would have met with more intense opposition.

Perdiguier's most systematic proposals appeared in the section of the *Livre du compagnonnage* titled "That Which Compagnonnage Has Been and That Which It Must Become."[46] His major challenge was to convince compagnons of the folly of their divisions. The notion that all workers of all trades shared certain interests was by no means generally accepted in the early nineteenth century. This idea contradicted the lived experience of workers in many skilled trades, for the largely artisanal nature of French manufacture reinforced diversity, making it difficult for workers to perceive or accept the relationship between themselves and workers in other trades. Generally, compagnons felt that they had benefitted from their individual societies, devoirs, and rites and failed to see their societies as equal and necessary parts of a whole. Heretofore, their aim had usually been the establishment of a monopoly on their trade in a particular town.

Perdiguier attempted to educate compagnons on the economic and social changes that had taken place since the Revolution. He explained that the labor pool had expanded, trades were requiring fewer skilled workers, and masters were able to hire less-skilled and unorganized workers, thus subjecting all workers to greater control and exploitation. He drove home the absurdity of battles between gavots and dévorants after which the victors thought it an honor to toil for a lower wage as long as they had outdone their rivals. "Understand, my friends, that in being divided we are weak and the object of scorn, and that in uniting we will be strong and respected, and that poverty will no longer dare to approach us. Let us unite then."[47] Yet, Perdiguier realized compagnonnage had often effectively regulated wages and working conditions by con-

46. Perdiguier, *Livre du compagnonnage,* 2d ed., 2:171–219.
47. Ibid., 2:204.

trolling hiring and the availability of skilled workers. Furthermore, driving out rival sects and creating monopolies did not always result in lower wages; the winners could sometimes set their price. Nevertheless, he maintained, the dictates of new conditions would inevitably mean greater competition for jobs, more sweated and unskilled work, and mechanization. Only a united compagnonnage, open to all workers, could maintain a strong bargaining position in this labor market.

Perdiguier presented concrete proposals for achieving unification. He suggested that compagnons du devoir and compagnons du devoir de liberté select about ten or fifteen "wise and capable men" who understood the fundamental principles of their devoir and who strongly supported the goal of unification. These deputies would meet to legislate a new code, a *nouveau devoir,* the product of their combined knowledge. The deputies would then draw up a constitution, laws, and regulations and reach agreement on the holidays and ceremonies to be celebrated. Finally, they would determine the "relationship of compagnons among themselves," including the administration of the new devoir, the degree of hierarchy among compagnons, and the kind of support to be given to one another during labor actions. Perdiguier believed each devoir's most positive features could be retained while eliminating all elements leading to division or dispute.

Perdiguier's description of each devoir's organization and ceremonies reflects his conviction that their differences were superficial. He thus concluded that men's "natural" ambition to rise above themselves would drive unification forward: "The task of combination that I propose is difficult but it is not impossible for men at the pinnacle of their century who understand humanity and their destiny on earth." More practical considerations—selection of delegates, ratification of a new devoir, and the federation of compagnonnage—were not discussed. The primary goal was to inspire enthusiasm and not to raise obstacles. Having proposed the unification of the devoirs, Perdiguier then proposed that compagnons cease selfishly restricting their organizations to a small elite and welcome all workingmen into the brotherhood, creating "compact and solid totality." New trades must be allowed to enter on an equal footing without the old bickering: "Compagnons, listen to me: if you come to blows over a little more or less seniority, you are wrong; for, you see, in our times, titles and parchments are not as worthy as the nobility of the heart and soul."[48]

Although he called for equality of trades and a nobility of talent over "birth," Perdiguier did not reject all aspects of discipline and hierarchy—sensitive issues at the root of much of the continuing hostility be-

48. Ibid., 2:206, 201.

tween novices and compagnons and between retired and active compagnons. Many retired compagnons (*anciens*) formed mutual aid societies with close ties to compagnonnage. Relations between active members (*jeunes* or *actives*) and anciens could be good and mutually beneficial. Some of the anciens had become masters (or employers) and favored the hiring of active compagnons; the masters' societies also lent money to the active societies. Anciens however, also began to exert undue influence on the actions and decisions of the jeunes. In 1843 a serious quarrel developed among compagnon joiners du devoir de liberté over the rank of dignitaire: anciens favored the rank; jeunes opposed it. Asked to arbitrate, Perdiguier eventually sided with the jeunes, finding the title meaningless and an unnecessary cause of division. This decision cost Perdiguier much support in his trade, for anciens dominated roughly one-third of the joiner's societies. In Toulouse the anciens won the struggle and gained control of the Mère, the registers, and the treasury.[49]

The anciens regarded Perdiguier as a radical, but his views on the Société de l'Union (or Union) demonstrate otherwise. This interurban mutual aid society had successfully broken away from compagnonnage in the 1830s and presented a serious challenge to the older association, continuing to recruit dissident compagnons long after its establishment. Perdiguier did not support the Union and was very skeptical of its claims to have eliminated the "mystery" and inequality of compagnonnage. In the *Livre du compagnonnage* he pointed out several contradictions between its doctrine and its practice. The Union's regulations, for example, stated that the association would have "no mysteries, no initiation, no distinctions," and yet some trades within the new association reintroduced—or never gave up—many such practices. The *sociétaires*, as they called themselves, still carried canes, wore "colors" (ribbons and sashes) identifying their position within the association, and adopted "other forms of compagnonnage" in their "new" association.[50] Perdiguier considered this a clear demonstration that workers still wanted and needed symbols and outward signs. These things need not create disharmony; they could stand as tangible proof of the skill and worth of all workers. Yet, compagnons were used to regarding these symbolic distinctions as fundamental to their identity. Uniting all compagnons would require equal regard for all their "colors" or the creation of a new set of common beliefs and symbols, a new "master fiction," in Geertzian terms.[51]

49. See, e.g., Briquet, *Agricol Perdiguier*, pp. 227–31; and Louis Claays, "Le Compagnonnage à Toulouse de 1800 à 1848" (Maîtrise, Université de Toulouse, 1969), pp. 71, 109–12, 152–55.
50. Perdiguier, *Livre du compagnonnage*, 2d ed., 1:49, 50.
51. Clifford Geertz, "Centers, Kings, and Charisma: Reflections on the Symbolics of Power," in *Culture and Its Creators: Essays in Honor of Edward Shils*, ed. Joseph Ben-David and Terry Nichols

Comments on the Union's emphasis on equality reveal further limits to Perdiguier's program. Perdiguier believed strict equality could undermine labor associations, which needed strong leadership to organize and direct their members. "All the members of the Société [de l'Union] are equal; in spite of this equality, order and peace are far from reigning among them," he noted. "Perhaps this proves that a well-arranged hierarchy is not harmful in an association of young men who all have more or less the same resources and more or less the same education. They are, consequently, all able to rise equally to any order and any position." Perdiguier, in contrast to many dissidents saw his compagnonnage as a potentially dynamic association whose hierarchy might actually encourage mobility by fostering healthy competition. Hierarchy, however, had to be based on talent: those whose merit was greatest would earn advancement.

This view was reinforced in his advice to the novices. Perdiguier counseled patience, stressing that all men who wished to become compagnons must first prove themselves worthy.

> I would dare, if the *aspirants* would hear me out, to give them this counsel: "If your compagnons sometimes act unjustly toward you, know how to be patient and suffer a little; this is only a novitiate, a time of testing through which all your leaders have passed. Instruct yourselves, behave yourselves and try to be received as compagnons as soon as possible. Once a compagnon, bring forth the new and progressive ideas that must rejuvenate your society in its government and in its spirit."[52]

Perdiguier's counsel was well meant but rather naive, given the anger of dissident novices. Whether the novitiate was actually worse than it had been or not, more and more novices found it increasingly harsh (or demeaning) and longer than the six months prescribed. In a cultural climate that emphasized an ethic of individual liberty and democratic mutuality, especially after 1830, many workers were not willing to tolerate a novitiate at all. Perdiguier's positive experience in compagnonnage, largely free from undue focus on status, undoubtedly confirmed his belief in the value of the initiation process and its tempering of spirit. He, however, had been initiated in 1824 after a six-month novitiate.

Part of Perdiguier's reluctance to change his views on the novitiate stemmed from his conviction that the strength of compagnonnage lay

---

Clark, pp. 150–71 (Chicago, 1977). See also Lynn Hunt's use of this concept in a revolutionary context in *Politics, Culture, and Class in the French Revolution* (Berkeley, 1984), pp. 87–119.

52. Perdiguier, *Livre du compagnonnage*, 2d ed., 1:49–50, 39–40.

in its corporate organization, whose unity consisted of an organic linking of different, hierarchically arranged parts. The organization of the Société de l'Union, by contrast, seemed to him to be derived from bureaucratic principles that lacked moral force. The Union had a president, and its members were "independents," but Perdiguier thought these were empty words, incapable of generating lasting solidarity, for they had cut the binding ties of body and family.

Perdiguier's continuing commitment to corporate and familial models informed his "Projet de règlement," written in 1846 or 1847, which proposed a plan of association whereby worker-members became the creators and owners of new businesses and workshops. Capital for the project would come from dues and, Perdiguier hoped, from investment by or low-interest loans from wealthy philanthropists. All members would choose the manager (*gérant*) and head (*chef*). A committee, under the manager's direction, would draw up the statutes. As membership and trades increased, new branches would form, each naming its own head. Perdiguier clearly articulated the relationship of these various parts to the whole, and body imagery reinforced his vision. "All the groups are interdependent and jointly liable [*solidaire*]; all together they form but one single association, of which the directing committee is the head and the various other groups are the body and the limbs." Article 18 invoked a family metaphor: "Members of all the groups are bound together by common interest and brotherhood."[53] Perdiguier found it logical and compelling to link current business practices and newer associational forms with compagnonnage's ideals of solidarity, brotherhood, and hierarchy.

Perdiguier always remained firm in his belief that compagnonnage had been a fundamental model for workers' associations, but by 1848 he had become far more engaged with the problems of the working class as a whole. He also realized he needed a more thorough understanding of the contemporary economic and political situation. This shift in emphasis evolved logically as his ideas matured in the 1840s and especially in the dynamic months of 1848 as his association with workers outside compagnonnage multiplied. His vision of the working class had been further enhanced by his connection with *L'Atelier* and his interaction with major literary and social thinkers—George Sand, Tristan, Pierre Leroux, Louis Blanc. The change in Perdiguier's approach to the organization of labor, however, was also provoked by compagnons' reactions to his proposed reforms.

53. The "Projet du règlement" was submitted to Louis Blanc in a letter of 18 March 1847 and was first published in Blanc's *Organisation du travail* (Paris, 1848), pp. 278–84, 280, 281.

REACTIONARIES AND DISSIDENTS

Although compagnons were usually willing to listen to Perdiguier's proposals, implementation remained difficult. Many younger compagnons thought reforming the "spirit" instead of the regulations and practices of compagnonnage would be a protracted approach with little hope of success. Even Perdiguier waited until 1861 to advocate greater equality between novice and compagnon. In the 1840s most novices realized they had little power to follow Perdiguier's call to "bring forth the new and progressive ideas which must rejuvenate [their] society."[54]

Less senior compagnons, while generally respecting Perdiguier's humanitarian views, were not enthusiastic about his advice. Many established compagnons, moreover, were openly hostile, inclined to respect neither his philosophy nor his advice. These self-proclaimed "traditionalists" felt that Perdiguier had revealed too much, had cast "pearls before swine" and profaned their sacred mysteries. Such compagnons believed that their words and practices derived their power from their mystery, even though, objectively, this secrecy was only relative. Previously, novice compagnons had generally accepted limits on their knowledge before initiation, but by the late 1820s, they were increasingly unwilling to remain unenlightened. Most of the old guard, though aware of their novices' discontent and its serious dangers, refused to make concessions, convinced that a more straightforward approach would only sap the strength of compagnonnage and lead to degeneration.

Some conservatives became activists for their cause: directly blocking progress or reform, refusing to accept the shoemakers, bakers, or other trades. Like Perdiguier, they expressed their views in poetry, song, and prose. According to these compagnons, reform would be a grave mistake; disclosing anything of their secrets was heresy. Perdiguier published some of these complaints in the second edition (1841) of the *Livre du compagnonnage* and defended his position. Even though he wanted people to know about compagnonnage, he had said little about initiations or oaths.[55] Not all compagnons who objected to his discussion of their practices, moreover, were completely opposed to reform. One Perodeaud (La vertu de Bordeaux) regretted that Perdiguier had written on the origin and foundation of several societies of which "he knew so little," for his presentation actually reinforced the images he wished to

54. Agricol Perdiguier, *Question vitale sur le compagnonnage et la classe ouvrière* (Paris, 1861), pp. 82–83; Perdiguier, *Livre du compagnonnage,* 2d ed., 1:39–40.

55. He reminded compagnons of his reticence again in a later work and portrayed himself as incapable of debasing himself by such a lack of discretion. *Histoire d'une scission dans le compagnonnage* (Paris, 1846), p. 151.

dispel: "Why present these doubtful statements, erroneous on nearly all points? Statements which they [the public] will only treat as fables. . . . The nineteenth century is a brilliant era of light, and it is in our general interest and that of the world to follow the course of progress. Thus, it is of the most urgent necessity that this matter be presented with as much clarity and wisdom as discretion allows." Perodeaud maintained that certain aspects of the rituals and secrets were beneficial but easily misconstrued by noninitiates. Even an ardent reformer such as Piron was not convinced that Perdiguier did the right thing in divulging mysteries: "You could have made several observations more favorable to our cause by using examples and citations more worthy of your subject. Moreover, your comments say nothing new to compagnons who already know about these things. . . .the errors which have slipped in, while scandalizing some, can only serve to feed the ignorance of others."[56] Piron may have thought that knowledge about ritual practice in his own society was the rule rather than the exception. Even were this so, the openness and understanding Piron's reform tried to establish was to apply only to members of a particular society, not to compagnonnage as a whole.

Both Piron and La vertu de Bordeaux believed that its ritual life was essential and meaningful to compagnonnage. While desiring some reform in these practices, they never wanted them eliminated or stripped to the bare minimum. Perdiguier agreed, but he believed that exposing some symbolic practices "no longer of this age" to the public would encourage (or shame) the compagnons to reform their worst abuses. He disclosed rituals and beliefs to demonstrate that apparently esoteric practices were informed by fraternal sentiments and principles that conferred value and dignity on labor. Perdiguier soon discovered, however, that despite his good intentions, he "created displeasure in all the societies and in my own as well as in the others."[57]

The compagnon joiners du devoir de liberté in Bordeaux, for example, were so incensed by the *Livre du compagnonnage* that they refused to distribute the copies Perdiguier sent them. Their first letter to him (20 January 1840), denied that the trades he discussed all had more or less the same "social organization" and expressed alarm lest the public regard all the societies as one. They also believed he had unfairly criticized his own society in his quest for objectivity. Even more critical letters followed. Although Perdiguier chose not to publish the worst of these attacks, he commented: "On 16 March I received a second letter from my confrères in Bordeaux. Their first letter was mild in comparison to

56. Perdiguier, *Livre du compagnonnage*, 2d ed., 2:12–13, 49: Perodeaud to Perdiguier, Paris, 9 January 1840, Piron to Perdiguier, Paris, 16 February 1840.
57. Ibid., 2:17–18, Perdiguier to Piron, Paris, 24 January 1840.

this. . . .people were seeking to raise prejudices and ill will against me. Anonymous letters and others from Paris and elsewhere were spread about in all the cities and presented me in the worst light."[58]

Some compagnons chose more direct means of defending compagnonnage against these "scurrilous" attacks. Albe Bernard, called Albigeois le bien aimé, an antireformist compagnon carpenter du devoir, used song to express his views. In "The Absurdities of the Regeneration of Compagnonnage," his sarcastic and satirical verses ridiculed three prominent reformers: Perdiguier; Pierre Moreau, leader and guiding spirit of the Union; and Jacques Gosset, père of the compagnon ironworkers (though never a compagnon himself) and author of a book on reform of compagnonnage.[59] Albigeois firmly believed that compagnonnage needed no reform; these reformers were vain men seeking personal glory. If their ideas were adopted, compagnonnage would be destroyed. Significantly, Albigeois was a carpenter, a member of a trade still well served by compagnonnage. His attack on reformers concluded with an unapologetic endorsement of traditional values:

> I still hear talk of compagnonnage
>> In their projects so superfluous
>> Of the emblems we misuse, the practices we abuse.
>> Before this regeneration
>> From the date of our foundation
>> Came "decency, obedience," our motto and allegiance.
>> Those who deride at compagnons' expense
>> Talk great absurdity and nonsense (repeat).
> It is of compagnonnage I sing today
>> And this my friends I say, despite our enemies,
>> Let progress pass us by.
>> Honor and glory, here's to the stuff of our memories.
>> A regeneration if authorized
>> On the basis of their enterprise,
>> Would indeed cause wonder and surprise
>> That compagnons could make such a blunder (repeat).

> Mais encor du Compagnonnage
> J'en entends blâmer les abus;

58. Ibid., 2:25, 55, Perdiguier, open letter to critics, 16 May 1840.
59. Albe Bernard (Albigeois le bien aimé), *Les Bêtises de la régénération du compagnonnage* (Paris, n.d. [1843]). See Jacques Gosset, *Projet tendant à régénérer le compagnonnage sur le tour de France: Souvenir à tous les ouvriers* (Paris, 1842). Strictly speaking, Moreau broke with compagnonnage without attempting to reform it, although he acknowledged its many valuable features. Some compagnons suspected Gosset of being a police informer; his reforms paralleled Moreau's, but he proposed to implement them within compagnonnage.

Sur les emblèmes, sur l'usage,
Tous leurs projets sont superflus.
La bienséance,
L'obéissance
Devancent la régénération.
C'est la devise
Qui fut soumise
A l'ère de notre institution.
Ceux qui narguent les Compagnons
Font de grandes Bêtises (bis).
Puisque sur le Compagnonnage
Je chante aujourd'hui, mes amis,
Laissons au progrès le passage
En dépit de nos ennemis.
Honneur et gloire
A nos mémoires;
Si pour une régénération
On authorise
Leur entreprise,
Gardons toujours notre fondation,
Car on dirait les Compagnons
Ont bien fait des bêtises (bis).[60]

This vigorous call to reject progress reinforced the tensions inherent in the rituals and origin narratives of compagnonnage. Such practices and texts could legitimate and encourage reconciliation, but they could also encourage more reactionary tendencies. The reformers faced a struggle against the many compagnons who continued to regard their associations as vital and meaningful despite (or because of) their hierarchical, exclusive, and aggressive features. Compagnons such as Albigeois—especially those in carpentry—believed that reform would undermine a tightly organized, effective association that gave them some economic leverage *and* memories "of honor and glory."[61]

Compagnons also wrote in anger against dissident compagnons and novices who broke away and formed their own associations. The poem *Le Compagnonnage et l'indépendance,* by an anonymous compagnon shoemaker, criticized "troublemakers" and defended the association while recounting an actual revolt of novice shoemakers-bootmakers in Marseille in 1837.[62] Maintaining that the novices had instigated the revolt

60. Bernard, *Bêtises,* pp. 3–4.
61. Nonetheless, even Albigeois would have a radical conversion in 1848, when he wrote the "Marseillaise de l'Union ouvrière."
62. *Le Compagnonnage et l'indépendance* (Avignon, 1838).

and brought its consequences on themselves, the author portrayed them as skeptics, abandoning themselves to unbelief. Although the poem made a plea for peace, it insisted the compagnons were justified in attacking the novices, who, in their ignorance, ridiculed the rituals. Prudent men who understood the meaning of these customs and beliefs knew their venerable order was worth far more than a chimerical independence.

The novices, said this poet, had created an irremediable rift by performing a false conduite, publicly blaspheming a sacred ritual with their "wild exaggeration" and "caricatures." The poem underscored the compagnons' dedication to their ceremonial life from the outset, describing a true conduite, "smiled on by heaven itself," with compagnons in the "fraternal circle," carrying "instruments of geometry" and "reeds" (one of Maître Jacques's symbols), uttering plaintive cries in a "language without words." The compagnons had long borne the rebels' "worthless threats" and "impudent chatter."

> Yet, when so boldly flaunted, a new scene appeared
> Where the sacred mysteries of their holy cult,
> Those respected signs so long venerated
> Served as base amusement to these vile adversaries,
> Rigorous means of action were at last necessary.

> Mais lorsque, sous leurs yeux vint s'offrir cette scène
> Où leur culte saint les mystères sacrés,
> Les signes respectifs qui lui sont consacrés,
> Servaient d'amusement à ces vils adversaires,
> Les moyens rigoureux parurent nécessaire.[63]

Violence followed, ending only when the novices murdered the noble Gascon l'île d'amour, who with his dying words begged the compagnons not to avenge him but to stop the bloodshed. This plea, reminiscent of Christ's (and Maître Jacques's) last words, ended the violence but not the schism. The author concluded that reform, independence, and change would ultimately destroy compagnonnage; he defended the present order against youth's impetuosity and desire for novelty. Again the message was that novices must endure patiently before playing a guiding role in compagnonnage.

The younger members, however, were generally unwilling to heed this message. Many made a complete break with compagnonnage rather than

63. Ibid., pp. 17, 89.

attempt to reform it from within. Even if reform had been more rapid, it would have been too narrow to suit many dissidents. Piron's reforms were conceived early, but never widely disseminated. By the 1840s when Perdiguier's campaign was under way, compagnonnage had already experienced its most serious schisms. Yet, dissidents who left to found new associations never entirely dissociated themselves from both the positive and negative elements of the spirit and practice of compagnonnage.

THE SOCIÉTÉ DE L'UNION

The creation of the Société de l'Union is a valuable illustration of the transformation of compagnonnage into a more "modern" labor association. Maurice Agulhon has called the Union the "intermediate link between the old compagnonnage and modern trade unionism." His definitive account of its origins is a major contribution, for the circumstances of the Union's founding were long in doubt. Perdiguier claimed that it began among novice joiners and locksmiths in Bordeaux in 1823. This remained the common version, despite the objections of its leader, Pierre Moreau.[64] Agulhon proves that the Union was founded in Toulon in 1830 and analyzes its development in that city's dynamic political and economic context.

Like compagnons, sociétaires were concerned with their history and insisted that public knowledge of their origins was essential to legitimate and define their association. Whereas compagnonnage's origin accounts were seen as fables by sociétaires, the Union's claimed to be rooted in fact. Yet, sociétaires also rewrote aspects of their schism to sever themselves from compagnonnage more sharply. The story of the founding is closely tied to Toulon's social and economic conditions in 1830 and to the contemporary state of compagnonnage. The Union emerged in the course of a major historical event, with parallels to the origins compagnonnage claimed for itself. For sociétaires, the event was the preparations in Toulon in 1830 for the Algerian expedition. Some compagnons traced their association to the building of the Temple of Solomon; others, to the construction of the cathedrals. In both cases, whether the circumstances were historical or mythical or both, the settings demanded the presence and participation of a multitude of workers. As will be seen in the next chapter, compagnons glorified and played upon the historical context of their origin narratives. Sociétaires, born in the new regime, presented their origins matter-of-factly.

64. Agulhon, *Ville ouvrière*, pp. 131–36; Perdiguier, *Livre du compagnonnage*, 2d ed., 1:49.

The schism arose over loyalty to the mère of the compagnon iron-smiths and locksmiths du devoir. Reluctantly, Mme. Martin, had leased larger accommodations to handle the influx of workers, primarily novices, arriving daily in Toulon. She had moved only after the compagnons assured her they would not desert her for another innkeeper. Conflicts, however, soon arose over the eating arrangements of compagnons and novices. According to Moreau, only six compagnons lived at the Mère, but they insisted on eating alone in the dining hall.[65] Mme. Martin dared to suggest that the novices, whose dining area was overcrowded, be permitted to eat with them. Highly insulted, the compagnons allegedly left the Mère immediately, engaged other lodgings, and ordered the novices to follow suit.

Several novices disobeyed the order, believing their place was with Mme. Martin, but the compagnons du devoir expelled them, calling them *espontons,* men guilty of "infamy or bad conduct." Convinced they were in the right, the novices accused the six compagnons of dereliction of duty. The masters exacerbated the break by supporting the novices and refusing to fire them. The compagnons du devoir of Marseille attempted to intervene, but too late to prevent a schism. The dissidents established a new organization based on "liberty and equality," principles that would be reinforced by the July Revolution. News of the "revolt" in Toulon spread quickly and stimulated enthusiasm for liberty and equality among other novices on the tour de France. Branches of the new Société de l'Union "sprang up in Lyon, Avignon, Marseille, Toulouse, Nantes, and Bordeaux."[66]

Moreau's account of the events emphasizes his personal disdain for compagnonnage, but the novices' opposition to many of its features is not unique. Although their action was too radical for Perdiguier, he and other reformers agreed with their critique of an all-too-common egotism that undermined fraternal principles. The dissidents had moved on to newer conceptions of fraternity and association. Agulhon comments that Toulon's "political atmosphere encouraged liberal thinking as opposed to the archaic authoritarianism of [compagnonnage]." Although Agulhon describes the Union as combining new and traditional features, he traces the schism itself to a split between liberals (novices) and traditionalists (compagnons). In 1832 the schism was compounded when a faction of liberal compagnons joined the novices' society.[67]

---

65. This account, which Agulhon accepts as essentially correct, appears in Pierre Moreau, *De la réforme des abus du compagnonnage et de l'amélioration du sort des travailleurs* (Auxerre, 1843), pp. 72–75.

66. Agulhon, *Ville ouvrière*, p. 132, esp. n. 27; Moreau, *Réforme*, p. 74.

67. Agulhon, *Ville ouvrière*, pp. 132, 133.

The extent of the sociétaires' liberalism is an important question. They were apparently more willing than compagnons to involve themselves in political matters; they openly announced their association and sought official recognition, perhaps believing that 1830 marked a new era for workingmen. In the 1840s, under Moreau's leadership the sociétaires joined politically and socially progressive movements. Moreau thought the Union could save workers from the internal strife of compagnonnage while preserving its fraternal and interurban bases. To a revitalized fraternal tradition, Moreau and the Union wanted to add liberty and equality, in the revolutionary tradition. Within the Union interurban connections were preserved, but trades were no longer divided by sects whose rivalries lay in the distant past. Each trade in the Union had a placement office (*bureau*) in every town on the tour, administered by three to seven members, depending on the number of sociétaires. Normally there would be at least a president, treasurer, secretary, and syndic, elected by secret ballot and majority vote and subject to recall.[68] The bureau placed incoming sociétaires in jobs without charging a fee ("tribute" as Moreau calls it).

The Union, like compagnonnage, had a relatively decentralized administration but enabled member trades to unite in a federative system. General headquarters were established in Lyon and each town on the tour had a central office that represented the whole association. A uniform code of regulations governed all the Union's trades and provided "fraternal support to those trades in need." According to a modern scholar, the Société de l'Union thus promoted equality and fraternity within a structured framework.[69] Perdiguier feared the Union's principles would produce anarchy, but Moreau said that Perdiguier was confusing sociétaires with "independents," or unaffiliated workers, who had no society and merely followed their individual wills. Each sociétaire had specific rights and responsibilities, prescribed not by a devoir but by the member's *contract* with the Union. Moreau believed that neither independents nor compagnons grasped the essence of the Union's strength, the great "unitary and universal principle present in nature itself"— equality, the force that bound sociétaires together.[70]

The sociétaires strove to root out inequalities, especially economic ones, between members. They drastically shortened the novitiate and greatly reduced admission fees in comparison to compagnonnage. Ac-

---

68. Moreau, *Réforme*, pp. 94, 75.

69. Ibid., p. 76; Jacques Marillier, "Pierre Moreau et l'Union," *Actualité de l'histoire: Bulletin de l'Institut français d'histoire sociale*, no. 5 (1953): 5.

70. Pierre Moreau, *Un Mot aux ouvriers de toutes les professions, à tous les amis du peuple et du progrès, sur le compagnonnage; ou, Le Guide de l'ouvrier sur le tour de France* (Auxerre, 1841), p. 22.

cording to the *Règlement général* of 1839, a worker could become a member, with almost no delay, for one and a half francs. The main condition for admission (article 10) was a thorough knowledge of the regulations and a willingness to abide by them. Article 9 listed the other conditions: candidates had to be at least sixteen years old, of "good habits and conduct," and possess a legitimate passport (or *carte de sûreté*) and a *livret* certified by all previous employers. The candidate had to be presented by a sociétaire who could testify to his good character and conduct (as in compagnonnage).[71] Unlike compagnonnage, however, the Union required no testing or humbling of the candidate's spirit, nor did sociétaires have to present a masterpiece as proof of their skill. Once initiated, new members were placed free and were paid the same rate as other sociétaires.

The Union's initiation was a simple ceremony. The candidate was brought before the other assembled members—and not at midnight or in darkness. He had to declare that he knew the regulations thoroughly and would, on his honor, observe them exactly and punctually. His sponsor then led him out of the room, returning to participate in the deliberation. The sponsor escorted the successful candidate back into the assembly, where the president, representing all the sociétaires, officially declared him a member of the Société de l'Union and presented him with a small printed copy of the regulations, to be affixed to his livret. The new sociétaire was to say: "It is with satisfaction that I receive this règlement, and I repeat in the presence of all the sociétaires the commitment that I have made to observe it."[72] He then signed and dated the society's register. This simple, secular contract never threatened dire consequences for its violation, but it was mandatory. Although not meant to transform the sociétaire, the initiation was a solemn moment that represented a serious commitment to the society and its aims.

Critics, however, doubted the force of this commitment. While praising the Union's *material* bases, the *Atelier* worried that "its moral guarantees had been neglected. . . . it was hardly realistic to banish, completely and in a day, old customs, traditional practices, and names given to compagnons in their initiations."[73] Such critics failed to understand that the sociétaires remained deeply committed to certain customs and practices of compagnonnage. Article 38 of the Union's 1839 règlement stated plainly that sociétaires owed each other "mutual peace,

---

71. *Règlement général de la société d'encouragement des ouvriers serruriers sous le titre de Société de l'Union* (Lyon, 1839), articles 5–10. Jacques Marillier, of the Institut français d'histoire sociale, graciously allowed me to examine a typewritten copy of this edition of the regulations. Most old regime trade corporations also required members to be of "good habits and conduct."

72. Ibid.

73. *L'Atelier*, March 1842, cited in Briquet, *Agricol Perdiguier*, p. 216.

goodwill, and much esteem and affection." Sociétaires continued to celebrate these sentiments at the Mère—most appropriately, given the circumstances of their origins.[74] Although sociétaires were loyal to their
mères, they tried to avoid the cycle of credit and debt which was a major
problem for many branches of compagnonnage. The Union's regulations stated that no more than three francs credit could be extended to
a member. Thus, although the Union kept the Mère, one of the oldest
traditions of compagnonnage, the relationship of mother and sons was
changing, from a more open-ended "familial" model to an affectionate
but more contractual one.

Like compagnonnage, the Union provided economic and fraternal
support for its sick or unemployed and mandated the sociétaires' attendance at a member's funeral. Those who failed to attend without a legitimate excuse were fined three francs, much as in compagnonnage.
The burial ceremony, however, eliminated elaborate symbolism.

Agulhon's account demonstrates that the Union prospered and spread
in the 1830s and 1840s. The moral force of equality was persuasive for
many workers. The Société de l'Union's records for the 1860s and
1870s, preserved in the Municipal Archives of Lyon, attest to continuing
strength. Yet, the transition from compagnonnages to the Union was not
always smooth. Many workers, even sociétaires, still longed for symbolic
garb and esoteric practice. Moreau's only concession to symbolism was
the association's seal: an interlaced compass and square over the image
of a handshake, surrounded by a laurel wreath, the words "Société de
l'Union, Union, Encouragement," the trade name, and the city. Under
Moreau's leadership, contests of skill, with prizes for the best work, were
instituted to encourage proficiency. Ironically, such competitions indicate that artisanal skill was not entirely beside the point. Moreau regretted that many sociétaires failed to take these contests seriously enough,
preferring to imitate compagnons and spend money on feast days, fancy
dress balls, and banquets.[75]

Moreau was disturbed that sociétaires, having withdrawn from compagnonnage, imitated some of its worst features. The Union's ultimate
aim was to unite all workers, and its members composed many songs of
unity and brotherhood. Nonetheless, he admitted that sociétaires continued to provoke fights: "The Union, overwhelmed by adversaries and
enemies, above all at the time of its foundation, also had its 'battle
songs.' The majority of these, however, were composed in the heat of

---

74. *Règlement général,* 1839, Articles 33, 12. Article 12 covers the choice of the mère, her
duties, and the society's obligations toward her.

75. Moreau, *Un Mot aux ouvriers,* pp. 25, 29; and AML, I² 47A, seal on the livret of M. Maus-
sion, attached to an 1852 *Règlement.*

combat itself."[76] Sociétaires and compagnons fought frequently and intensely until 1848, especially in Toulon and Lyon, where compagnonnage remained strong and compagnons continued to resist and resent sociétaires' encroachment on "their" prerogatives. The Société de l'Union thus appeared to many observers but one more rite of compagnonnage, further fragmenting the working class.

Moreau and his fellow sociétaires, however, insisted that their society was driven by the strongest of moral forces—equality—the only principle capable of generating lasting worker solidarity. Guided by this principle, sociétaires dissociated and differentiated themselves from compagnonnage, discarding customs judged to be hierarchical, divisive, and elitist. Moreau believed the sociétaire's simple statement of allegiance had binding force because all members were equal and had the same duties from the moment they joined the association. Yet the persistence and tenacity of compagnonnage is some indication that equality was not an attractive concept for all skilled workers. To discover what principles and values remained compelling to compagnons, I look, finally, to their origin narratives, to "read" how they constructed their history and culture.

76. Moreau, *Réforme*, pp. 83, 84.

CHAPTER 8

The Mythic Past and Present

The workers of compagnonnage must sacrifice their idols
on the altar of good sense.

—Jean-Baptiste Arnaud
compagnon baker, 1859

In the course of his tour de France in the 1830s, Jean-Baptiste Arnaud's experience as a compagnon du devoir "proved [to him] that the
secret societies of Compagnonnage were incompatible with progress."[1]
Although Arnaud, also known as Libourne le décidé, found some support for his view that compagnonnage must give up its symbolic side,
many more compagnons would defend, rework, and elaborate on their
claims to ancient legends and practices. From the 1830s on, articulating
and defining origins became a particularly active pursuit for individual
compagnons and their societies. As early as 1818, however, compagnonnage's antiquity was vigorously asserted.

Writing to the mayor of Marseille in May 1818, a group of journeyman
artisans calling themselves the gavots, vehemently protested a recent
edict that banned their meetings and their association, the compagnons
non du devoir. The gavots were amused that the mayor, with his recent,
temporal, and fleeting authority, dared to abolish their ancient association: "More than two thousand years ago," they wrote, "the gavots Received the Light; they date their origin to the temple of Solomon, the
wisest of Kings, who was their founder," and "the compagnons du devoir
are even more ancient." Therefore, they warned, "it would be in vain
should [the mayor] wish to put an end to either their operations or our
own."[2]

1. Jean-Baptiste Arnaud, *Mémoires d'un compagnon du tour de France, contenant plusieurs dissertations sur le devoir, entre l'auteur et plusieurs compagnons tailleurs de pierre et charpentiers* (Rochefort,
1859), foreword, n.p.
2. AM Marseille, I²136, 24 May 1818, gavots to mayor, Marseille.

How could the gavots make this amazing claim of august and luminous origin? And what of the compagnons du devoir, "even more ancient" than the gavots? Arnaud's rationalism would insist it made no difference who the "fathers and founders of compagnonnage" were, for the "past, and especially the past of 2,000 years ago, was unimportant."[3] But other compagnons disagreed and used their version of the past to empower them in the present. Workers united in compagnonnage constructed a culture of sociability and solidarity out of existing materials. Starting from the base of a shared work experience, compagnons also generated their practices from Judeo-Christian and popular religious beliefs, corporate and familial models, and gender alliances and oppositions. Their constructions were no mean feat given the barriers separating the French. Moreover, the regional variations in language and trade practices common in the old regime persisted well into the new regime. By fashioning its own family and country where young, male adherents could become the sons of a new mère and père and *pays*, compagnonnage generated pervasive and deep ties among an important segment of workers, enabling them to assert their demands against their masters.

As seen, however, the unity of compagnonnage and its success as a vehicle of labor organization had quite obvious limits. The first serious rivalries, between compagnons du devoir and non du devoir (dévorants and gavots) emerged in the late seventeenth century and became a dominant feature of these associations from at least the mid-eighteenth century on, with a newer rival, the enfants de Père Soubise (also compagnons du devoir) joining the fray. According to the origin narratives, the compagnons of each rite became the fictive sons of a powerful father: Solomon, Maître Jacques, or Père Soubise. Each rite sought to control its trades on the tour de France while defending their "father's" reputation. A song of the enfants de Maître Jacques, for example, urges his compagnons to destroy Solomon's followers "because they did not have good blood." Such opposition and insult gave compagnons opportunities to display virility, bravado, and frequently, aggression.

Nomenclature became vitally important in the nineteenth century (see Table 8.1). Compagnons non du devoir were known as gavots but increasingly called themselves compagnons du devoir de liberté (or *compagnons de liberté*) and *enfants de Salomon*. Various of their trades and especially joiners and locksmiths were called gavots; stonecutters were called *loups* (wolves) and *étrangers* (strangers). Compagnons du devoir were enfants de Maître Jacques. Various of their trades were known as dévorants; joiners and locksmiths were *chiens* (dogs), and stonecutters

---

3. Arnaud, *Mémoires d'un compagnon*, foreword.

TABLE 8.1. Some common designations for the sects of compagnonnage

Compagnons du devoir	Compagnons non du devoir
1. *Enfants de Maître Jacques* (children of Master Jacques) Also called:	1. *Enfants de Salomon* (children of Solomon) Also called:
a *dévorants* (followers of the duty, devourers): various trades	a *gavots* (heretics, mountain people): various trades
b *chiens* (dogs): various trades	b *loups* (wolves), and *étrangers* (strangers): stonecutters
c *loups-garoux* (werewolves), and *passants* (those who pass): stonecutters	
2. *Enfants de Père Soubise* (children of Father Soubise) Also called:	
a *bon drilles* (good fellows), *chiens* (dogs), and *passants* (those who pass): carpenters	
b *renards* (foxes) for novice carpenters	

were *loups-garoux* (werewolves) and *passants* (those passing). The compagnon carpenters of the enfants de Père Soubise (children of Father Soubise) were known as *bon drilles* (good fellows) and passants; the aspirants in this trade were *renards* (foxes). Clearly, these names reveal the complexities and oppositions set up and perpetuated within compagnonnage and also the importance of the name itself. Sects disputed fiercely for dominance in its trades on the tour, but these quarrels were not only, not even primarily, clear-cut economic struggles, although they may have begun as contention for control of a limited labor market. Compagnons in trades with no economic conflict of interest (for example, stonecutters and joiners), but in opposing devoirs, insulted and attacked one another simply because they were defined as opponents.

Until the 1820s and 1830s these hostilities did not gravely impair the efficacy or importance of compagnonnage because one devoir tended to gain ascendancy in each trade on the tour. As the last two chapters have shown, however, in the context of the Revolution and its aftermath, this internecine warfare weakened the association. Newer forms of labor organization, emerging in the more open political climate, began to supplant the old brotherhoods, but compagnonnage also undermined itself by reinforcing its divisions and antagonisms. Such divisions had mirrored and "fit" the culture of corporate society, built on privilege, difference, and distinction. Devising ways to privilege oneself over others (even quite similar others) was customary in the old regime but appeared less acceptable in postrevolutionary society. Nevertheless, compagnons focused on what police called "age-old hatreds"; each sect claimed to be the true "faith," and each elaborated its origin narratives to reinforce its claim. In this chapter I work through a number of these accounts—from the eighteenth to the nineteenth century—to see what they reveal about how compagnons constructed and made sense of their lives as skilled workers and adult males.

Defining the Origin Narrative

Origin narratives—some scholars have called them myths—are accounts concerned with explanations of how something came to be. The compagnons called their origin narratives by various names: histories, legends, stories, origin accounts. There is no simple correlation between historical experience and the constructed reality in such narratives, but they make authentic and revealing—although nonliteral—claims about a group's cultural reality and beliefs. Imaginative elements are rooted in their cultural and material context, and the belief systems encoded in origin narratives are not detached from but enmeshed in the workings of a particular society. The content of origin narratives is informed by aspects of a society's system of classification; their narrative form reflects the social processes that produce, maintain, or destroy that system.[4]

Early references to the origins of compagnonnage are few and fragmentary. The most detailed accounts were codified in the early nineteenth century when certain aspects of its culture were coming to seem anachronistic. The origin narratives of the three major sects of compagnonnage reveal a pervasive sociocultural debt to Catholic symbol and ritual and to early modern trade corporations and confraternities. They encode the transformation of symbols and practices common to these in-

4. My analysis and interpretation of origin narratives has been influenced by a number of works, e.g., Terence Turner, "Oedipus: Time and Structure in Narrative Form," in *Forms of Symbolic Action: Proceedings of the 1969 Annual Spring Meeting of the American Ethnological Society*, ed. Robert F. Spencer (Seattle, 1969), pp. 26–68; and Turner, "Myth as Model: The Kayapo Myth of the Origin of Cooking Fire," paper presented at the meeting of the Association of Social Anthropologists, Oxford, July 1973; Dan Sperber, *Rethinking Symbolism* (Cambridge, 1974); Edmund Leach, *Political Systems of Highland Burma* (Boston, 1965); and Claude Lévi-Strauss, *The Savage Mind* (London, 1966), *The Raw and the Cooked* (London, 1969), *Structural Anthropology* (New York, 1967), esp. pp. 202–28 ("The Structural Study of Myth"), and *From Honey to Ashes* (London, 1973). I use the term *structure* to denote the meaningful content of social systems, not simply "form" or "surface" structure but the formal aspect of meaningful relations existing among the various elements of a given social system—and particularly its symbolic elements. Cf. Turner, "Myth as Model," p. 5.

stitutions to create an original association with distinctive needs and goals. The most detailed narratives also refer to Protestantism, the Templars, and Masonry. Traces of these relationships are embedded in the origin narratives and when deconstructed, reveal fundamental relationships between compagnons and other social groups, compagnons' views on labor and its organization and on the ordering of the social and cultural world.

Although, as Edmund Leach points out, ritual and myth are interrelated cultural products, "myth regarded as a statement in words, 'says' the same thing as ritual regarded as a statement in action," compagnons generally viewed ritual as more sacred and more secret than the origin narratives, despite their import, and many examples survive (see Appendix 2).[5] Perdiguier, for example, virtually silent on initiation rituals, provides fairly extensive accounts of the "legends," although he is somewhat reticent in discussing those of his own rite and trade. His motivation for presenting these accounts, however, remains somewhat ambiguous.

On the one hand, Perdiguier seems to be searching for the lost key to a once-united compagnonnage. "It is very certain," he once remarked, "that in other times compagnonnage was not cut up as it is in our days."[6] On the other hand he recognized the problems generated by the retelling and persistence of these legends. Narratives that established, legitimated, and reinforced rivalries and divisions were recited, told, or very commonly, sung during initiation or leave-taking ceremonies, on feast days, at meetings, or while sharing a bottle of wine in a cabaret, keeping hatreds fresh. In telling these stories, therefore, Perdiguier tried to discredit them and to discourage belief in aspects of them.

Yet, the *Livre du compagnonnage* in effect helped make these narratives even more central to the life of compagnonnage, as well as widely known to the public.[7] Following the general introduction, the opening twenty-five pages of the book are devoted to a discussion of the various societies of compagnonnage and their origins. Perdiguier deemphasizes or discounts the symbolic, the implausible, or even the Freemasonic. Furthermore, he takes a critical stance on what he calls "fables," even with regard to his own rite (at least in trades not his own). For example, he swiftly dismisses the stonecutters du devoir de liberté who "pass themselves off as the oldest [trade] in Compagnonnage. There's an old fable about where some say it's a question of Hiram, others say it's Adoniram;

5. Leach, *Political Systems*, pp. 13–14.
6. Agricol Perdiguier, *Histoire d'une scission dans le compagnonnage* (Paris, 1846), p. 7.
7. While it is difficult to determine how important these origin accounts were for actual compagnons, Perdiguier and others make a convincing case that they were central to the nineteenth-century compagnon's identity.

therein one finds crimes and punishments: but I leave this fable for what it's worth." Perdiguier likewise gave little credence to the legends of the compagnons du devoir. Their accounts of Maître Jacques and Père Soubise included much that "would not stand up to serious scrutiny."[8] But many compagnons objected to Perdiguier's views and questioned their accuracy. The carpenters du devoir criticized a "certain little story of M. Perdiguier" as full of errors: he and others "could not obtain exact information and [thus] invented some extraordinary fictions."[9]

In the following discussion I rely on Perdiguier's accounts as my base narrative but supplement them with those provided by other compagnons, particularly compagnons du devoir. As I outline and analyze each of the major origin narratives, I discuss how different sources inform my understanding of how compagnons constructed and reshaped their history. The most important of these other sources were published by the compagnon carpenters du devoir in 1843 and by a compagnon stonecutter du devoir, Victor-Bernard Sciandro (La sagesse de Bordeaux) in 1850.[10] Almost all sources agree there are two major variants. The first traces the origins of compagnonnage to the building of the Temple of Solomon (tenth century B.C.). Both compagnons du devoir and non du devoir have such an account. The second major variant finds the origins in the building of the cathedral of Orléans (thirteenth century). Whereas some texts may trace the compagnonnage of some or all trades to the Middle Ages, Perdiguier supplies the most detailed account.[11]

THE TEMPLE OF SOLOMON

Enfants de Salomon

Perdiguier begins the text of the *Livre du compagnonnage* with his version of the "origins of the first societies." Compagnonnage recognized three founders, Solomon, Maître Jacques, and Père Soubise, all linked to the building of the temple. Perdiguier begins simply and directly with

8. Agricol Perdiguier, *Le Livre du compagnonnage, contenant des chansons de compagnons, un dialogue sur l'architecture, un raisonnement sur le trait, une notice sur le compagnonnage, la rencontre de deux frères, et un grand nombre de notes*, 2d ed., 2 vols. (Paris, 1841), 1:31, 28.

9. Les CC. [Compagnons] passants charpentiers, à leurs FF:: du vrai compag:: de l'aimable tour de France, *Notice historique sur le compagnonage* [sic] *primitif, comme base fondamentale des sociétés* (Paris, 1843), p. 71.

10. Ibid.; Victor-Bernard Sciandro, *Le Compagnonnage: Ce qu'il a été, ce qu'il est, ce qu'il devrait être* (Marseille, 1850), pp. 15–19; and Jean Marquet, ed., *Notice historique sur la fondation de la société de l'union des travailleurs de tour de France* (Tours, 1882–89). See also Appendix 2.

11. For Perdiguier's version of the "Orléans" narrative, see his *Question vitale sur le compagnonnage et la classe ouvrière* (Paris, 1861), pp. 26–27; cf. his *Histoire d'une scission*. For other accounts tracing compagnonnage's origins to the Middle Ages see Appendix 2, nos. 9–10.

what his society, the devoir de liberté, believes about its origins. The stonecutters, joiners, and locksmiths, he says, "recognize Solomon [as their founder]; they say that this king gave them a Devoir to reward them for their work, and fraternally united them in the enclosure of the Temple, the work of their hands."[12] Perdiguier's rhetorical presentation and structural organization reveal his esteem for the compagnons du devoir de liberté: he privileges their account as the model and basis from which the other accounts (and, by implication, other societies) developed and deviated.[13]

Perdiguier's account is based on his reading of the biblical story (1 Kings 5:13–18) and Furne's *Biographie universelle*. Perdiguier recalls Solomon's appeal to Hiram, king of Tyre, for the cedars of Lebanon and for a highly skilled artisan (identified as another Hiram), to work on the temple. Solomon called to Jerusalem great numbers of the finest workers, specifically stonecutters and builders, and ordered them to construct the temple of the finest materials. Hiram, according to Perdiguier, was a worker-architect, an "expert and able man, who knew how to work in gold, silver, bronze, iron, stone, wood, in scarlet, in purple, in fine linen and crimson, and who knew how to make all manner of engravings and designs, and all the things anyone described to him." He personally designed parts of the temple which required seven and a half years and "innumerable workers" to complete. Foreign workers alone numbered 153,000.[14] The narrative discusses the temple's construction and embellishment and then evaluates Solomon's strengths and weaknesses. Nowhere does Perdiguier specify exactly how Solomon founded the devoir de liberté; he contents himself with the vague statement I have quoted.

Other accounts are more forthcoming. The details they supply deviate further from the biblical account and bring the origins of the enfants de Salomon more into line with the Freemasons'.[15] All the accounts of

12. Perdiguier, *Livre du compagnonnage,* 2d ed. 1:20.
13. Perdiguier's view can be contrasted to that of the gavots of Marseille, who accepted the compagnons du devoir as the oldest members of compagnonnage. Letter to the mayor, AM Marseille, I²136, 24 May 1818.
14. Perdiguier, *Livre du compagnonnage,* 2d ed., 1:22, 24, 23–24. Cf. 2 Chronicles 2:13–14. The compagnons' narratives confuse or conflate this Hiram with Adoniram, the agent in charge of the levy of workers sent to Lebanon. Perdiguier says the foreign workers were in addition to the thirty thousand Israelites levied to gather the cedars of Lebanon.
15. "Les Origines: 1° Les Enfants de Salomon," in Emile Coornaert, *Les Compagnonnages en France du Moyen Age à nos jours* (Paris, 1966), pp. 341–43. Coornaert does not cite his sources, but he relied on Etienne Martin Saint-Léon, *Le Compagnonnage: Son histoire, ses coutumes, ses règlements, ses rites* (Paris, 1901), pp. 2–10, and obtained "communication des documents secrets dont lecture est donnée aux nouveaux compagnons en vue de leur révéler les origines traditionnelles de leurs sociétés" (p. 342). As noted earlier, direct transmission of Masonic culture and practice to compagnonnage cannot be established in the prerevolutionary era. Perdiguier says contact occurred between Masonic lodges and assemblies of compagnons during or after the Revolution. Agricol Perdiguier, *Le Livre du compagnonnage,* 3d ed., 2 vols. (Paris, 1857), 2:75.

compagnons du devoir de liberté, including Perdiguier's, portray Solomon as a wise king who wanted to build a temple modeled on the tabernacle of Moses to honor and glorify God. The more detailed accounts explain that such disorder and confusion reigned among the work force called to Jerusalem, that lazy and unskilled workers were paid as much as good ones. Thus, Solomon or, some say, the worker-architect Hiram gave each qualified worker an "assignation" for payment and a password for identification. When Hiram found a candidate who merited advancement, a special ceremony was performed beneath the temple among the workers already "received," and the initiate was given a new rank and password.

This situation did not last. Three apprentices, unable to advance by merit, became jealous of Hiram and planned to force him to reveal the masters' password on threat of assassination. One night, the three gathered in the temple; each in turn confronted Hiram with his demand. Hiram refused each time, and at every refusal was struck with the tool each apprentice carried. The third blow killed him. The assassins later buried him in a secluded place, having dug three graves: one for Hiram's body; the second for his clothing; and the third for his cane, a *jonc marin*. They planted a branch of acacia on his tomb. That evening nine compagnons went looking for the absent Hiram. Drawn by the acacia's fragrance, they quickly discovered the murder. Solomon was notified; the "word" (that is, password) was changed. Wearing white leather aprons and gloves, the compagnons performed an elaborate mourning ritual, reinterring Hiram in a bronze tomb bearing many emblems and symbols including a golden triangle and the inscription "To the Glory of the Great Architect of the Universe."[16]

The structural relationships expressed in this narrative can be summarized in three major points. First, it presents a highly favorable image of skilled workers and assigns great value to their creations. Second, it establishes a new secret and hierarchical order. Finally, the order continues as an independent association after its Christ-like leader suffers martyrdom. The narrative thus contradicts and opposes commonly held notions about work and workers in French society. Particularly in the old regime, but also well into the nineteenth century, manual labor was a mark of low status and a symbol of pain and penitence. Although the construction work portrayed in the narrative is a type of art, it is nonetheless hard, physical labor.[17] The narrative implies that it is honorable and even glorious if done with skill.

16. Coornaert, *Compagnonnages*, p. 343. Only the initial letters of this common Masonic motto were engraved on the tomb.

17. William H. Sewell, Jr., *Work and Revolution in France: The Language of Labor from the Old*

But labor must be organized to be fruitful. The theme of potential disorder among workers resonated both before and after the Revolution. In French society, workers were often portrayed as unruly and inferior beings. The narrative depicts a positive vision of orderly organization, which protects the workers and ensures that work will be completed. The control and ordering of the work force involves the workers' consent and elevation. Order is not imposed from above: Solomon creates an association, but workers join it voluntarily and understand its terms. The compagnons' narrative thus expresses the need for and benefits of association.

The compagnons who created this narrative construct an association that elevates and honors work and workers. The workers in this narrative, as opposed to those in the biblical account, are not slaves; they are not levied but "called." The notions of being "chosen" and "called" are reminiscent of the Protestant idea of calling as vocation, further enriching and extending the narrative's possible meanings and resonance. The impressive temple is chosen to represent work; Hiram, the order's founder, is a man of wisdom and talent who is not degraded by his labors. The compagnons' association, again, is given, not imposed; qualified workers can choose to enter it. But not all can enter. This order is secret, reinforced and transmitted by ritual, with code words to exclude nonmembers. The artisans' order is not only secret and exclusive but also hierarchical (apprentices, journeymen, and masters), mirroring the structure of old regime trade corporations and the hierarchy present in many nineteenth-century compagnonnages. The spatial configuration of the initiation in the narrative incorporates and reinforces this hierarchy and depicts order as relatively fixed and unchanging. Workers do not leave the temple after Hiram's death to spread the order to other workers and other places.

Although many of the narrative elements undeniably recall aspects of trade corporations and confraternities, connections between these institutions and compagnonnage are not highlighted. Rather, the language and imagery link compagnons to a secret society of some prestige, Freemasonry. This rhetorical slant may represent a late eighteenth- or nineteenth-century recasting of earlier origin legends. The result is to distance and distinguish compagnonnage from trade corporations, which were not only the province of masters but also abolished by the Revolution.[18]

Regime to 1848 (Cambridge, 1980), pp. 22–25, maintains that the work in the narrative, although skilled labor, is really art and not quite the same as work.

18. See Mary Ann Clawson, *Constructing Brotherhood: Class, Gender, and Fraternalism* (Princeton, 1989), pp. 53–83, for the important ties between Masonry and trade corporations in the eigh-

Another possible nineteenth-century element is the threat posed by unskilled workers, depicted as competitors and usurpers who can advance only by force. This theme would have had much resonance in the world of nineteenth-century artisans. The narrative elaborates the motif of the encroachment of the unskilled: three apprentices use their tools to commit a brutal murder rather than create a work of art. Hiram's assassination, however, like Christ's Crucifixion, was the necessary step for founding a new order. Christian themes and symbolism pervade this narrative episode, but Hiram, unlike Christ or Christian martyrs, dies to guard a secret not to spread a new truth. His death is a warning to other initiated workers that they too must be prepared to die to defend secrets.

The burial episode expresses the significance compagnons attached to proper fulfillment of this rite of passage. Masonic symbolism—the acacia (symbolizing hope and immortality), the white clothing, the triangle, and the inscription on the tomb—is used liberally in this passage. One minor but key difference centers on the acacia: in the Masonic account Hiram's followers plant the acacia on the tomb, whereas in the compagnons' account the assassins leave the acacia. This device allows the assassins to show remorse and belated reverence for Hiram; the acacia quickly leads the compagnons to the body, which they then bury properly. In the compagnons' narrative, even "rebels" may repent and eventually be reconciled to the established order.

Enfants de Maître Jacques, Enfants de Père Soubise

Perdiguier's account of the origin of the two rites of compagnons du devoir, also set at Solomon's temple, is quite detailed. He begins with the life of Maître Jacques who was born in Carthage and traveled widely in Greece, Egypt, and Palestine "in his youth," during which time he became a highly skilled stonecutter. After traveling twenty-one years, he arrived in Jerusalem (at age thirty-six) and was named master of the stonecutters, masons, and joiners. Maître Jacques sculpted columns of the temple decorated with figures from the Old Testament and from his own life. At the temple, he became associated with another skilled master, Père Soubise, whose trade and achievements are not discussed. The

---

teenth and nineteenth centuries. Her discussion focuses on the Anglo-American context but is also relevant for France. She analyzes how Masonry provided a context for elites to experiment in and explore both science and philosophy. Compagnonnage allows us to consider something of the reverse—how compagnons reaped cultural or social benefits by creating or using a connection with Masonry. Unfortunately, French connections between Masons and artisans have not been the subject of a major study. The philosophes, some of whom were Masons, were concerned with science and its relation to the crafts, but their interests remained more theoretical than in England, where scholars, scientists, and inventors often actively associated with artisans.

temple completed, Maître Jacques and Père Soubise, swearing mutual and eternal allegiance, sailed from Jerusalem with a band of disciples. Père Soubise's envy of Maître Jacques's talents and popularity soon drove them apart. Maître Jacques landed at Marseille with thirteen compagnons and forty disciples; Père Soubise stopped at Bordeaux with an unknown number of followers.[19] Each leader gave his followers a devoir. For three years after the rupture Maître Jacques and his followers traveled widely, constantly on guard against the attacks of Père Soubise's followers.

Afterward, Maître Jacques retreated to the grotto of Sainte-Baume in Provence, where Mary Magdalene was said to have died. There he met his end, betrayed by one of his own disciples, Jéron, sometimes called *Jamais* (never). One morning while Maître Jacques was praying in a secluded area, Jéron approached and gave him the kiss of peace, a signal for five disciples of Père Soubise to attack. The assassins threw themselves on Maître Jacques, stabbing him five times with their swords. As he lay dying, Maître Jacques enjoined his disciples to forgive his enemies. He gave his disciples the kiss of peace, telling them to do likewise to those they received as compagnons. He promised to watch over his followers as long as they never forgot him and remained faithful to God and the devoir. Maître Jacques was forty-seven; the year was 989 B.C.[20]

The disciples prepared an elaborate funeral ceremony, lasting three days. His body was placed on a bier, carried to the desert, and exposed for two days. A fire, kept burning with alcohol and resin, was lit around the sarcophagus. On the way to the desert the cortege met with a violent storm and passed through forests and mountains. Arriving at Maître Jacques's final resting place, the compagnons made the stations of the cross.[21] They performed their rituals at the graveside. Placing bread, wine, and meat in the tomb, they then covered it with huge rocks further secured with heavy iron bars. Then they lit a great fire and threw their torches and the other funerary objects into it. Dividing up by trade, the disciples went their separate ways; each received a piece of Maître Jacques' clothing:

> His hat, to the hatters
> His tunic, to the stonecutters
> His sandals, to the locksmiths

19. Perdiguier points out this gross anachronism in a footnote, remarking that Marseille was founded about 600 B.C. and Bordeaux about 300 B.C. *Livre du compagnonnage*, 2d ed., 1:28. The temple was built circa 959–52 B.C.

20. Ibid., 1:29.

21. Perdiguier makes no reference to this anachronism: the date is supposedly 989 B.C., nine centuries before the Crucifixion.

His coat, to the joiners
His belt, to the carpenters
His staff, to the wheelwrights.[22]

It was believed, though never confirmed, that Père Soubise instigated the crime. He shed tears on Maître Jacques's tomb and led the pursuits of the assassins, mitigating suspicions of his guilt.

In this narrative, as in the first, labor is glorified; a noble founder-worker is martyred; a devoir is established; religious and secret imagery and practice inform the action. The second narrative provides a sense of historical reality by means of specific dates, ages, and numbers—even though these facts are almost always inaccurate.[23] Maître Jacques emerges as historical figure of great proportions: scenes from his life vie with those of the Old Testament patriarchs, and at the same time he resembles the central figure of the New Testament, Jesus. Although Maître Jacques can symbolically represent both God the Father and God the Son, it is the Christ-like parallels that dominate his adult life and death. After Maître Jacques, Père Soubise pales by comparison. His very title, Père, is another anachronism, a Christian and clerical title far less appropriate than "Master" for the head of a group of workers. Yet, compagnonnages had similarities with lay religious orders, which indeed had "reverend fathers" as their heads. Maître Jacques, despite a secular title, is a supremely religious figure in both word and deed.

Themes of rupture, hostility and spatial separation permeate this narrative, structuring the rites of Maître Jacques and Père Soubise. The devoirs here are less well defined than the one in the first legend; they are not necessarily hierarchical or secret, largely because Maître Jacques has such a close resemblance to Christ. Although he has "compagnons and disciples," the distinction is not explicitly defined or known as it would be with "compagnons and apprentices." This silence generates an important ambiguity. No direct command, moreover, orders compagnons to keep the devoir secret. Finally, nothing is said about Père Soubise's devoir, although one assumes it is analogous to that of Maître Jacques. Again, as in the first narrative, this lack of specificity is a device that could permit eventual reconciliation.

This narrative's images and content are much more clearly Judeo-Christian than Masonic, and New Testament themes of the betrayal and

22. Perdiguier, *Livre du compagnonnage*, 1:30. He notes the incongruity of giving Maître Jacques' belt to the carpenters, who were enfants de Père Soubise.
23. Not only someone like Perdiguier could have discovered these inaccuracies. The wealth of material—books, pamphlets, songbooks—written by a wide variety of compagnons, particularly from the 1820s on, reveals their relatively high level of literacy and their intense interest in their associations and in history in general.

death of Christ predominate. Thus, although the narrative is set before the birth of Christ, the "law" invoked here is that of the New Testament. Ideally, then, Maître Jacques's followers should organize themselves on the principles of brotherhood and equality. Other aspects of the narrative, such as how the devoir is transmitted, bear out this conclusion. At least prior to Maître Jacques's death there is no mention of secret initiation; rather, the devoir is passed on through the kiss of peace, uniting members in one spiritual "family." Again, ideally, the overriding principle that informs this rite is Christian charity, or love.

The devoir is somewhat elaborated and developed during the burial episode. As in the first narrative, the leader's burial is a central event in the devoir's history. Maître Jacques's burial required many difficult and epic trials reminiscent of Hiram's trials in the first narrative and of potential trials in an actual initiation. During the burial episode Christian, pagan, and popular ritual, symbolism, and practice intermingle. The need for secrecy, after the founder's death, is revealed by the pains taken to conceal Maître Jacques's tomb from the profane. By contrast, the usually secretive enfants de Salomon buried Hiram in a tomb openly displaying their society's major symbols. Maître Jacques's disciples, unlike Hiram's, however, left the temple and would be unable to guard the tomb. Their scattering exemplifies the continued life and vigor of compagnonnage and parallels the work of Jesus' disciples. This final episode may signify that, like Christianity, the compagnons du devoir's association would not be exclusive and might actively recruit new members. Even within the narrative context, the devoir is increased: first Maître Jacques is master of "stonecutters, masons, and joiners"; at the account's end, his clothing is divided among six trades—hatters, stonecutters, locksmiths, joiners, carpenters, and wheelwrights. Even losing the masons, his trades have doubled.

In fact, most of the trades in compagnonnage belonged to the rite "du devoir." Yet, discrepancies exist between the narrative line and the historical organization of compagnonnage. First, the carpenters, although compagnons du devoir, were enfants de Père Soubise, at least in the nineteenth century. Thus, including them in the list of trades in the narratives may imply the potential unity of all compagnons du devoir, a time when they were all children of Maître Jacques. This same list is also significant because the trades named were all staunch defenders of their rights and privileges as the oldest societies of compagnonnage. With the exception of the hatters, however, these claims are not borne out in early historical evidence. Carpenters seem to have been fully organized rather later than other compagnonnages—perhaps only from the mid- to late eighteenth century. The narrative's final episode, thus, demonstrates how compagnons created, manipulated, and rewrote their own history. Finally, the creation of a potential framework for reconciliation in the last episode cannot be ignored. Carpenters (enfants de Père Soubise) are given some of Maître Jacques's clothing; Père Soubise himself displays remorse and sorrow over his former friend and colleague's death; and some enfants de Maître Jacques were willing to allay their suspicious of Soubise because of his actions. Père Soubise's pursuit of the assassins, his own disciples, is also a sign that hostilities might be ended. This pursuit, however, is problematic, for Maître Jacques did not want his enemies pursued. Perhaps, neither Père Soubise nor his compagnons could be as Christ-like as Maître Jacques. Ambiguities in these cultural scripts gave actual compagnons the flexibility to vary their future relationships of opposition or cooperation.

THE CATHEDRAL OF ORLÉANS

Enfants de Maître Jacques and Enfants de Salomon

The next narrative traces the origins of compagnonnage not to the temple of Solomon but to the building of the cathedral of Orléans. It gives a history of the major schism between compagnons non du devoir and the more senior compagnons du devoir. Some nineteenth-century compagnons claimed that the temple legends were fabrications, but the Orléans account was "true history."[24] Although aspects of the third narrative appear plausible, however, particularly in comparison with the earlier narratives, they cannot be historically documented.

According to this account, the original and oldest body of compagnons was the enfants de Maître Jacques, founded in the fifteenth century by Jacques de Molay (sometimes called Jacques Molière), the last grand master of the Knights Templar. The Templars were a rich and powerful order—a state within a state—famous as the architects of the great cathedrals. In the East during the Crusades they were initiated into many secret practices. Eventually, they came into conflict with King Philippe le Bel (Philip IV), who abolished them and ordered Jacques de Molay burned at the stake.[25] Before his death, he gave a rule (règle, as in mo-

24. Coornaert, Compagnonnages, "Les Origines," p. 346, and "Opinions d'un charpentier," p. 348.
25. The Templars were a famous lay religious and military order (known also for their important banking activities) who protected pilgrims during the twelfth-century crusades. They were disbanded in 1312 and their leader, Jacques de Molay, was burned at the stake in 1314 in the reign of Philippe le Bel (1283 to 1314). The order was also accused of practicing sodomy. See Norman Cohn, Europe's Inner Demons (New York, 1975), pp. 85, 89. Despite some glaring factual and chronological discrepancies, this narrative reveals some knowledge of the Templars' history.

nastic orders) to the compagnons (including masons, stonecutters, and carpenters) working on the cathedrals.

The enfants de Salomon, far from being the oldest compagnons were insurgents: insubordinate to master workmen and even to Jacques de Molay, they revolted against his "rule" in 1401 during work on the cathedral of Orléans. Prior to their mutiny, the rebels sometimes called themselves "compagnons of the Temple," but whether in reference to Solomon is not known. The schism was rooted in general disagreements, especially over religious issues. The rebels accused the compagnons du devoir of failing to uphold the original devoir and of swearing allegiance to the Catholic church, in return for the church's support of their aims.[26]

Forced to flee, the rebels took the name gavots, which is given two etymological derivations: first, from the boats, called *gavotages,* used in their flight; and second, from the *gaves* (gorges) in the Pyrenees where they took refuge. Before leaving, the rebels named their adversaries *chiens* (dogs), too pliant and too disposed to renounce the original devoir for a new one. The compagnons du devoir gladly accepted this name, claiming dogs were models of obedience and fidelity; they scorned the rebellious gavots, calling them *"loups* [wolves], independent and severe . . . heretics and mountain people."[27] The gavots found "wolves" a good name, for they remained proudly independent. Thus resulted a division between the compagnons du devoir and the gavots, also called compagnons non du devoir.

Like the temple narratives, this one introduces a powerful founder for the association, setting the scene at the construction site of a noble edifice with spiritual and artistic value. It differs from the first two, however, in significant ways. First, work on the cathedral is not discussed. Second, Jacques de Molay is not a skilled worker and has very little contact with his followers; his compagnons do not (or are not allowed to) bury their founder. Diverging from the pattern in the previous narratives, the central role of work and the founder's life recedes: their importance is assumed and suggested schematically. This narrative also lacks elaborate symbolism and emerges as a more "realistic" account. Yet, as in the first two cases, history is created and reshaped to meet compagnons' needs.

26. The name "compagnons of the Temple" might refer to the Parisian quarter of the Temple, which had its own canonical jurisdiction. Some seventeenth-century compagnons had sought protection there. There is no evidence that the event portrayed in this narrative occurred; the cathedral was built in the thirteenth century. At this point the narrative takes on distinct overtones of the French religious and civil wars, especially in the late sixteenth century, when the Catholic League was most active against Huguenots.

27. Perdiguier, *Question vitale,* pp. 26–27. Cf. Fernand Braudel on the negative stereotypes of mountain dwellers, *The Mediterranean and the Mediterranean World in the Age of Philip II,* 2 vols. (New York, 1966), esp. 1:35–38, 44–47.

The key episodes define the devoir, engage in debate over correct interpretation, and articulate relationships among various groups.

This narrative implies that compagnonnage will share the glory, power, and troubles of the Templars, with which it is linked.[28] Somewhat like the Templars, compagnonnages could be seen as a "state within a state" and were frequently in conflict with church and state authorities. In the narrative, however, compagnons du devoir bow down in obedience to the church. Moreover, Templars (a lay religious order) and compagnons are initially linked by a shared rule, presumably like that of a monastic order, but this rule is soon replaced by a "devoir." The relationship between the Templars and compagnonnage is critical, but the two groups are not synonymous, nor are compagnons presumed subordinate to Templars.

The conflict and schism at the heart of this narrative reflected realities present in the compagnonnages from at least the eighteenth century and increasingly insistent in the nineteenth century. The narrative makes a further analogy with religious schism: the dévorants representing the Catholics, and the gavots, the Protestants. The devoir is thus likened to a religion, the one true religion. But who are the "true believers"? This narrative, according to Perdiguier, is generally considered to "belong . . . to the enfants de Maître Jacques," and its initial and final episodes confirm this attribution. The intermediate episode, however, in which gavots accuse dévorants of overweening loyalty to the church, is more ambiguous. Further, compagnons du devoir seem pleased to be associated with established order if it benefits compagnonnage; they accept the appellation "dogs" and give it a positive connotation. The final episode is fairly well balanced: gavots also take an abusive title, "wolf," and transform it into a term of praise. Thus, the compagnons who are "dogs" remain within the cathedral confines, upholding the devoir; the "wolves" become outsiders but consider themselves heroes valiantly defending the original devoir.[29]

28. Some authors claim operative Masonry can be traced to the Templars' dissolution, but the evidence is extremely tenuous. Paul Naudon, for example, argues that former Templars allegedly joined the corporations of various building trades; speculative Masonry supposedly grew out of these operative groups in the seventeenth and eighteenth centuries. Naudon, *Les Origines religieuses et corporatives de la franc-maçonnerie* (Paris, 1964), pp. 9, 113–15. See also René Le Forestier, *La Franc-maçonnerie templière et occultiste aux XVIIIe et XIXe siècles* (Paris, 1970); and Demeter Gérard Roger Serbanesco, *Histoire de la franc-maçonnerie universelle: Son rituel, son symbolisme* (Paris, 1963). In any case the Orléans narrative presents compagnons as the French equivalent of operative masons; thus, as in the first temple narrative, compagnons and compagnonnage are effectively linked with Freemasonry in the reader/listener's mind.

29. Perdiguier, *Question vitale*, pp. 26–28. The epithets "dogs" and "wolves" have wider cross-cultural meaning in Indo-European folklore, posing interesting questions about cultural transmission. I have not found dogs and wolves commonly used as oppositional terms of honor/opprobrium in France. On the ability to valorize epithets given in insult, see Marie-Louise Sjoes-

Cumulatively, the narrative creates a mutable account capable of favorable interpretation by both devoirs. Most significant, it constructs a common origin. Gavots, the supposed heretics, chide other compagnons for straying from the true devoir—establishing a parallel with the Reformation. As a gavot, Perdiguier says the "compagnons who were the most resolute, with the most conviction, unwilling to submit to the new order of things were treated as rebels, although they were upholding the ancient law, the original devoir, the spirit of tolerance, religious philosophy; [the rebels] were subject to violent persecutions."[30] Although Perdiguier emphasizes elements of freethinking or deism in the gavots' practices, *all* brotherhoods of compagnonnage were at least nominally Catholic. Most compagnons, du devoir or gavot, went further: they commonly attended mass together on Sunday, celebrated masses on patron saints' days, and buried and prayed for their dead with Catholic rites. The seventeenth century witnessed some Protestant influence in compagnonnage, and this, coupled with the present narrative and Perdiguier's beliefs, may lead to the easy assumption that de-Christianization or anticlericalism was stronger among gavots than dévorants. References to the reformed religion were not limited to gavots, however. There are examples of compagnons from both devoirs with preferences for skepticism, deism, or Protestantism.[31] Ultimately, in their lives and narratives, gavots showed no greater spirit of toleration than their enemies.

A COMPARATIVE READING

All three narratives examined here expound two central concepts—the dignity of labor and the need for association—in a context of belief which is essentially Judeo-Christian. Labor, whether on temples or cathedrals, is dedicated to the glory of God and man. Noble and Christlike figures establish voluntary associations that protect the status of skilled labor; the two major founders are then martyred for their beliefs.

---

tedt's discussion of the "hero inside the tribe" and the "hero outside the tribe" in her study of medieval Celtic society, *Gods and Heroes of the Celts*, trans. Myles Dillon (Berkeley, 1982), chaps. 6 and 7. Whether compagnons were "dogs" or "wolves," mourners of both sects sometimes howled during burial rites. Survivals of animal totemism in nineteenth-century *urban* culture are rare and could have reinforced the esoteric image of compagnonnage.

30. Perdiguier, *Question vitale*, p. 26.

31. One of the earliest references to Huguenots among compagnons du devoir (1654–55), as noted in Chapters 2 and 3, is the "Serment des selliers" (BN, Coll. Dupuy, no. 775, fol. 274 v°). I have found no record of gavots at that time. Ménétra, an eighteenth-century compagnon du devoir, portrays himself variously as a skeptic, a deist, and a practicing (albeit generally anticlerical) Catholic. Sciandro, a nineteenth-century compagnon du devoir, praises the Reformation.

In all three narratives, compagnonnage legitimates itself by appropriating the symbols and practices of the church, trade communities, and confraternities. This borrowing of shared cultural materials made compagnonnage more comprehensible and acceptable to its members, particularly in the old regime. Simultaneously, however, by transmuting and adapting these materials, compagnonnage differentiated itself from other French corporate bodies and its sects from one another.

Although the Orléans narrative is less detailed and complex than the others, it provides an incisive exploration of beliefs and divisions. Schism arises not over desires for power or advancement, as in the first two, but over the devoir, the organizing principle and code of compagnonnage itself. This account gives compagnonnage a common origin while revealing an enmity that will probably divide it forever into warring sects, just as the Reformation irretrievably split Catholicism. But myths are not scripts for action, although lived and constructed experience interact dynamically. These origin narratives encoded and reflected certain structures and relationships existing within (and between) various sects and between compagnonnage and the rest of French society. For example, the Orléans narrative establishes putative relationships between compagnonnage and the Templars, the church, and the state. Origin accounts thus can suggest the range of actions that appeared plausible and legitimate to compagnons in dealing with one another and the wider society. These interactions could potentially be redefined by different devoirs, trades, or generations of compagnons. The narrative symbolism is multivocal, permitting manipulation and reinterpretation to respond to the strategies and needs of particular groups of compagnons at different times.

The origin narratives introduced and reinforced the structures and beliefs of compagnonnage and were learned, at least in part, during initiation rituals. These narratives were also quasi-sacred charters bestowing status, privilege, or legitimacy on certain sects or trades. The workers specifically mentioned in all three narratives (stonecutters, carpenters, metal workers) were all in construction trades and required skill, training, and strength to practice their crafts. By the nineteenth century these were the most prestigious and best-paid trades of compagnonnage. Historically, however, these were not its "ancient and original" trades. As has been seen, the first compagnonnagelike associations emerged among cutlers (sixteenth century). A century later the Sorbonne condemned four more trades—shoemakers, hatters, tailors, and saddlers—for practicing "compagnonnage"; only the hatters also appear in an origin narrative.[32] Carpenters and metal workers (other than locksmiths),

32. Significantly, shoemakers are absent from the origin narratives, although Maître Jacques could have left them his sandals just as he left the hatters his hat. Masons (i.e., stonemasons),

moreover, were not fully active in compagnonnage until the eighteenth century; the imposing stonecutters apparently were not organized as compagnons until well into that century.

Yet, in the nineteenth century carpenters and stonecutters insistently claimed and were often believed to be the oldest and most important trades in compagnonnage.[33] This trope is common in history and myth: kings and noblemen often commissioned histories or privileged those legends that legitimated their powers and prerogatives. The status of the carpenters was enhanced, moreover, by their patron, Saint Joseph, a major saint and one close to Christ himself.[34] The carpenters' compagnonnage remained powerful until the late nineteenth century, but their insistence on privilege led to narrowness and exclusivity, exacerbating conflict among compagnons and between compagnons and other workers. Nonetheless, the creators of the origin narratives, by selecting workers who *could* have built temples and cathedrals potentially extended their valuation of labor to all the trades of compagnonnage. Compagnons presented an enduring image of themselves and their social contributions as important and honorable, in sharp contrast to the common view of work and workers. Yet, the negative depiction of those outside one's sect encouraged destructive brawls among workers. Origin narratives thus reinforced the weaknesses of compagnonnage as well as its strengths in the postrevolutionary era.

Nineteenth-Century Initiation Rituals

Initiations underwent a reshaping and elaboration, similar to that of the origin narratives. Some late eighteenth- and nineteenth-century initiation accounts incorporated aspects of the origin narratives. Others ended with a reading of a lecture (*la morale*), based on these legends.[35] Although initiations, with their standard elements and format, are apparently less malleable than narratives, we have already seen a significant

---

who were mentioned in the narratives, were rarely organized into compagnonnage and generally formed independent associations.

33. Théodore Barrière's play *Les Charpentiers* (1847), discussed in Chapter 1, provides evidence of how the status and antiquity of the carpenters in compagnonnage was accepted in public discourse. A pivotal song in act 1, scene 1, is noteworthy for stating that when the "devoir ordered it," the carpenters upheld their honor by "breaking [i.e., defying] the Sorbonne." The stanza suggests a reading of Perdiguier for the 1655 condemnations but also an interpretation of that history based on the carpenters' version of things.

34. Perhaps the Catholic church aimed to create a similar connection by designating May first as the feast of Saint Joseph the Worker. This rather obvious attempt to co-opt organized labor's most symbolic holiday and invest it with traditional religious meaning occurred after World War II.

35. E.g., Toussaint Guillaumou, *Les Confessions d'un compagnon* (Paris, 1864), p. 37.

range of variation in them. The three accounts I turn to now bear that
out: the first emphasizes Masonic elements; the second, harsh physical
hazing; the third, less extreme on both scores, is perhaps closer to the
norm. Like the origin narratives, these initiation accounts reveal how
compagnons established community and created opposition through incorporation and exclusion.[36] These narratives also accent the dilemmas
compagnons faced in trying to understand, transform, and yet preserve
the ritual process from old regime to new.

Joiners and Locksmiths du Devoir de Liberté, Toulouse

Joseph Pradelle (Toulousain la fraternité), a twentieth-century compagnon turner, in 1941 published an elaborate account whose source
cannot be fully authenticated.[37] Pradelle, who wrote extensively on
compagnonnage, claims this initiation was employed "throughout the
old regime." Emile Coornaert and Roger Lecotté generally consider
Pradelle's work reliable, but some doubts remain because this narrative is permeated by Masonic imagery, not found in other eighteenth-
century sources on compagnonnage. I thus judge this to be a very
late eighteenth- or, more likely, an early nineteenth-century account.
There is a preamble before the *setting* is outlined. The novice is instructed:

> The initiation is a ceremony of the utmost solemnity for the
> compagnons, for it is by means of this that we begin the initia-
> tion into our sacred Mysteries of the Devoir de liberté, founded
> by the great King Solomon, when he ordered the building of the
> magnificent Temple of Jerusalem. We must thus celebrate it with
> the greatest possible pomp in order to give the *Récipiendaire* lofty
> ideals following from the maxims we wish to teach him. (pp.
> 135–36)

The initiation chamber is intricately decorated and the four cardinal
points marked on the floor. On the east is a temple erected in honor of
Solomon, and a portrait of the king in all his glory hangs within. Before
this stands a throne, with a semicircular table at its foot. A fine cloth
covers the table and on it is placed a book of the devoir. Seven torches
are arranged in a straight line behind the table. Also in front of the

36. Cf. Susan G. Davis, *Parades and Power: Street Theatre in Nineteenth-Century Philadelphia* (Philadelphia, 1986), p. 15.
37. Joseph Pradelle, "Réception des compagnons menuisiers et serruriers de devoir de liberté
sous l'ancien régime à Toulouse," *Mémoires de l'Académie des sciences, inscriptions, et belles-lettres de
Toulouse*, ser. 13, 3 (1941): 135–53, hereafter cited in the text.

temple is a large tableau of the construction of the temple in Jerusalem, including a scene of Hiram whispering the password into the ear of a compagnon and giving him a special handshake.

In the middle of the room, "Solomon," played by the premier compagnon wearing a royal robe and a crown, sits on a magnificent throne. He holds the compagnons' colors (ribbons) and a (large architectural) compass in his hands. Solomon is surrounded by three compagnons; the scene is framed by laurel garlands and is lit by four candles. At a distance from the throne are pieces of architectural design made by joiners and locksmiths. All the initiated compagnons, arranged in rank order, are in the room, formally dressed and wearing their colors. Some compagnons, playing the role of *satellites* (attendants), are armed with gleaming swords: they have a coat of arms drawn on their chest and wear little but a coat of mail. Finally, two "guards," armed with lance and shield in the left hand, stand beside the temple's entrance. Dressed in "either Turkish or Greek" costume, they also have coats of arms drawn on their bodies. Other geometric designs are traced on the floor of the room.[38]

In the first stage of *separation* the rôleur brings all those ready and willing to be initiated to the premier compagnon in an undecorated assembly room. The rôleur asks them a set of questions stressing the finality of the step they are about to take. The subjects, who have prepared their answers in advance are told that after initiation "there will be no time for regret," nor will they be able to meet with compagnons of other sects. If the novices agree to these conditions, they say: "We desire to be compagnons du devoir de liberté" (pp. 136–37). They leave the room while the compagnons deliberate on their personal merits and professional skills. If they are judged acceptable, the premier compagnon informs them when and where to report for their initiation, telling them to be "properly dressed." Unworthy subjects are led away, never to be received as compagnons.

The second stage of separation occurs when the subjects arrive as instructed. Reexamined on their resolve, they are told they will be strictly subject to the society's laws: its "primordial" law is to sustain and support the society at all times. Each who is willing to go forward picks a "godfather" and "godmother" (both compagnons) and then leaves the room. Each subject will be called forward individually to undergo the ritual. First, however, each submits the new name he has chosen to the godparents and the society for approval and pays twenty-five francs for the initiation. The first aspirant separates himself from the others and

---

38. The sometimes elaborate staging of initiations (esp. here and in the seventeenth-century accounts) reveals the importance of the element of "spectacle" in ritual. The compagnons proved marvelously resourceful.

is blindfolded by his godfather. The godfather takes the aspirant's left hand, the godmother his right hand, and he is led to the "temple."

The *transition* begins when the godfather makes overtures to enter Solomon's chamber by knocking on the door, in series of threes. There is no response. Finally, the godfather calls out: "Solomon! Solomon! Solomon!" Solomon, in an angry and haughty tone, eventually tells these "bold and profane" mortals to leave this "place of light" or face instant death. The godfather continues his entreaties, claiming to be a compagnon "nourished" on Solomon's principles. Finally, the door is opened. The godparents hold the aspirant tightly, for there is danger ahead; they lead their charge around the room several times, encountering flashes of light, strange noises, and sounds of fighting. The godparents eventually manage to lead the aspirant to the temple's entrance. The aspirant kneels, but Solomon orders these profane ones to flee. Again the godfather intercedes; the temple gate is opened.

Solomon immediately turns against the aspirant, ordering his guards to seize this "enemy"; they tie him up and push him to the ground. The godparents plead for mercy, but Solomon orders the aspirant executed. All is silent as the aspirant is led to a deserted part of the room. The godfather manages to rescue the aspirant and lead him back to the temple. Similar "struggles" continue for some time. Finally, the aspirant is brought before Solomon and told to raise his hands toward the king, who allows the aspirant to be untied. He remains blindfolded as Solomon questions him about his desire to become a compagnon. At times the godfather whispers the proper answers to his charge. If Solomon and the others judge the candidate to be sincere, they say: "Let him see the light!" As the blindfold is removed, two attendants rush forward, pressing their sword points against the aspirant's chest to demonstrate that he faces death if he betrays his oath. Kneeling, the aspirant raises his left hand, places his right hand on the Bible and swears "before God, to the Body of Compagnons here assembled, never to reveal to any living being that which I have seen and heard, and that which I see and will see after this, on the pain of having my heart pierced by these two swords and my name held in abomination by all the faithful Compagnons of the Tour de France" (p. 148).

In *incorporation* the aspirant actually "receives the light" through baptism. Before that occurs all the compagnons assemble in the room in rank order. Their demeanor is serious. The aspirant sits in front of "Solomon," now revealed as the premier. The initiate's godfather sits to his right, his godmother to his left. He swears to support his godfather, godmother, and the society's interests at all times. The premier sings a long "poem"; during one verse wine is poured over the aspirant's head as he is baptized "in the name of the Grand Architect and Great King Solomon." The paper bearing his new name is placed in a glass: he swallows the paper, drinks to the health of all, and they drink to his. After each aspirant goes through the same procedure, all reassemble to learn the symbolism of the figures and setting (pp. 150, 151–53).[39]

Most initiation rituals are intended to create loyal adherents to a new social group. The present example, however, is striking in at least four regards. First, this case emphasizes the separation of the novice. Second, it rigorously examines his motives. Third, it insists on his complete allegiance to compagnonnage but with little reference to other social groups (the church, the family). Finally, this account is most distinctive for its complexity, length, and Masonic symbolism.

The drawing out of the ritual in this case intensifies many of its elements. The aspirant is more clearly separated from his previous social position than in other examples. The account repeatedly stresses that he is entering a new society that will become the major focus of his daily life and warns the subject of the gravity of this step. The godparents, particularly the godfather, help separate him from the outside world as a necessary prelude for his "reception of the light." Mind and body are prepared for a new life of "enlightenment." Far more than the chamois dressers' nineteenth-century initiation, which also includes some Masonic elements, the "Pradelle account" concentrates on the ritual subject's transformation into a "new" person by means of an elaborate, highly symbolic procedure, which includes threats and physical hazing. The novice is harassed, frightened, kept in darkness, and reminded of his worthlessness. He is surrounded by men in foreign dress: these Turkish (or Greek) chain-mail-garbed figures are meant to be grand and rather frightening, although they undoubtedly struck some novices as ridiculous. These characters emphasized the distance between those in authority in the society and those seeking admission to it, contrasting the rights of members to the weakness of aspirants. Novices may have been impressed by this ceremony (or suspended any reservations) because of the prestige implied by its Masonic symbolism and language. Moreover, the text depicts this initiation as quite an extravaganza. The compagnon joiners and locksmiths infused their initiations with drama and entertainment reminiscent of *The Magic Flute*.[40]

39. In the "Explication des hieroglyphes," compagnons learn that "tout ce que vous voyez est un symbole": e.g., "Le compas, l'équerre, le niveaux tracés sur le plancher ... vous représentent à la fois, la justice, la science et l'égalité"; and "ces sept colonnes sont une double allégorie disant que la construction du temple dura sept ans et ensuite qu'il y avait dans ce temple sept degrés de dignité." This marked Masonic symbolism makes it likely that much of this ceremony dates from the early nineteenth-century.

40. Cf. Clawson on nineteenth-century American fraternal orders as conscious creators and

After these elaborate trials, the subject was put to the final test, the oath. The present account, compared to earlier ones, further elevates the oath's importance. The society appropriated new powers: it wrested the subject's allegiance from other institutions and duties and transfered them to itself, claiming the power of life and death over the subject should he betray compagnonnage. This direct expression of power, more implicit in earlier ceremonies, could reflect anxiety about controlling the initiate in a changing world of labor and its organization.

Further Masonic and deist elements emerge in the final phase when the subject is baptized in the name of the "Grand Architect." Solomon, the non-Christian king, is central, and Christian symbolism is weaker than in previous accounts, presenting a characterization of compagnons du devoir de liberté as less churchgoing and more freethinking than compagnons du devoir. These characteristics emerged in the Orléans narrative as well when the enfants de Maître Jacques called the gavots "heretics." While retaining the essentially Christian formulations of baptism and communion, this initiation broadened its symbolic base and shifted it away from Catholicism. The proliferation of pagan, occult, Hebrew, and even pseudoscientific imagery doubtless resulted from contact, direct or indirect, with Freemasonry.

The joiners and locksmiths' account reveals strong concerns about hierarchy, authority, and discipline. Structurally, such issues were less important in seventeenth-century initiation accounts, although none of these early cases were egalitarian. The premier compagnon's authority was already well established even in the seventeenth century, but in the Pradelle account there is a greater emphasis on order and rank than in other eighteenth-century accounts. The room itself, for example, is decorated according to a geometric plan and all the compagnons stand in rank order. Solomon's role and authority are preponderant; Maître Jacques was not equally dominant in initiation accounts of compagnons du devoir. The concerns of the present account were also expressed to some extent in other nineteenth-century texts on initiation and in the postrevolutionary organization and orientation of compagnonnage. Yet, that this ceremony could have been practiced in roughly the same era as the revised initiation of the chamois dressers indicates the range of variation possible in the symbolic practices of compagnonnage. As minor

---

providers of entertainment in their rituals. See *Constructing Brotherhood*, pp. 17–18, and chap. 7. She calls these rituals, especially in the later nineteenth century, a type of "mass media entertainment." Fraternal orders in the United States such as Masons, Elks, and Odd Fellows were "marketing a standardized entertainment product" (pp. 17–18). In the compagnonnages, drama and entertainment were important but not "marketed," largely because these were far more closed and limited organizations.

as these variations seemed to outsiders, each differentiated one sect or trade from the others and built formidable barriers to a united association.

Carpenters du Devoir, Enfants de Père Soubise, 1884

In Pradelle's account the complex symbolism encodes the principles of authority and elitism in terms closely linked to Masonic sources. These principles are thus potentially identifiable within a context of enlightenment and progress. Another account, published in 1909 by Henri Bricheteau, presents an initiation in which the principles of authority and elitism are taken to extremes. The author castigates the symbols and practices of this initiation as an archaic and unwholesome tradition that vitiated the positive aspects of compagnonnage.[41] Bricheteau, writing under the pseudonym of Jean Connay, is, however, far from impartial. His punning pseudonym sends a double message. While "j'en connais" means "I know about it," "con" is also a popular term for "dope" or, more crudely, "asshole." Bricheteau's pseudonym can thus stand not only as a proof of his bona fides but also as a warning: "I know about this now, but I was duped, I was a *con:* don't you be."

Born in 1882 in Paris, Bricheteau was a carpenter who became a member and later the secretary of the Union des charpentiers de la Seine, a syndicalist organization bent on challenging the supremacy of compagnonnage in this trade. When he wrote his first anticompagnonnage tract in 1909, "Connay" described himself as a former compagnon carpenter who had been initiated as a *bon drille* in the compagnons du devoir and enfants de Père Soubise. He quit, however, because of "serious injustices and anachronisms."[42] Connay's work was published by the Union des charpentiers de la Seine and bore the approval of an introduction by Léon and Maurice Bonneff, who were already well known and respected for their works on labor and social questions. The Union des charpentiers' campaign against compagnonnage continued in 1911 with *Comment on devient compagnon du devoir,* an abridged version of Connay's earlier work. I have not been able to verify that Bricheteau was actually a member of compagnonnage; nevertheless, some of his claims about the enfants de père Soubise are at least partially supported in other sources.

41. Jean Connay [Henri Bricheteau], *Le Compagnonnage: Son histoire, ses mystères,* preface by Léon Bonneff and Maurice Bonneff (Paris, 1909). For a brief biographical note on Bricheteau, see Jean Maitron, general ed., *Dictionnaire biographique du mouvement ouvrier français: Troisième partie: 1871–1914 De la Commune à la Grande Guerre* (Paris, 1973), 11:58.
42. Connay, *Le Compagnonnage,* preface.

Without denying the past grandeur and vigor of compagnonnage, Connay deplored its present state, graphically portraying its harsh initiations and unequal treatment of aspirants and lower-ranking compagnons. He vehemently condemned the castes and divisions and denounced the practice of allowing bosses to attend workers' meetings. This last accusation cannot be confirmed, although retired compagnon carpenters who had become entrepreneurs probably continued to frequent their former society. The bon drilles, nonetheless, remained a powerful unit with which other labor organizations had to contend. Connay exaggerates in claiming they controlled two-thirds of the work sites, but other sources reveal that the vitality and authority of compagnonnage was significant among carpenters up to World War I. Many unaffiliated carpenters, moreover, continued to accept its leadership in labor disputes.[43]

Connay's magnification of the strengths and weaknesses of compagnonnage may be read as the negative testimony of an experience the author found personally offensive. In a somewhat similar but more sophisticated vein, the novelist Henry Poulaille, whose father was a carpenter and mother was a chair caner, attacked compagnonnage as violent and reactionary. Poulaille's *Pain quotidien, 1903–1906* (1939) serves as a rare fictional representation of compagnonnage in the artisanal trades, particularly carpentry, before the Great War. The author presents a debate between two brothers, both carpenters: Henri is a syndicalist; Alexandre is a compagnon, an enfant de Père Soubise. They agree that compagnons possess "admirable professional qualities," but each brother believes his association defends the "honor" of carpentry best. Henri is a member of the relatively new Union syndicale—a fictionalized Union des charpentiers. He finds it incredible that in the twentieth century, there could be "imbeciles who stuffed their heads with stories like those of your Père Soubise. . . . I don't buy stuff like that," and he underlines his disdain by laughing. Alexandre says his society safeguards "team spirit [*esprit d'équipe*], the duty of solidarity." Henri counters that compagnons are divided among themselves: solidarity was limited to the compagnon's particular society. Henri and the Union syndicale embody values the novel characterizes as progressive and positive; their top priority is to fight recruitment into compagnonnage.[44]

43. Ibid., p. 133. Cf. France, Direction du Travail, *Les Associations professionelles ouvrières*, 4 vols. (Paris, 1899), 1:123–25; and Pierre du Maroussem, *Charpentiers de Paris: Compagnons et indépendants*, vol. 1 of *La Question ouvrière*, 4 vols. (Paris, 1891–94), pp. 127–49. For compagnonnage's importance in carpentry before 1848, see Dudley Channing Barksdale, "Parisian Carpenters and Changes in Forms of Work, Culture, and Protest, 1789–1848" (M.A. thesis, University of North Carolina, Chapel Hill, 1978).
44. Henry Poulaille, *Le Pain quotidien, 1903–1906* (Paris, 1939), pp. 42–43.

Compagnonnage also continued to be a major force in the late nineteenth and early twentieth century leather industry. The archivist Henri Lemoine, writing in 1928 on the state of compagnonnage among chamois dressers, said the association was "violently attacked by syndicalism at the beginning of the [twentieth] century [and] has almost completely disappeared." Even the Confédération Générale du Travail (C.G.T.), which had been founded only in 1895 but was already France's largest labor union, thought it crucial to undermine any remaining attractions of compagnonnage in a France where much industry continued to be small scale and linked to artisanal traditions. The C.G.T. thus claimed that the secret ceremonies and especially the initiation in the leather trades were a series of hazings "as crude as they were brutal." If there is some truth to this accusation, the chamois dressers must have dramatically revised both of the earlier versions of their initiation ceremonies I have examined. Lemoine ventured no opinion, but cited the comment of a labor inspector who found compagnons in the leather trades "extremely reserved" ("d'une discrétion absolue") about their initiations, which seems to imply that they had something of a less than suitable nature to hide.[45]

Investigative studies by the French labor department (the Direction du travail) partially overcame such reserve, obtaining testimony from present and former compagnon carpenters du devoir about their initiations by asking them to verify accounts similar to the one Connay would present roughly ten years later. Some compagnons flatly denied the existence of harsh initiation tests; the majority, however, claimed that only parts of the investigators' facts were wrong, that physical trials were becoming less rough, or that only moral tests were now practiced (suggesting that severe tests had once existed). A major Parisian businessman, formerly a *conseiller, prud'homme,* and compagnon carpenter du devoir, declared he would never again consent to be initiated as he had been—even for ten thousand francs. The labor department took this testimony as indirect confirmation of their account's validity.[46]

In general, however, severe hazing and crude or even obscene practices were apparently not a major feature of these initiations before the nineteenth century, particularly compared to those of early modern youth groups, confraternities, or trade communities. Had the compagnons' initiations been as rowdy and ribald as the initiations, pranks, and

---

45. Henri Lemoine, "Le Compagnonnage dans l'industrie des cuirs et peaux: La Société secrète des compagnons du devoir, blancheurs-chamoiseurs [*sic*]," *Syndicat général des cuirs et peaux de France, Bulletin mensuel,* 29, no. 264 (20 November 1928): 663.

46. Direction du Travail, *Associations professionelles* 1:124. Connay (1909) also admitted that some of the harshest physical aspects of the initiation had been modified by the turn of the century.

charivaris reported for confraternal or trade associations (especially those of the printers), I am convinced some evidence would have surfaced. We cannot be absolutely certain that "crude and brutal" aspects of earlier initiations did not escape contemporary investigations or diligent researchers; it seems clear, however, that prior to the nineteenth century these initiations were not primarily designed to humiliate or harm the novice.

Whatever the remaining strength and attraction of compagnonnage, and whatever the truth about its rituals, Connay and his syndicalist sponsors wanted an end to the association. Connay's work thus spared no details, especially scatological ones, to convince his readers that compagnonnage was both ridiculous and barbaric. I recognize his intent, biases, and exaggerations, but I also accept the reasonable possibility that the carpenters' initiation in the later nineteenth century had developed along the lines Connay reports. The basic elements and structure of his testimony are present in other works on the carpenters and their associations.[47] Connay's work is, moreover, useful as a "tribute" to the power of compagnonnage; it is unlikely he would have been so fiercely critical of a weak and unimportant institution. The "eccentricities" of the brotherhoods had been written about, but not with Connay's combination of anger and disdain. Workers who continued to join may have disliked elements of the organization, but they believed it protected their interests. Novices (like some young fraternity men) may have derived pleasure from the coarseness of the ceremony—if not in the actual moment, then in its retelling or in the anticipation of forcing future novices to submit to *their* will.

The carpenters du devoir usually conducted a group initiation of their aspirants, called *renards* (foxes),[48] annually, around the feast of Saint Joseph (18 March), the carpenters' patron saint. Connay's account describes an 1884 initiation beginning on the eve of the feast of Saint Joseph. The *setting* was the Mère and other places, too, for the whole procedure took nine nights and ten "passages" to complete. All the major tests occurred in a dark, undecorated room in the cellar. When not going through a passage, the renards were sequestered in a dormitorylike room, hidden from the street, called the *renardière*. Other parts of the initiation were performed in the Mère's assembly room.

47. Direction du Travail, *Associations professionelles* 1:123–25; and Maroussem, *Charpentiers de Paris*, pp. 127–49.
48. The carpenters du devoir de liberté claimed that their nickname, *renards de liberté*, originated when they broke away from the carpenters du devoir. The bon drilles called them *renards* in scorn, but the rebels proudly took the name identifying themselves with foxes, who were clever and independent. Cf. the use of *chiens* and *loups* in the Orléans narrative, p. 287.

The actual phase of *separation* began as the renards ate dinner together on the eve of the feast of Saint Joseph. Separated from all others but their examiners, they went through the entire ceremony as a group. After dinner they learned songs of compagnonnage until called to begin the initiation.

Transition began when the renards were brought into an assembly room and made to kneel before a table at which a number of compagnons were sitting. Each renard was questioned—name, origins, work experience. The compagnons judged the aspirant's masterpiece and, if it was acceptable, ordered him to construct a project on the spot. Successful novices were sent to the *commissaire* of Père Soubise and gave him their papers, *livrets,* and any possessions (for example, money, watches) they were carrying. The initiation had no fixed cost: the renard "bargained" for the price of each of the ten passages. The whole process could total over a hundred francs, paid on the final day of the ceremony.

The renards were assigned numbers by which they were ranked and addressed throughout the remaining initiation. The first night they were put in the renardière: their faces were decorated with charcoal, and they were made to sing far into the night. At dawn, the renards washed and prepared for Mass to celebrate the feast day of Saint Joseph. In the procession to the church they carried the platform holding the society's chef-d'oeuvre and the sanctified bread to be offered in the Mass. That evening there was a banquet and a ball to which the renards were sometimes invited; if not invited, they were put in the renardière to await the start of their trials.

The severity and intensity of the trials increased each night. Although the renards were baptized and swore their oaths to the society on the third night during the very first passage, the little baptism (*petit baptême*), their trials were hardly over. Some testing and hazing occurred before this "little baptism," but the most rigorous hazing took place *after* it—a sequence different from that found in earlier initiation accounts. The tests seem to have been imposed less to evaluate the initiate's valor or loyalty before entry than to debase him and subject him to the society's full authority.

The little baptism had a number of parts. The renard was first blindfolded, put in a barrel and rolled around the room, then carried into another room filled with noise and uproar and dropped on the floor. Père Soubise, greatly angered to be so disturbed, began to berate and castigate the renard for daring to approach this "sacred place." When Père Soubise was finally appeased, the renard was asked to swear to renounce God and his father and mother, for, he was told, "you have no need of them with us."[49] He was also to swear to kill and steal for the society if necessary. If he refused to so swear, he was roughed up; if he persisted in his refusal, he was threatened with death. If the renard capitulated, he was berated for cowardice and lack of principle: "Get out of here then! Dirty beast, deprived of good sense, you disgusting being, what do you want us to do with you? Confide our secrets in you, after you have renounced your family and promised to steal and kill?" (p. 144). Eventually, the renard was allowed to take the final oath: "I swear before God and the worthy compagnons never to speak or to divulge any of the secrets that might be confided to me." Then he learned some iconography—for example, that the initials U.V.G.T., often found on compagnons' diplomas, ribbons, and certificates, stood for "Union, Virtue, Genius, and Labor," the principal values encoded in the origin narratives. In preparation for the baptism, he chose a new name as well as a *représentant* and *adjoint* (deputy and assistant deputy), who took the place of the godfather and godmother of other accounts. The renard next drank an elaborate toast to the health of the représentant and the adjoint. Then, as he knelt, still blindfolded, the compagnons poured water over his head, saying: "I baptize you in the name of Père Soubise, and all his little *soubiseaux*" (p. 145).

The other passages possess these same elements of rough play and slapstick. Renards, for example, are made to "jump" for Père Soubise, are decorated with charcoal, doused with buckets of water in the facetious *grand baptême,* rolled around the room in barrels. Slapstick was most prevalent during the daytime and the minor passages. Such "play" was used to denigrate, frighten, and fatigue the renards. Other practices went beyond play: compagnons carved a "Z" on the renard's back with a sharp tool and forced him to swallow sawdust and drink wine while lying on his back, toasting the compagnons conducting the ceremony.[50] Throughout the initiation, but especially in the last two passages, compagnons violently flagellated the renards.

Other procedures were less physically taxing but more frightening or humiliating. In at least three passages, the renard was threatened with castration or underwent simulated castration. The sixth passage, the "gutter and apron of the roofer," found the renards naked and in a circle on their hands and knees. A candle was placed in the renard's anus, and the renard behind him removed it with his teeth—a maneuver called "bolting and unbolting the staircase." If the renard successfully completed these tests, he reached the ninth night and tenth passage.

49. Connay, *Compagnonnage,* p. 143, hereafter cited in the text.
50. Connay says the "Z" was a carpenter's mark "signifying the process of returning or bringing back" (ibid.).

Incorporation occurred during the second phase of the tenth passage with the "Descent of the Crown." The crown, symbolizing the society's glory, and the would-be compagnons' ribbons and sashes had been suspended from the ceiling in a basket on the eve of the feast of Saint Joseph. The renards, clean and dressed up, entered the room; the premier compagnon released the basket, allowing the colors to float down on the new compagnons. At this precise moment renards became compagnons. To mark the event, they embraced the senior compagnons; all joined hands and danced around in a circle, singing:

> There are no more renards, mère,
> No more renards at your place.
> There are only compagnons, mère,
> Only compagnons at your place. (p. 173)

The initiation was at an end.

The most striking difference between this initiation and previous cases is its emphasis on physical punishment and humiliation. In initiation rituals per se, physically taxing and humiliating trials are not uncommon. According to Victor Turner, such ordeals are intended as a "destruction of the [subjects'] previous status . . . a tempering of their essence in order to prepare them to cope with their new responsibilities and restrain them in advance from abusing their new privileges."[51] The brutality of the compagnon carpenters' trials seems so extreme compared to tests in other trades of compagnonnage that we tend to suspect Connay of exaggeration or fabrication of certain details. Yet, these trials are no more harsh than can be found in other cultures' initiations—or in those of some twentieth-century American fraternities and gangs. Given the doubts about the source of the account, it is difficult to ascertain the carpenters' motives. In "tempering" initiates by standards they regarded as harsh but necessary, Connay indicates that compagnons allowed their more sadistic tendencies to emerge.[52]

Homoerotic and homosexual elements, rarely seen this openly in compagnonnage, add to this initiation's complexity. Beyond the most obvious episode, which simulated anal intercourse—"bolting and unbolting

---

51. Victor Turner, *The Ritual Process: Structure and Anti-structure* (Chicago, 1969), p. 103.

52. Pierre Moreau also claimed aspirants often suffered gravely during initiations: he said he knew a shoemaker who went insane after his initiation and a baker who died during his. *Un Mot aux ouvriers de toutes les professions, à tous les amis du peuple et du progrès, sur le compagnonnage; ou, Le Guide de l'ouvrier sur le tour de France* (Auxerre, 1841), p. 17. While neither Moreau nor Connay are disinterested sources, their accounts may have served the compagnons' purposes. Rumors of esoteric and harsh initiations could make compagnonnage appear powerful: if an association held the power of life and death over its members, it could be imagined as equally powerful against its enemies.

the staircase"—junior and senior males embrace one another and dance together. The young males are reminded of their inferiority by being "de-sexed" or placed in a submissive, female role. Although brother-hoods of compagnonnage were never publicly accused of sodomy or homosexuality (as were the Templars), male bonding and camaraderie played a critical role in these organizations. This initiation's homoerotic features helped to fuse the young novices into a united cohort. Their sequestration kept them together in the liminal setting of the *renardière*, where they ate and slept (or were kept awake). They learned many of their new society's beliefs and precepts for behavior as they sang songs that could be seen as a secular form of prayer and praise. Finally, al-though the carpenters' liminal phase is far more limited in scope and duration, it is reminiscent of the sequestration of young males in many African circumcision rituals.[53]

In another departure from other examples, renards are baptized be-fore rigorous testing, in the transitional period. Baptism is not the cap-stone (as in other cases) but almost an entry into the ritual. Furthermore, in this account the incorporation phase is comparatively brief, probably because the bon drilles kept initiates in the lower grade of *reçu* for a significant period. Rigorous testing was thus a sign that even "received" compagnons remained in a continuing "transitional" status, undergoing more testing before achieving the higher rank of *fini*.

The transitional period before and during the little baptism, in the first three nights, is, nonetheless, significant, for the renard's loyalties to the wider society are questioned. The renard can give no answer the compagnonnage accepts as correct.[54] Compagnons did not want a mem-ber without moral scruples; yet, simultaneously, they wanted one who could be loyal to compagnonnage above all other institutions—church, state, or family. This paradox mirrors the position of compagnonnage in French society. Although these semiclandestine associations were de-pendent on members' allegiance, compagnons could not sever them-selves from the wider world of production to which they also belonged. The interrogators forced the renard to confront the ambiguity and mar-ginality he faced as a compagnon.

In general this initiation account is quite secular in tone. The little baptism is done in the name of Père Soubise and his *soubiseaux*, not in

---

53. For example, Victor Turner, *The Forest of Symbols: Aspects of Ndembu Ritual* (Ithaca, 1967), chap. 7, "*Mukanda:* The Rite of Circumcision." Obviously vast differences exist. Yet, novices are forged into a liminal group more explicitly in this account than in any others available in com-pagnonnage. See also, Victor Turner, "Variations on a Theme of Liminality," mimeographed paper, Institute for Advanced Study, Princeton, November 1975.

54. The test of questions that have no correct answer is found in other ritual performances. Cf. Victor Turner, *Chihamba, the White Spirit* (Manchester, England, 1962).

the name of God; the godparents of earlier initiations are replaced by the deputy and assistant deputy—political-administrative terms. The actual incorporation of new members takes place in the "descent of the crown," when the new compagnons are covered in the society's glory and their colors and joyfully embrace and dance. No pseudocommunion or shared meal occurs during this part of the ceremony. In sum, this account has few overtly Christian elements; its extended transitional period, extreme hazing, homoerotic elements, and secular incorporation make it fundamentally different from the other cases I have examined.

Shoemakers du Devoir, 1833

I end with this narrative because it is one of the best available examples of an initiation based on personal testimony. Toussaint Guillaumou (born about 1815), a dedicated compagnon shoemaker, recounts his 1833 initiation in his 1864 memoirs.[55] As with Ménétra's *Journal,* questions of memory and revisions of the past arise. By 1864 Guillaumou was only about fifty, but he had lived through the shoemakers' struggle to be recognized as compagnons and through failed attempts to unify compagnonnage. Beyond these more particular failures was the larger failure of 1848 and the subsequent overthrow of the Second Republic. At the time he was writing, Guillaumou fully recognized the limitations of compagnonnage as a labor association and had a fairly critical and freethinking perspective on its mysteries. Finally, as a devoted man of '48 and social democrat, Guillaumou may have been somewhat embarrassed to admit his true feelings about the ceremony—even if he remembered them well.

Despite these problems, Guillaumou's account is certainly the most complete of the few accounts written by a compagnon about his initiation.[56] That he chose to "expose" *(dévoile)* his initiation was unusual. As noted, neither Ménétra nor Perdiguier did so in any detail. Perdiguier remains discrete about his initiation even in his later works. Guillaumou still felt some compunction about revealing the details of his initiation

55. Guillaumou, *Confessions,* pp. 24–38; the citations in the following account are all taken from these pages. Coornaert reprints Guillaumou's account, but mistakenly dates it 1835. *Compagnonnages,* pp. 388–93.

56. E.g., the compagnon baker Jean-Baptiste Arnaud, who was critical of secret societies such as compagnonnage, nonetheless says only that he was initiated in 1836 into the "mysteries of Compagnonnage" and received a "baptism joining me for life to the Enfants de Maître Jacques" (*Mémoires,* p. 54). Victor-Bernard Sciandro, who writes much on origin narratives, says little about its rituals and makes no reference to his own experience. The "Mémoires d'un travailleur bas-normand," ed. Gabriel Désert, *Annales de Normandie,* no. 1 (1969): 59–77, and no. 2: 155–78, recounts the life of Pierre Ameline, a compagnon *chaudronnier* (boilermaker) who made his tour de France from about 1836 to 1844.

in 1864, for he spent nearly a page discussing the pros and cons of his disclosure. He finally concluded, "I cannot today take seriously the mysterious nonsense that others have already unveiled and which my reason refuses to consider a secret." Nonetheless, his reading of and reaction to his initiation are neither simple nor unambiguous. Discussing the case of an aspirant initiated after him, he reveals how much the experience and response of individuals could differ. Moreover, Guillaumou himself took compagnonnage very seriously and as a novice had very high expectations of its ceremonies: "I had heard so much exalted talk and celebration of the joy of the compagnons' mysteries that I thought they would put me in seventh heaven." Finally, despite his disillusionment, he remained a compagnon and continued to fight for the recognition of the shoemakers. Guillaumou's reactions to and comments about his initiation are even more important than the details he provides—details that will now seem quite familiar.

Guillaumou was received in Nîmes at Christmastime in 1833 in the midst of a citywide strike in a number of trades. The shoemakers had joined the strike and only five compagnons and about a dozen aspirants were left in town. Deciding to go ahead with his initiation, Guillaumou borrowed twenty francs from his parents and used ten francs he had saved to pay for his board at the Mère to cover the thirty-franc reception fee. The appointed night, he arrived all dressed up at the Mère at about ten thirty. There he met another aspirant, Rochefort, who was also going to *faire le saut* (make the jump). Guillaumou, punningly noted that if you changed the spelling to *sot* (fool), it would have been more on the mark, but Rochefort was *enchanté* by the whole idea. The initiation itself began at midnight, when two compagnons appeared with canes and ribbons. As the eldest aspirant in the city, Guillaumou went first. His hat was removed, and the compagnons made as if to undo his hair. Guillaumou thought this was quite droll since he had a short haircut and not the longer hairstyle, drawn up in a ribbon, common in the eighteenth and early nineteenth century. He followed the compagnons into a room that he knew to be the Mère's attic. He said (obviously from later experience) that the room wasn't really suited for the ceremony; usually it was conducted in a basement with several "compartments." At the back of the attic was a temple made out of bedsheets. Guillaumou handed over all his personal effects and agreed to be blindfolded "without any emotion." Then began a series of tests; Guillaumou presents himself as always being a step or two ahead of his initiators, cleverly seeing through most of the traps set for him.

He was led around the attic, being made to lower his head or raise his feet high to avoid obstacles—"nocturnal gymnastics that began to bore me a bit." His guide then led him to the temple where there followed three "knocks" on the sheets; Guillaumou tells us knowingly that someone obviously hit the table or the floor. He endured some more twists and turns around the room to the accompaniment of noise and howls, and the odor and smoke of incense were beginning to suffocate him. Finally, he was pushed into a chair and his interrogation by the premier compagnon (whose voice Guillaumou recognized) began. One of Guillaumou's tests challenged his religious loyalties. Asked if he were a Catholic, Guillaumou answered that he wasn't devout but had received the sacraments. The compagnons told him most novices were like him and that compagnonnage was a religion much older than Christianity which had "preserved its purity across the ages." After lecturing Guillaumou for a while, the compagnons proposed that he quit Christ for the compagnons' religion. Guillaumou thought "the logic dubious . . . [and] saw a trap." He responded that although he was a bad Catholic, it was the religion of his father and mother whom he dearly loved; to renounce it seemed a crime. He said he wanted to accept the compagnons' religion but had to know its principles first. Guillaumou thought the compagnons seemed embarrassed by this answer; they threatened to throw him out. He was violently seized and knocked about the room a bit more. Guillaumou became impatient and began to resist. He was sternly told he didn't know where he was; to which he said, "By God! I'm in the père's attic, and all your fuss is wearing me out and boring me." Eventually, the compagnons, satisfied with his firm resolve, brought him back to the temple. They told him all this had been a test. "I suspected as much," Guillaumou reports dryly.

Guillaumou recounts one other major test: he was asked if he would be willing to counterfeit money should the society need funds. He again suspected a trap and refused, knowing the "society too honest for any such crime, one severely punished by law." This attitude apparently offended the compagnons, who all agreed to put Guillaumou out; one, however, said that Guillaumou now knew too much, and it would be better to strangle him. He was lifted from his seat and someone actually began to choke him hard. Guillaumou claims he didn't take this threat seriously, but when the stranglehold continued, he had some doubts and resisted. Tearing off his blindfold and grabbing his chair, he began to fight "like a devil." When the compagnons finally calmed him down and brought him back in the temple (quite a bit the worse for wear), the rest of the tests went quickly. The most affecting part of the initiation for Guillaumou seems to have been when he was told the story of the brave Mouton Coeur de Lion, who, "for devotion to compagnonnage," died in prison in Rochefort for a crime he didn't commit. Guillaumou was impressed with this "severe virtue" and thought he would be equal to such sacrifices for the *société*—all the while inwardly reserving the right to act according to his free will.

The oath was similar to the shoemakers' seventeenth-century oath but even closer to the oaths recited by the other trades condemned in that century. Guillaumou rose to repeat it after the premier compagnon: "I swear before God and the compagnons listening, never to divulge to father, mother, brother, sister, or to anyone, the secrets confided to me. Not to engrave them on stone, marble, or any metal." Again with irony Guillaumou adds, "They didn't mention paper." After repeating the oath three times, he was warned that anyone who betrays it deserves "*Death!*"—and the other compagnons swore to this. Finally the "neophyte" was asked what he wished and was prompted in a whisper by another compagnon, "The light!" The blindfold was removed, and in the blinding light of seven candles standing on the temple's improvised altar, the candidate usually found he had sworn his oath on a crucifix.

Guillaumou repeated his oath yet again, and then, kneeling, received his colors. The red one represented "Maître Jacques' blood, shed for the good of all, in the plains of Provence." The other ribbon, blue, represented the "union and concord that reigns in the tour de France among all the compagnons." Guillaumou had to admit that this meaning was "more beautiful than true." He chose three compagnons, a godfather, godmother, and *curé*, each of whom proposed a new name.[57] He was flattered by the name "ami du courage" proposed by a fourth compagnon, but finally picked his godfather's choice, "le bien-aimé du tour de France," both to please his sponsor and because he believed the name united the best traits of all the proposed names. He was then baptized "in the name of the Father, the Son, and the Holy Spirit . . . brave compagnon, enfant de Maître Jacques." But Guillaumou's tests were not quite finished: he was made to drink a large "chalice" full of wine, water, and a large quantity of pepper and salt. He reports drinking the cup "boldly" down to the last drop, "disguising as much as possible the grimace that this horrible drink produced." His colors were pinned to his chest, and he received the "kiss of alliance from [his] new brothers" who assured him he was now a compagnon. Guillaumou skeptically remarks, "I was obliged to believe it. However, I doubted it." The whole ceremony had taken about an hour and a half, but Guillaumou had to wait outside the chamber until Rochefort's initiation ended. Newly re-

57. I have found no seventeenth-century references to curés (see p. 89, fn. 14); eighteenth-century usage is rare, but the term appears in, e.g., *traits carrés* (AMM, B 1309/73, 10 November 1760, compagnons charpentiers [du devoir]).

ceived compagnons could not attend receptions of aspirants in their cohort.

While waiting, Guillaumou questioned a compagnon about the "mysteries," but with little result. The compagnon found him too curious and told him he would learn more shortly and the rest while on his travels. Guillaumou concluded that this compagnon, like so many others, really "didn't know anything." When he was finally let back into the chamber he found a very pale, shaken, and even ill Rochefort, who was "so overcome with emotion" that he barely had the strength to tell Guillaumou his new name, Francoeur. The two new compagnons then had to kneel quite a long time on the tile floor, in front of the altar, first to hear the reading of *la morale* and then to receive and learn the symbolism of their *affaires* (diplomas). The lecture essentially recounted the story of Maître Jacques's assassination at the hands of the *margageats* (rebels). The compagnons were told to pardon these schismatics, "tormented as they were by remorse." Guillaumou found much of this tedious; he was tired and his knees hurt. The ceremony ended with the entry into the chamber of some compagnons visiting from another city. At the time he had thought that the ceremony was all right, but "I confess that I expected better."

Guillaumou's later reflections on these initiations were somewhat more positive and granted their moral purpose. He accepted the necessity of examining proposed members on their capabilities, conduct, and finances. The tests taken while blindfolded represented one's passage through "the tortuous roads . . . of life with the ignorance of inexperience." To gauge character, moral worth, and loyalty, seductive traps were laid, enabling the compagnons to learn about the aspirant's resolve to do good or evil. Guillaumou thought these tests also guarded the novice against vice and kept him from the "weaknesses afflicting humanity." He thus found the initiation's *intentions* praiseworthy but questioned whether most compagnons were able to translate and understand them properly in the actual ceremony. Furthermore, he objected to useless aggravations and believed aspirants ought not to be endangered or injured. Initiations too often became "saturnalia" and lost their serious purpose. One of his most damning conclusions was that these "so-called *secrets*" were counterproductive: "They can only encourage dangerous prejudices [and] stand in the way of the development of harmony and intelligence which the working class needs to perfect its skills and create for itself the place its importance demands in the great human society."

Yet, we cannot leave Guillaumou's observations about initiations without juxtaposing them to those of another contemporary compagnon. Pierre Ameline (born 1812), a compagnon boilermaker, who wrote his memoirs in the 1840s, revealed very different sentiments about his initiation, which took place in 1839. Ameline, from a relatively comfortable rural background, became a highly skilled worker who built and repaired engines and distilling machinery. Although he did not discuss the details of his initiation, he called the time during which he created his masterpiece and underwent his reception "the week I cherish and esteem most of my life. I could only appreciate it as I grew older."[58] To this testimony we can add Guillaumou's comments on the initiation of Rochefort who was "enchanted" with the whole idea of the initiation and also quite shaken up by the tests and the hazing that Guillaumou took in stride. Guillaumou, however, presents Rochefort as a sort of trusting (if not simpleminded) rural fellow—which might have been a typical view held by urban workers.

Thus, it becomes exceedingly difficult to know how compagnons in general reacted to their initiations. As bizarre or foolish as these rituals may have seemed to some in the postrevolutionary world, the middle-class fraternal associations that prospered in the same era performed rites that could be considered equally inane. To return to Jean-Baptiste Arnaud, whose words opened this chapter, the ceremonies, legends, and symbols of compagnonnage were "ridiculous" and its secrecy "incompatible with progress." He recognized, however, that the most critical problem was how workers used their symbols: as long as such emblems "were tied to absurd prerogatives, we will always be divided and unfortunate."[59]

GENERAL CONSIDERATIONS ON BECOMING A COMPAGNON

The initiation accounts and origin narratives of compagnonnage illustrate at least three critical areas of understanding: first, the importance of these texts and practices for individual compagnons; second, their importance for the community of compagnonnage, its unities and disunities; and finally, the historically constructed and variable nature of supposedly immutable practices and texts. The individual experienced the transformation of initiation through the sequential phases of the ritual process. Separation removed novices from their usual social posi-

58. Désert, "Mémoires," no. 2: 170.
59. Arnaud, Mémoires, foreword, n.p.

tions; transition prepared them for their new lives as compagnons; incorporation placed them as changed beings in a new society and more fully instructed them in that society's beliefs. The ritual subjects' characteristics were ambiguous during the liminal phase; they were in a cultural realm with few or none of the attributes of their past or coming states. They could no longer be associated with the normal roles or positions attributed to similar beings in either the society they were leaving or the one they were entering. In the drama of the ritual, novices forsook family, country, religion—in effect, their social and cultural pasts. A liminal person, furthermore, possessed nothing: novice compagnons gave up some or all of their property: pockets were emptied; part or all of their clothing was removed; they had no insignia or titles indicative of particular ranks or roles. Ordeals and humiliations rendered them passive, humble, and willing to accept punishment.

Such trials worked to destroy novices' previous status. They shaped new beings who could cope with new responsibilities while warning them against the abuse of their new privileges and knowledge. During the liminal phase the novices lost their position on the social scale; they were stripped of their old attributes and subjected to a temporary drop in status—"a lowering in order to go higher."[60] Reaggregated into a new society, the compagnon was given new rights and obligations; he was expected to learn the norms and beliefs of compagnonnage as encoded in origin narratives and to uphold the devoir. Theoretically, the new compagnon became an equal in a powerful all-male brotherhood, obliged to render mutual aid, respect, and "love" to his brothers. Yet, at least by the early nineteenth century, this brotherhood was more formally hierarchical than before, and members could advance only slowly in rank.

Initiation was the first and perhaps most important step in creating a community of compagnons who would serve their society well; narratives of their origins and beliefs reinforced this community. The very existence of this illegal association was essentially dependent on its members' loyalty and discretion in the face of secular or religious investigations. As seen, compagnons sometimes broke their oaths or made fun of their beliefs; yet, neither church nor state was able to suppress compagnonnage permanently. And there is some negative evidence on the efficacy of these oaths: information on the symbolic practices of compagnonnage is limited.

The initiation, in whole and parts, along with the recitation and singing of legends served an even more vital function than secrecy for com-

60. Turner, *Ritual Process*, pp. 95, 103.

pagnonnage. Such practices and texts created a strong sense of legitimacy for this unauthorized association in the framework of the highly structured corporate society of early modern France. This need for legitimation intensified in the nineteenth century when the demise of corporate society made it more difficult for any group to retain its corporate identity. Lacking church or state sanction, compagnons used initiations, songs, and narratives to forge powerful, moral communities worthy of their members' loyalty.

Furthermore, initiation accounts and origin narratives reveal compagnonnage to be an institution bound by many of the same principles and symbols found in other corporate groups in old regime France. Before 1789 many journeymen took oaths of allegiance when entering confraternities; almost all had been baptized, had received Holy Communion, and knew the common Christian symbols. Like the church, compagnonnage claimed the power to damn those unfaithful to it; like the state, it pursued and punished those who broke its laws. Moreover, as seen in some late eighteenth- and nineteenth-century initiations and narratives, the infusion of Masonic elements enhanced these workingmen's brotherhoods with a sense of legitimacy, status, and importance. Compagnonnage adapted shared cultural materials not to integrate itself into French society but rather to make itself into an established and comprehensible association.

Finally, the degree to which the rituals and narratives underwent historical change remains a somewhat open question. The available documentation—particularly the initiation accounts of the joiners and locksmiths du devoir de liberté, the carpenters du devoir, and the two examples of the chamois dressers du devoir—indicates that initiations were altered in new directions sometime in the late eighteenth and nineteenth centuries. As seen in the last chapter, part of the chamois dressers' aims in revising their rituals was to make them more meaningful to their postrevolutionary members. This early nineteenth-century ritual largely exchanged one symbolic language for another, the Christian for the Masonic. It also substituted a hierarchy based on random chance for one based on seniority. And as noted, the chamois dressers may even have developed a third form of initiation, another significant revision adding the dimension of physical hazing not apparent in either previous version.

In the case of the chamois dressers these symbolic modifications appear to have been intentional and more abrupt ruptures than evolutionary transformations. Mary Ann Clawson has uncovered one possible motivation for "tinkering" with symbolic materials. In fraternal orders in the United States she finds that "the chief product distinguishing one order from another was the ritual. . . .The orders altered and revised their rituals periodically in attempts to make them more appealing and thus to improve their competitive position."[61] But it is not evident that most societies of compagnonnage were as deliberate about making these modifications as in Clawson's study.

Compagnons' musings and writings about origins are a more compelling case of the conscious desire to explain how and why differentiation occurred as well as to construct who they (and the "others") were. Similarly, whether planned or accidental, distinctions that appeared in ritual practice were central to the identity of each society of compagnonnage. Differentiation seems to have accelerated in the nineteenth century, encouraged perhaps by competitive pressures from other kinds of labor associations and the deskilling of trades. The very harshness of the compagnon du devoir's initiation, for example, could have had a desirable short-term effect of limiting the numbers of highly skilled carpenters. At the same time, it seems apparent that a not insignificant number of young men accepted—perhaps even welcomed—these ordeals as a means of proving their honor and virility and were proud of having endured and "passed." Even the skeptical Guillaumou wanted to be "tough" in his initiation. He fought back, showed no pain, and contrasted himself favorably to his pale and shaken co-initiate.

Whatever their precise historical evolution, these practices and texts all reveal an inner dynamic of synchrony and diachrony; more critically, both initiations and narratives display the compagnons' ability to fashion complex cultural "products." These rituals, from the seventeenth to the nineteenth century, moreover, had an important continuity of meaning and function. They fraternally joined an aspirant to his fellow compagnons and made him responsible to his devoir. In this sense initiations do not vary dramatically over these two centuries. The late eighteenth- and nineteenth-century initiation accounts differ from earlier ones perhaps less in terms of content than in terms of the cultural context, which was increasingly unconducive to their performance.

Each of these later initiations also provides information on the beliefs of the particular society of compagnonnage. For example, in Pradelle's account, initiation elevated the new compagnon's status with dramatic symbolic displays while locating him in a hierarchical and ordered system. This initiation's Masonic language and practice also tended to el-

---

61. Clawson, *Constructing Brotherhood*, p. 17 and chap. 7, where she discusses the mechanics of this process.

evate the status of this compagnonnage by associating it with an elite organization. The initiation firmly established the society's power over its members and impressed the initiate with his obligations.

Authority in this case, however, unlike the carpenters' initiation, is exhibited far more symbolically than physically. Which form of "instruction" had the greater impact on the novice? Pradelle, for example, notes more esoteric details were only revealed to the new compagnon after the ceremony; young renards immediately felt the trace of the "Z" on their backs—and bore the physical mark of their initiation. But both novices were probably affected by the pomp and complexity of their own ceremony, and most likely, neither fully understood its meaning, as Guillaumou claimed. Whether they thought it impressive, annoying, or foolish, novices had to submit to initiation in order to enter into compagnonnage and receive its benefits and protections.

The chamois dressers' early nineteenth-century revision of their initiation is a valuable account because it articulates an attempt to make ritual comprehensible and meaningful by the reform of language. Piron believed the initiate should learn the meaning of the symbols used. Significantly, Piron's society was attempting to reduce a growing authoritarian and hierarchical emphasis in compagnonnage, even though the 1767 initiation account of this association was not particularly marked by these tendencies. As Piron himself noted, his reforms were responding to both positive and negative effects of the Revolution. In sharp contrast to this approach, compagnon carpenters du devoir renewed a commitment to authority and hierarchy both in the claims they asserted as a society of compagnonnage and in their rituals. According to Connay, senior members were allowed to humiliate novices and abuse them physically. Novices were kept in a transitional state for nine days, repeatedly forced to prove their worth and only gradually incorporated into the society. The account of the shoemakers' initiation falls somewhere in between these two, with its desire to retain the mystery of initiation (including its tests) while providing some analysis of its meaning. Yet, even when a society of compagnonnage satisfied at least some of the aspirants' questions about its rituals, curious and intelligent workers (such as Guillaumou) still might not be content or convinced. If some initiations became harsher at the end of the nineteenth century, perhaps it was an attempt, in a more skeptical age, to retain the mystery and enforce the blind obedience compagnons believed necessary.

Variations in initiation accounts and origin narratives tell us something of the economic and social needs and the cultural context of compagnonnages. Although further study of particular trades might reveal specific events influential in the creation of distinctions between them, many differences appear to have been randomly generated or chosen in opposition to the practices of another devoir or trade. Although initiations did not change radically, they were gradually transformed, becoming more elaborate and more secular as compagnonnage entered the nineteenth century. The revolutionary era, as a time when compagnons were more effectively silenced than ever before, was a critical period for this process of adaptation and resistance to new cultural practices.

The same differentiation, creation of solidarity and worth, and cultural preservation and transformation are evident in origin narratives. All the legends glorify skilled labor, but they use different historical, cultural, and spiritual contexts to create varying images of compagnonnage. The contradictions between the two major variants are never resolved in the narratives themselves. Different versions of these narratives existed, to be thought about and puzzled over without ever being completely integrated. The initiation ritual, on the other hand, often had to assimilate divergent traditions and symbolisms—for example, Christian and Masonic—in one performance. As a dynamic performance susceptible to immediate response and reaction, the initiation may have been more sharply influenced by cultural change and pressures. Nevertheless, it is the origin narratives, not the initiation accounts, that more explicitly confront contemporary issues—changes in modes of production, skill levels, and the organization of labor—albeit through the filters of the temple of Solomon or the cathedral of Orléans.

Origin narratives and initiation rituals—the key charters of compagnonnage—were open to various transformations throughout its history. Although initiations and legends articulated ties with the past, compagnons were not isolated or alienated from contemporary contexts. Nevertheless, there were real limits to their ability to change the value and meaning given to work and its organization. The brotherhoods fostered positive beliefs in mutuality, the dignity of labor, artisanal creativity, and resistance to exploitation by masters, bosses, or the market. Yet, the inflexibilities of compagnonnage were clearly problematic: its societies excluded many workers, restricted its younger members' status and power, and emphasized male bonding in a manner that encouraged aggression and tended to distance compagnons from "decent" women (except as tolerant mères) and family (except as pseudosons and pseudobrothers).

The initiation and origin accounts thus reveal much about issues confronting artisan members and *their* perceptions, choices, and responses. The origin narratives, particularly in the nineteenth century, when they were fully articulated, had an especially strong resonance for compagnons. All these texts emphasize the need to create order, protect skilled workers, and fight threats from competitors, rebels, and usurpers. Yet, more extensive knowledge about compagnonnage, spread by Perdiguier and other compagnons who sang and wrote about it, may have turned some workers—members and nonmembers—away from it, just as it motivated others to try to reform it and still others to defend its "traditions." In the event, compagnons generally chose to maintain rather than transform their associations profoundly, a choice which meant compagnonnage would not serve as the vehicle for a progressive, united labor movement. Yet, whatever compagnons did not do, they did create—as artisans and mythmakers. They told not the tale others might have wished to hear but one that compelled attention nonetheless, for it was a history constructed and reconstructed out of their practice of compagnonnage as brothers, rivals, and members of the wider culture.

CHAPTER 9

Epilogue and Conclusion

> This insatiable thirst for profit, this frenetic desire for gold
> is the essence of . . . *competition*. It seizes all, destroys all and
> devours all for its own benefit!!! What then will become of
> the unfortunate worker????
>
> —CC. passants charpentiers, 1843

I began my story of compagnonnage with the glory and fraternal emotion of 1848. At least superficially, the great reconciliation symbolized the aims that the Revolution would bring all France: liberty, equality, a new unity. Yet, the compagnons' hopes for reform and reconciliation were dashed, as were, less permanently, the hopes of the working class as a whole. Compagnonnage proved unable to heal its divisions or to enact far-reaching reform, more for internal than for external reasons. After 1848 the visibility and strength of this old labor association generally declined. Although compagnonnage remained powerful in several trades until the early twentieth century, one scholar has called 1848 "an apotheosis that crowned and put an end to its temporal existence."[1]

1848 AND THE SPIRIT OF RECONCILIATION

My initial discussion of the reconciliation of compagnonnage in 1848 was framed largely in the optimistic views of those outside the organization. As my subsequent analysis of the practices and perspective of the compagnons themselves has demonstrated, however, any serious reform would have required a profound remaking of these brotherhoods. Lasting unity between the sects would have required a realistic assessment of their most critical problems: divisions that cross-cut trades; hostility be-

---

1. Rémi Gossez, "Le Compagnonnage en 1848 d'après des documents inédits," *Compagnonnage* (May 1950): 7.

tween novices and established members; elitism that rejected many types of workers and trades; conflicts between reformers and reactionaries; and finally, beliefs and practices that created and reinforced obstacles to unity and reform. Given these odds, why would anyone think reform and reconciliation possible? Perhaps compagnons and outsiders alike misjudged the depth of the divisions. Perhaps reformers counted on Perdiguier or the Revolution itself to solve all their problems.

Certainly, some compagnons could forcefully articulate the social dangers of an unregulated economy, with its "insatiable thirst for profit," driven by blind, all-encompassing competition, regardless of workers' heightened misery.[2] The problem for compagnonnage would be to control similarly destructive rivalry and competition in their own midst. In 1840 a compagnon wrote to Perdiguier: "There are things in compagnonnage which have become ridiculous [and] one must keep in step with the times. . . .The trouble is that each *corps d'état* is marching alone, as individuals, while we must march together, collectively. However, I am convinced that the Compagnons du Devoir will unite, and that this antipathy which exists among the various trades, will disappear confronted by the reason of wise and enlightened men."[3]

And once the Revolution began, the spirit of "marching collectively" seemed to have no limits. Even Albigeois le bien aimé, the diehard antireformer and author of *Les Bêtises de la régéneration de compagnonnage,* had what might be called a conversion experience in 1848. His "Marseillaise de l'Union ouvrière" went well beyond the reformist hymns in praise of unification and reform of compagnonnage in the image of the new republic. Albigeois spoke passionately to every member of the working classes on the urgent need to break down *all* rivalries. Evoking the miserable conditions of labor for the *prolétaires* under the "yoke of tyranny," he threatened "the monsters who have abased us," presenting "the worker whose arms flashed in the eyes of the despots of France." He urged that "all talent, all industry, Devoir, attribute, foundation, be mingled in the union created in honor of the nation."[4]

That a proud carpenter and bon drille such as Albigeois could undergo this radical political shift must have been both heartening and

2. Les CC. [Compagnons] passants charpentiers à leurs FF:: du vrai Compag:: de l'aimable tour de France, *Notice historique sur le compagnonage* [sic] *primitif, comme base fondamentale des sociétés* (Paris, 1843), p. 31.

3. Agricol Perdiguier, *Le Livre du compagnonnage, contenant des chansons de compagnons, un dialogue sur l'architecture, un raisonnement sur le trait, une notice sur le compagnonnage, la rencontre de deux frères, et un grand nombre de notes,* 2d ed., 2 vols. (Paris, 1841), 2:76, letter from Varnier, dit Beau désir le gascon, compagnon *cloutier* du devoir, 11 October 1840.

4. Albe Bernard (called Albigeois le bien aimé), "La Marseillaise de l'Union ouvrière," in *Chansons compagnonniques composées par le citoyen Dénat, dit La franchise de Castelnaudary,* ed. Dénat (Paris, n.d. [1848]), pp. 5–7.

troubling to those who wanted a powerful and united compagnonnage. Would compagnonnage be the workers' union or would it be superseded and engulfed by that union? The compagnons' dramatic demonstrations of solidarity on 20 March at the place de la République and 21 May at the Fête de la Concorde—of peace and labor—swept away divisions by the power of emotion, but constructing a united compagnonnage and defining its relationship to the rest of the working class would require many hours of mundane meetings and debates that tended to dissolve unity in a sea of discord. Such everyday efforts, less dramatic than the great "journées," were also somewhat less ephemeral. Most notably, compagnons in Paris founded the Club des compagnons de tous les devoirs réunis to serve as the major vehicle for reform and reconciliation. The club, explicitly open to the rites and devoirs of all trades, was the major organizing force behind the impressive patriotic demonstration of 20 March: its first manifesto invited compagnons of all sects and trades to meet for the public march, asking that "the veil of forgetfulness separate us from a sad and bloody past, and that the hand of Fraternity guide us henceforth toward a shining future." The writers exhorted compagnons to show France and even the rest of Europe that compagnonnage "had not always been rightly appreciated and that it also could understand the way of progress." Beyond this, the organizing committee of the club proposed a list of candidates for the Constituent Assembly.[5]

Among the most dynamic leaders of the club were Dénat (La franchise de Castelnaudary), a compagnon stonecutter of the devoir de liberté, president of the organizing committee, and Toussaint Guillaumou, the secretary, who had tirelessly led the shoemakers' fight for official recognition. Perdiguier was also a member, but after his election to the Constituent Assembly, he became more involved in politics and the social question on a national level. His own energy and personal integrity, combined with the celebrity he enjoyed from his writings and the patronage of George Sand, had made him a strong candidate for the assembly. Resoundingly elected both for the constituency of the Seine and for that of his native Vaucluse, he chose to represent Paris, believing that he would be more accessible to the needs of the working class.[6] Perdiguier's prominence was a source of pride and publicity for the compagnons and lent great prestige to their plans, even as he moved away from the immediate concerns of compagnonnage.

5. *Aux compagnons de tous les devoirs et de tous les corps d'état* (Paris, n.d. [1848]). Gossez, "Compagnonnage en 1848" (May 1950): 7.
6. Anfos Martin, *Agricol Perdiguier, dit Avignonnais-la-vertu: Sa vie, son oeuvre, et ses écrits* (Cavaillon, 1904), p. 165. Martin cites a letter written by Perdiguier to his electors in the Vaucluse, 13 May 1848.

Guillaumou, wounded on the barricades of the Palais Royal in February, devoted himself to the logistics of unification. That he could still believe in this possibility after the shoemakers' travails and rejections says as much about the intense attachment many compagnons had for their societies as it does for the spirit of 1848. Nonetheless, Guillaumou wanted a compagnonnage that would benefit all workers, a society informed with republican ideals and zealous in their defense. Although not elected to the assembly, he remained an active participant in the short-lived Second Republic. Guillaumou may also have had a key role in composing the address presented to the provisional government on 20 March. In any event, according to Jean Briquet, Perdiguier had little direct influence on those "fiery words" that portrayed compagnons, "blackened with the gunpowder of the barricades" and swearing to uphold the republic, serve the "Common Mother," and repulse tyranny.[7] The speech's passionate rhetoric and emphasis on willing sacrifice sought to absolve compagnons' past errors and grant them a united future in *this* republic. Their incessant battles, they said, had perhaps been instigated by the successive governments of "the past half century," eager to divide or corrupt a "mass of united workers which could have been an obstacle to their plans." In themselves, the authors asserted, the societies of compagnonnage were "entirely democratic, teaching virtue, humanity, and fraternity."[8]

The roughly eight thousand to ten thousand men drawn from twenty societies of compagnonnage, who had participated in the procession, seemed a living testimony to the sincerity of these words. The *Démocratie pacifique* found it significant that only a day earlier, on 19 March, the compagnon carpenters had celebrated their traditional patronal day of Saint Joseph. In a sense this *particular* festival was a partial catalyst for the moving and *general* display of brotherhood witnessed the next day: "Under the influence of yesterday's festival, and above all of a revolution made in the name of fraternity, compagnons of all the devoirs, rivals and almost enemies up to this day, embraced each other while forswearing all their quarrels."[9] But as the fervor of 20 March dissipated, the Club des compagnons faced severe obstacles to implementing the ideals expressed in the address to the provisional government.

Only twelve of the twenty societies that had participated in the procession sent representatives to the next planning meeting of the club.

7. Jean Briquet, *Agricol Perdiguier: Compagnon du Tour de France et Répresentant du Peuple (1805–1875)* (Paris, 1981), p. 226. The complete text of this address appears in Cynthia M. Truant, "Compagnonnage: Symbolic Action and the Defense of Workers' Rights in France, 1700–1848" (Ph.D. diss., University of Chicago, 1978), appendix 1, p. 319.

8. AN BB³⁰ 300, pièce 1848.

9. *La Démocratie pacifique*, 21 March 1848, unpaginated [page 3].

The constitution that emerged from the club's normally moderate and peaceable deliberations remained far from the "radical fusion of all the Compagnonnages" which Guillaumou identified as its initial goal.[10] Concerned with maintaining something of each devoir's and trade's sovereignty and traditions, the delegates came up with an ambiguous articulation of institutional relationships within a loose confederation. One member proposed the creation of a small central committee to consist of seven permanent members (article 13) plus a delegate from each society. Under this plan there would also be regional committees in the major cities of the tour de France. The role of these committees, however, was not well defined; they seemed destined to be centers for information exchange rather than decision making.[11]

Article 12, which dealt with economic relations between compagnons of different societies on the tour de France, provided virtually the only concrete statement of aims. It decreed that all compagnons of whatever devoir or society would be allowed to work in all parts of France and that there would be no further banishments or brawls. The constitution clearly acknowledged that competition between workers in the same trade harmed all workers and benefited employers. Thus, "no society will be allowed to work in any region with the intention of competing with its brothers [*frères*] to lower the price of work simply to facilitate the placement [of a particular sect] in that region."[12] The compagnons actively attempted to adapt their thinking and practice to the economic and social realities facing them. Nevertheless, their fundamental labor strategy remained control of hiring. This approach did not necessarily entail limitation of numbers of compagnons and societies or the perpetuation of hierarchical divisions among the membership, but the constitution's framers failed to confront these issues in the document. Similarly, nothing was said about accepting less-skilled workers into compagnonnage or about the increased job competition among skilled workers. Lack of attention to these points reveals that there were no tangible plans to expand the scope or increase the membership of compagnonnage.

As the Club des compagnons worked on its constitution in April and May, members joined a wide spectrum of compagnons and other workers to prepare for the Fête de la Concorde on 21 May. Perhaps they believed the massive, peaceful demonstration of all labor might bring a large number of compagnons together again as had the reunion of 20 March. The May demonstration might provide the élan to advance the tedious

10. Briquet, *Agricol Perdiguier,* p. 228.
11. Gossez, "Compagnonnage en 1848" (April 1950): 6 and (May 1950): 7.
12. Ibid. (May 1950): 7.

practical work of unification, and might inspire compagnons to "fit" themselves into the larger "family of workers" as Pagnerre had exhorted them to do on 20 March.[13] Dénat (now president of the club) wrote the "Marseillaise des compagnons de tous les devoirs réunis," and thousands of copies of this rousing appeal for immediate "*re*-unification" were printed and distributed along the parade route on 21 May. Dénat's anthem spoke not of blood or rising up against the ferocious enemy but of compagnons, no longer divided by "categories," "marching under the same standard," forgetting their discord and being united in "peace" and "love."

> We have crossed the barrier to the place
> Where holy Fraternity
> Has shown us from afar her banner,
> held in the hands of Liberty. (repeat)
> If someone out of weakness
> Refuses to be our friend,
> Let us wait for him to be become strong
> And let us guide him by wisdom.

> Nous avons franchi la barrière,
> Où la sainte Fraternité
> Nous montrait de loin sa bannière
> Dan les mains de la Liberté. (bis)
> Si quelqu'un voulait par faiblesse
> Refuser d'être notre ami,
> Attendons qu'il soit affermi
> Et guidons-le par la sagesse.

Dénat's language fused Christian love and republican virtue; he hailed united compagnons who practiced fraternity and called out "Long live Equality" as a "sublime example to the world."[14]

The roughly three hundred thousand men and women of the working classes who paraded through Paris from nine in the morning until late evening on 21 May seemed to their observers to be inspired by a similar sort of vision. Press reports portrayed this mass of citizens in glowing terms. The *Démocratie pacifique* constructed and then deconstructed oppositions among participants and spectators: "The bourgeoisie and the proletariat, the people and the army, men and women, all the classes of the population, of the French nation, vied with each other in enthusi-

13. *Le Moniteur universel*, 21 March 1848, p. 651.
14. Dénat, "La Marseillaise des compagnons," in *Chansons compagnonniques*, pp. 1–2.

asm, union, and devotion to the republican fatherland."[15] The immense spectacle was an intense moment of unity and equality, but within a few weeks, many looked back on it as poignant but also naive and doomed. The Fête de la Concorde was the last of the massive, nonviolent demonstrations of the working classes in the Revolution; it took place as radicalism was increasing among workers and only days after the failed invasion of the assembly (15 May). The elections in April had put a conservative Constituent Assembly in place, and now, the day before the festival, the assembly openly began debating the fate of the workshops. In the days and weeks after the festival, as the workers' anger and fears grew, the words of Dénat's anthem, urging peaceful social transformation and distancing the rhetoric of violent revolution, took on overtones of nostalgia. Yet, Dénat's language and imagery formed a powerful strand of the revolutionary discourse, and many held to his ideals until June. But with the abolition of the workshops on 21 June and the bloody insurrection of 24–26 June the militancy of Albigeois's "Marseillaise" came to seem far more appropriate.

Dénat's belief in the power of reason and love could not produce the miracle of "holy Union" even for the societies of compagnnonage, much less for all workers. The club's constitution was in essence complete before the insurrection of 24–26 June but the chaos of those days and the repressions that followed put aside approval and implementation for months. In October 1848 the "Constitution fraternelle compagnonnique et sociale des devoirs réunis" was signed in Paris by fifteen compagnons who represented five trades and each of the three rites. The constitution was not submitted for general ratification until March 1849 when thirty-five societies of compagnonnage on the tour de France reviewed its provisions. The opposition was almost immediate. Aspirants and compagnons generally found the proposed reforms too abstract and too sweeping. Even though the constitution had actually done little to reorganize compagnonnage, it had failed to include safeguards for the rights of individual societies. Most feared that one powerful trade in the region would come to dominate all the others. Aspirants were dissatisfied with the constitution's almost total disregard of their specific problems and complaints, and the reactionary members opposed the entire document, claiming it changed too much. When the final vote for reconciliation was taken, twenty societies abstained, eight voted for, and seven against.[16] Guillaumou believed the constitution, although imperfect,

15. *La Démocratie pacifique*, 22 May 1848, p. 1; see also the *Moniteur*, 23 May 1848, pp. 1123–24.

16. Emile Coornaert, *Les Compagnonnages en France du Moyen Age à nos jours* (Paris, 1966), p. 76.

would eventually have "made way for an era of fraternity and force in compagnonnage that the times seemed to favor—especially given the influence of the highly worthy and active men in all the societies."[17]

The failed constitution was a discouraging conclusion to the years of reform preceding 1848 which accented the tension between the desire for reconciliation and the inability to achieve it. The events of 1848 forced the compagnons who most ardently wished for unity to confront the degree and complexity of change that would be necessary to accommodate meaningful reform. Moreover, while compagnonnage struggled with its internal problems in the years before 1848, competing models of labor organization had become well established, providing a far wider choice of association than was possible at the beginning of the century. Workers could enjoy the benefits of association without submitting to the more negative and less effective practices of compagnonnage. Such workers saw little purpose in reconstructing a form of organization they considered obsolete. Reformist compagnons regretted the loss of workers who might have reinvigorated compagnonnage, without always recognizing how much the compagnonnages had done to drive them away. The Second Empire soon made any dispute over the form of workers' organization moot, and in the series of repressions that followed, many compagnons felt—as perhaps they had during the great Revolution—that security lay in their traditions, however imperfect they might seem to the rest of the working class.

Perdiguier, who had supported the social democratic cause and sat with the Mountain in the assembly, was arrested a few days after the coup d'état in December 1851. He had remained loyal to the working class to the end: in September he had been among the very few members of the assembly to oppose the assault on the ten-hour day.[18] Thus, on 9 January 1852 his name appeared on a list of eighty-four proscribed representatives. Sent into exile, Perdiguier lived first in Belgium, where he wrote his memoirs, and then in Geneva. Although influential friends in Paris—Eléonore Blanc, Ange Guépin, George Sand—offered to negotiate for his pardon, Perdiguier was initially reluctant. He refused, as an innocent man, to dishonor himself by asking pardon of the guilty. Finally, ill health and concerns about the welfare of his family pushed him to accept his friends' intercession. He was pardoned toward the end of 1855 and returned to Paris in early December. Bitter about the overthrow of the republic and discouraged about the decline of compagnon-

---

17. Toussaint Guillaumou, *Les Confessions d'un compagnon* (Paris, 1864), p. 234.

18. Ibid., pp. 170–71. The Mountain of 1848 was named in memory of those Jacobin deputies, followers of Robespierre, who sat in the upper seats of the Convention during the first Republic (1792–94).

nage, he nonetheless mustered the enthusiasm to write and speak about the association almost until his death in 1875.

COMPAGNONNAGE AFTER 1848

With a few exceptions, compagnons wrote little in the nineteenth century about their fleeting engagement in the Revolution of 1848. And no organized attempts at institutional unification were attempted again until the end of that century. Pleas like those of the compagnon baker Jean-Baptiste Arnaud, who in his 1859 memoirs called on the workers of compagnonnage to "sacrifice their idols on the altar of good sense," were generally ignored.[19] Compagnons could not or would not forsake the ritual practices that both informed and divided their brotherhoods. Perdiguier felt sure that rituals could be made to unite compagnonnage. Perhaps he was recalling the festivals of 1848. Yet, when he published the text of his play, Les Gavots et les Devoirants in 1862, its grand scene of "reconciliation" (see frontispiece) was not a recreation of revolutionary days but a model for the future "grands fêtes" of compagnonnage.[20] The play seems to have grown out of an article written earlier the same year in which Perdiguier recalled the terrible battles of compagnonnage, now largely ended, and focused on the "sentiments of union and fraternity" seen in the festivals of various trades of the association.[21] These festivals, sponsored by one sect but embracing guests from rival devoirs, were emotional moments that "brought [compagnons] together, let them know, appreciate, love one another. They serve progress [and] the unity of compagnonnage." These performances were thus not "dreams," but "practical reality."[22] Such celebrations must be the nucleus for general festivals that included all devoirs and rites.

Perdiguier worked out this idea in Les Gavots et les Devoirants. The play, set in the suburbs of a provincial city (in this case Bordeaux) and adamantly not Paris, revolved around a concours (competition of skill) between sects and the "impossible" love of a dévorant for the daughter of a gavot. The play attributes the negative features of compagnonnage to

19. Jean-Baptiste Arnaud, Mémoires d'un compagnon du tour de France, contenant plusieurs dissertations sur le devoir, entre l'auteur et plusieurs compagnons tailleurs de pierre et charpentiers (Rochefort, 1859), foreword, n.p.
20. Agricol Perdiguier, Les Gavots et les Devoirants; ou, La Réconciliation des compagnons (Paris, 1862), especially pp. 69–75, for the scene of reconciliation.
21. Perdiguier, "Les Fêtes patronales dans le compagnonnage: Tailleurs de pierre et autres corps," Le Siècle, 7 January 1862, fol. 2r and v.
22. Ibid., fol. 2v. This conviction may have been informed or reinforced by memories of 1848 when the celebration of the feast day of Saint Joseph preceded and helped invigorate the mass reconciliation of 20 March.

the schism (which Perdiguier dated back to Orléans in 1401), but it neither describes recent history nor proposes practical reforms. The climax, an elaborately staged reconciliation of the "divided families," unites the warring rites by means of another rite—a marriage between the compagnon dévorant and his sweetheart of the gavot sect. The lithograph by Dorléans, printed at the same time as the play, prominently features the women associated with compagnons and compagnonnage (mères, sweethearts, wives) in the foreground. More than a fraternity, compagnonnage was now a family in which married compagnons, their "mothers," and all their founder-fathers (Père Soubise, Solomon, and Maître Jacques)—represented by statues on the dais in the center of the image—represented domestic harmony. This was an important shift from compagnonnage's abortive reconciliation in 1848 where no women had been similarly visible.[23] After the defeats of 1848 Perdiguier may have believed in the need for a familial discourse that represented the domesticating influence of mothers and the wise authority of fathers. Later generations of compagnons may have found this representation appealing, for, at the Musée du Compagnonnage and in some printed documentation, the Dorléans lithograph is captioned " 'La Réconciliation des Compagnons,' place des Vosges, à Paris en 1848."[24] This label, apparently attached in the twentieth century, recasts the lithograph as a revered memento of 1848, one of the most ennobling episodes in the history of compagnonnage.

Neither the memory, the representation, nor the reality of these celebrations created more than ephemeral emotional solidarity. Nevertheless, compagnonnage retained some of its former importance in larger cities, notably in the building trades, through the first decades of the Third Republic. Among carpenters, the enfants de Père Soubise continued to attract a considerable membership to the end of the nineteenth century, despite the enmity of the C.G.T. and the Union des charpentiers. Compagnonnage, said Jean Connay, "no longer responded to the economic necessities of our time and . . . is an instrument of division among workers."[25] Yet, up to World War I many young carpenters still trusted in compagnonnage, despite the probability of severe hazing and

23. Joan Scott convincingly demonstrates the centrality of models of the family and male-female relations in the construction of social(ist) theory. She attentively deconstructs the ambiguities, oppositions, and alliances embedded in these utopian visions. *Gender and the Politics of History* (New York, 1988), pp. 108, 111. Perhaps informed by aspects of this discourse, Perdiguier's play offers compagnons a wider range of choices in family and gender relations.

24. In 1848 the place des Vosges was renamed the place de la République. There are two copies of the lithograph at the Musée du Compagnonnage, one of which is featured in the central entry and the other, better copy, in the section Fêtes et Souvenirs.

25. Jean Connay [Henri Bricheteau], *Le Compagnonnage: Son histoire, ses mystères* (Paris, 1909), p. 6.

humiliation in its initiations. The proponents of modern labor unions found its attractions difficult to accept and harder yet to explain.

In roughly the same era diverse groups of reformers carried on Perdiguier's vision. In the last decade of the nineteenth century, for example, a compagnon blacksmith du devoir, Abel Boyer, realizing that "some homogenization of rites was essential to any collective action," worked to establish the new Union compagnonnique. The 1920s saw some revival of debate and discussion on the future of compagnonnage in new journals such as *Le Compagnonnage du tour de France,* first published in 1919, leading to the establishment of the Fédération générale du compagnonnage in 1922. But the rites continued their disputes and their decline. Neither the Union compagnonnique (1889) or the Fédération générale (1922) accomplished their larger goal as Steven Zdatny defines it, to "reinfuse the life of the working class with the *esprit compagnon.*" Nonetheless, these new associations kept compagnonnage alive, albeit in a limited way, sometimes by becoming a sort of cultural appendage for compagnons who now saw no contradiction in also joining the C.G.T.![26]

In the Vichy era, some compagnons, backed by Pétain, tried to reverse the decline, capitalizing on a supposed bond between Vichy's "corporatism" and the corporate origins of compagnonnage. Jean Bernard, a compagnon stonecutter du devoir and a devout Catholic, was prominent in this effort. In 1941 in Lyon he founded the journal *Compagnonnage,* which portrayed compagnonnage as a lay brotherhood whose members were pious, conservative, obedient, and subservient to the state. Bernard's reconstructed compagnonnage incorporated material from the origin narratives of the compagnons du devoir into his writing and speeches. Mottoes suggestive of order and virtue were scattered throughout the journal. Slogans calling compagnonnage "the most social creation of which I know" and "a civic order of workers" attempted to demonstrate that the association was entirely compatible with the aims of the new regime.[27]

Bernard's vision only tangentially coincided with the past practices and beliefs or the contemporary views of compagnons. The societies of compagnonnage were at once too independent and too complex to be subsumed under Bernard's categories. More critically, societies of compagnonnage had a long historical tradition of resistance to control

---

26. Steven Zdatny, *The Politics of Survival: Artisans in Twentieth-Century France* (Oxford, 1990), pp. 19–20.

27. See, e.g., Jean Bernard, "La Communauté, la règle, l'ordre," *Compagnonnage* (July 1942 and August 1942), pp. 1–3. The first quotation is attributed to Pétain; the second to Bernard. This journal should not be confused with *Le Compagnonnage: Journal mutualiste, professionel, philosophique, et littéraire* (Montauban) which began publication in 1920.

by economic and social "superiors." The traditional and stubborn refusal of compagnonnage's branches to be directed by an established central office of a trade continued even under occupation. Bernard's ideas
thus never dominated the organization as a whole. "His" compagnonnage was known as the Association ouvrière des compagnons du tour de
France. After the war the charge that the Association ouvrière, under
Bernard, had collaborated with Vichy created new ideological obstacles
to unity. And as most members of the Association ouvrière had been
enfants de Maître Jacques, old structural divisions between rites and devoirs were reinforced on new grounds.

Compagnonnage still exists today, still divided into three organizations
that maintain rather separate identities. The divisions, however, differ to
some degree from the historical ones. The Association ouvrière is composed primarily of compagnons du devoir (descendants of the enfants
de Maître Jacques) but also includes other compagnons du devoir who
consider themselves the heirs of the enfants de père Soubise. The former
compagnons du devoir de liberté are now principally organized in the
Fédération compagnonnique des métiers du bâtiment. Finally, the Union compagnonnique, the smallest of the three organizations, includes
members of both devoirs. These new organizations keep some traditions
alive and generate interest in the association and its practices. The Association ouvrière and the Fédération compagnonnique in particular
have prospered in conjunction with restoration projects of French national monuments. Twentieth-century compagnons have also profited
from a resurgence of interest in artisanal crafts and traditions. With government support the Association ouvrière and the Fédération compagnonnique also provide technical training and education for young
craftsmen who still complete a tour de France (or even foreign intern-
ships) and make a chef-d'oeuvre. These compagnons carry on the skills
and practices of earlier centuries while learning new techniques and
modern designs.

THE LEGACIES OF COMPAGNONNAGE

The brotherhoods of compagnonnage grew notably in the eighteenth
century, largely in response to the rise of merchant capitalism and the
expansion of regional economies. Their organizations could sometimes
profit from the vulnerability of masters in the *corporations des métiers* who
needed a steady supply of relatively skilled workers. Yet, master artisans,
themselves often threatened by the cheaper, varied, and more innovative
production of rural and foreign competitors, sought ways to control

workers and reduce their wages and "rights." Moreover, growing divisions in the corporations between large- and small-scale masters, the former working to undermine trade regulations and the latter jealousy guarding their precarious status, tended to ensure that journeymen continued to be dependent workers. Before 1789, unmarried itinerant journeymen remained minors under French law, and they were usually unable to settle down or marry until they had established themselves as masters, an increasingly impossible goal. In these conditions the brotherhoods of compagnonnage played a vital and legitimizing role.

Compagnonnage gave its members an arena in which to oppose masters' paternal power and assert their own status as adult males, thus escaping, to some extent, their dependent status. In the workshop itself compagnons could not always remove themselves from the discipline and training of the shop's head—whether master, mistress, or master's wife. In the eighteenth century, however, by limiting their discourse on and interaction with "fathers" (whether as founders or innkeepers) and by confining most of their contact with women outside the workshop to "mothers" and (sometimes shared) prostitutes, compagnons underplayed their subordination and reinforced the superiority of their fraternity. Although the compagnons' *mères* had a key role in compagnonnage, it was primarily to give care and not to impose discipline. Ultimately, the compagnons' relationship with their mères, even when deeply informed by sentiment, retained its contractual and economic quality. Finally, the compagnons' definitions of labor and honor were gendered male. Their narratives excluded women completely: the most exalted and important forms of work glorified in these narratives required great strength coupled with artistry and skill—qualities almost always defined as masculine. Frequent internecine brawling and bravado further proclaimed the compagnons' virility and defiance of society's attempts to repress their "debaucheries."

The need for fraternal bonding and the rituals used to achieve it may have become more pronounced in the nineteenth century. Their public processions were still very much male affairs, although there was a somewhat greater visibility of mères, as witnessed in the frontispiece and in nineteenth- and twentieth-century group photographs, though not photographs of public rituals.[28] The compagnons' conceptualization of labor and its organization as essentially male domains and their sentimentalization of the women in their (private) lives varied little from contemporary gender constructions. As male bonding and concepts of

28. See, e.g., figs. 5, 6, 8, in Coornaert, *Compagnonnages*. The many photographs on display in the Musée du Compagnonnage in Tours also show that in public *ritual* performances, mères were almost always absent.

fraternity became more politically informed in the early nineteenth century, especially after 1830, so too did the role of female domesticity. For example, although the plays discussed in Chapter 1 were not written by compagnons, they made the women in the compagnons' lives central to the workers' moral regeneration and integration into civilized society. This approach took a fascinating (if not pre-Freudian) twist in the 1884 comic opera, *La Mère des compagnons,* by Henri Chivot and Alfred Duru.[29] The unusually young, pretty mère of the compagnon carpenters ends up marrying a compagnon (when she could have married a viscount) and thus perfectly fuses the roles of wife and "mother," remaining loyal to her "boys" as the mère des compagnons after her marriage.

Like the contradictions between fraternity and domesticity, the tensions between fraternity and political organization became more marked in the nineteenth century. Whereas societies of compagnonnage were slow to adopt democratic political ideologies, many individual compagnons were influenced by the growing politicization of the working classes. Some, such as Agricol Perdiguier, recognized that compagnonnage, as one of the earliest labor associations, could provide a model of interurban labor organization which could function under most conditions of political repression. Compagnonnage actively contested economic and social relations and constructed its own definitions of them. Some beliefs and practices of compagnonnage informed the debates on the social question before 1848; some of its members (or former members) successfully transformed its societies. The members of the Société de l'Union, for example, adapted the fraternal model of compagnonnage under the inspiration of the new political ideas of republicans and socialists in the 1830s and 1840s. The great outpouring of sentiment— from writers, workers, and the general public—which greeted compagnonnage in 1848 bore witness to the popularity of the ideals of solidarity and fraternity. The projected unity of "all its little republics" had a wide appeal. Ironically, however, this tribute came at a moment when compagnonnage was in decline, its major contributions to the labor movement almost at an end. Nevertheless, whether or not compagnonnage contributed directly to the later trade union movement, many labor organizations retained a not insignificant degree of symbolic practice and imagery.[30]

This shrinking of compagnonnage even before 1848, except in a few

29. Henri Chivot and Alfred Duru, *La Mère des compagnons* (Paris, 1884), comic opera in 3 acts and 4 tableaux, first presented in Paris at the theater of the Folies Dramatiques, 15 December 1880.

30. See Eric J. Hobsbawm and Terence Ranger, eds., *The Invention of Tradition* (Cambridge, 1983).

trades, can in part be linked to the reorganization of production which began in the eighteenth century. The abolition of the corps des métiers in the Revolution, the deskilling of artisanal trades and the widespread practice of subcontracting in the nineteenth century undoubtedly accelerated the decline. But this pattern of decline was linked as much if not more to changes in political culture. Compagnonnage began to lose potential membership as many young workers came to prize equality over the hierarchical structure and impenetrable practices of its brotherhoods. Workers, of course, never rejected the concept of brotherhood: fraternalism remained a powerful metaphor of organization. But by the late 1820s and 1830s external and internal critics began to complain that compagnonnage was dominated by an exclusivity and hierarchy that undermined fraternity and diminished its ability to act against exploitative labor conditions or to unite a broader spectrum of artisanal workers.

To understand the direction that compagnonnage took—and failed to take—in the nineteenth century, I have traced its culture and practice from their early manifestations to their postrevolutionary adaptations. Although most compagnons seem to have seen the dangers of the Revolution for their association, a few wished to glorify its—and their— possibilities. A pamphlet called "Le Compagnonnage Moderne," written in the 1860s, expressed a view akin to that found in the 1848 address to the provisional government: that compagnonnage was originally "the democratic society par exellence," an institution that "belonged to the people, and was of the people." This anonymous author believed that "the French revolution . . . should have been the point of departure for a new era of compagnonnage." Instead, he sadly noted, it had been as fatal to compagnonnage as it was to other old regime institutions, which, at some point, compagnonnage had come to resemble. After the Revolution, compagnonnage retained its marks of privilege and its prerogatives as it fomented new battles among its societies.[31] The present book offers a different history. Compagnonnage was never a "democratic" association. Its societies both adapted and contested revolutionary practices and culture. Dispersed and temporarily defeated by the Revolution, compagnons attempted to recreate and reinforce their former associations. During or soon after the revolutionary period, it appears that their symbolic texts and practices were elaborated and revised, perhaps to ensure that their "secrets" would be kept from their enemies, perhaps to make their meaning and purpose more transparent.

But the problem was complex, for these societies wanted to survive and legitimate themselves as fraternal and corporate institutions at a

31. AML, I²47A, "Compagnonnage, 1821–1869," piece no. 36, undated, anonymous ms.

time when revolutionary principles promoted fraternity but called for the end of corporatism. Compagnonnage was shaped by early modern European institutions—the church, confraternities, and corps des Métiers—which themselves drew on models of the body and the family. Like all these sources and models, compagnonnage incorporated both hierarchical and egalitarian principles. After the Revolution, however, compagnons could not and did not cling to old memories and habits only. They incorporated some features of postrevolutionary society into their associations: compagnons increasingly called their brotherhoods "societies" and adopted more bureaucratic postrevolutionary terminology. They tightened discipline and organization and standardized and regularized record keeping, communications, and practices. In general, compagnons reestablished their brotherhoods as viable, if limited, labor associations in the early nineteenth century.

Yet, most societies of compagnonnage were not primarily interested in serving as vehicles for the united organization of labor, despite their new experiences and analyses of postrevolutionary economy and society. Instead, they were eager to emphasize their own primacy over other workers. The result was somewhat restructured rituals and an increased emphasis on the origins of compagnonnage, which were written down, discussed, and circulated as never before. These narratives, often with negative consequences, articulated the nature and purpose of each sect, validated its existence, and attempted (sometimes successfully) to elevate the status and priority of certain trades, such as carpentry, within compagnonnage. By adopting terms and symbols from Freemasonry, as all their origin narratives did to some degree, compagnons linked themselves to an elite association. The implications of this connection could be both liberal (for example, Masonry's links to the Enlightenment and freethinking) and exclusivist. The origin narratives also helped formalize issues of seniority, leadership, and privilege which had previously been more fluid. Nonetheless, the legends and rituals remained complex and multivocal, perpetuating and encoding the more positive features of mutuality and solidarity as well as the less savory aspects of compagnonnage.

There was, however, an increasing struggle over who would control the interpretation of these texts and practices. In the 1820s and 1830s many aspirants refused to submit to the rule of compagnons, and schism and defection were the results. Tensions between societies grew as well. Most sects remained reluctant to admit new trades, if not openly hostile. The dominant trades were generally unwilling to undertake any significant reform, thus expediting their own decline. Such decisions limited membership and reduced the significance of compagnonnage in trade union history, but they preserved a fraternal organization that remained meaningful for its adherents and instructive to its students. Compagnons exercised a degree of conscious choice in rejecting both reform and the idea of "progress," refusing to change their practices to conform to contemporary culture. Compagnonnage did change in the nineteenth century, but often to reinforce its views and practices. Those who remained within the largely "unreformed" brotherhoods apparently did not regret their choice. Their anxieties about social and cultural change, their adherence to corporate values in a capitalist world, their rejection of unskilled and factory labor expressed views at once progressive and retrograde.

The failure of the reform movement may ultimately have been tied to or been inherent in the original structures of the fraternally and ritually created units within compagnonnage. These brotherhoods evolved in a world whose legitimating principles—corporate distinctions and privilege—were no longer those of the contemporary social order. Yet, nineteenth-century brotherhoods, such as the Masons in Great Britain and the United States, could retain elaborate (and equally incongruous) ritual and remain widely popular. This persistence of and delight in ritual is even more intriguing in a supposedly pragmatic Anglo-American culture, less attuned to and more suspicious of such practice than the French. In part Anglo-American acceptance of such ritual is explained by the values of the new nineteenth-century political order, which were often based on the bonds and construction of fraternalism, which Masonry had done much to encourage. In France, the fraternalism so important in compagnonnage was transformed by the terms of the legal and (sometimes) political equality for adult males as defined in the French Revolution, and it continued to play a major role in social and labor organizations.

Another important component of the new fraternalism was unity. Although no fraternity ever included all potential brothers and almost all excluded any "sisters." Even though Masons, Odd Fellows, and Elks asserted principles of white male superiority, they did not adamantly maintain principles of hierarchy and exclusivity with regard to applicants of essentially the same social class. Compagnonnages, unlike these fraternal orders, labelled certain workers "inferior" and sought to exclude them to enhance their own sense of identity and economic advantage. But compagnons were increasingly unable to control competition from unskilled workers by barring them from their ranks, and these exclusivist beliefs and practices limited their membership and eventually sapped their strength in most trades. Instead of moving toward a broadly based fraternalism, compagnons seemed locked in endless permutations of fratricide.

In a sense compagnons became, as Norbert Elias remarks about prerevolutionary French elites, "imprisoned by [their own] institutions."[32] Compagnons may have feared that too much—or even any—change in their beliefs and practices would utterly erode their brotherhoods, would turn them into something other than compagnonnages. Although their associations were rejected by the majority, they still had a clear utility and meaning for a minority. Compagnons may have made a virtue of necessity, defining themselves as the last of the "true" artisans. In the first half of the nineteenth century this not insubstantial minority found that their societies provided mutual aid, legitimated their worth, and defended their economic interests. These achievements cannot be minimized in an era when all workingmen's associations in France led a very precarious existence, and few of them could gain concessions for workers. Those who broke from compagnonnage, however, insisted that the benefits of association could exist in a less ritualized and more egalitarian context. Despite the formation of new and rival associations and despite continuing internal dissensions, compagnonnage continued to fill the needs of this significant minority of the artisanal labor force at least into the 1830s and 1840s. Books, pamphlets, poems, and songs written by articulate and sensitive compagnons such as Perdiguier kept more positive aims alive while spreading a new message of reform and unity.

Thus, categorizing compagnonnage as "archaic" minimizes its fulfillment of deeply felt needs in the working class. From at least 1700 to 1848, the autonomous and highly structured societies of compagnonnage, almost alone among labor organizations, provided mutual aid and labor defense through a strong interurban network. Compagnons themselves constructed these brotherhoods and dedicated them not only to the pursuit of "independence" and economic well-being but also to their own vision of a social and cultural order based on the dignity of labor. Early compagnonnages gave workers a voice and a defense against their increasing subordination in the corps des métiers and brought them to the brink of newer forms of unionism in the mid-nineteenth century. When compagnonnages could go no further as vehicles of labor organization, they continued to instruct contemporaries and descendants about the unexpected ways in which class consciousness develops, or fails to develop.

The rituals and origin narratives, while retaining many corporate and old regime values, also embodied beliefs specific to compagnonnage itself as well as its particular sects and trades. These "charters" stressed

32. Norbert Elias, *The Court Society* (New York, 1983), p. 275.

the dignity of labor and laboring men and their need for independent associations to promote and defend their prerogatives. The discourse of the narratives and rituals emphasized the almost sacred character of the all-male brotherhoods. As the family metaphor was played out, mères and pères formed a context not for parental authority but for the economic and social interrelation of (ideally) equal "brothers." Although fathers and, in particular, mothers were respected and often loved, the compagnons only rarely called themselves "sons" and were not directly subject to the authority of these fictive parents. They remained economically and morally obliged to their innkeepers, but this obligation was mediated by the brotherhood. As time went on, "elder" brothers (more senior compagnons) increasingly began to take on more paternal authority, and younger workers increasingly resented them.

Newer liberal and socialist associations seemed more appropriate responses to economic and social conditions in the nineteenth century, and the strategies, tactics, and beliefs of compagnonnage became less acceptable and perhaps less comprehensible, even to the artisan. Nonetheless, compagnonnage, throughout its history, gave workers, employers, police, and the public, a dramatic example of workers' ability to understand and contest their assigned roles in the social order. Even in the nineteenth century, although their rituals had come to seem reactionary and even bizarre, the solidarity and force shown by compagnonnage gave other labor associations a living model to confront, critique, and sometimes copy. Compagnonnage was a resource for workers as they rethought the problems, processes, and potential involved in the organization of labor.[33]

Compagnons demonstrated early on that workers themselves had the ability to create associations that revised the range of their assigned social and economic status within the larger social and cultural order. Finally, as one of the few corporate institutions that survived the French Revolution, compagnonnage provided a complex example of the adaptation, accommodation, and resistance that could occur in the transition from pre- to postrevolutionary society. The brotherhoods of compagnons—working, plotting, striking, and brawling, but also singing, joking, remembering, and writing—enliven our reading of French history and enrich our understanding of the complex processes and possibilities of social and cultural creation from old to new regimes.

33. Cf. the way Natalie Z. Davis interprets the concept of "woman on top"—in literature, play, festival, folklore, reality—as a private and public resource that "renewed old systems but also helped change them into something different." *Society and Culture in Early Modern France* (Stanford, 1975), pp. 150–51.

Initiation Accounts, Sources

This appendix serves as a bibliography of the major texts on the initiations of compagnonnage from the mid-seventeenth to the early twentieth century currently available for public examination. The appendix reveals slight variations in some of the earliest texts and the relatively limited body of public texts extant on this subject.

1. Compagnon shoemakers du devoir, 21 September 1645: A four-page, untitled printed pamphlet (n.p., n.d. [Paris, 21 September 1645]) presented by master shoemakers to the doctors of the Faculty of Theology concerning the compagnons "du devoir" in their trade (BN, 4° FM 35348). I will refer to this pamphlet as "Compagnons du devoir, cordonniers"; like no. 5, below, this document begins with the words "Les abominables impietez." Another, somewhat abridged version of this piece exists (n.p., n.d. [Paris, 21 September 1645]); it begins with the words "Les Compagnons d'un certain Mestier" (BN, E. 3488). Roger Lecotté reproduced this version in "Les Plus anciens imprimés sur le compagnonnage," *Bulletin Folklorique de l'Ile de France (Paris)*, 1968, 4th ser., no. 4, pp. 67–68.

2. Compagnon shoemakers du devoir, 13 May 1648: A printed *sentence* in response to a complaint brought by the Confraternity of Saints Crespin and Crespinian, in *Extraict des registres de l'officialité de Paris*, 13 May 1648 (BN, E. 3489 [Paris, 1648]).

3. Compagnon shoemakers du devoir, 1 July 1648: Registration of decision of 13 May 1648 (no. 2, above), in *Extraict des registres de l'officialité de Paris*, 1 July 1648, BN, E. 3485 (Paris, 1648).

4. Compagnon shoemakers du devoir, 1651: [Abbé] Célestin Douais, "Le Pseudo-baptême et les pseudo-serments des compagnons du devoir à Toulouse en 1651," *Mémoires de l'Académie des sciences, inscriptions, et belles-lettres de Toulouse*, ser. 9, vol. 5 (1893): 432–58, based on documents in the episcopal archives of Toulouse.

5. Compagnon saddlers du devoir, 1654: "Serment des selliers de la ville de Bordeaux," BN, Collection Dupuy, no. 775, fols. 272r and v, n.d. [1654], followed by a "Note relative au serment secret prêté par les selliers de Bordeaux lors de leur réception comme compagnons," fols. 274r and v, 1654.

6. Compagnon shoemakers, hatters, tailors, saddlers, and cutlers du devoir, 1655: A four page printed pamphlet titled *Résolution des docteurs de la faculté de Paris, touchant les pratiques impies . . . pour passer compagnons, qu'ils appellent du devoir, depuis peu reconnues et advouées par plusieurs desdits Mestiers*, BN, D. 1074 (Paris, 14 March 1655). Another version of the *Résolution*, which includes additional material on the hatters and a section on the cutlers not found in other seventeenth-century sources is reproduced in Pierre Varin, *Archives législatives de la ville de Reims: Collection de pièces inédites pouvant servir à l'histoire des institutions dans l'intérieur de la cité* (Paris, 1840–52), part 2, vol. 2: *Statuts, 1514–1699*, 2:249–55.

7. Compagnon coopers, c. 1700: Joseph Pradelle, "Legendes, initiations, règlements, moeurs, et coutumes du compagnonnage," Musée de vieux Toulouse, mss. Cahier 13, dated May 1941.

8. Compagnon turners du devoir, 1731: *Livre de règles*, article 41, "Concernant la Réception," and article 42, "Concernant le serment de fidélité au Devoir," in Emile Coornaert, *Les Compagnonnages en France du Moyen Age à nos jours* (Paris, 1966), pp. 375–77; he cites the Archives de l'Association ouvrière as his source.

9. Compagnon tailors, 1743: Joseph Pradelle, "Moeurs et coutumes—Compagnonnage," Musée du vieux Toulouse, mss. Cahier 7, n.d.

10. Compagnon chamois dressers du devoir, c. 1766–67: BN, MSS. Collection Joly de Fleury, 421, fols. 366–74, "Lettre en forme de dénonciation au ministre publique, d'une compagnie, ou association formée dans les villes de Châlons, Angers, et Le Mans sous le nom de compagnons blanchers ou chamoiseurs du devoir." Edited and published by Paul-M. Bondois, as "Un Compagnonnage au XVIIIe siècle," in *Annales historiques de la Révolution française*, 6 (1929): 588–99.

11. Compagnon leather dressers (*mégisseurs*) du devoir, 1782: AM Troyes, FF Supplément, Police investigation of initiations and activities of compagnons *mégisseurs*, 1782.

12. Compagnon joiners and locksmiths du devoir de liberté, before 1789: Joseph Pradelle, "Réception des compagnons menuisiers et serruriers de devoir de liberté sous l'ancien régime à Toulouse," *Mémoires de l'Académie des sciences, inscriptions, et belles-lettres de Toulouse*, ser. 13, 3 (1941): 135–53.

13. Compagnon chamois dressers du devoir, c. 1815: AD Seine, 4 AZ 1068, four ms. registers, "Devoir des compagnons blanchers et chamoiseurs réunis," register 2, fols. 69–83. These registers have been published under the name of the compagnon who completed their redaction: J.-F. Piron, *Devoir des compagnons blanchers et chamoiseurs réunis* (Paris, 1990 [1840]).

14. Compagnon locksmiths du devoir, 1820s: Pierre Moreau, *Un Mot aux ouvriers*

de toutes les professions, à tous les amis du peuple et du progrès, sur le compagnonnage; ou, Le Guide de l'ouvrier sur le tour de France (Auxerre, 1841), p. 17.

15. Compagnon shoemakers du devoir, 1833: Toussaint Guillaumou (called Carcasonne le bien aimé), *Les Confessions d'un compagnon* (Paris, 1864), pp. 29–38.

16. Compagnon carpenters du devoir de liberté, c. 1840–41: Coornaert, *Les Compagnonnages*, pp. 384–85; he cites the Archives de l'Union compagnonnique as his source.

17. Compagnons du devoir (no trade given), Bordeaux, 1842: Direction du Travail, *Les Associations professionnelles ouvrières*, 4 vols. (Paris, 1899–1901), 1:118–20.

18. Compagnon shoemakers du devoir de liberté, mid-nineteenth century: Direction du Travail, *Les Associations professionnelles ouvrières*, 4 vols. (Paris, 1899–1901), 1: 120–22.

19. Compagnon shoemakers du devoir de liberté, mid-nineteenth century: *Le Secret des compagnons cordonniers dévoilé* (Paris, 1858).

20. Compagnon turners du devoir, c. 1870: Coornaert, *Les Compagnonnages*, pp. 383–84; he cites the Archives de l'Union compagnonnique as his source.

21. Compagnon carpenters passants du devoir, 1880s: Direction du Travail, *Les Associations professionnelles ouvrières*, 4 vols. (Paris, 1899–1901), 1:123–24. Cf. Pierre du Maroussem, *Charpentiers de Paris: Compagnons et indépendants* (Paris, 1891), pp. 127–49.

22. Compagnon carpenters du devoir, enfants de Père Soubise, 1884: Jean Connay [Henri Bricheteau], *Le Compagnonnage: Son histoire, ses mystères* (Paris, 1909), pp. 135–73.

23. Compagnon harness makers du devoir, c. 1890: Auguste Bâtard (called Nantais la belle conduite), *Souvenirs d'un apprenti* (Paris, 1960), pp. 102–4.

Origin Narratives, Sources

Many more texts on the origins of compagnonnage than on its initiations are open to scholarly examination, most of them in published form. The following list is the sample on which I based my analysis and interpretation of the compagnons' constructions of their history and identity, but it also represents the most important and extensive texts on this subject.

1. Auguste Bâtard (Nantais-la-belle-conduite), *Souvenirs d'un apprenti* (Paris, 1960), pp. 135–37.

2. Robert Ingham Clegg, *New Revised Edition of Mackey's History of Freemasonry* (New York, 1921), 1:158–61, "The Temple Legend."

3. Les CC. [Compagnons] passants charpentiers, à leurs FF:: du Vrai Compag:: de l'aimable tour de France, *Notice historique sur le compagnonage* [sic] *primitif, comme base fondamentale des sociétés* (Paris, 1843), p. 71.

4. Gavots to the mayor of Marseille, AM Marseille, I²136, 24 May 1818.

5. "Legendes de Salomon, de Maître Jacques, et de Père Soubise," in Emile Coornaert, *Les Compagnonnages en France du Moyen Age à nos jours* (Paris, 1966), pp. 341–45.

6. Albert G. Mackey, *Encyclopedia of Freemasonry,* 1916 ed., article "Compagnonnage."

7. Etienne Martin Saint-Léon, *Le Compagnonnage: Son histoire, ses coutumes, ses règlements, ses rites* (Paris, 1901), pp. 2–10.

8. Pierre Moreau, *De la réforme des abus du compagnonnage* (Auxerre, 1843), pp. 94–95, 99–100.

9. "Opinions d'un charpentier designé comme arbitre, et accessoirement, d'autres compagnons," in Coornaert, *Les Compagnonnages,* pp. 347–48.

10. "Les origines d'après un compagnon passant tailleur de pierre [de Maître Jacques]," in Coornaert, *Les Compagnonnages,* pp. 346–47.

11. Agricol Perdiguier, *Le Livre du compagnonnage,* 2d ed., 2 vols. (Paris, 1841), 1: 20–49.

12. Perdiguier, *Mémoires d'un compagnon,* introduction by Alain Faure (Paris, 1977), pp. 290–93.

13. Perdiguier, *Question vitale sur le compagnonnage et la classe ouvrière* (Paris, 1861), pp. 26–28.

14. Victor-Bernard Sciandro [La-sagesse-de-Bordeaux], *Le Compagnonnage: Ce qu'il a été, ce qu'il est, ce qu'il devrait être* (Marseille, 1850), pp. 15–19.

15. Joseph Voisin [Angoumois], *Histoire de ma vie et 55 ans de compagnonnage* (Tours, 1931), pp. 30–50.

Bibliography of Primary Sources

Among his many works on compagnonnage, two bibliographical essays by Roger Lecotté are indispensable to research on this subject: his "Essai bibliographique sur les compagnonnages de tous les devoirs du tour de France" (in *Compagnonnage: Par les compagnons du tour de France*, ed. Raoul Dautry [Paris, 1951]) cites over one thousand primary and secondary references to compagnonnage. Lecotté's *Archives historiques du compagnonnage* (Paris, 1956) is an excellent guide to more than four hundred primary printed and manuscript sources as well as to paintings, artifacts, and chefs d'oeuvre of compagnons from the sixteenth to the twentieth centuries. My own bibliography is, by comparison and necessity, more selective and lists only the most relevant manuscript and primary printed sources examined for this study.

ARCHIVES NATIONALES

AB XIX 981. Conseiller du roi, commissaire au Châtelet, 1724.
AD XI 18. Edits, arrêts, lettres patentes (imprimés), 1783.
AD XI 65. Maîtrises et jurandes, communautés des arts et métiers (imprimés), 1791.
BB[18] 1114–1558. Procureurs généraux, 1825–48.
BB[30] 299–317. Affaires politiques, adresses et pétitions, 1848.
C 70. Assemblée nationale, notes et minutes, 11–20 June 1791.

C 71. Assemblée nationale, minutes, procès-verbal, 9 June 1791.
D IV 51. Pétitions à l'Assemblée constituante, 1790.
D XXIXbis 18. Officiers municipaux, correspondence général, 1791.
F^7 3765. Bulletins de police généraux, 1809.
F^7 4236. Compagnonnage, affaires départementales, 1804–13.
F^7 9786–87. Objets généraux, affaires départementales, 1817–27.
F^12 1560. Police des ouvriers, 1791–1825.
Y 13016. Etablissements de répression, arts et métiers, 1789.

ARCHIVES DÉPARTEMENTALES

Bouches du Rhône. 208 U. Cour d'appels. Procédures divers, 1822–25.
——. J 2213. Cahier d'enregistrements des compagnons de Toulon, 1826–28.
——. 1204 U. Tribunal de Toulon. Grèves, 1826–28.
Côte d'Or. BB II. Archives judiciaires, 1540.
——. U II. Assises. Interrogations, dépositions, 1805–6.
——. U V. Tables des arrêts criminelles, 1811–50.
Gironde. 1–13 B. Ordonnances, arrêts, pétitions, 1709–85.
——. 12 B 280. Registre des compagnons serruriers du devoir, 1741–42; C 3708. Registre des compagnons serruriers du devoir, 1757–61.
Haute-Garonne. C 150. Ordonnance sur les compagnons du devoir et les gavots, 1730.
Rhône. BP 3613–23: Sénéchausée/Criminel; 10 M: Affaires politiques, associations, 1851–82.
Seine. 4 AZ 1068. Cinq registres, compagnons blanchers et chamoiseurs du devoir [c. 1838–40].

ARCHIVES MUNICIPALES

Bordeaux. Fonds Delpit 70. Concours des compagnons, 1744.
Dijon. B 185–396. Minutes, ordonnances communales, 1552–1762.
——. G 10–219. Extraits des registres de la chambre du conseil, 1608–1785.
Lyon. HH, arts et métiers, FF, police; I2 47A. Compagnonnage, l'Union, et coalitions des ouvriers, 1821–69.
Mâcon. HH 11. Compagnons menuisiers non du devoir, 1753–58.
Marseille. FF 206. Compagnons du devoir, 1740–87.
——. I^2 136–37. Compagnonnage, compagnons du devoir, 1789–1819.
Nantes. HH, arts et métiers; FF, police; I^2, police.
Toulouse. II^7-II^9. Rapports, commissions de police, 1793–99; II^58-1, Jugements de la police correctionnelle, 1799–1827; 2 Q 5, Règlements de divers sociétés de bienfaisance de Toulouse, 1808–43.

PRIVATE ARCHIVES

Archives Pierre Moreau. Institut français d'histoire sociale, Paris.

PUBLISHED SOURCES

Appel à tous nos frères de la corporation des ouvriers cordonniers et bottiers de la ville de Paris, sans distinction de sociétés. Paris, 1848.

Arnaud, Jean-Baptiste. *Mémoires d'un compagnon du tour de France, contenant plusieurs dissertations sur le devoir, entre l'auteur et plusieurs compagnons tailleurs de pierre et charpentiers.* Rochefort, 1859.

Aubert. *Chansons des bons drilles.* Paris, 1848.

Audiganne, Armand. *Les Ouvriers en famille; ou, Entretiens sur les devoirs et les droits du travailleur dans les diverses relations de sa vie laborieuse.* Paris, 1863.

Aux compagnons de tous les devoirs et de tous les corps d'état. Paris, [1848].

Barrière, Théodore. *Les Charpentiers.* Paris, 1847.

Bâtard, Auguste-René (called Nantais la belle conduite). *Souvenirs d'un apprenti.* Paris, 1960.

Bernard, Albe (called Albigeois le bien aimé). *Les Bêtises de la régénération du compagnonnage.* Paris, [1843].

Berreyer, Pierre-Antoine. *Affaire des charpentiers: Plaidoyer en faveur des ouvriers accusés du délit de coalition (23 août 1845).* Paris, 1845.

Bonvous, Auguste. *Les Compagnons du devoir, un programme: Etude sociale sur les corporations compagnonniques de Maître Jacques et du Père Soubise.* Angoulême, 1900.

Boyer, Abel (called Périgord coeur loyal). *Le Tour de France d'un compagnon du devoir.* Paris, 1957.

Boyer, Adolphe. *De l'état des ouvriers et de son amélioration par l'organisation du travail.* Paris, 1841.

Capus (called Albigeois). *Conseils d'un vieux compagnon à son fils prêt à partir pour le tour de France; ou, La Fin déplorable d'un enfant de Soubise.* Tours, 1844.

Carpentras le coeur fidèle. "Discours pour l'installation d'un premier compagnon serrurier [du devoir] à Chartres, 1833," ed. Maurice Jusselin. *Compagnonnage* (June 1950): 5.

Chovin de Die, François (called Le Dauphiné). *Le Conseiller des compagnons.* Paris, 1860.

Club compagnonnique: Convocation pour le 8 avril. Paris, 1848.

Le Compagnonnage et l'indépendance. Avignon, 1838.

Les CC. [Compagnons] passants charpentiers à leurs FF:: du vrai compag:: de l'aimable tour de France. *Notice historique sur le compagnonage* [sic] *primitif, comme base fondamentale des sociétés.* Paris, 1843.

"Les Compagnons du Tour de France," in *L'Illustration,* 22 November 1845, pp. 183–85, and 29 November 1845, pp. 203–6.

Connay, Jean [Henri Bricheteau]. *Le Compagnonnage: Son histoire, ses mystères.* Preface by Léon Bonneff and Maurice Bonneff. Paris, 1909.

Cornu, E. (called La constance de Dijon). "Souvenirs de réception, 1866." *Union compagnonnique,* 19 May 1907.

Dautry, Raoul, ed. *Compagnonnage: Par les compagnons du tour de France.* Paris, 1951.

Dénat (called La franchise de Castelnaudary). *Chansons compagnonniques.* Paris, n.d. [1848].

Dennery [a.k.a. D'Emery or D'Ennery], Adolphe Philippe, and Pierre-Etienne Piestre [called Eugène] Cormon. *Les Compagnons; ou La Mansarde de la cité.* Paris, 1846.

Désert, Gabriel, ed., "Mémoires d'un travailleur bas-normand, première moitié du XIXe siècle," *Annales de Normandie,* no. 1 (1969): 59–77 ("Souvenirs de jeunesse") and no. 2 (1969):155–78 ("Le Tour de France d'un compagnon chaudronnier, 1836–1844"). Désert has edited portions of the memoirs of a compagnon boiler-maker, Pierre Ameline.

Desnoyers, C.-H.-Edmond [a.k.a. E. D. de Biéville]. *Les Dévorants.* Paris, 1843.

Doinel, Jules, and Camille Bloch, eds. *Archives du Loiret: Inventaire sommaire des archives départementales.* 4 vols. Orléans, 1900.

Edeline, René (called Tourangeau la franchise). *Les Compagnons du tour de France.* Paris, 1964.

Encyclopédie méthodique: Jurisprudence, police. 9 vols. Paris 1782–91.

Egron, Adrien-César. *Le Livre d'ouvrier: Ses devoirs envers la société, la famille, et lui-même.* Paris, 1844.

Giraud, Auguste-Ambroise. *Réflexions philosophiques sur le compagnonnage et le tour de France.* Paris, 1846.

Gosset, Jacques [a.k.a Jean] (called Le Père des forgerons). *Détails sur quelques compagnons forgerons relativement à leur changement de Mère (15 août 1843).* Paris, 1843.

———. *Projet tendant à régénérer le compagnonnage sur le tour de France: Souvenir à tous les ouvriers.* Paris, 1842.

Guillaumou, Toussaint (called Carcasonne le bien aimé du tour de France). *Les Confessions d'un compagnon.* Paris, 1864.

Helyot, Pierre [Père Hippolyte]. *Histoire des ordres monastiques, réligieux, et militaires et des congrégations séculières.* 8 vols. Paris, 1714–19.

Isnard, Emile. *Documents inédits sur l'histoire du compagnonnage à Marseille au XVIIIe siècle.* Vol. 4 of *Mémoires pour servir à l'histoire du commerce et de l'industrie,* ed. Julien Hayem. 4th series. 5 vols. Paris, 1911–17.

Isambert, François-André, et al., eds. *Recueil général des anciennes lois françaises depuis l'an 420 jusqu'à la révolution de 1789.* 29 vols. Paris, 1822–33.

Lebrun, [Père] Pierre. *Histoire des pratiques superstitieuses qui ont séduit les peuples et embarassé les sçavans.* 2d ed. augmentée par J. Bellon. 4 vols. Paris, 1732–37. Vol. 4: *Recueil des pièces pour servir de supplément à l'histoire des pratiques superstitieuses.*

Lespinasse, René, and François Bonnardot, eds. *Le Livre des métiers d'Etienne Boileau.* Paris, 1879.

Lockroy, Joseph-Philippe, and Jules de Wailly, *Deux compagnons du tour de France.* Paris, 1845.

Marquet, Jean, ed. *Notice historique sur la fondation de la société de l'union des travailleurs de tour de France.* Tours, 1882–89.

Mavidal, M. J., and M. E. Laurent, eds. *Archives parlementaires de 1787 à 1860.* 1st ser. 2d ed. 82 vols. Paris, 1879–1913.

Ménétra, Jacques-Louis. *Journal de ma vie.* Ed. Daniel Roche. Paris, 1982.

———. *Journal of My Life.* Ed. Daniel Roche. Trans. Arthur Goldhammer, with a foreword by Robert Darnton. New York, 1986.

Moreau, Pierre. *Un Mot aux ouvriers de toutes les professions, à tous les amis du peuple et du progrès, sur le compagnonnage; ou, Le Guide de l'ouvrier sur le tour de France.* Auxerre, 1841.

———. *De la réforme des abus du compagnonnage et de l'amélioration du sort des travailleurs.* Auxerre, 1843.

Nadaud, Martin. *Mémoires de Léonard, ancien garçon maçon.* Bourganeuf, 1895.

Perdiguier, Agricol (called Avignonnais la vertu). *Appel aux compagnons.* Paris, 1873.

———. *Devoir de liberté: Chansons de compagnons et autres.* 2 parts. Paris, 1834–36.

———. *Les Gavots et les Devoirants; ou La Réconciliation des compagnons.* Paris, 1862.

———. *Histoire d'une scission dans le compagnonnage.* Paris, 1846.

———. *Le Livre du compagnonnage, contenant des chansons de compagnons, un dialogue sur l'architecture, un raisonnement sur le trait, une notice sur le compagnonnage, la rencontre de deux frères et un grand nombre de notes.* 1st ed. Paris, 1839; 2d ed. 2 vols. Paris, 1841; 3d ed. 2 vols. Paris, 1857.

———. *Mémoires d'un compagnon.* Ed. and with an introduction by Alain Faure. Paris, 1977 [1854–55].

———. *Question vitale sur le compagnonnage et la classe ouvrière.* Paris, 1861.

Piron, Jean-François (called Vendôme la clef des coeurs). *Chansonnier du tour de France, dédié aux compagnons du devoir.* Paris, 1879 [originally published 1840].

———. *Devoir des compagnons blanchers et chamoiseurs réunis.* Paris, 1990 [based on the early nineteenth-century mss.].

Poulaille, Henry. *Le Pain quotidien, 1903–1906.* Paris, 1939.

Riancey, Henri de. "Du Compagnonnage: Son passé, son présent, son avenir." *Le Correspondant: Recueil périodique: Religion, philosophie, politique, sciences, littérature, beaux-arts,* vol. 12, 10 October 1845, pp. 45–80, and 24 October 1845, pp. 202–36.

Sand, George. *Le Compagnon du tour de France.* Paris, 1841.

Sciandro, Victor-Bernard. *Le Compagnonnage: Ce qu'il a été, ce qu'il est, ce qu'il devrait être.* Marseille, 1850.

Le Secret des compagnons cordonniers devoilé par les C.C. du devoir, les sociétaires, les indépendants, les compagnons de liberté et ceux de l'ère nouvelle, réunis en société de secours mutuels à Paris. Paris, 1858.

Simon, Claude G. *Etude historique et morale sur le compagnonnage.* Nantes, 1853.

Sue, Eugène. *Le Juif errant.* Illus. A. Ferdinandus. 2 vols. Paris, 1845.

Tristan, Flora. *L'Union ouvrière.* Paris, 1843.

Varin, Pierre. *Archives législatives de la ville de Reims: Collection de pièces inédites pouvant servir à l'histoire des institutions dans l'intérieur de la cité.* Paris, 1840–52. Part 2, vol. 2: *Statuts, 1514–1699.* Paris, 1847.

Vibert, Lionel, ed. *The Constitutions of Freemasons* [1723]. London, 1923.

Voisin, Joseph (called Angoumois). *Histoire de ma vie et 55 ans de compagnonnage.* Tours, 1931.

Zaccone, Pierre. *Histoire des sociétés secrètes, politiques, et religieuses . . . suivie d'un précis historique sur le compagnonnage.* 2 vols. Paris, 1866 [1847].

Index